Surrealist women's writing

Manchester University Press

Surrealist women's writing

A critical exploration

Edited by

Anna Watz

MANCHESTER UNIVERSITY PRESS

Copyright © Manchester University Press 2020

While copyright in the volume as a whole is vested in Manchester University Press, copyright in individual chapters belongs to their respective authors, and no chapter may be reproduced wholly or in part without the express permission in writing of both author and publisher.

Published by Manchester University Press
Oxford Road, Manchester M13 9PL

www.manchesteruniversitypress.co.uk

British Library Cataloguing-in-Publication Data
A catalogue record for this book is available from the British Library

ISBN 978 1 5261 3202 4 hardback
ISBN 978 1 5261 6715 6 paperback

First published 2020
Paperback published 2022

The publisher has no responsibility for the persistence or accuracy of URLs for any external or third-party internet websites referred to in this book, and does not guarantee that any content on such websites is, or will remain, accurate or appropriate.

Typeset
by New Best-set Typesetters Ltd

Contents

List of figures	page vii
Notes on contributors	ix
Acknowledgements	xii
Introduction Anna Watz	1
1 'The dung beetle's snowball': the philosophic narcissism of Claude Cahun's essay-poetry Felicity Gee	17
2 Identity convulsed: Leonora Carrington's *The House of Fear* and *The Oval Lady* Anna Watz	42
3 Recasting the human: Leonora Carrington's dark exilic imagination Jeannette Baxter	68
4 Colette Peignot: the purity of revolt Michael Richardson	87
5 Suzanne Césaire's surrealism: tightrope of hope Kara M. Rabbitt	103
6 Kay Sage alive in the world Katharine Conley	122
7 Outside-in: translating Unica Zürn Patricia Allmer	142
8 Ithell Colquhoun's experimental poetry: surrealism, occultism, and postwar poetry Mark S. Morrisson	156
9 Leonor Fini's abhuman family Jonathan P. Eburne	179
10 'Open sesame': Dorothea Tanning's critical writing Catriona McAra	210

11 Magic language, esoteric nature: Rikki Ducornet's
   surrealist ecology   225
   Kristoffer Noheden

Index   246

Figures

1.1 Claude Cahun, *Self Portrait (Near a Granite Wall)*, 1916. © Jersey Heritage Trust 2020. *page* 18
1.2 Claude Cahun, Table of Contents from *Aveux non avenus*, Éditions du Carrefour, 1930. © Jersey Heritage Trust 2020. 22
1.3. Claude Cahun, *Self Portrait (Lower Body, Seaweed, and Le Pere)*, 1932. © Jersey Heritage Trust 2020. 26
1.4 Claude Cahun, *Self Portrait (Crouched Naked in Rock Pool)*, 1930. © Jersey Heritage Trust 2020. 35
2.1 Max Ernst, page 15 from *A Little Girl Dreams of Taking the Veil* (1930), trans. Dorothea Tanning, Dover Publications, Inc., 1982. © Estate of Max Ernst / Bildupphovsrätt 2020. 49
2.2 Leonora Carrington, *Femme et oiseau*, 1937. Oil on canvas. © Estate of Leonora Carrington / Bildupphovsrätt 2020. 57
4.1 Georges Bataille, Colette Peignot, and Georges Ambrosino, c. 1936. Photographer unknown. 92
5.1 Suzanne Césaire. Date and photographer unknown. 107
7.1 Unica Zürn, *Das Haus der Krankheiten*, n.p., from Unica Zürn, *Das Haus der Krankheiten*. © Verlag Brinkmann & Bose, Berlin 1986. 147
7.2 Unica Zürn, *The House of Illnesses*, trans. Malcolm Green, p. 55. © Verlag Brinkmann & Bose, Berlin 1986 / Atlas Press, London 1993. 148
7.3 Unica Zürn, *Plan des Hauses der Krankheiten*, n.p., from Unica Zürn, *Das Haus der Krankheiten*, © Verlag Brinkmann & Bose, Berlin 1986. 148
8.1 Ithell Colquhoun, cover of *Grimoire of the Entangled Thicket*, 1973. 168
8.2 From *Wood and Water*, vol. 2, no. 7, 1983. 170

9.1 Leonor Fini, *Sphinx Philagria*, 1945. Oil on canvas. © Artists Rights Society (ARS), New York / ADAGP, Paris 2020. 183

9.2 Leonor Fini, *Étude pour* Mourmour, 1976. Ink, watercolor, and wash. © Artists Rights Society (ARS), New York / ADAGP, Paris 2020. 188

9.3 Stanislao Lepri, *Les Voyeurs*, 1949. Oil on canvas. © Artists Rights Society (ARS), New York / ADAGP, Paris 2020. 191

9.4 Leonor Fini, *Sphinx Amalbourga*, 1942. Oil on canvas. © Estate of Leonor Fini / Artists Rights Society (ARS), New York / ADAGP, Paris 2020. 193

9.5 Leonor Fini, *Les Stryges Amaouri*, 1947. Oil on canvas. © Artists Rights Society (ARS), New York / ADAGP, Paris 2020. 193

9.6 Leonor Fini, *Rogomelec*, 1978. Oil on canvas. © Artists Rights Society (ARS), New York / ADAGP, Paris 2020. 203

9.7 Leonor Fini, *The Angel of Anatomy*, 1949. Oil on canvas. © Artists Rights Society (ARS), New York / ADAGP, Paris 2020. 203

10.1 Dorothea Tanning, *Woman Artist, Nude, Standing*, 1985–87. Oil on canvas. Collection of The Destina Foundation, New York. © Estate of Dorothea Tanning / ADAGP, Paris, and DACS, London 2020. 215

10.2 Dorothea Tanning, *De quel amour (By What Love)*, 1969. Tweed, metal, wool, chain, and plush. Musée National d'Art Moderne, Centre Georges Pompidou, Paris. © Estate of Dorothea Tanning / ADAGP, Paris, and DACS, London 2020. 217

10.3 Dorothea Tanning, page 4 from the exhibition catalogue *Ouvre-Toi*, 1971. Ink, coloured ink, and wash on paper. Collection of The Destina Foundation, New York. © Estate of Dorothea Tanning / ADAGP, Paris, and DACS, London 2020. 220

Notes on contributors

Patricia Allmer is Professor of modern and contemporary art history at the University of Edinburgh. She has taught, published, and curated extensively on surrealism and its legacies. Her books include *René Magritte* (Reaktion Press, 2019) and *Lee Miller: Photography, Surrealism, and Beyond* (Manchester University Press, 2016), and her curatorial projects include *Taking Shots: The Photography of William S. Burroughs* (2014; The Photographers' Gallery / Prestel), and *Angels of Anarchy: Women Artists and Surrealism* (Manchester Art Gallery, 2009 / Prestel).

Jeannette Baxter is Reader in modern and contemporary literature at Anglia Ruskin University, Cambridge. Working at the intersection of literature, history, politics, and surrealist studies, she has published a number of books and articles on authors such as J.G. Ballard, Leonora Carrington, Alan Burns, Kazuo Ishiguro, Ian McEwan, and W.G. Sebald. She is currently working on a book-length project on the British surrealist anti-fascist novel.

Katharine Conley is the author of numerous articles and books on the surrealist movement, including *Surrealist Ghostliness* (University of Nebraska Press, 2013), *Robert Desnos, Surrealism, and the Marvelous in Everyday Life* (University of Nebraska Press, 2003), and *Automatic Woman: The Representation of Woman in Surrealism* (University of Nebraska Press, 1996). Recent articles and book chapters include 'Collecting Ghostly Things: André Breton and Joseph Cornell' (*Modernism/Modernity,* 2017); 'Photographic Automatism: Surrealism and Feminist (Post?)Modernism in Susan Hiller's *Sisters of Menon*' (in *Intersections: Women Artists/Surrealism/Modernism*, Manchester University Press, ed. Patricia Allmer, 2016); 'Value and Hidden Cost in André Breton's Surrealist Collection' (*South Central Review*, 2015). She is Professor of French and francophone literature at William & Mary, Williamsburg.

Jonathan P. Eburne is the editor of *ASAP/Journal* and Professor of comparative literature, English, and French and francophone studies at the Pennsylvania

State University. He is the author of *Outsider Theory: Intellectual Histories of Unorthodox Ideas* (University of Minnesota Press, 2018) and *Surrealism and the Art of Crime* (Cornell University Press, 2008), and co-editor of four other books: *Leonora Carrington and the International Avant-Garde* (with Catriona McAra, Manchester University Press, 2017); *The Year's Work in Nerds, Wonks, and Neocons* (with Benjamin Schreier, Indiana University Press, 2017); *The Year's Work in the Oddball Archive* (with Judith Roof, Indiana University Press, 2016); and *Paris, Capital of the Black Atlantic: Literature, Modernity, and Diaspora* (with Jeremy Braddock, Johns Hopkins University Press, 2013). He lives in central Pennsylvania, USA.

Felicity Gee is Senior Lecturer in modernism and world cinema at the University of Exeter. She is the author of the forthcoming monograph *Magic Realism, World Cinema and the Avant-Garde* (Routledge, 2021), and has published widely on surrealist literature, affect theory, and avant-garde film. She was awarded a British Academy grant to conduct archival research in Cuba, on the interdisciplinary work of Alejo Carpentier. Her research straddles film, art history, and literary studies, and her current projects investigate the collaborative work of modernist writers and artists that takes place across and between media.

Catriona McAra is University Curator at Leeds Arts University. She was awarded her doctorate in History of Art at the University of Glasgow, followed by a postdoctoral fellowship at the Institute for Advanced Studies in the Humanities (IASH), University of Edinburgh. She has published extensively on the art and literature of Dorothea Tanning and Leonora Carrington with a particular interest in feminist aesthetics and surrealist legacies in contemporary practice. She is author of *A Surrealist Stratigraphy of Dorothea Tanning's Chasm* (Routledge, 2017), and co-editor with Jonathan P. Eburne of *Leonora Carrington and the International Avant-Garde* (Manchester University Press, 2017). Recent articles on Tanning include 'Glowing Like Phosphorus: Dorothea Tanning and the Sedona Western' in *Journal of Surrealism and the Americas* 10:1 (2019).

Mark S. Morrisson is Professor and Head of English at Penn State University. He is author of *The Public Face of Modernism: Little Magazines, Audiences, and Reception 1905–1920* (University of Wisconsin Press, 2001); *Modern Alchemy: Occultism and the Emergence of Atomic Theory* (Oxford University Press, 2007); *Modernism, Science, and Technology* (Bloomsbury Academic, 2016); and numerous articles and chapters; and he is co-editor, with Richard Shillitoe, of *I Saw Water: An Occult Novel and Other Selected Writings by Ithell Colquhoun* (Penn State University Press, 2014). Morrisson is a past editor of the Penn State University Press series *Refiguring Modernism: Arts, Literatures, Sciences* and a past co-editor, with Sean Latham, of the *Journal of Modern Periodical Studies*. Early in his career, he enjoyed a role in the founding of the Modernist Studies Association, and he returned at mid-career to its board as President. He currently sits on the Executive Board of the ADE.

Kristoffer Noheden is Research Fellow in the Department of Media Studies, Stockholm University. He is the author of *Surrealism, Cinema, and the Search for a New Myth* (Palgrave Macmillan, 2017) and some twenty articles and book chapters on surrealism, as well as co-editor, with Abigail Susik, of the forthcoming volume *Surrealism and Film after 1945: Absolutely Modern Mysteries* (Manchester University Press). Noheden's current book project concerns animals and ecology in surrealist art, film, and writings from 1919 to 2018. He is co-curator of the exhibition *Alan Glass: Surrealism's Secret* (Leeds Arts University, 2021).

Kara M. Rabbitt serves as Associate Provost at William Paterson University of New Jersey, a public regional institution in the New York metropolitan area. Specialising in francophone Caribbean literature, with related expertise in nineteenth-century French poetry, Rabbitt has published and presented in the USA and internationally in these areas of research. She was awarded an American Council on Education fellowship for the 2019–20 academic year, completing a research project on adult learners.

Michael Richardson is currently Visiting Fellow at Goldsmiths University of London. He has published widely on surrealism.

Anna Watz is Senior Lecturer in English literature at Linköping University, Sweden. She is the author of *Angela Carter and Surrealism: 'A Feminist Libertarian Aesthetic'* (Routledge, 2016), as well as numerous articles and book chapters on Angela Carter, Leonora Carrington, and second-wave French feminism. She is currently preparing a monograph on the intersection between surrealist women's art and writing of the 1970s and the emergence of poststructuralist feminism and theories of *écriture féminine*.

Acknowledgements

I am immensely grateful to Rikki Ducornet for allowing me to use her exceptional artwork for the cover of this book. Her generosity and enthusiasm for the project made the final stages of the editorial process a delight. Furthermore, I extend warm thanks to Manchester University Press editor Matthew Frost for his support. I also want to thank all the contributors, as well as the anonymous reviewers whose insightful comments improved the volume greatly.

I gratefully acknowledge the Swedish Research Council (2018-01419) for supporting my editorial and scholarly contribution to this volume.

Introduction

Anna Watz

As is well known, most women who participated in surrealist activities received little critical recognition until the 1970s, when feminist interventions in art and literary scholarship demanded a thoroughgoing revision of previous critical narratives. In Anglo-American criticism, the work of Gloria Feman Orenstein was pioneering in challenging and rewriting the previously largely male canon of surrealist works.[1] Orenstein's intervention was followed in 1985 by Whitney Chadwick's immensely influential book *Women Artists and the Surrealist Movement*, which introduced to the anglophone public the visual work of, amongst others, Eileen Agar, Leonora Carrington, Ithell Colquhoun, Nusch Éluard, Leonor Fini, Valentine Hugo, Dora Maar, Lee Miller, Meret Oppenheim, Valentine Penrose, Kay Sage, Dorothea Tanning, Toyen, and Remedios Varo.[2] The 1990s saw an upsurge in scholarly work on surrealist women's art – a trend that is still not showing any signs of waning. Indeed, art by women surrealists is still an immensely popular topic of research, resulting both in scholarly publications and in a wealth of gallery exhibitions; the last decade has witnessed a great proliferation of feminist-curated shows dedicated to surrealist women artists.[3] Moreover, these women's work is frequently invoked to showcase how surrealism anticipated currently highly topical subjects, such as ecocriticism and a critique of anthropocentrism.[4]

Many of the artists mentioned above worked across multiple media, such as painting, sculpture, photography, and writing; yet historiographies since the 1970s have tended to foreground the visual aspects of this oeuvre. The idea for the present volume emerged as a reaction to this imbalance; I wanted to carry out a critical investigation of surrealist women's writing that did not place this genre in a subordinate position vis-à-vis visual art, but instead considered it on its own terms and merits. Penelope Rosemont's 1998 anthology *Surrealist Women: An International Anthology* was pivotal in showcasing the rich and varied body of written work – fictional, critical, poetic – by women associated with the surrealist movement. Yet, despite Rosemont's brilliant work in presenting and promoting the importance of the writing of these women surrealists, they have attracted far more attention from the public as visual artists, and, moreover, received much more critical consideration by art historians than by literary scholars. And perhaps, as Rosemont herself concedes, this seeming preference for their visual output is neither strange nor accidental: 'The reason is obvious: paintings, photographs, collages, and objects move around in the world unencumbered by language barriers.'[5] Additionally, many of their texts have been out of print since their publication (often in very small print-runs) and are hence difficult to get hold of.

Surrealist Women's Writing: A Critical Exploration aims to demonstrate the extensiveness of writing by women associated with the surrealist movement – in terms of genres and styles as well as thematic concerns. It endeavours to showcase the historical, linguistic, and culturally contextual breadth of this writing, as well as to highlight how the specifically surrealist poetics and politics that characterise these women's work intersect with and contribute to contemporary debates on, for example, gender, sexuality, subjectivity, otherness, anthropocentrism, and the environment.

The focus in this volume on previously under-studied aspects of women surrealists' production – namely their rich and multifaceted written bodies of work – should not be understood as an attempt to contest earlier critical narratives; indeed, feminist art-historical scholarship from the 1970s up to the present has been instrumental both in introducing previously rather unknown women surrealists to a wider public and in writing these artists into official narratives of surrealism. These efforts have indeed been truly invaluable. The goal of the present volume is to add another dimension to these existing narratives by reading surrealist women's artistic output through a new lens: literature. The title of the volume, *Surrealist Women's Writing: A Critical Exploration*, is an explicit homage to Rosemont's groundbreaking and inspiring anthology. I hope that this collection of essays – the first to focus exclusively on the writings of certain women affiliated with surrealism – will function as a critical companion piece (albeit less comprehensive) to Rosemont's book.

The gesture of separating writing from the visual arts, however, is neither unproblematic nor straightforward. As is well known, surrealism itself was a radically interdisciplinary movement, and, as has already been suggested above, several of its members worked in many different media. Thus, even though scholars tend to find their critical perspectives circumscribed by disciplinary training and affiliation, such separations do not necessarily suit surrealism itself. I therefore want to stress that the focus of this book on *writing* is motivated solely by academic reasons; the surrealist women discussed here did not necessarily see the fields of the visual and the textual as distinct and separate from each other. Indeed, the visual and literary production of many of these artists can be seen to comment and expand on each other, a complexity continually and explicitly addressed by the chapters in this volume.

'Women's art'?

I am a painter, not a woman painter. I am independent.[6]
Leonor Fini

Looming large in my corner is the phenomenon of Women Painters.[7]
Dorothea Tanning

As outlined above, surrealist women's visual art has received increasing scholarly and curatorial attention since the 1970s, a development that has fostered its popularity amongst general audiences. Despite the de facto positive effects of the emergence of the feminist art-historical construction and promotion of 'women's art' for these artists, many of those still alive and active at this point remained highly critical of the category and its reliance on the strategy of separation of the genders (Catriona McAra, in Chapter 10, offers a perceptive analysis of the tensions generated by this intersection in the late twentieth century of living surrealist figures and revisionary critical perspectives). Dorothea Tanning was particularly outspoken about her unwillingness to be categorised as a 'woman artist', regularly refusing inclusion in exhibitions and art-historical publications focusing exclusively on women. As she complains in a 1990 interview with Carlo McCormick: 'I've written statements by the dozens, I've written savage letters to all kinds of earnest people who wish to include me in this category, and I just can't talk about it anymore. I'm not against women, far from it. I'm against these confused people, doing that.'[8] Her 'savage letter' responding to Lea Vergine's invitation to participate in her 1980 exhibition (and subsequent catalogue) *L'Altra metà dell'avanguardia 1910–1940* (The Other Half of the Avant-Garde 1910–40) is a case in point:

> I cannot, with good will or conscience, take part in an exhibition that concerns itself with only half of humanity (women), while excluding the other half (men).
>
> By the way, what exactly makes me a woman? It seems as if a medical exam is required in order to take part in a project like yours. Above all today when imposture is so common that a person one thinks is a woman could turn out to be... a man!
>
> Please trust that if my paintings have ever been shown at women's art exhibitions, it is without my knowledge. Alas! How does one prevent such things![9]

Several other artists, for example Leonor Fini and Meret Oppenheim, have voiced similar misgivings about the category of 'women's art', arguing that such pigeonholing perpetuates women's 'exile' from the writing of history.[10]

It is of course true that the addition of the modifier 'woman' to the category of 'artist' signals something outside of and other to a 'universal' subject position. While we have become accustomed to terms such as 'women's art' or 'women's writing', we would consider terms such as 'men's art' or 'men's writing' to be absurd. Divorcing women's art and literature from the universal might be seen to suggest, at least for the surrealists cited above, that they are distinctly different from (and implicitly lesser than) men's art and writing, which occupy the position of 'universal'. It is thus understandable that Tanning, Fini, Oppenheim, and others found the prospect of confinement in the category of women's art extremely patronising and belittling. It is also likely that they feared that if their work was pigeonholed as women's art, spectators and reviewers would be biased in their interpretations of it.

As justified as these fears might have been, however, the fact that women artists associated with surrealism today enjoy much more popular appreciation as well as critical recognition than they would have without the feminist art-historical intervention of the 1970s and 1980s cannot be ignored. It might be fruitful to view the construction of the category of women's art (or literature) as a first performative step, which *makes visible* previously neglected art and literature produced by women. More than that, even though the term women's art or literature seemingly perpetuates the separation of women from the norm, it could also be argued that it implicitly performs a critique of the masculine bias of the 'universal'. Thus, rather than perpetuating women's exile from 'official' narratives, we might say that scholarship that focuses on women's art or literature holds up a critical mirror to this exile. Moreover, we should also note that such a focus does not seek to exclude or marginalise non-women artists or writers (as Tanning suggests above) but endeavours rather to readjust a historical and systemic imbalance: exhibitions and scholarship that focus on women artists or writers should be viewed as gestures of inclusion of women rather than exclusion of men.

When women are included in official narratives on the same terms as men, the category of women's art might no longer serve a critical purpose (or at least not the same as it serves today). Sadly, we have not yet arrived at this point. As Patricia Allmer observes:

> A cursory survey of large-scale surrealist exhibitions and publications indicates, nevertheless, that these [women] artists have still not secured guaranteed places within the field mapped by general surveys of both surrealism and modernism. Their under-representation ... suggests that the extensive work done on women artists has failed to alter the preconceptions of male creative authority and

male discursive power that control and organize the institutions of art history, exhibition-curation, and critical writing.[11]

Thus, categories such as women's art or women's literature still serve an important critical function, however much we might wish that they were no longer needed.

'By the way, what exactly makes me a woman?'

For contemporary feminist scholars, the problem with categories such as women's art or women's literature is not so much their segregationist tendencies as their implicit invocation of a shared female identity and a set of universal experiences common to all women – an essentialist tendency also picked up and critiqued by Tanning in her fierce response above ('what exactly makes me a woman?'). Most feminists today understand gender as a social construction without biological origin or essence, which, in the words of Judith Butler, is 'performatively produced' by repetition and 'compelled by the regulatory practices of gender coherence'.[12] Thus, to speak of 'women' as a stable category denoting essential characteristics might be seen not only as misguided but as perpetuating sexist stereotypes. Moreover, as Butler notes,

> If one 'is' a woman, that is surely not all one is; the term fails to be exhaustive, not because a 'pregendered' person transcends the specific paraphernalia of its gender, but because gender is not always constituted coherently or consistently in different historical contexts, and because gender intersects with racial, class, ethnic, sexual, and regional modalities of discursively constituted identities. As a result, it becomes impossible to separate out 'gender' from the political and cultural intersections in which it is invariably produced and maintained.[13]

Thus, as Butler and subsequent queer, intersectional, and postcolonial feminist theory demonstrate, not only is any ontology pretended by the term 'woman' (or even 'women') a fiction; the category might also be seen to obfuscate differences between regional, social, racial, or historical circumstances, while perpetuating a problematically universalist and transhistorical understanding of gender and sexuality.

The third-wave feminist questioning of the term 'woman'/'women' has been essential in exposing the problems that may result from uncritically assuming a shared universal female identity. At the same time, feminist scholarship cannot operate without a critical language to name instances of oppression resulting from hegemonic or patriarchal structures. We therefore continue to need the term 'women', although we must employ it self-consciously and all the while acknowledging its constructedness. We might think of this usage in terms of 'strategic essentialism', a critical strategy proposed by the postcolonial theorist Gayatri Chakravorty Spivak. This approach, which Spivak famously described as 'a *strategic* use of positivist essentialism in a scrupulously visible political interest',[14] involves employing categories such as 'women' in order to mobilise agency for marginalised groups, while simultaneously guarding against the rhetoric of fixed and universal identities. Butler, in *Bodies that Matter* (1993), similarly proposes that terms denoting sex, race, and gender might be self-consciously re-employed in ways that ultimately undercut the violence they have historically enacted:

> In this sense, the argument that the category of 'sex' is the instrument or effect of 'sexism' or its interpellating moment, that 'race' is the instrument or effect of 'racism' or its interpellating moment, that gender only exists in the service of heterosexism, does *not* entail that we ought never to make use of such terms, as if such terms could only and always reconsolidate the oppressive regimes of power by which they are spawned. On the contrary, precisely because such terms have been produced and constrained within such regimes, they ought to be repeated in directions that reverse and displace their originating aims ... Occupied by such terms and yet occupying them oneself risks a complicity, a repetition, a relapse into injury, but it is also the occasion to work the mobilizing power of injury, of an interpellation one never chose.[15]

Acutely aware of the problems inherent in the terms 'women' and 'women's writing', I have chosen the title *Surrealist Women's Writing: A Critical Exploration* for such strategic reasons. I am keenly aware that the writers discussed in this volume were formed by a variety of gendered discourses, which were in turn shaped by cultural, linguistic, historical, social, and racial factors. Clearly 'being a woman' in Paris in the 1920s was not the same thing as it was in Fort-de-France in the 1940s or in New York City or Cornwall in the 1980s.

Moreover, woman is in some ways a problematic sex/gender assignment for certain of these writers; indeed, as Claude Cahun (Lucy Schwob) famously announced: 'Masculine? Feminine? It depends on the situation. Neuter is the only gender that always suits me.'[16] In Cahun's photographic self-portraits, the artist sometimes appears in masculine attire and sometimes in exaggeratedly feminine costume and make-up. At other times the gender of Cahun's photographic persona is impossible to fit into a binary masculine–feminine system. As Katharine Conley aptly points out, Cahun's 'autobiographical self-representations ... [blur] the boundaries, categories and norms of established sexualities and ages ... When we look at her photographs, collages and self-portraits, we wonder whether we are seeing a woman or a man, a young or an old person, someone who is healthy or sick, a human being or an object.'[17] Thus, the inclusion of Cahun in a collection of essays devoted to women's writing in itself signals the unstable boundaries of the definition and meaning of this concept.

Conscious of the risk of complicity and repetition, *Surrealist Women's Writing*, then, proposes a strategic use of the term women's writing – one that aims to highlight a body of work that to date has been doubly marginalised – because surrealist women have historically attracted less critical attention than surrealist men and, also, because surrealist writing has received less consideration than surrealist visual art.

Scope and delimitations

The chapters in this volume discuss the written work of ten women associated with surrealism: Claude Cahun (1894–1954), Leonora Carrington (1917–2011), Colette Peignot (1903–38; also known by her pseudonym Laure), Suzanne Césaire (1915–66), Kay Sage (1898–1963), Unica Zürn (1916–70), Ithell Colquhoun (1906–88), Leonor Fini (1907–96), Dorothea Tanning (1910–2012), and Rikki Ducornet (b. 1943). The collection thus spans writing in English, French, and German from the 1920s to the 1990s by surrealist women based in France, Britain, the USA, Martinique, and Mexico.

Part of the aim of this book is to foreground writing by women who are otherwise mainly known for their visual production. For instance, Leonor Fini's visual output, which includes paintings, drawings, costumes, and masks, is currently a popular topic amongst feminist art historians, while the three novels she published in the 1970s have hardly received any mention at all. (Only one of them, *Rogomelec*, has appeared in English translation, and only very recently, in 2020.) Kay Sage's uninhabited architectural landscapes are well known; less well known are her plays (written in English) and poetry (in English, French, and Italian). Moreover, even though the British surrealist Ithell Colquhoun's novels and poetry have received some critical attention, she is primarily associated with her canvases and collages exploring occult themes and the unconscious.

Claude Cahun and Dorothea Tanning have recently come under critical scrutiny as literary writers, in *Reading Claude Cahun's Disavowals* (2013) by Jennifer L. Shaw and *A Surrealist Stratigraphy of Dorothea Tanning's Chasm* (2017) by Catriona McAra. Yet both artists and writers are nevertheless still chiefly thought of as visual artists. Cahun's provocative and gender-bending photographic work, which was serendipitously found amongst the possessions of Cahun's partner Marcel Moore after the latter's death in 1972, was 'rediscovered' by scholars in the late 1980s, and has since become hugely *en vogue*, probably because of how closely it seems to chime with contemporary theories of gender and sexuality. Shaw aptly describes the development thus:

> Cahun entered the pantheon of Surrealism as one of several forgotten women artists, but because she was 'rediscovered' at precisely the same moment when contemporary artists and scholars were exploring the politics of identity, her work also took on a different kind of importance. Claude Cahun became something of a cult figure – a heroine for art historians and critics with allegiances to postmodernism, feminism and queer theory.[18]

However, while such approaches are fruitful, Shaw suggests, they might not be able to 'go far enough'; 'If we end our analysis by pointing out the ways that Cahun's and Moore's photographs seem to prefigure our own postmodern interests, we lose sight of the specific aims of the project.'[19] As Shaw aptly demonstrates, the 'failed autobiography' *Disavowals, or Cancelled Confessions* (1930) showcases these other dimensions of Cahun's ambitious project. In addition to *Disavowals*, Cahun also published fiction, critical writing, and theory (most of which remains untranslated); as Rosemont points out, Cahun was indeed 'the principal pioneer in ... the preeminently masculine domain of theory and polemic ... Her prowess as a critical thinker and polemicist is formidable.'[20] Tanning's oeuvre, too, might be better understood when taking into consideration her only novel *Chasm* (2004), which she, as McAra shows in her compelling monograph, worked on for most of her career.[21] In addition to *Chasm*, Tanning also wrote autofiction, critical writing, and a large body of poetry.

Leonora Carrington's multi-genre oeuvre is currently receiving much attention from critics as well as general audiences – her fame amongst the latter group was certainly intensified by the 2017 publication of the bestselling biography *The Surreal Life of Leonora Carrington*, authored by the artist's grand-niece Joanna Moorhead.[22] It is also significant that most of her non-English writing exists in English translation; moreover, most of her writing is currently in print.[23] Parts of Carrington's literary oeuvre have been absorbed into mainstream literary circles, notably the short story 'The Debutante', which has appeared in several collections of feminist short stories,[24] and the novel *The Hearing Trumpet*, which has been reissued numerous times, most recently by Penguin in 2005, published with an introduction by the acclaimed novelist Ali Smith. Amongst critics, in addition to 'The Debutante' and *The Hearing Trumpet*, the memoir *Down Below* has also received considerable attention, although the rest of Carrington's substantial literary body of work remains comparatively under-studied. Jonathan P. Eburne and Catriona McAra's edited volume *Leonora Carrington and the International Avant-Garde* (2017), however, is devoted equally to Carrington's visual art and writing, and might signal a new and more interdisciplinary direction in scholarship on Carrington.[25]

Rikki Ducornet and Unica Zürn are primarily pigeonholed as literary writers, although both have also produced a considerable amount of pictorial work. Ducornet's fiction is situated at the intersection between surrealism, postmodernism, and magic realism and is frequently discussed alongside the writing of novelists such as Angela Carter and Italo Calvino. Zürn's autobiographic as well as fictional writing (some of which is available in English) often explores themes of violence and illness. The dissection of sentences in her anagram poetry, as Renée Riese Hubert observes, evokes an analogous disarticulation of the body, a thematic that Zürn developed in dialogue with her partner Hans Bellmer.[26]

Despite her extensive body of work, Zürn, however, is probably best known as Bellmer's partner and muse. And indeed, she is not the only woman surrealist who seems to be remembered mainly through her association with a male writer or artist. This is certainly true of the two non-fiction writers under scrutiny in this volume: Suzanne Césaire and Colette Peignot. The writing of both these women has unfortunately been overshadowed by the male writers with whom they associated. The feminist and anticolonial surrealism of Césaire reverberates through her contributions to the Martinican journal *Tropiques*, which she co-founded and edited with her husband Aimé Césaire in 1941. Yet, out of the couple it is usually Aimé Césaire who is foregrounded – both in surrealist and in postcolonial scholarship. The same is true for Peignot, who is often referred to as the muse of Georges Bataille and Michel Leiris (she was also Bataille's lover). Her writing was published only posthumously, under the pseudonym Laure – a name chosen by Bataille and Leiris to avoid the censure of Peignot's brother, who wanted her writing to remain unpublished. The continued affiliation of surrealist women with their more famous male partners is yet another reason why we still need the academic category of women's art or writing – critical narratives need to undo these knee-jerk associations, which tend to confine the woman artist in the role of muse, wife or lover, whose art or writing risk becoming seen as minor appendages to those of their male partner.

The selection of writers covered in this volume is of course far from comprehensive; there are numerous surrealist women writers who unfortunately fall outside its scope. The most conspicuous and regrettable omission is probably Joyce Mansour, one of postwar surrealism's most prolific poets and prose writers. Other important authors missing from the volume are Emmy Bridgwater, Marianne van Hirtum, Nelly Kaplan, Annie Le Brun, Nora Mitrani, Valentine Penrose, Gisèle Prassinos, Alice Rahon, Eva Švankmajerová, and Simone Yoyotte. A glance at the table of contents of Rosemont's *Surrealist Women* reveals several other absences. *Surrealist*

Women's Writing: A Critical Exploration is thus not a comprehensive critical history of surrealist women's writing; rather, it offers sustained analyses of the written work of a selection of women associated with surrealism. It is to be hoped that the future holds more critical work in the field of surrealist women's writing, which takes the writers unfortunately neglected here into consideration.

Although *Surrealist Women's Writing* is the first edited volume critically to focus solely on surrealist women's writing, it is of course not the first book to address this topic in some form. Susan Rubin Suleiman's discipline-shaping *Subversive Intent: Gender, Politics, and the Avant-Garde* (1990) argues that much avant-garde or surrealist writing by women engages in a parodic dialogue with earlier, male avant-garde artists and writers. This 'double allegiance' allows women writers, Suleiman suggests, to appropriate the subversive energy of earlier (male) avant-garde works while simultaneously parodying their gendered blind spots.[27] The most prominently featured surrealist woman in Suleiman's book is Leonora Carrington; elsewhere, however, Suleiman has also examined the writing of Gisèle Prassinos and Nelly Kaplan through the same interpretative lens.[28] Some of the written work of Carrington, Prassinos, and Joyce Mansour is covered in *Surrealism and Women* (1991, ed. Mary Ann Caws, Rudolf Kuenzli, and Gwen Raaberg), although most of the essays in the collection focus on visual art.[29] Katharine Conley's *Automatic Woman: The Representation of Woman in Surrealism* (1996) offers insightful readings of the autofiction of Carrington and Unica Zürn, and Natalya Lusty's elegantly argued *Surrealism, Feminism, Psychoanalysis* (2007) foregrounds Carrington's literary representations of transgression in the larger context of surrealism and feminism.[30] The 2013 special issue of *Mélusine*, subtitled *Autoreprésentation féminine*, also contains a few essays devoted to the writing of surrealist women, most notably that of Cahun and Carrington.[31] Although it is mainly devoted to visual art, Patricia Allmer's edited volume *Intersections: Women Artists/Surrealism/Modernism* (2016) also features essays on the writing of Cahun, Lise Deharme, and Carrington.[32]

The eleven chapters of *Surrealist Women's Writing* are organised in a loosely chronological order. In Chapter 1, Felicity Gee reads the writing of Claude Cahun, and in particular *Disavowals* (1930), as a philosophical testing of the boundaries both of the written word and of the self. Adopting Pierre Mac Orlan's designation of the textual fragments in *Disavowals* as 'poem-essays and essay-poems', Gee demonstrates how Cahun's work dialectically engages the realms of the poetic and the philosophical in order to provide a radical commentary both on the intimately personal and on aspects of society, politics, culture, and gender in the early twentieth century – a commentary that still holds relevance for the twenty-first-century reader.

Chapters 2 and 3 are devoted to the writing of Leonora Carrington. In Chapter 2, Anna Watz reads Carrington's French short stories published in the volumes *The House of Fear* (1938) and *The Oval Lady* (1939) as an active engagement with surrealist theories of collage and subjectivity, as they were articulated by André Breton and Max Ernst. The chapter argues that, whilst Carrington's stories participate in surrealist experiments with 'convulsive identity', they simultaneously express an ambivalence about the the effects for women of the surrealist exaltation of passivity, irrational abandon, and non-agency. Ultimately, the chapter suggests, Carrington's engagement with and extension of the theories and practices of Breton and Ernst demonstrate that surrealist theory is not a 'male project', as has sometimes been argued; moreover, it proposes that such theory includes implicitly feminist elements.

Jeannette Baxter, in Chapter 3, adopts a politico-historical perspective on a selection of Carrington's English narratives written after her relocation from Paris to New York, and, eventually, to Mexico ('White Rabbits', 1941–42, *The Stone Door*, 1976, and 'The Happy Corpse Story', 1971). Not only were these works written in exile, Baxter argues – they are at core about exile experiences. By juxtaposing what she calls Carrington's 'dark exilic imagination' with writings on the topic of exile by Hannah Arendt, Theodor W. Adorno, and Edward Said, Baxter teases out a disquiet haunting Carrington's narratives regarding what it means to be human in a time of war, displacement, horror, and cruelty. For Baxter, these exile writings not only illuminate Carrington's own personal history but provide a poignant reflection on the radical uncertainties of the modern human condition.

In Chapter 4, Michael Richardson examines the writing of Colette Peignot, which to a great extent revolves around the notion of the sacred. Richardson demonstrates how Peignot's understanding of the sacred was elaborated in response to Michel Leiris's foundational essay 'The Sacred in Everyday Life' (1938) and surrealist ideas about myth and the marvellous, but also that it was intensely inflected by her own personal experience. Peignot's notion of the sacred is predicated on 'communication', a term which for Peignot signifies a paradoxical or dialectical oscillation between extremes: a simultaneous movement towards other people and away from them and the presence of death in the most vital moments of life.

Suzanne Césaire's writing is the subject of Chapter 5. Kara M. Rabbitt here explores Césaire's engagement with surrealism in her essays published between 1941 and 1945 in the journal *Tropiques*, which employ surrealism as a literary, cultural, and political tool with which to construct a distinctly Martinican cultural identity. Rabbitt's chapter demonstrates not only Césaire's immense importance as a cultural figure in Martinique but also how her anti-imperialist writings constitute some of the most sustained engagements with surrealism produced in the Caribbean context.

In Chapter 6, Katharine Conley investigates the hitherto largely unknown and critically neglected poetry of Kay Sage. Focusing on poems that feature animals (most importantly birds, which stand in for Sage herself), Conley reveals a new and perhaps surprising thematic aspect of Sage's oeuvre – a concern with connections with other beings, which stands in contrast to the solitary landscapes depicted in her paintings. Through perceptive close readings of these animal poems, Conley shows how Sage's crafty French–English wordplay engenders a multiplicity of meanings and instances of double entendre. While on the surface appearing simple, these poems are in fact multifaceted reflections on human life and experience.

Patricia Allmer's Chapter 7 is concerned with the issue of untranslatability in the prose – both autobiographical and fictional – of Unica Zürn. This chapter takes issue with how existing English translations of Zürn's German works evidence lexical and syntactical translational choices that reduce the complexity of these texts to autobiographical reflections of the author's life. In this way, the more abstract, philosophical themes in Zürn's writing, as well as her intertextual references to German literary works and their adaptations into different media, are lost. Through careful textual analysis, Allmer exposes these translational shortfalls and demonstrates the works' own preoccupation with the very issue of untranslatability.

In Chapter 8, Mark S. Morrisson focuses on Ithell Colquhoun's hitherto largely unknown poetic oeuvre. Challenging received critical narratives regarding the supposed disappearance of surrealist and modernist poetic efforts in Britain after the Second World War, until the British Poetry Revival in the 1960s and 1970s, Morrisson reveals that Colquhoun regularly published automatic or esoteric surrealist poetry in various literary periodicals and little magazines from the 1940s through the 1980s. The chapter not only sheds light on previously neglected aspects of Colquhoun's work but also constitutes a revision of the historiography of British postwar poetry and its relationship to surrealism.

Jonathan P. Eburne, in Chapter 9, explores the three novels that Leonor Fini published in the 1970s – *Mourmour* (1976), *L'Oneiropompe* (1978), and *Rogomelec* (1979). Reading these texts as autofictions that offer mythologised versions of Fini's artistic life, Eburne demonstrates how they, like her art and domestic life, ultimately explore what Fini herself terms the abhuman. Fini's abhumanism rejects compulsory and reproductive heterosexuality, instead favouring queer, incestuous, polyamorous, and cross-species erotic intimacies that involve the animal, the vegetal, and the mineral. However, it is not a call to political action; rather, as Eburne shows, it functions in terms of perversion – not only of normative sexuality and humanist ideology, but also of political engagement and militancy.

In Chapter 10, Catriona McAra offers a reading of Dorothea Tanning's little-known non-fiction writing from the 1970s, 1980s, and early 1990s, which critically engages with intellectual history, artists, and artistic movements. The chapter frames Tanning's critical writing in relation both to her visual work and to revisionary feminist perspectives on surrealism that, like Tanning's written work, started emerging in the 1970s. Despite the fact that Tanning herself proclaimed that she was suspicious of feminism, McAra demonstrates that her critical writings – read alongside her visual and fictional output – indeed manifest a feminist politics still pertinent in the twenty-first century.

Kristoffer Noheden, in Chapter 11, considers the fiction of Rikki Ducornet from an ecocritical perspective. Focusing in particular on the novels *The Stain* (1984), *Entering Fire* (1986), *The Jade Cabinet* (1993), and *Phosphor in Dreamland* (1995), Noheden argues that Ducornet's writings engage occult knowledge systems in order to present an ecological and non-anthropocentric worldview in which nature and different lifeforms are deeply interconnected. Positioning Ducornet's narratives in the context of surrealism's ecological imperative, this chapter urges us, through Ducornet, to turn our careful attention to the interplay and language of humans and animals, as well as nature in a broader sense.

The chapters in this collection demonstrate that women associated with surrealism produced writing across a variety of genres – fiction, autobiography, poetry, philosophy, and theory as well as criticism. Taken together, the chapters illustrate the richness and complexity of this extensive body of work. In her introduction to *Surrealist Women*, Rosemont expresses concern that isolating surrealist women's production from that of men might involve an attempt to divorce these women from the surrealist movement as a whole. 'Ironically', Rosemont writes, 'the old (mostly male) critics who ignored or minimized women in their studies of surrealism are not that different from these newer (often female) critics who ignore or minimize surrealism itself in their studies of women who took part in it. Each of these one-sided and erroneous views reinforces the other, and both prop up the insidious fiction that surrealism is yet another "Men Only" movement.'[33] This narrative is continually contested in the chapters in this collection, all of which examine their writers through the lens of surrealism; together, these chapters constitute a powerful statement about the crucial importance of women participants in the surrealist movement.

Notes

1 See, e.g., Gloria Feman Orenstein, 'Women of Surrealism', *The Feminist Art Journal* (Spring 1973), pp. 15–21; 'Art History and the Case for the Women of

Surrealism', *Journal of General Education* 27:1 (Spring 1975), pp. 31–54; and *The Theater of the Marvelous* (New York: New York University Press, 1975).
2 Whitney Chadwick, *Women Artists and the Surrealist Movement* (London: Thames & Hudson, 1985).
3 Recent exhibitions include *Angels of Anarchy: Women Artists and Surrealism* (Manchester City Gallery, Manchester, 2009–10); *Unica Zürn: Dark Spring* (The Drawing Centre, New York, 2009); *Surreal Friends: Leonora Carrington, Remedios Varo and Kati Horna* (Pallant House Gallery, Chichester, 2010); *Double Solitaire: The Surreal Worlds of Kay Sage and Yves Tanguy* (Katonah Museum of Art, New York, 2011); *In Wonderland: The Surrealist Adventures of Women Artists in Mexico and the United States* (LACMA, Los Angeles, 2012); *Leonora Carrington: The Celtic Surrealist* (Irish Museum of Modern Art, Dublin, 2013–14); *Leonora Carrington* (Liverpool Tate, Liverpool, 2015); *Dorothea Tanning: Web of Dreams* (Alison Jacques Gallery, London, 2014); *Claude Cahun: Beneath this Mask* (The Southbank Centre, London, 2015); *Leonor Fini: Réalisme Irréel* (Weinstein Gallery, San Francisco, 2015); *Ithell Coquhoun: Image and Imagination* (Penlee House Gallery, Penzance, 2016); *Gillian Wearing and Claude Cahun: Behind the Mask Another Mask* (National Portrait Gallery, London, 2017); *Leonor Fini: Theatre of Desire, 1930–1990* (Museum of Sex, New York, 2018); *Dorothea Tanning: Behind the Door, Another Invisible Door* (Museo Reina Sofía, Madrid, 2018, and Tate Modern, London, 2019); *Greta Knutson Tzara – I Nytt Ljus* (Norrköpings konstmuseum, Norrköping, Sweden, 2019); *Claude Cahun* (Mjellby Konstmuseum, Halmstad, Sweden, 2019); and *The Female Gaze: Women Surrealists in the Americas and Europe* (Heather James Fine Art, New York, 2019).
4 As Penelope Rosemont argues, '[e]cological concerns engaged the Surrealist Movement as a whole almost from the start … But it is primarily the women in surrealism who stressed these matters, and it is they who deserve credit for making the ecological critique an integral part of the surrealist project'. Penelope Rosemont, 'Introduction: All My Names Know Your Leap: Surrealist Women and Their Challenge', in Penelope Rosemont (ed.), *Surrealist Women: An International Anthology* (Austin: University of Texas Press, 1998), p. li.
5 Penelope Rosemont, 'In the Service of Revolution, 1930–1939', in *Surrealist Women*, p. 47.
6 Quoted in Peter Webb, *Sphinx: The Life and Art of Leonor Fini* (New York: The Vendome Press, 2007), p. 273.
7 Dorothea Tanning, *Between Lives: An Artist and Her World* (New York and London: W.W. Norton, 2001), p. 334.
8 *BOMB Magazine* 33 (Fall 1990), https://bombmagazine.org/articles/dorothea-tanning/, accessed 13 December 2019.
9 Dorothea Tanning quoted in Lea Vergine, *L'Altra metà dell'avanguardia 1910–1940: Pittrici e scultrici nei movimenti delle avanguardie storiche* (Milan: Gabriele Mazzotta editore, 1980), p. 276; translation mine; ellipsis in the original.
10 See Chadwick, *Women Artists and the Surrealist Movement*, p. 12; Judith D. Suther, *A House of Her Own: Kay Sage, Solitary Surrealist* (Lincoln: University

of Nebraska Press, 1997), p. 235; and Penelope Rosemont, 'All My Names Know Your Leap', in *Surrealist Women*, p. xxx. We should also remember that some women artists whom we now associate with surrealism were themselves reluctant to accept the label surrealist.
11 Patricia Allmer, 'Introduction', in Patricia Allmer (ed.), *Intersections: Women Artists/Surrealism/Modernism* (Manchester: Manchester University Press, 2016), p. 3.
12 Judith Butler, *Gender Trouble: Feminism and the Subversion of Identity* (1990. New York: Routledge, 2007), p. 33.
13 Butler, *Gender Trouble*, p. 6.
14 Gayatri Chakravorty Spivak quoted in Stephen Morton, *Gayatri Spivak: Ethics, Subalternity and the Critique of Postcolonial Reason* (Cambridge: Polity Press, 2007), p. 126.
15 Judith Butler, *Bodies that Matter: On the Discursive Limits of 'Sex'* (New York and London: Routledge, 1993), 123.
16 Claude Cahun, *Disavowals, or Cancelled Confessions*, trans. Susan de Muth (London: Tate Publishing, 2007), p. 151.
17 Katharine Conley, *Surrealist Ghostliness* (Lincoln: University of Nebraska Press, 2013), p. 45.
18 Jennifer Shaw, *Reading Claude Cahun's* Disavowals (Aldershot: Ashgate, 2013), p. 6.
19 *Ibid.*, p. 7.
20 Rosemont, 'In the Service of Revolution', p. 48.
21 Catriona McAra, *A Surrealist Stratigraphy of Dorothea Tanning's* Chasm (London and New York: Routledge, 2017).
22 Joanna Moorhead, *The Surreal Life of Leonora Carrington* (London: Virago, 2017).
23 The year 2017 saw the reissue of Carrington's short stories in *The Complete Stories of Leonora Carrington* (St Louis MO: Dorothy, a Publishing Project) and *The Debutante and Other Stories* (London: Silver Press).
24 See, e.g., Angela Carter (ed.), *Wayward Girls and Wicked Women* (London: Virago, 1986), and Jessica Amanda Salmonson (ed.), *What Did Miss Darrington See? An Anthology of Feminist Supernatural Fiction* (New York: The Feminist Press at CUNY, 1989).
25 Jonathan P. Eburne and Catriona McAra (eds), *Leonora Carrington and the International Avant-Garde* (Manchester: Manchester University Press, 2017). Eburne's monograph *Surrealism and the Art of Crime* (Ithaca: Cornell University Press, 2008) also deals to a substantial degree with Carrington's writing.
26 Renée Riese Hubert, *Magnifying Mirrors: Women, Surrealism, and Partnership* (Lincoln: University of Nebraska Press, 1994), p. 150.
27 Susan Rubin Suleiman, *Subversive Intent: Gender, Politics, and the Avant-Garde* (Cambridge, MA: Harvard University Press, 1990), p. xvii.
28 Susan Rubin Suleiman, 'Surrealist Black Humor: Masculine/Feminine', *Papers of Surrealism* 1 (2003), www.research.manchester.ac.uk/portal/files/63517385/surrealism_issue_1.pdf, accessed 5 January 2020.

29 Mary Ann Caws, Rudolf Kuenzli, and Gwen Raaberg (eds), *Surrealism and Women* (Cambridge, MA: The MIT Press, 1991).
30 Katharine Conley, *Automatic Woman: The Representation of Woman in Surrealism* (Lincoln: University of Nebraska Press, 1996); Natalya Lusty, *Surrealism, Feminism, Psychoanalysis* (Aldershot: Ashgate, 2007).
31 Georgiana Colvile and Annie Richard, ed., *Autoreprésentation féminine*, special issue of *Mélusine*, no. 33, 2013.
32 See Jonathan P. Eburne, 'Savage Balm: Claud Cahun and Lise Deharme', and Victoria Ferentinou, 'Trespassing Boundaries: Liminality, Hybridity and the Quest for Identity in Leonora Carrington's *The Stone Door*', in Patricia Allmer (ed.), *Intersections: Women Artists / Surrealism / Modernism* (Manchester: Manchester University Press, 2016).
33 Rosemont, 'All My Names Know Your Leap', p. xxx.

1

'The dung beetle's snowball': the philosophic narcissism of Claude Cahun's essay-poetry

Felicity Gee

Published in Paris, 1930, Claude Cahun's *Aveux non avenus* is a work 'virtually entirely dedicated to the word adventure',[1] although given that it took a decade to write (1919–29) it is also an evidential text of refashioning, of cancellations and additions. Translated as *Disavowals, or Cancelled Confessions*,[2] it breaks ostensibly with traditions of autobiography or confessional writing through experimentation with form on the one hand, and a deliberately misleading and forking investigation of the self on the other. It is an expansive collection of writings – poems, diary entries, notes on dreams and nightmares, Socratic dialogue, mini-essays on modern politics, gender, love, and human avarice. Cahun did not believe that the hallowed and fetishised form of autobiographical writing could constitute a life lived. As Jennifer L. Shaw argues, 'it would be wrong to interpret her work as a reflection of her biography. Personal experience informs it, but it is complex, referential, paradoxical and often ironic. Even her most directly political writings never sit still for the reader.'[3] Consequently, rather than providing a series of chronological self-portraits,[4] *Disavowals* dwells on absences and illusions, splitting and multiplication, hunting down '[t]he void bang in the middle' of the self.[5] In so doing, Cahun addresses and challenges fear by fidgeting, leaping, and galloping over extensive ground and numerous stylistic and thematic regions. What is astonishing in this spatio-temporal feat is the book's depth, which at no point is compromised by its breadth. *Disavowals* is an intensely profound work that rewards the reader with a tender lyricism, supported with sharp philosophical observation. This chapter explores the potential impact of Cahun's radical politics for the reader in the twenty-first century. It considers the manifold ways in which *Disavowals*, in particular, keeps reinventing itself. The text, illustrated with striking, provocative photomontages, never stops. Its 'prismatic'[6] narcissism and labyrinthine turns beg the reader to begin again, to trace a different path through the ideas, and to draw new conclusions.

Born Lucy Renée Mathilde Schwob in Nantes, France, in 1894, the niece of the symbolist writer Marcel Schwob, Cahun begins publishing with a

1.1 Claude Cahun, *Self Portrait (Near a Granite Wall)*, 1916.

new name that reflects a gender-neutral identity, and establishes a perspective from which to interrogate and play with fixed ideas of the female and feminine.[7] Cahun's ambivalence regarding the socio-hegemonic ley lines determining gender is frequently humorously rendered: 'Shuffle the cards. Masculine? Feminine? It depends on the situation. Neuter is the only gender that always suits me.'[8] Aided in areas of design and image reproduction by stepsister Marcel Moore (née Suzanne Malherbe – the two became lifelong lovers, friends, and intimate collaborators), Cahun categorised *Disavowals* as 'a psychological and moral experiment'.[9] As Shaw details, the book was originally published in an edition of five hundred copies, and copies of photographs documenting its launch at the Librarie José Cortí in Paris are kept in the Cahun archive at the Jersey Heritage Trust. Shaw notes how reproductions of the photomontages from the book shared window space with Max Ernst's *La Femme 100 têtes* (1929) and the magazine *Bifur*.[10] Much has been written on Cahun's gender, the use of masks and costume, and the direct strategy of polymorphous performance in their work, to which this chapter is indebted.[11] Departing from these intriguing aspects of performance and self-fashioning, this chapter prioritises instead Cahun's *textual* politics. It considers what the meandering word-paths, the returns and repetitions of moral, ethical, social, and sexual politics might tell us about a distinct form of poetics that eschews shame or embarrassment and enacts a deeply philosophical dialogue on selfhood as well as on contemporary European society. In particular it draws upon the affective shifts that proliferate in and between the words and layers of ideas, and which ask the reader to reflect upon life not as a fixed subject but as a conduit of knowledge, desire, passion, and argument. Ultimately, Cahun's is a poetics that is political, didactic, elusive, funny, and intensely affecting. The questions they create are not simply about male, female, lesbian, androgynous, transvestite subjects and positions, but articulate the burgeoning axes of difference that exist between human subjects, other human subjects, and the world.

Disavowals offers a radical sexual/textual politics[12] born out of a fierce intellectual engagement with modernist form and its predecessors (classicism, romanticism, symbolism). It shares the spirit of the modernist poem, which, according to Toril Moi, is characterised by 'its abrupt shifts, ellipses, breaks and apparent lack of logical construction … [the] kind of writing in which the rhythms of the body and the unconscious have managed to break through the strict rational defences of conventional social meaning'.[13] This is not to say that *Disavowals* is devoid of reason – quite the contrary – but that the thread of reasoning often breaks to enjoy digressive and experimental ideas, which may or may not cohere and coalesce. Cahun asks the reader to face not only her own perceived lack but, more widely, to consider the often invisible and indeterminate aspects at the heart of modern existence. This is clearly outlined towards the end of *Disavowals*, in chapter IX (subtitled 'We get the god we deserve, unfortunately for us'), in the interlude 'Snowball'. They write:

> A rolling stone gathers no moss, but covers the original form in clay where gravel sticks, debris, so well bound together by the movement, so thoroughly incorporated, that its form is no longer visible, nor its point of origin. The dung beetle's snowball grows fatter, hardens, suffices to set off an avalanche. Whoever wishes to strip his soul bare must expect to see the dubious amalgam completely fall apart in his hands.
>
> This surgical blade with which analysis or religion arms us against ourselves will it encounter an ivory core – or just rubbish, rubbish, piles of rubbish all the way into its unrecognisable centre, dust swept along the wind?[14]

Cahun's tongue-in-cheek wordplay takes the concept of the uprooted, shifting stone and reveals its paradoxical nature. Fantasised in this verse as being pure (as snow), precious and strong (as ivory) with an original core value, the stone (human) in its modern setting can only gather debris, growing fat (greed and lack of rigour) and becoming unrecognisable. When subjected to interrogation and moral questioning, Cahun asks whether this boulder of excrement will only reveal layer upon layer of rubbish, its value scattering in veils of indiscernible dust upon the wind, with no residual aura. A damning portrait of the modern human reimagined as a dung-beetle's ball, Cahun highlights the Sisyphean task of attempting to negotiate selfhood in an era of increasingly consumer-driven culture, where often narrow definitions of gender were reproduced in advertising, popular entertainment, and art. The jarring juxtaposition of satire and melancholy, of purity and filth, rapid movement and slow amalgamation, solid and ephemeral forms, is exemplary of their ability to unpick social reality at its seams. For Cahun, nothing is fixed, nothing is certain, and if we stare hard enough in the mirror, the world, its history, and its rules begin to unravel. Whether the writing is a response to consumer capitalism, discoveries in sexology, a questionnaire posed in *Minotaure* by the surrealists,[15] or interrogating classical narratives on femininity, Cahun's rapier wit and refreshing honesty shatter preconceptions of what it is to be a modernist woman writer, just as their photographic oeuvre challenges the oft-discussed misogyny of surrealist artists who favour women as muses. As Elza Adamowicz reminds us: 'The medium of photomontage undoes specularity by fabricating an open, unresolved, and composite self'; this surfeit of faces, Adamowicz wryly observes, is Cahun's 'femme 100 têtes': 'less the hapless, headless female body of a Max Ernst than the hundred-headed body of the empowered female subject'.[16]

Disavowals is a textual collage that offers the antidote to the dung-beetle's snowball, where the 'void bang in the middle' of self, and, by extension, society, is replaced by an aura, returned to us through Cahun's surgical knife – literally and emotionally cutting. Slips and shards of objects, snippets of dialogue, and reworkings of mythical tales fan out in generous abundance. Where the dung-beetle's ball is comprised of sedimented, cloying layers, Cahun's textual layers free the source materials from any binding context, reinvesting them with new potential and encouraging new associations and emotions to emerge for the reader. Walter Benjamin valued the work of surrealists at a time when the mass reproduction of cultural objects threatened a loss of aura, or uniqueness: 'Every day the urge grows stronger to get hold of an object at very close range by way of its *likeness*, its reproduction.'[17] Benjamin's consideration of an elimination or 'withering' of 'aura' in early twentieth-century culture finds that 'authentic' existence has been supplanted by 'a plurality of copies' whereby a work of art, or an object, ceases to 'transmit' 'its testimony to the history [and tradition] it has experienced'.[18] Cahun understood the need to mobilise the modes of production available to them – illustration, photography, poetry, performance, sculpture, critical writing, photomontage – in order to re-conduct aura back to the public through a polysemic mode of address. In other words, the traditions and histories of their references to classical and popular culture when juxtaposed into a poetic counterpoint retain the authenticity (Benjamin's 'aura') of their origins because they have been revivified through Cahun's artistry and politicised perspective. In the essay 'Prenez garde aux objets domestiques' written for *Cahiers d'art*, a companion piece to their contribution to the 1936 *Surrealist Exhibition of Objects* at the Charles Ratton Gallery in London, Cahun reveals a democratic, surrealist approach to modernity:

> I insist on the primordial truth: one must oneself discover, manipulate, tame, and construct irrational objects to be able to appreciate the particular or general value of those displayed here. That is why, in certain respects, manual laborers may be in a better position than intellectuals to understand them, were it not for the fact that the whole of capitalist society – communist propaganda included – diverts them from doing so. And that is why you are beginning to dig into your pockets, and perhaps to empty them out on the table.[19]

Here we must begin with ourselves, the objects in our pockets and littered about our houses, the natural objects that form backdrops to our daily routines. These sentiments find an earlier release through the creative practice enacted in *Disavowals*, an indirect and surrealist approach to modern, capitalist life. On the dust jacket for the Tate edition of *Disavowals*, Dawn Ades declares Cahun 'a major surrealist writer and radical theorist of sexuality', and to this I would add philosopher: 'For myself I'm interested in making the game more complicated. Those who live by the tongue have discovered a way of talking that replaces action, that's even more simple – and less compromising.'[20] Complexity is precisely how Cahun manages to weave poetry and philosophy into searching, essayistic treatises, which, as I will demonstrate, push at the boundaries between the disciplines of poetry, art history, theory, and philosophy.

At the very end of *Disavowals*, Cahun writes the words:

> Dear Strangers, keep your distance: I have only you in the world. And me? What about me? ...' someone shouts: myself. My beautiful future, the unhoped for reserve, comes to me. Present already past, you who evade me, one moment more respite ... Provided that it's not too late.[21]

It is all too easy to read oneself into the gaps in this free verse, the self and the other locked into the crucial moment of a promised alignment that may already have passed. The giddy vertigo of a spatio-temporal tension in which past selves and future selves dance at arm's length is an acute realisation of the idea of potential. Potential is always ahead, something to come, but the desire for it is ever present. These ideas chime with the rather low-grade photograph of a dirt road with a vanishing horizon that accompanies the table of contents directly following this verse at the end of *Disavowals*. The

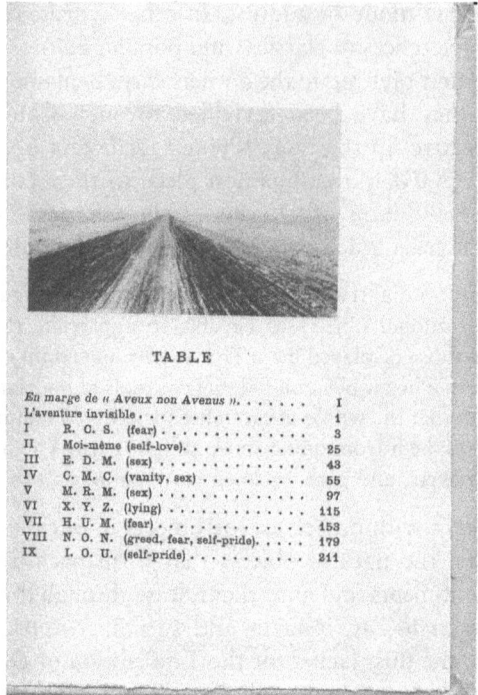

1.2 Claude Cahun, Table of Contents from *Aveux non avenus*, Éditions du Carrefour, 1930.

photograph acts as a coda, or a return, to the opening sentence: 'The invisible adventure.'[22] The words quoted above discuss an adventure into the self, which is poised on the point of becoming both in and against the ebb of time, an idea that is doubled in the photograph where the self in human form is replaced by the horizon, the gaze fixed on a landscape devoid of human presence. The image is suggestive of movement passed; it bears the traces of prior journeys etched in white over the charcoal surface of the road. It also evokes potential movement towards a future, where the cropped perspective – entering the path *in medias res* – urges the viewer forward towards the horizon, towards the 'invisible adventure'. It is interesting as a metaphorical image in that it replaces the reflective surface required of Narcissus with the horizon – centripetal introspection to centrifugal potential. Roger Cardinal has remarked of Cahun's landscape photographs (numerous examples of which were taken on Jersey) that they are shot 'as if the edge of the land were a zone especially conducive to transformation, a place where known things yield readily to a thrilling differentness, an enthralling indecisiveness of polymorphousness'.[23] The photograph is a contemplative image in that it seems to index Cahun's detailed philosophical adventures into the self, but then leaves the body behind, leading forwards into thought abstracted. The monochrome reproduction of the view lends a rather sombre tone, and, coupled with Cahun's refrain, 'Provided that it's not too late', encourages introspective reflection that cleverly incorporates the previous pages back upon itself. In chapter II, for example, we might fold the following words back into the photograph: 'It's all about converging lines. They don't meet for long. Where they stop is arbitrary. Continue to bring these lines to life, each in its own direction: you will correctly call them divergent.'[24] The relationship between image and text is always taut and philosophical, regardless of whether it is comedic, dramatic, or dark. Here it manages to evoke invisibility, what is felt, but not necessarily present, or what is fantasised and fleeting. By careful design, the original dust jacket of the 1933 edition wraps this philosophical working through of the visible and invisible, with *calligrammes*[25] of the book's title – the front cover arranged as a crossroads (the starting point) and the back arranged in the form of a circular clock with a minute and second hand, seeming to expand the words 'Provided that it's not too late'.

The French writer Pierre Mac Orlan's essays on photography and the *'fantastique social'* or social fantastic ruminate on the camera's ability to condense the mood and preoccupations of an epoch. He argues that 'the mystery that emanates from certain sights, certain people, and certain objects does not spring just from the power of revelation that a human brain can possess'[26] but is *witnessed* through the camera lens. We know that the camera held important sway for Cahun, providing testimony for the enactments of self. The camera, both machine and audience, realised ideas based in a love of theatre, classical myth, and literature, as well as developing elements of surrealist practice such as the privileging of chance and the radical power of unexpected juxtaposition. An amateur photographer (evidence in the Jersey Heritage Trust archive shows that photographs were sent away and developed commercially rather than processed in a personal darkroom), Cahun used the camera as an intermediary in order for multiple real and fantasised identities to proliferate. As Agnès Lhermitte notes regarding *Disavowals*, 'the interior space of Claude Cahun is constructed in the text through juxtaposition and superimposition of diverse angles of viewing, a prismatic vision', and the photomontages contribute 'the merciless mental exploration that cut Cahun's body into tiny pieces'.[27] Mac Orlan, a fan of Marcel Schwob and frequent visitor to the salons of Montmartre and its spectacles, seems to nurture a predilection for nightlife and its phantasmagoric allure, focusing more closely on the milieu of Cahun's mise-en-scène. In his preface to the first French edition of *Disavowals*, he seems to align Cahun's spirit with the spirit of Parisian nightlife that is so dramatically rendered in the photographer Eugène Atget's ghostly nightscapes of the city. He imagines Cahun as a wanderer of the night: 'This night broods over a strange congress of sometimes tender, sometimes furious forms and ideas. A philosophical orchestra plays discreetly. At dawn, all of this disappears.'[28] Undeniably evocative, Mac Orlan's romantic imagining of Cahun as barely human *flâneuse*[29] fails to apprehend the solidity of the ideas accompanying these migratory adventures. Cahun is interested not in revealing the mysterious elements of life that Mac Orlan discusses in 'Élements de fantastique social' (1929) per se but in capturing acts of transformation and recording the relationship between self and other, where other is by turns one's own psyche, the exterior environment, one's lover (who sometimes assists in the taking of the photograph or is imagined in interior dialogue), or a fictional figure drawn from long ago. Nevertheless, Mac Orlan's description of *Disavowals* as containing a series of 'poem-essays' or 'essay-poems' is evocative, revealing a deeper connection with the philosophical direction of Cahun's mysterious twists and turns. He writes:

> *The sum total of poem-essays and essay-poems* contained in this publication ... is the equivalent of the more or less regulation 300 pages of an adventure novel ... Ideas trace elegant parabolas to end in a tragic unfolding, *exploding without a sound* ... The characters that evolve in this funeral procession are not exactly phantoms. More exactly, *these are apparitions whose weight, nonetheless, can be calculated*, who cannot evade the touch of a hand.[30]

Despite its moments of romantic hyperbole, Mac Orlan's overall verdict on *Disavowals* understands the temerity with which Cahun writes, and highlights the text's conscious difficulty, an observation many scholars have echoed in their own reactions to it; Kate Kline, for example, refers to 'the erratic, confused, and confusing rhythm of the text', which nevertheless 'convincingly communicates the incoherence of reality'.[31] Mac Orlan's is an intimate and intellectual engagement with the writing, keenly picking out the emotional and affective, as well as the critical and narrative, strategies deployed by Cahun. But it is the almost casual mention of 'poem-essays and essay-poems' ('*poème-essais et essai-poèmes*' in the original) that stopped me in my tracks. To my mind Mac Orlan's compound nouns encapsulate perfectly the poetic and philosophical tension that courses through *Disavowals*, moving unceasingly back and forth between the condensation of personal sensory intensities and more sprawling, investigatory prose linked to socio-political and cultural aspects of early twentieth-century life. Here Mac Orlan alludes to the symbolist conceit of the melancholy heart which could be said to correspond to Cahun's frustration and bitterness in negotiating life with love, particularly in chapter

III, where a long-form poem entitled 'Morose Delights' ribbons through various acts of voyeurism and physical involvement with lovers:

> From now on one will ponder
> whether morose delight,
> passed through the sieve of time
> isn't preferable to pleasure.
> It is the juice of it,
> the corrupted liquid
> concentrated, purified,
> stronger and more lasting.[32]

A poetic treatise on memory and forgetting, 'Morose Delights' speaks of the maturation of pain over time, and the role of art in immortalising a favourable view of love (classical statues serve as key examples) that serves to aid in forgetting and prepares one to repeat the process over again. But Cahun's reflective moroseness shifts to something more intense in the following chapter (IV), where it reflects on how art can also obfuscate and conceal:

> Where love is concerned, it's up close that illusion corrupts our senses.
> In direct proportion to the distance he puts between himself and his beloved, the lover's thoughts circle love's fantasy, getting smaller and smaller – centre at last, stand still.
> And his thoughts see that there is nothing, that they were moving round a void, that they exist alone.[33]

Here Cahun crafts a baroque conceit of decorative illusion, or *engaño* – deceit, *trompe l'oeil*, trickery – that proliferates in layers around the void, which in turn represents a fear of emptiness, nothingness, the *horror vacui*. In this particular passage, Cahun investigates the traps of love, the suffering entailed therein, and the pleasurable humiliation in deceit. The surface, like Cahun's layered selves in the 'ludicrous merry-go-round'[34] of repeated encounters with the mirror, is illusory: a 'baroque exhibitionism'[35] that is tethered to the anxiety, not of existing at the margins but of not existing at all. The acute fear of illusory reality here extends to the human figure, the couple. I read this passage as a moment of impasse, where the philosophical enquiry into the idea that one *is not seen* by the world results in a fleeting illusion of self in love. This is not, of course, simply about love, it is also about the fear of a version of the world that does not accept the fantasies of its subjects, of a society that fails to recognise the power in them.

Mac Orlan's allusion, above, to Cahun's proliferating ideas (and selves) as a series of apparitions is unusual in that it unexpectedly attributes weight and measure to a phenomenon (the apparition) which is associated with palimpsestic weightlessness. He reinforces the concept of the poem-essay/essay-poem by measuring Cahun's writing in terms of its power to impress

1.3 Claude Cahun, *Self Portrait (Lower Body, Seaweed, and Le Pere)*, 1932.

upon the reader. He hereby lays claim to a kind of writing, an essayism, which weighs and measures ideas through experiment and repetition. The etymology of the essay or *essai* dates to the twelfth-century Vulgar Latin base *exagium*, meaning a weighing, or weight, and the verb *exigere*, to try, test, examine. Contemporary usage derives from the Middle French usage of *essai*, furthered by Michel de Montaigne's collected work *Essais* (commencing in 1572). The essay is not about a definitive conclusion, or the exhaustion of its subjects; rather it is more often determined by digression, tangential experiment, and multiple, intertextual references and forking paths. It is thought in becoming – beginning, repeating, trying, failing – levelled against an implied other, audience or reader. Brian Dillon, in his self-reflexive long-form essay *Essayism*, describes how the essay performs 'a combination of exactitude and evasion. A form that would instruct, seduce, and mystify in equal measure.' He urges his reader to '[i]magine a type of writing so hard to define its very name should be something like an effort, an attempt, a trial ... Imagine what it might rescue from disaster and achieve at the levels of form, style, texture and therefore, at the level of thought.'[36] Throughout *Disavowals*, the Cahun-character, seemingly determined by their corporeal body, searches for weight and for meaning in mirrors and in dreams; Cahun the philosopher-poet/poet-philosopher weighs the world in spite of 'the horror of the unknown' and the internal fear that '[m]y thoughts were not strong enough'.[37] The slippage between the self as a part of an objective reality and the self as an abstract concept is noted in Maurice Merleau-Ponty's *The Visible and the Invisible*, whereby '[t]o touch *oneself*, to see *oneself* accordingly – is not to apprehend oneself as an object, it is to be open to oneself, destined to oneself (narcissism)'.[38] Cahun's *Disavowals* attempts to – *essaie de* – touch the centre, the core of selfhood, but gestures towards something in the invisible, the vanishing horizon. This is no less real than the self in the mirror, or the troubling limbs or bodily appearance of which they are so critical in *Disavowals*. Deeply philosophical, Cahun's text – which, we should recall, was begun in 1919 – tests out Merleau-Ponty before *The Visible and the Invisible* is even written. Both clearly obsessed with the same issues, Cahun's philosophical journey nevertheless has more at stake because it is written from a socialised female perspective that is desperate to step outside these constraints. Extension from the body through the mind is, as Virginia Woolf, Djuna Barnes, H.D., Gertrude Stein, Simone de Beauvoir and others proved, essential to really see oneself. Cahun tempers a detailed, meandering prose with affective, emotional verse. The result is enlivening and dynamic, the poetry seemingly, like the photomontages and Cahun's wider photographic oeuvre, punctuating the flow at particularly introspective moments of jealousy, anxiety, lust, or fear.

Mac Orlan skilfully avoids privileging essays over poems or vice versa by inserting a hyphen to denote equity between the two modes of expression. Similar checks and balances arise between the fields of poetry and philosophy, framed through aesthetic and literary studies. For centuries, for example, literature has produced poet-philosophers such as Titus Lucretius Carus (99–c. 55 BCE), Georg Philipp Friedrich Freiherr von Hardenberg (1772–1801, known by his penname Novalis), Percy Bysshe Shelley (1782–1822), Paul Éluard (1895–1952), or Audre Lorde (1934–92). In his consideration of the use-value of poetry for the discipline of philosophy, Peter Lamarque muses on the ways in which the complexity of poetry (especially modernist poetry) opens up space for philosophical enquiry: 'in poetry we attend to the finegrainedness of language, its textures and intricacies, its opacity; in conveying thought-processes, and we find value in the experience that it affords'.[39] Equally, philosophers borrow from poetic tradition to condense complex ideas into compelling images; it is simply not the case that philosophy elucidates while poetry obfuscates – modern philosophers such as Gilles Deleuze (1925–95) and Félix Guattari (1930–92) or Hélène Cixous

(b. 1937) have shown how poetry enters the discourse of philosophy. In the case of the latter, it has been argued that her philosophical rigour sometimes takes 'the parameters of thinking and writing' to their 'outer edges', while 'her approach signals a productive exchange with that which escapes the binds of logocentric discourse'.[40] Cahun's fierce ripostes and philosophical rigour in the modern(ist) epoch determine the parameters for self-fashioning, but importantly also define the parameters for what constitutes as avant-garde, or new, which includes essayistic poetry illuminating the strictures of gender denominations. As Mina Loy writes: 'Poetry is prose bewitched, a music made of visual thoughts, the sound of an idea.'[41] Cixous in interview remarked that '[f]or me, theory does not come before, to inspire, it does not precede, does not dictate, but rather it is a consequence of my text, which is at its origin philosophico-poetical, and it is a consequence in the form of compromise or urgent necessity'.[42] It is important for Cahun that the 'urgent necessity' to communicate may take various forms, not only poetry and philosophy but also the essayistic and journalistic. And although Cahun's views on lesbianism, femininity, masculinity, eroticism, or politics may seem very direct and unabashed, even to the twenty-first-century reader, it is via the 'indirect' means of modern art and writing that their audience is hoped to reflect more deeply.

Cahun's first published book of essay-poetry, *Vues et visions*, printed in the literary magazine *Mercure de France*, 1919, is a doubled narrative of prose poems illustrated beautifully by Moore. Tirza True Latimer has observed how, even from this early publication, Cahun combines '*views*' – real places in space and time visited while holidaying with Moore (in Le Croisic) – with the mythical *visions* of classical antiquity (Rome). Taking a Sapphic turn, Latimer explains that '[t]he adoption of antiquity as a point of reference, while, redolent of mainstream high culture and the interwar *rappel à l'ordre*, would also have resonated within Paris's gay subcultures'.[43] Moore's illustrations of nude women in classical and modern styles frame Cahun's paired verses. Something similar is enacted much later, in 1951, in the poem-collage-novel written and illustrated by Valentine Penrose (née Boué), *Dons des féminines* ('Gifts of the Feminine'), which imagines the travels of Rubia and María Élona based on Penrose's intimate affair with Alice Rahon (albeit with Rahon's role imagined and not materialised in the same manner as Cahun and Moore's). Such important texts as *Vues et visions* and *Dons des féminines* demonstrate the collaborative creative labour of a lesbian poetics, which reinvents male-dominated terrain (André Gide, Jean Cocteau, Max Ernst's collage novels, Georgio de Chirico's modern imagining of antiquity) through adventure and travel. This intimate, yet direct form of address is unapologetic in its show of love, of contrastive moods signalled in the real and the utopian spaces, and uncompromising in its inventive, and what Latimer terms 'covert', deployment of form.[44] Shaw reads into the book a 'female, lesbian counterpart to the "Greek love" evoked by the Uranian poets', referenced in Cahun's unpublished 'Jeux uraniens' ('Uranian Games', aka 'Amor amicitiae', begun in 1913),[45] which attempts to push lesbianism out of the shadows into the light beyond the divisive lines segregating same-sex love towards a perfect love.[46] This utopian image corresponds to the episode in Plato's *Symposium* where Aristophanes recounts the mythical story of love and sexual difference. Platonic love exists in perfect symmetry represented in the figure of the androgyne – the third sex – where female and male attributes unite into a whole. After the splitting of the androgyne into male and female halves (socialised love), it remained possible, according to Aristophanes, for non-heterosexual love to develop in same-sex directions:

> such a nature is prone to love and ready to return love, always embracing that which is akin to him. And when one of them meets with his other half, the actual half of himself ... the pair are lost in an amazement of love and friendship and intimacy, and one will not be out of the other's sight, as I may say, even for a moment: these are the people who pass their whole lives together; yet they could not explain what they desire of one another.[47]

'Amor amicitiae' is dedicated 'À RM [Renée Mathilde] son ami Claude Cahun' and is structured as a dialogue between the lover 'l'aimé' and the friend 'l'ami', representing the instinctual lust and philosophical[48] journey of Sapphic love, where male and female attributes shift according to mood and perception. The dialogue evokes the rhythm of falling (in love and friendship with the other), a kind of spherical movement into which the subjects of love are interpellated, by turns mortal and imaginary:

> C'est le monde renversé: tu m'as jeté à terre [...] Les yeux levés au ciel [...] Comprenez donc enfin où votre divinité réside? Est-ce dans le sillon, le vent, la mer, ou plutôt dans l'art d'une symphonie humaine? Pourquoi vouloir excepter l'humanité seule de l'ordre universel? Ami, chacun porte sa nature en soi et ne songe qu'à la combattre.[49]
>
> (The world is turned upside down: you threw me to the ground ... Eyes lifted to heaven ... So do you finally understand where your divinity resides? Is it in the furrow, the wind, the sea, or rather in the art of the human symphony? Why would you want to exclude humanity alone from the universal order? Friend, everyone carries their own nature within them, and thinks only of fighting it.)

The battle to which Cahun returns again and again is with oneself as much as against society; their essayistic poetry here enacts a constant, and positive, back-and-forth within a cellular, elliptical movement that contains self and lover, male and female, playing also with the trope of the 'mannish' lesbian. Both 'Amor amicitiae' and *Vues et visions* adopt dialogue as a literary form through which the subject's inner voice (usually identifying as male) is imagined in the form of the lover, as well as in the form of abstract Nature. The final refrain of *Vues et visions* repeats across both real and imagined spaces (Le Croisic and Rome), the text spanning the double-page layout, but with a deliberate shift in gender from 'ami' to 'amie': 'La douleur se calme et se change en un battement d'ailes qui se raientit et s'efface. Ingrat, je vais quitter cette ami/amie qui me chante et me berce et m'endort' ('The pain subsides and changes into a beat of the wings that slows down and fades away. Ingrate, I will leave this friend who sings to me, rocks me and sends me to sleep').[50] Cahun's spatio-temporal imagining, their elliptical working out, is not purely utopian in its realisation, but returns to the Cahun-character who is unable (yet) to succumb fully to pleasure ('Ingrat'/'ungrateful') because they are still tied to the experience of suffering; the verse imagines love fading into a slow beat, carried by a pair of wings. Platonic love, like self-love, is potentiality, energy, 'le feu de l'action' ('the fire of the action'),[51] but pain, lack of action, is still able to hamper or destroy it.

Cahun's involvement in the Parisian surrealist avant-garde is evidenced in writings such as the essay 'Les Paris sont ouverts' ('Place Your Bets'), which appeared in the February 1933 issue of the Association des écrivains et Artistes révolutionnaires (AEAR, Association of Revolutionary Artists and Writers) and was dedicated to Leon Trotsky.[52] Cahun had been introduced to Breton in 1932 by Jacques Viot and contributed to Georges Bataille and Breton's *Contre-Attaque* (1935–36); they were friends with Breton and Jacqueline Lamba, Robert Desnos and Tristan Tzara. Later in the unpublished text 'Confidences au miroir' (1945–46) they recall the power of surrealism around the time of the Paris group's ideological struggles with the Parti communiste français (PCF, French Communist Party). This particular free-form essay charts Cahun's increasing engagement with anti-bourgeois, anti-fascist ideologies, but it also weaves in drifting thoughts about the value of art, fame, René Crevel's tragic suicide, a friendship with Henri Michaux, among other concerns.[53] It is an entirely different kind of writing from *Disavowals*, less poetic although still brimming with literary references, more a dialogue between certainty and uncertainty – an essay or treatise *on* poetry. But despite their obvious fit with surrealism in terms of its radicality and nonconformism, Cahun never followed any group or faction to the letter, instead following their own instinctual paths. Michael Löwy distinguishes Cahun as 'an individualist and libertarian character ... [who] could not accept the authoritarian Marxism represented by the leadership of A.E.A.R.' nor Louis Aragon's sympathising with Stalinist Communism,[54] which is when, like Breton (who was also expelled from the group), they seek inspiration in Trotsky. There is a direct link between the ideas in 'Les Paris' and 'Prenez garde', which called for a democratisation of art, and willingness to make irrationality and incongruity part of everyday praxis. In 'Les Paris' Cahun's poetics shifts to provocation, extending beyond the figure of the couple and gender politics (which, it should be noted, are still very much evident in all their work) towards a new focus: how to reach a reading public, and promote revolutionary spirit through words on a page. This is, of course, a complex question perennially levelled at artists, and asked of surrealism in particular, given its insistence on a revolutionary poetics. In Breton's words:

> the independence of art – for the revolution
> the revolution – for the liberation of art once and for all[55]

For Breton and others, surrealism *is* revolution, and where Cahun saw this fail in Aragon's allegiance with Communism, they believed sufficiently to push for their own categorisation of what it meant to be revolutionary as an artist – *'l'action indirecte'* ('indirect action'). Poetry should not be propaganda, argues Cahun. Propaganda is a direct form of poetry (song verses, popular metre) hijacked for jingoistic, nationalistic, and populist forms of persuasion. As it lacks subtlety, Cahun continues – their voice seemingly rallying against the forces of state marketing and capitalist advertising – this kind of blunt address cannot win over the masses; indirect poetry on the other hand requires people to think, and only by thinking can true change, and revolution, be achieved. This is an example of how Cahun deliberately incorporates gaps, ellipses, or obfuscation into their writing with the purpose of encouraging the reader's active participation:

> It's done by starting it up and then letting it break down. That obliges the reader to take a step further than he wants to by himself. The exits have been blocked, but you leave him the trouble of opening the front door. Let him desire, says Breton.[56]

Suggestive of finding one's way in a labyrinth, the path towards meaning is embedded in the desire to move away from the self, away from a clear path. To 'let' the reader desire is to deliberately create uncertainty, often the result of provocation, titillation, and lack designed in the verse. To open Cahun's 'front door' is to submit to a challenge, one that, for this reader, forcibly unblocks any limits imposed by expectation. Cahun understood the value of shock when unleashed upon a society cowed by shame and guilt, and their accounts of desire are also carnal and unapologetic: 'poetry … seems undeniably an inherent need of human, and even of animal, nature, a need undoubtedly linked to sex instinct … a constant bundle of changing relationships between poetic and social evolution'.[57] The first part of 'Les Paris' is subtitled 'La poésie garde son secret' ('Poetry Keeps Its Secret'), and indeed I feel that, where photography has exposed Cahun's complex relationship with real and ontological selves, poetry is Cahun's secret, passionate, weapon: 'Poems cannot be called "revolutionary" or "not revolutionary" except insofar as, in their very inmost selves, they represent the people, the poets who created them. All poetry is poetry of circumstance. ... poets in their own way act upon people's sensibility. Their attack is more cunning: but even their most oblique blows can be fatal.'[58] Cahun alludes here to the instinctive and uncensored aspects of poetic writing, as well as to the deliberation and cunning involved in addressing a reader. Poetry allows Cahun's innermost thoughts to materialise, which, as in their photographs, condenses such a wealth of material in its references and emotional swells that it is not immediately accessible and requires excavation, opening up a dialogue with the reader. The way in which they describe this creative process might arise out of surrealist chance – circumstance – but it is designed to be clever, wilfully difficult and misleading in order to catch the reader off guard. This is not automatism, as the decade it took to develop *Disavowals* clearly demonstrates, but a critical practice predicated on layers, repetition, and by turns reasoned and aesthetically overloaded language. In the essay-poem 'Chanson sauvage' ('Wild Song') published in *Mercure de France* in 1921, Cahun demonstrates how early on in their career as a writer a rebellious Dada spirit anticipated complex theoretical philosophies: 'Vers mon Verbe de révolte, à chaque mot rétif, vers le désordre defensive de mon esprit, pour que tu ordonnes ses gestes barbares' ('Towards my Word of revolt, to every stubborn word, towards the defensive disorder of my mind, so that you order its barbarous gestures').[59] What would much later become the bedrock of poststructuralist theory – the study of thinking through language in order to challenge any notion of meaning or truth as closed, or fixed, thereby embracing the instabilities and gaps in systems of knowledge – was already in evidence in their essay-poems written about commodity capitalism, homosexuality, and the power of artistic revolt. In the dialogic verse of this 'song', the other – 'mon enfant' – is characterised as fearless, smiling, and with disarming confidence, while the speaker is rebellious, cynical, and abrasive. Whether 'mon enfant' is a lover or part of the speaker's extended self, the structures of difference – the refusal to cement identity in a single likeness of the self but rather to present it in a series of human and non-human entities – produce an essayism that is marked by the poetic refrain of an eternal return back to the self. Each return is predicated on difference, on a shift, a new layer, a new twist of perspective. Cahun is most revolutionary in turning the binary into the sphere – in other words, in opening up for the reader a space (the song is set against a vast sea, and a city, which flaps wings fashioned from rows of factories) where flux, rebellion, but also Platonic love, undermine grand narratives of order. Later this is romantically reimagined as 'Pink magic' in *Disavowals*.⁶⁰ Cahun's secret is that poetry can be abstract and difficult, while also adopting an intimate and philosophical lyricism.

What I mean to say here is that Cahun negotiates, and constantly redefines, the meaning of revolution and of selfhood through permeable frameworks of difference, rather than likeness, as I also underline in relation to the concept of Benjaminian aura, above. What is revealed in mirrors, behind reflections, or between objects, relies on a friction, a gap, or fissure, in order to re-evaluate and expand their ideas. What Jacques Derrida would later cleverly term as *différance*, a linguistic term that assumes irreducibility as the genesis for any modern analysis of logocentrism, seems relevant (in spite of its lack of discourse on gender specifically) in relation to Cahun's own linguistic fashioning of modern (gender-neutral) philosophy. Derrida proposes that one can know 'where "we" are' only if we start from the 'concept of *play*': 'announcing, on the eve of philosophy and beyond it, the unity of chance and necessity of calculations without end'.⁶¹ Cahun's *post-scriptum* to 'Les Paris' insists that debates on poetry remain open, and (in line with surrealism) emphasises that play and creativity supersede any goal of fixed meaning. In Chapter I of *Disavowals* an image of the soul as collage (the invisible, irreducible reimagined as an object) reveals a propensity of post-structuralist dissection *avant la lettre*: 'Indiscreet and brutal, I enjoy looking at what's underneath the crossed-out bits of my soul. Ill-advised intentions have been revised there, become dormant; others have materialized in their place.'⁶² Arguably, their approach to writing, as well as to photography, is incredibly sophisticated and ahead of its time. Poetry, Cahun suggests, is a form of short cut which is capable of generating intensity such as that associated with extreme suffering or sexual love, and which 'intervenes' in the indirect knowledge of the universe generated by philosophical thought or enquiry.⁶³ It is clear that indirect action must involve both philosophical and poetic discourse. Mac Orlan's description of *Disavowals* as a collection of 'poèmes-essais' or 'essais-poèmes' is therefore relevant across Cahun's oeuvre. Stopping short before a full-blown philosophical treatise emerges, nevertheless their writing tends towards the meandering, indirect probing of philosophical thought often found in shorter essay forms. As Dillon notes regarding an essayistic writing practice: 'It seems quite clear to me now that all my escape routes, actual and textual, were leading me back to where I began.'⁶⁴ The love of repetition finds purchase here, as well as in the repetitive rhymes and refrains of their verse. The two, as Mac Orlan's hyphen insists, are inseparable, just as Cahun and their Cahun-character. What makes Cahun's writing unique is how their dialogic self-fashioning – a kind of ekphrastic self-portraiture – by turn smooths and deliberately raises up the join between the essay and the poem. At nodal points in *Disavowals* – punctuated by ellipses and broken into stanzas by the graphic stars, hearts and eyes inserted in the original manuscript – the poetic and the essayistic meet, before separating again. Sometimes this is supposed to be jarring, as in the metamorphic leap between objective and subjective perspective, vernacular and ancient descriptions of love, or in this surrealist image:

> – He suffered with daring; he died without complaint… (I am a masochist and I screamed so loudly with joy that your feeble human ears couldn't hear a thing.)
>
> Guillotine window.
>
> A sheet of glass. Where shall I put the silver? Here or there; in front or behind the window?[65]

And at other times this shift is seamless, such as the rapid interchangeability between 'I' and 'God' and 'You'. Whether held in a close-up or at a distance, speaking from behind or in front of the mirroring glass, the subject of the shifting portrait plays with the reader, acutely aware of their craft and mode of address. For Michel Beaujour the self-portrait is a 'complex literary type' that asserts the subject's 'absolute difference' to the world; and the writer of the self-portrait, he continues, 'is unhoused from the start', marginalised in their exteriority, locked into the mirrors of a memory archive refashioned as conceptual discourse.[66] His is a rather bleak summation of portraiture, where polymorphous and fantastic facets of the subject belie a dispossessed self. But within these traps of self-fashioning is also something new that resists:

> There is no self-portrait that is not at grips with the *thing* or *res:* the commonplace. The self-portrait ineluctably sets itself up as topography or description, a scanning and destruction of *places,* which implies a rhetorical, mythological, and encyclopedic horizon. This amounts to saying that the self-portrait is always absolutely modern. The place, the stupidities, which the subject can utilize as his foils, as his dialectical raw material show him at grips with the Other who haunts him and from whom he tries to escape – that encyclopedia is constantly modified even if only superficially, according to fashionable ideologies and local traditions.[67]

This description helpfully outlines the dialogic and dialectical process of condensation in Cahun's essay-poetry, all of which, of course, does not occlude Cahun's photographs from the poetic. A photograph fixes the subject, whether already still, or in frozen motion, and the version of the subject is held by the viewer's gaze to be hunted down. The poet does not show himself or herself so clearly, but presents abstracted thoughts, which may

1.4 Claude Cahun, *Self Portrait (Crouched Naked in Rock Pool)*, 1930.

coalesce into a readable 'image' or escape into the following sentence, snaking in and between the synapses. Often Cahun, the subject of a portrait, places their body within or alongside forms of nature, abstracted or occluded. They can be found – arms protruding from a rocky boulder (*Je tends les bras*, 1932) – as a doubly exposed image of body placed against rock, a naked version of Aristophanes' androgyne on the sand, umbilically bound by seaweed, or framed by the exotic Jersey Island fronds of St Brelade's Bay (c. 1939). In *Self Portrait (Crouched Naked in a Rock Pool)* (1930) Cahun is positioned between two rocky formations, crouched looking over their left shoulder obliquely into the still water (Figure 1.4). The water is dark and flat, while the protruding rock and Cahun's body are exposed in strong white light. The swimming cap on their head creates an optical illusion, seemingly cast in porcelain, turning Cahun into a shelled creature, with a protected head and fleshy body. The body is twisted slightly, showing sinewy musculature, and nothing in the portrait signals comfort or ease. Unlike the more deliberately narcissistic portraits where reflection or doubling is heightened, here the viewer is indirectly discouraged from reading any fixity into the composition. The eye roves among the bleached-out parts of the image, the body opens the door to a poetic verse in which all that is usually protected – by clothes, by socialisation, by categorisation – has been exposed. The image appeals to nature, to a wild and strangely erotic and tender form. Cahun's profile turns aslant from the viewer, refusing to be caught and fixed. They are not female, their vagina likened to a sea creature, but they *are* sea creature. The effect is one of slippage rather than performance or staging, and this is what makes it poetic; the environment is condensed within the self, and the self is folded within the environment. Increasingly through the 1930s, Cahun's photographs posit the expansion of the self within the wider frame of Nature, and the Cahun-character becomes smaller, more distant, at times melding with or disappearing into the landscape that surrounds them. In *Disavowals*, this diminishing figure reflects on power beyond the self: 'Metaphysical cowardice. You've had enough of the sky above your head, and the wind of vertigo bends your knees. In such a state, you don't give a damn about truth, about the earth… it is enough to reassure you that the lookout calls from the crow's nest: Horizon!'[68] The answers are not to be found in gods, or in Nature, when all that exists or matters is I, a narcissism that, unlike that of the ill-fated Narcissus who 'didn't know how to go beyond appearances', attempts to find self-love. It can be said that the essay-poems/poem-essays in *Disavowals* fill in some of the gaps created by Cahun's photographic images, but any presumed 'evidence' of an expanded thought process in their writing actually brings with it more questions than it answers. This is comically illustrated in a section entitled 'I am in training, don't kiss me' clearly referencing Cahun's most iconic self-portrait, which ends inevitably with a 'who knows?'[69]

In conclusion, Cahun devised many routes via which to follow their 'invisible adventure' and these are inexhaustible, not simply due to the volume of permutations by which one can apprehend the ideas, but inexhaustible meaning indefatigable – bursting with energy. Clearly inspirational to the twenty-first-century reader interested in gender politics, Cahun's prolific oeuvre also opens the reader up to new ideas on class politics, aesthetics, and consumer culture. Their work has inspired further dialogue in works such as Barbara Hammer's film *Lover Other: The Story of Claude Cahun and Marcel Moore* (2006) – a quasi-documentary on Cahun and Moore's lives – and Sarah Pucill's films *Magic Mirror* (2013) and *Confessions to the Mirror* (2016) – which dialogically expand *Disavowals* and 'Confidences au miroir' through moving images. For Pucill, a visual artist, Cahun's multiplicity opens up possibilities for authorship – 'a theorist before her time': 'I see her as a writer and a thinker. She saw herself as Cassandra because what she was saying had to do with the future. She's responding to Freud's theories of narcissism from a female queer point of view.'[70] In *Magic*

Mirror, Cahun remains for Pucill an active participant in a dialogue on the genre of autobiography, thereby never becoming the objective study of the documentary. In the recent exhibition *Gillian Wearing and Claude Cahun: Behind the Mask Another Mask* at the National Portrait Gallery in London (2017), the Turner Prize-winning artist Wearing's self-portraits are brought together with Cahun's for the first time, curated by Sarah Howgate. *Behind the Mask Another Mask* sees Wearing explore her own practice through Cahun's performance portraits, enacting a 'spiritual camaraderie'.[71] As well as these explorations through visual art, the writer Rupert Thomson's novel *Never Anyone But You* (2018)[72] experiments with a somewhat voyeuristic fan-fiction that imagines Cahun's life, drawn heavily from their self-portraits. Each of these examples evinces a love affair with Cahun's work, and, like Cahun who applies their creativity with and against others – whether Moore, Judith, Echo, Narcissus, Gide, Havelock Ellis – each writer and artist holds up *Disavowals* or the self-portraits as mirrors, to *see differently*. In our present moment, modes of writing and creative expression have become more hybrid, ever searching for a means to face the void in our time, to reflect the world back in provocative and authentic work. Auto-fiction, auto-theory, film-philosophy, and scholarship in interdisciplinary fields such as the medical humanities, history of the emotions, or psycho-geography are just a few examples of the interpenetration of form and approach in recent art and literary trends. Many of these impulses for intermedial work can be traced in Cahun's essay-poems and poem-essays, which 'exceed' the 'passage from symbolism to surrealism' and anticipate 'the most advanced preoccupations of our times'.[73] Many of the conundrums faced by Cahun in the early twentieth century exist today, and their deliberate motion to refute and refuse any categorisation or fixity serves as inspiration at times when autonomy, aura, or affect seem compromised. 'No point in making myself comfortable' writes Cahun, wryly, as we return to the beginning.[74] Their legacy is the key to thinking otherwise.

Notes

1 Pierre Mac Orlan, Preface to *Aveux non avenus*, p. XXIV. Reprinted in Jennifer Mundy, 'Introduction', in Claude Cahun, *Disavowals or Cancelled Confessions*, trans. Susan de Muth (1930; London: Tate Publishing, 2007), p. vii.
2 Jennifer L. Shaw brilliantly suggests that the title could also be read phonetically as '*Veux non à Venus*' or 'Wish no to Venus', which could be seen as 'rejecting the mainstream constructions of femininity, beauty and love associated with the ideal emblematized by the goddess Venus', thereby launching 'a critique of idealization'. Jennifer L. Shaw, *Reading Claude Cahun's Disavowals* (Farnham: Ashgate, 2013), p. 105.

3 Jennifer L. Shaw, *Exist Otherwise: The Life and Works of Claude Cahun* (London: Reaktion Books, 2017), p. 9.
4 Debates regarding Cahun's photographic oeuvre have explored the genesis of their 'self-portraits'. The issue of whether the photographs where Cahun takes up the position of sitter are self-portraits – clearly costumed and staged according to their personal, philosophical views on identity – or portraits taken by Marcel Moore in collaboration – Moore's shadow falls across some of the shots – has been of interest to scholars. See, for example, James Stevenson, 'Claude Cahun: An Analysis of Her Photographic Technique', in Louise Downie (ed.), *Don't Kiss Me: The Art of Claude Cahun and Marcel Moore* (London and Jersey: Tate Publishing and Jersey Heritage Trust, 2006), pp. 46–55, and Tirza True Latimer, 'Claude Cahun's Mirror in the Lens', *The Gay and Lesbian Review Worldwide* 18:1 (2011), pp. 19–23.
5 Cahun, *Disavowals*, p, 2.
6 Agnès Lhermitte, 'Postscript: Some Brief Observations', in Cahun, *Disavowals*, p. xxii.
7 To date critical responses to Cahun's work have tended to deploy the female pronouns she/her. However, given Cahun's deliberate move to identify as gender-neutral there is a strong case to use the pronouns they/them. Given the defiant and determined attitude to unpick social fixity regarding gender norms which manifests in Cahun's writing, as well as the overt and confrontational photographic portraits that refuse to align with an idea of birth sex, this chapter takes the decision to engage with this fluidity by assigning the neutral pronouns. Intentionally, this is also designed to underline the underlying philosophical and critical elements of their work. Cahun's work is essential to any study of feminist modernisms and women's writing, and in using these pronouns the feminist work is not diminished or evaded; rather it continues Virginia Woolf's work in *Orlando: A Biography* (1928) where a utopian dream of freedom and multiplicity is achieved by disregarding and expanding parameters and boundaries designed to fix sex and gender. Ultimately, as Cahun's biographer François Leperlier has noted, they take 'sexual "indeterminateness" to the limit'. François Leperlier, *Mise en scène: Claude Cahun, Tacita Dean, Ginia Nimarkoh*, trans. Simon Pleasance (London: Institute of Contemporary Arts, 1994), p. 20.
8 Cahun, *Disavowals*, p. 151.
9 Letter to Adrienne Monnier, 20 June 1928. Quoted in Mundy, 'Introduction', p. 117.
10 The only publication of Cahun's (self-)portraits during their lifetime was *Frontière humaine* for *Bifur*, 5 (1930), about which Katharine Conley has written in her article 'Claude Cahun's Iconic Heads: from "The Sadistic Judith" to Human Frontier', *Papers of Surrealism* 2 (Summer 2004), pp. 1–23.
11 See, e.g., François Leperlier, *Mise en scène*; François Leperlier (ed.), *Claude Cahun: Écrits* (Paris: Jean Michel Place, 2002); Elza Adamowicz, '"Sous ce masque, un autre masque": Claude Cahun's Photomontages', in Kathryn Banks and Joseph Harris (eds), *Exposure: Revealing Bodies, Unveiling Representations*

(Frankfurt am Mein: Peter Lang, 2004), pp. 49–61; Conley, 'Claude Cahun's Iconic Heads'; Tirza True Latimer, *Women Together / Women Apart: Portraits of Lesbian Paris* (New Brunswick: Rutgers University Press, 2005); Downie (ed.), *Don't Kiss Me*; Carolyn Topdjian, 'Shape-Shifting Beauty: The Body, Gender and Subjectivity in the Photographs of Claude Cahun', *Resources for Feminist Research* 32:3–4 (2007), pp. 63–81; Lizzie Thynne, 'Indirect Action: Politics and the Subversion of Identity in Claude Cahun and Marcel Moore's Resistance to the Occupation of Jersey', *Papers of Surrealism* 8 (Spring 2010), pp. 1–24; Emily Apter, 'Towards a Unisex Erotics: Claude Cahun and Geometric Modernism', in Anna Katharina Schaffner and Shane Weller (eds), *Modernist Eroticisms: European Literature after Sexology* (London: Palgrave, 2012), pp. 134–49, among many others.
12 *Sexual/Textual Politics: Feminist Literary Theory* is the title of the feminist theorist Toril Moi's influential 1985 book (New York: Routledge, 2002).
13 Moi, *Sexual/Textual Politics*, p. 11.
14 Cahun, *Disavowals*, pp. 194–5.
15 See 'Réponse à L'enquête: "Quelle a été la rencontre capitale de votre vie?"', *Minotaure* 3–4 (December 1933). Reprinted in Mary Ann Caws (ed.), *Surrealist Painters and Poets: An Anthology* (Cambridge, MA: MIT Press, 2001), p. 143.
16 Adamowicz, '"Sous ce masque, un autre masque"', p. 58, p. 51.
17 Walter Benjamin, 'The Work of Art in the Age of Mechanical Reproduction' (1936), in Hannah Arendt (ed.), *Illuminations: Essays and Reflections*, trans. Harry Zorn (1955. London: Pimlico, 1999), p. 217; emphasis added.
18 Benjamin, 'The Work of Art', p. 215.
19 Claude Cahun, 'Beware of Domestic Objects', trans. Guy Ducornet, in Penelope Rosemont (ed.), *Surrealist Women: An International Anthology* (London: Athlone Press, 1998), p. 60. Cahun contributed three objects to the exhibition, since lost, including *Un air de famille* and the arresting sculpture now known as 'Object'. See Jill Shaw, 'Notable Acquisitions at the Art Institute of Chicago', *Art Institute of Chicago Museum Studies* 35:2 (2009), pp. 70–1.
20 Cahun, *Disavowals*, p. 149.
21 *Ibid.*, p. 204.
22 *Ibid.*, p. 1.
23 Roger Cardinal, 'The Imaging of Magic', in Patricia Allmer (ed.), *Angels of Anarchy: Women Artists and Surrealism* (Munich: Prestel, 2009), p. 38.
24 Cahun, *Disavowals*, p. 28.
25 After Guillaume Apollinaire's book of free verse typographical poems titled *Calligrammes: Poèmes de la Paix et de la Guerre* (Paris: Mercure de France, 1918).
26 Pierre Mac Orlan, 'Elements of a Social Fantastic' (1929), in Christopher Phillips (ed.), *Photography in the Modern Era: European Documents and Critical Writings, 1913–1940*, trans. Robert Erich Wolf (New York: The Metropolitan Museum of Art/Aperture, 1989), pp. 31–3.
27 Lhermitte, 'Postscript', pp. xxi–xxii.
28 Mac Orlan, 'Preface', p. xxvi.

29 See Lauren Elkin, *Flâneuese: Women Walk the City in Paris, New York, Tokyo, Venice and London* (London: Penguin Random House, 2016). In this important repositing of the turn-of-the-century art of *flânerie*, or aimlessly wandering, Elkin takes the 'male privilege' assigned to this activity – epitomised in the works of writers such as Charles Baudelaire, Louis Aragon, Georges Bataille, and André Breton – and reassesses the act of wandering the streets through her own experiences, as well as those expressed in the works of female writers and filmmakers.
30 Pierre Mac Orlan, 'Preface', pp. xxiv–xxvi; emphasis added.
31 Katy Kline, 'In or Out of the Picture: Claude Cahun and Cindy Sherman', in Shelley Rice (ed.), *Inverted Odysseys: Claude Cahun, Maya Deren, Cindy Sherman* (Cambridge, MA: MIT Press, 1999), p. 74.
32 Cahun, *Disavowals*, p. 39.
33 *Ibid.*, p. 76.
34 *Ibid.*, p. 1.
35 Leperlier, *Mise en scène*, p. 20.
36 Brian Dillon, *Essayism* (London: Fitzcarraldo Editions, 2017), p. 12.
37 Cahun, *Disavowals*, p. 78.
38 Maurice Merleau-Ponty, *The Visible and the Invisible*, ed. Claude Lefort, trans. Alphonso Lingis (Evanston: Northwestern University Press, 1968), p. 249. Merleau-Ponty was working on this unfinished manuscript when he died, and it was first published posthumously under the title *Le Visible et l'invisible* in 1964.
39 Peter Lamarque, 'Semantic-Finegrainedness and Poetic Value', in John Gibson (ed.), *The Philosophy of Poetry* (Oxford: Oxford University Press, 2015), p. 36.
40 Anthea Buys and Stefan Polatinsky, 'The Provocation of Hélène Cixous: Philosophy in Poetic Overflow', *Mosaic: An Interdisciplinary Critical Journal* 42:4 (December 2009), p. 80.
41 Mina Loy, 'Modern Poetry' (1923), in Roger L. Conover (ed.), *The Lost Lunar Baedeker: Poems of Mina Loy* (New York: Farrar, Straus, & Giroux Inc., 1997), pp. 157–61.
42 Kathleen O'Grady, 'Guardian of Language: An Interview with Hélène Cixous', *Women's Education des femmes* 12:4 (Winter 1996–97), p. 7.
43 Latimer, *Women Together / Women Apart*, p. 77.
44 *Ibid.*, p. 81.
45 Claude Cahun, 'Amor amicitiae', in François Leperlier (ed.), *Claude Cahun: Écrits* (Paris: Jean Michel Place, 2002), pp. 487–95.
46 Shaw, *Exist Otherwise*, p. 41.
47 Plato, *Symposium*, trans. Benjamin Jowett, *Project Gutenberg*, www.gutenberg.org/files/1600/1600-h/1600-h.htm, pp. 105–6.
48 Plato's 'yet they could not explain' tallies with Cahun's essayistic drive here: the will to explain, to find answers is always present.
49 Cahun, 'Amor amicitiae', p. 490, p. 493. My translation.
50 Cahun, *Vues et visions*, in Leperlier (ed.), *Écrits*, pp. 120–1.

51 Cahun, 'Amor Amicitiae', p. 494.
52 The essay was expanded and republished by José Corti in May 1934.
53 See Claude Cahun, 'Confidences au miroir', in Leperlier (ed.), *Écrits*, pp. 571–624.
54 Michael Löwy, *Morning Star: Surrealism, Marxism, Anarchism, Situationism, Utopia* (Austin: University of Texas Press, 2009), p. 67.
55 André Breton (co-written by Leon Trotsky and co-signed by Diego Rivera), 'Manifesto for an Independent Revolutionary Art' (1938), in André Breton, *Free Rein*, trans. Michel Parmentier and Jacqueline d'Amboise (Lincoln: University of Nebraska Press, 1995), pp. 30–3.
56 Claude Cahun, 'Place Your Bets', quoted in Thynne, 'Indirect Action', p. 4.
57 Claude Cahun, 'Poetry Keeps Its Secret' (an extract from 'Place Your Bets'), trans. Guy Ducornet, in Rosemont (ed.), *Surrealist Women*, p. 54.
58 *Ibid.*, p. 54.
59 Claude Cahun, 'Chanson sauvage' (1921), in Leperlier (ed.), *Écrits*, pp. 460–1. 'Chanson sauvage' was originally published in *Le Mercure de France*, a journal for which Cahun wrote between 1914 and 1927.
60 Cahun, *Disavowals*, p. 102.
61 Jacques Derrida, 'Différance', in Jacques Derrida, *Margins of Philosophy*, trans. Alan Bass (1972. Chicago: University of Chicago Press, 1984), p. 7.
62 Cahun, *Disavowals*, p. 6.
63 Cahun, 'Les Paris', in Leperlier (ed.), *Écrits*, p. 32.
64 Dillon, *Essayism*, p. 93.
65 Cahun, *Disavowals*, p. 25.
66 Michel Beaujour, *Poetics of the Literary Self-Portrait*, trans. Yara Milos (New York: New York University Press, 1991), p. 25, p. 5, p. 18.
67 *Ibid.*, pp. 15–16.
68 Cahun, *Disavowals*, p. 184; ellipsis in the original.
69 *Ibid.*, p. 185.
70 'Sarah Pucill / Magic Mirror: Interviewed by Anna McNay', *Photomonitor* (May 2014), www.photomonitor.co.uk/2014/05/magic-mirror/, accessed 2 June 2014.
71 Gillian Wearing and Sarah Howgate, 'Gillian Wearing in Conversation with Sarah Howgate', in *Gillian Wearing and Claude Cahun: Behind the Mask Another Mask* (London: National Portrait Gallery Publications, 2017), p. 171.
72 Rupert Thomson, *Never Anyone But You* (Toronto: Corsair, 2018).
73 François Leperlier, 'Afterword', trans. Susan de Muth, in Cahun, *Disavowals*, p. 215.
74 Cahun, *Disavowals*, p. 1.

2

Identity convulsed: Leonora Carrington's *The House of Fear* and *The Oval Lady*

Anna Watz

'Who am I?' This question famously opens André Breton's *Nadja* (1928) and reverberates throughout surrealism's various artistic expressions.[1] Indeed, a troubling of identity in the light of Sigmund Freud's theories of the unconscious is a key facet not only of Breton's oeuvre but also, for example, of Marcel Duchamp's alter-ego experiments, Claude Cahun's self-portraits, the collage novels of Max Ernst, and, as I will argue in this chapter, the early short stories of Leonora Carrington (1917–2011).[2] Carrington wrote most of her short fiction during the years 1937–39, when she lived with Ernst in Saint Martin d'Ardèche in the south of France. With the notable exception of the novella *Little Francis*, these stories were written not in Carrington's native English but in French. Only six stories were published at the time of their composition (with Carrington's sometimes foreign-sounding syntax and grammatical errors unchanged), in the slim volumes *La Maison de la Peur* (*The House of Fear*, 1938) and *La Dame ovale* (*The Oval Lady*, 1939). Both volumes featured accompanying illustrations by Ernst, who also wrote a foreword to *The House of Fear*.

This chapter focuses on the stories in these two publications, all of which share a distinctive narrative perspective: they are told by a first-person narrator-observer, who seems to be a foreigner to the action of the narrative itself.[3] Often this narrator is suspended on the very edges of the story, passively watching the events play out between other characters – sometimes uncomprehendingly, sometimes dispassionately, and sometimes in a state of intense fear. The stories typically end abruptly with the narrator left petrified before a scene of violence. The peculiar narrative perspective and the lack of narrative resolution are not only characteristic of the stories in these two collections but one of the hallmarks of Carrington's short fiction.[4] Yet I choose, in this chapter, to focus only on the stories in *The House of Fear* and *The Oval Lady*, in order to analyse them in relation to their formal frame (which crucially includes Ernst's collages) as well as to tease out thematic resonances and echoes across the stories.

Carrington's emergence as an artist, in the mid- to late 1930s, has often been associated with revolt – against the bourgeois normativity of her upbringing, against religion, and, in particular, against her conservative father – and her prewar writing has often been read by critics as a dramatisation of such rebellion. Whitney Chadwick stated in a 1986 article that '[f]rom the beginning [Carrington's] revolution was a private one, having nothing to do with Marx, Freud, or Surrealist theorizing. It was a direct frontal assault not on the family as an institution, but on one particular family, hers'.[5] Much subsequent critical work on Carrington's early stories (and paintings) has seized on this biographical explanation. Without dismissing these autobiographical resonances, my own analysis of these stories in this chapter will by contrast focus precisely on what their dramatised revolt has to do with what Chadwick calls 'Surrealist theorizing'. The stories in *The House of Fear* and *The Oval Lady*, I suggest, self-consciously participate in the surrealist project of questioning identity through their portrayal of a disrupted or 'convulsed' self. As I will show, Carrington's unsettling of subjectivity engages directly with surrealist ideas about the self, especially as they were developed in theoretical and artistic work by Breton and Ernst. Yet Carrington's involvement in the surrealist discourse of unsettled identity is at times fraught with ambivalence and uncertainty. Whereas Breton and Ernst envision psychic, and by extension social, revolution resulting from their troubling of identity,[6] several of Carrington's stories contain a critical reflection on the gendered and political blind spots of such a project.

Scholarly work on *The House of Fear* and *The Oval Lady* is still relatively limited, with the notable exception of the large critical attention given to the fierce and comic story 'La Débutante'. This story was included by Breton in the 1950 revised edition of his *Anthology of Black Humor*, and it has subsequently been republished as part of both surrealist and feminist anthologies.[7] Feminist scholars have tended to interpret the story as a triumphant and gruesome revenge on the patriarchal logic of the British upper middle classes and their repressive codes of femininity. But to make the savage feminist victory of 'La Débutante' synecdochally represent all of Carrington's writing of this time is to gloss over its ambivalence and complexity. The other stories in *The House of Fear* and *The Oval Lady* are concerned with a less straightforward kind of revolt – one that is locked in dialogue with surrealist theories of subjectivity.

Surrealism and identity

As David Lomas has convincingly argued, 'the question(ing) of identity resounds across the surrealist project, but for the surrealist artist or writer there were no ready-made answers. Indeed, the hypothesis of an unconscious, of the subject's radical determination by an elsewhere ... seemed to render obsolete the ethical and philosophical imperative to know thyself'.[8] Freud's theory of the irrational unconscious helped the surrealists elaborate artistic aims and techniques that they hoped would liberate the subject from bourgeois constraints and repressions and allow desire and the imagination free expression.

Many surrealist ideas about how to compel the conscious, rational ego to retract and thus allow irrational unconscious impulses and desires free rein involve simulating a state of passivity. André Breton, in his first *Manifesto of Surrealism* (1924), famously defines surrealism as 'psychic automatism in its pure state' and goes on to suggest, under the subheading 'Secrets of the Magical Surrealist Art', that surrealist writing involves putting oneself 'in as passive, or receptive, a state of mind' as possible.[9] Surrealist artists and writers, on this view, become 'simple receptacles of so many echoes, modest *recording machines*'.[10] Ernst incorporates the endorsement of artistic passivity in his discussion of the new techniques frottage and collage in the pivotal essay 'Beyond Painting' (1936), blurring the lines between what constitutes creativity, activity, and passivity. 'In the measure of my activity (passivity)', he states, 'I contributed to the general overthrow of those values, which in our time, have been considered the most established and secure'.[11] As Ernst here suggests, not only is psychic passivity essential in the surrealist practices of frottage and collage, but it also enables a kind of revolt of the mind.

The practice of collage is central to Ernst's thinking about identity.[12] Paraphrasing Comte de Lautréamont's famous aphorism 'as beautiful ... as the chance encounter of a sewing machine and an umbrella on a dissecting table',[13] Ernst, in 'Beyond Painting', offers the following explanation of the purpose and effect of collage:

> A ready-made reality, whose naive destination has the air of having been fixed, once and for all (a canoe), finding itself in the presence of another and hardly less absurd reality (a vacuum cleaner), in a place where both of them must feel displaced (a forest), will, by this very fact, escape to its naive destination and to its identity; it will pass from its false absolute, through a series of relative values, into a new absolute value, true and poetic: canoe and vacuum cleaner will make love. The mechanism of collage, it seems to me, is revealed by this very simple example. The complete transmutation, followed by a pure act, as that of love, will make itself known naturally *every time the conditions are rendered favorable by the given facts: the coupling of two realities, irreconcilable in appearance, upon a plane which apparently does not suit them.*[14]

Threaded through Ernst's discussion of collage in this essay is the question of what constitutes the self. Breton had speculated in an early essay, written in conjunction with Ernst's first solo exhibition in Paris in 1920, that Ernst's work might offer the possibility of an 'escape from the principle of identity', a remark which Ernst enthusiastically reiterates in 'Beyond Painting', calling it 'prophetic'.[15] Seeking to unsettle the humanist philosophical tradition, which saw stability, coherence and autonomy as characteristics of a self that was capable of self-knowledge, Ernst ventures that the meeting of two irreconcilable realities 'on an apparently antipathetic plane' in collage provokes an 'exchange of energy ... which might be a broad flowing stream or a shattering stroke of lightning and thunder'; this exchange, Ernst states, constitutes identity itself.[16] He closes his essay with yet another paraphrase, this time of Breton's surrealist maxim, found at the end of *Nadja*, 'Beauty will be CONVULSIVE or will not be at all'.[17] 'IDENTITY', Ernst proclaims, 'WILL BE CONVULSIVE OR WILL NOT EXIST'.[18] What Ernst calls 'identity' here, then, is a sudden experience of the world and the self as essentially contradictory; it is thus a fundamental *questioning* of traditional notions of identity and coherent selfhood based on a rational relation to the surrounding world.

Like Breton's concept of convulsive beauty, Ernst's convulsive identity is crucially inflected by his extensive knowledge of psychoanalysis and passionate reading of theories on hysteria. To experience convulsive beauty or convulsive identity might thus be described as feeling the self split into contradictory fragments. For Breton, such an experience is often visualised through a juxtaposition between frenzy and stasis. In *Nadja*, he explains that convulsive beauty is 'neither dynamic nor static ... Beauty is like a train that ceaselessly roars out of the Gare de Lyon, and which I know will never leave, which has not left.'[19] In the first chapter of *L'Amour fou* (1937), he further elaborates: 'There can be no beauty, as far as I am concerned – convulsive beauty – except at the cost of affirming the reciprocal relations linking the object seen in its motion and in its repose ... I regret not having been able to furnish, along with this text, the photograph of a speeding locomotive abandoned for years to the delirium of a virgin forest.'[20]

For Ernst, convulsion is often visualised or represented as a splitting of the hysterical subject, or, as Elza Adamowicz has argued, as 'the self [existing] within the other and the other within the self'.[21] Ernst's three collage novels – *La Femme 100 têtes* (*The Hundred Headless Woman*, 1929), *Rêve d'une petite fille qui voulut entrer au carmel* (*A Little Girl Dreams of Taking the Veil*, 1930), and *Une semaine de bonté* (*A Week of Kindness*, 1934) – can be read as his working through of questions of hysteria and identity, which he would later theorise in 'Beyond Painting'. While all three collage novels also showcase Ernst's self-professed identification with the figure of the female hysteric,[22] it is the middle one, *A Little Girl Dreams of Taking the Veil*, which, according to Lomas, constitutes Ernst's 'most sustained treatment of the hysteria topos'.[23] This work chronicles the dream of the protagonist Marceline-Marie, who is radically confused about her own identity; as Lomas observes, 'in the course of her dream, [she] never succeeds in wholly identifying with either of her dual selves whom she alternately refers to as "moi" and "ma soeur"'.[24] In the preface to the novel, Ernst writes that Marceline-Marie's 'double first name is of prime importance in the evolution of the dream that follows. Because it is probably due to the troubles provoked by the coupling of the two names of such a very different signification that we will see her slit herself up the middle of her back from the very beginning of the dream and wear appearances of two distinct but closely related persons.'[25] As is evident in his analysis of Marceline-Marie's double-barrelled name, hysteria is for Ernst strongly connected to collage in that it involves a juxtaposition of two incongruous elements resulting in psychic disruption.

As is already evident, much surrealist discourse unquestioningly adopted the early psychoanalytic association between hysteria and femininity. Consequently, the troubling of identity sought by Breton and Ernst in their experiments with automatism, hysteria and passivity was often conceived as simulating a 'feminine' subject position. This identification with what was perceived as a feminine sensibility was thus seen as a way for the male artist to challenge and subvert not only the bourgeois-patriarchal-capitalist social order but also his own masculine subjectivity. During feminism's second wave, scholars started to question this surrealist veneration of women generally, and of the hysteric and the *femme-enfant* especially, which was now seen as symptomatic of a patriarchal bias that construed women as inherently more passive and irrational than men – indeed, as man's other, or as a 'second sex', to cite Simone de Beauvoir.[26] This critique was certainly accurate; yet it must be remembered that the surrealists were deeply critical of the gender norms promoted by post-Second World War France. As Amy Lyford points out, '[t]he postwar society in which the surrealists lived was rife with images promoting traditional social roles for men and women: images of robust manhood and female maternity cropped up everywhere as if they were antidotes to the terrible memories evoked by the sight of veterans' wounded bodies'.[27] Thus, even though the surrealist idealisation of 'feminine passivity' was indeed problematic, it would be erroneous to suggest that 'male surrealism' actively promoted patriarchal values and traditional notions of masculinity; the masculine position inhabited by these arists in their art and writing is anything but stable and in control. At the same time, despite their aversion to traditional articulations of masculiny, none of the surrealists was of course immune to the influence of contemporary gender norms and conventions. Carrington's stories ambivalently navigate the doubly fraught terrain of late 1930s gender norms and surrealism's veneration of femininity. In some ways, as this chapter will suggest, Carrington's stories anticipate aspects of second-wave feminism's critique not merely of surrealism but of patriarchal society generally.

As I will demonstrate, *The House of Fear* and *The Oval Lady* overtly and actively engage with Breton's preoccupation with images of simultaneous frenzy and stasis as well as Ernst's investment in collage as a way to elicit a hysterical subjectivity or 'convulsive identity'. The fact that both volumes were illustrated by Ernst further aligns them with the surrealist project of subverting the notion of the autonomous self. However, Carrington's two volumes also differ from one another in one important respect. Whereas *The House of Fear*, to which Ernst wrote the preface, demonstrates a much more straightforward artistic investment in Ernst's and Breton's vision, *The Oval Lady* incorporates an implicit critique of the exaltation of passivity, and by extension of femininity. The recurrent motif of female passivity and silence in the latter volume forms a poignant commentary on the gendered stakes in hysteria and convulsive identities. Thereby anticipating both Beauvoir's and the second-wave feminist demystification of the socially constructed otherness of women, the stories in *The Oval Lady* might be read as a reflection on surrealism's masculine bias, but, more productively, as a critique of the patriarchal structure of Carrington's contemporary society in a wider sense.

The House of Fear

Leonora Carrington wrote the stories collected in *The House of Fear* and *The Oval Lady* (as well as several other short stories that remained unpublished at the time) during her relationship with Max Ernst. Much has already been written about this relationship. Some critics argue that the union ultimately hampered Carrington's own creative expression. For instance, Carrington's biographer, Joanna Moorhead, claims that, by 1940, Carrington 'had worked out an important and essential truth about being a woman who was also an artist: if she stayed with Max she would be dwarfed by him'.[28] Robert Belton goes as far as to suggest that Carrington's work of this time is hopelessly flawed by 'the corrupted vocabulary of male Surrealism', of which Ernst is clearly construed as a main proponent.[29] Most feminist scholars, however, while acknowledging the uneven power balance between the young female artistic 'apprentice' and the much older and established male 'master', have sought to foreground Carrington's artistic autonomy vis-à-vis Ernst.[30] My proposition that Carrington actively engages with Ernst's ideas about identity and collage in these stories does not in any way render them derivative or suggest that her artistic agency was compromised; instead, it aims to demonstrate that surrealist theory was never an exclusively masculine domain.

The presence of Ernst is particularly strong in the earliest volume, *The House of Fear* (published in 1938). Not only does the volume contain a preface and collages by Ernst, but the story itself (henceforth referred to as 'The House of Fear') exists in a tentative intertextual relation with as well as mirroring formal elements of Ernst's collage novels. The story is narrated by an ungendered first-person narrator, 'a very boring person' and 'recluse', who is unexpectedly halted by a horse in the street and invited to the yearly party at the Castle of Fear later that evening.[31] The party is a Lewis Carrollesque affair, to which the narrator guesses that 'all the horses in the world had come'. Fear, the mistress of the house, is also revealed to look 'slightly like a horse, but … much uglier' and to wear a 'dressing gown … made of live bats sewn together by their wings'.[32] The fact that bats usually signify fear in the Carrington bestiary, making appearances in several other stories (e.g. 'The Debutante' and 'Uncle Sam Carrington'), further reinforces Fear's already terrifying countenance.

The frightened horses and the equally terrified narrator are now at the mercy of Fear and the bizarre rules of a game she has apparently spent the past year devising. She dictates:

> You must all count backwards from a hundred and ten to five as quickly as possible while thinking of your own fate and weeping for those how have gone before you. You must simultaneously beat time to the tune of 'the Volga Boatmen' with your left foreleg, 'The Marseillaise' with your right foreleg, and 'Where Have You Gone, My Last Rose of Summer?' with your two back legs. I had some further details, but I've left them out to simplify the game.[33]

Responding to these instructions, the previously petrified horses in mass rapture begin 'to beat their hooves as if they wanted to descend to the depths of the earth'. The narrator, however, remains on the periphery: 'I stayed where I was, hoping [Fear] wouldn't see me.'[34]

This absurd game is simultaneously funny and uncanny; even though Fear's seemingly nonsensical instructions are humorous, we are nonetheless left with the uncomfortable feeling that the horses are acting like automata – robbed of all free will of their own. This sense is reinforced by the narrator's terrified attempt to escape the Medusa-like 'great eye' of Fear ('she had only one eye, but it was six times bigger than an ordinary eye') by staying immobile.[35] The only options here are complete stasis or automatic compliance; the forced loss of self that is implicit in both options is indeed fearful.

The contradictory experience of frenzy and stasis here recalls both Breton's description of convulsive beauty and Ernst's account of the troubling effect on the psyche of bringing two planes of existence into conflict with each other in collage. The most unsettling part of the story, however, is its closing sentence; frozen in the midst of this seemingly programmed ecstasy, the narrator offers the unfinished pronouncement that '[i]t went on like this for twenty-five minutes, but…'.[36] This interrupted finishing sentence closely echoes several of the captions to the plates in *The Hundred Headless Woman* and *A Little Girl Dreams of Taking the Veil*, which similarly end with a conjunction (most typically 'and') followed by an ellipsis (Figure 2.1). Even though Ernst's caption sentences are often concluded syntactically on the following page, the fact that different parts of a sentence are often logically incompatible or that the collages held together by a split caption appear wholly unrelated, adds to the experience both of contradiction and suspense. Like the incongruous clauses or picture elements of a surrealist *cadavre exquis*, the narratives of Ernst's collage novels do not progress teleologically; instead of providing resolution they produce perturbation and confusion. In addition to this, many of the collage images portray characters arrested in mid-action, frozen like statues. Indeed, as Lomas has pointed out,

The father: "Your kiss seems adult, my child. Coming from God, it will go far. Go, my daughter, go ahead and …

2.1 Max Ernst, page 15 from *A Little Girl Dreams of Taking the Veil* (1930), trans. Dorothea Tanning, Dover Publications, Inc., 1982.

'[f]rozen immobility ... introduces a factor of suspense, or deferral of the climactic moment, which characterises the narrative structure of the collage novel in general'.[37] A sense of petrification, thus, marks Ernst's collages and their accompanying captions, as well as the affective experience of the viewer.

The recurring petrification that is both represented in and effected by Ernst's collage novels is clearly linked to his favouring of psychic passivity as an ideal condition for the artist to inhabit, as discussed above. Both instances are, moreover, intimately tied to his concept of convulsive identity – an experience of the self not as autonomous and coherent but as split into contradiction with itself, or ruled by an otherness within. This notion also fundamentally informs Carrington's 'The House of Fear'. The story, as we have seen, ends with the narrator frozen in mid-chaos, unable to join the enraptured horses in their frantic dance. Perhaps we can read this scene as signifying a clash within the self, between the conscious, 'very boring' ego with their 'enormous intelligence'[38] and the violently irrational unconscious, ruled by 'automatic' impulses beyond the control of the rational mind. More important, however, is the effect of this contradiction on the reader; we are left reeling in the same frenzied suspension as the narrator, the 'but...' that ends the story obstructing any sense of narrative resolution; all that is available by way of conclusion is a paradoxical state of frenzied stasis. This contradictory state strongly resembles Ernst's characterisation of collage as a collision between two irreconcilable realities on a plane unsuitable to both – preconditions he deems essential for the attainment of convulsive identity.

In his preface to *The House of Fear*, entitled 'Loplop Presents the Bride of the Wind', Ernst invents an alter ego for Carrington, akin to his own alter ego, the birdlike creature Loplop (who features in many of his collages).[39] 'Who is the Bride of the Wind', Ernst asks; 'Can she read? Can she write French without mistakes? What wood does she burn to keep herself warm?'[40] He continues: 'She warms herself with her intense life, her mystery, her poetry. She has read nothing, but drunk everything. She can't read. And yet the nightingale saw her sitting on the stone of spring, reading. And though she was reading to herself, the animals and horses listened to her in admiration.'[41] As Natalya Lusty has astutely observed, Ernst 'presents [Carrington] here as a *conducteur merveilleusement magnétique*, a term used to describe the function of the *femme-enfant* for the male surrealist imagination'.[42] The *femme-enfant* was a key surrealist muse figure, whose 'closeness to mystery and sexuality', in the words of Marina Warner, 'formed the crux of Surrealist doctrine'.[43] Breton, especially, repeatedly invoked the *femme-enfant* as 'the only one in whom resides the state of absolute transparency of vision',[44] but, as Warner has pointed out, Ernst too was in awe of this figure (as can be seen, for example, in *A Little Girl Dreams of Taking the Veil*).[45] Ernst's characterisation of Carrington as the Bride of the Wind in the preface to *The House of Fear*, casts her, as Lusty argues, as the supreme surrealist muse: irrational, eroticised, and mysterious.

Ernst's 'introduction' of Carrington in this preface was presumably aimed at integrating her definitively into the surrealist circle.[46] As Lusty also notes, Carrington's choice to write in French, 'a language in which she was far from fluent despite having been taught at home by a French governess, indicates a certain pragmatic move in terms of her association with the Surrealists';[47] we might thus conclude that at this point she was eager to be included as an active participant in the movement of which she had become an ardent admirer while studying art in London a few years earlier. *The House of Fear*, I propose, is perhaps Carrington's most earnest attempt at writing herself into 'the surrealist project', as it would have been defined at the time. Her appropriation of Ernst's primarily visual collage technique for her own short story mode might thus be read as an active alignment with surrealism's contemporary aims and theories, but more importantly it demonstrates that surrealist theory and the surrealist quest of troubling identity were never exclusively masculine projects.[48]

The Oval Lady

Composed around the same time, the stories in *The Oval Lady* (published in 1939) bear strong similarities to 'The House of Fear'. Indeed, most of the stories in *The Oval Lady* revolve around the emotional state of fear. Although 'The House of Fear' is the only story in Carrington's published oeuvre to end on a truncated sentence (mirroring the captions of Ernst's collage novels), the stories in *The Oval Lady* parallel the effect of suspense by ending in mid-action. Another striking resemblance is the narrative perspective; all five stories in *The Oval Lady* feature a first-person narrator positioned on the margins of the action.

However, while the narrator of 'The House of Fear' is ungendered, the narrators of all the stories in *The Oval Lady* are female (and bear a noticeable resemblance to Carrington herself). Another aspect that distinguishes the volumes from one another is the critique, in *The Oval Lady*, of culturally assigned gendered norms, and, by extension, their oblique distancing from the surrealist elevation of female passivity and irrationality. Although Carrington later dismissed the impact of the surrealist muse cult on her early work, claiming that she 'didn't have time to be anyone's muse' because she 'was too busy rebelling against [her] family and learning to be an artist',[49] it is clear from these (and other) early stories that the constraints on women imposed by surrealism as well by patriarchal culture generally required artistic working through.⁵⁰ Thus, whereas 'The House of Fear' seems to align itself with Ernst's and Breton's ideas regarding convulsive identity fairly straightforwardly, the stories in *The Oval Lady* engage with these ideas much more ambivalently.

In the title story, the anonymous narrator reveals herself to the reader as an observer, positioned in front of a window as if regarding a framed painting. Inside the window frame, a very thin, tall lady, with a sad and oval face, stands completely still. Like Breton's description of convulsive beauty as 'neither dynamic nor static', this image is frozen while at the same time trembling with movement, due to a shivering feather in the woman's hair. 'My eyes kept being drawn to the quivering feather', the narrator states: 'it was so restless in the window, where nothing was moving!'⁵¹ The window frame here functions as a literal frame for the visual image, and the narrator's overt admission of being a spectator implicates the reader in the same gaze.

The lady in the window presents an enigma to the narrator, who is 'devoured by curiosity' and 'irresistible desire' to step into the frame herself. Deborah B. Gaensbauer reads this curiosity as an 'overwhelming compulsion to trespass', seeing the narrator as an 'unabashedly nosy Alice-in-Wonderland-like character ... [who] vault[s] the barriers of old rules and hierarchies to penetrate the fantastic realms reserved for dreams and hallucinations or well-kept family secrets'.⁵² Yet, inside the stately and stifling home of the Oval Lady, named Lucretia, the narrator does not do much to defy any rules, but rather, as we shall see, freezes in the face of patriarchal control.

Lucretia herself, however, defies patriarchal rule with all her might, starving herself for the sole purpose of spiting her father, who has forbidden her to play with her beloved wooden rocking horse, Tartar. Flying in the face of her father's prohibition, she turns herself into a white horse to join Tartar in frenzied play. She also invites her tame magpie, Matilda, in from the outside, and her entry into the room brings in masses of newly fallen snow. The previously sad, bored, and angry Lucretia who stood immobile by the window now 'laughed with joy and danced madly around in the snow',⁵³ revivified by the ecstatic play as well as, presumably, the transgression against her father.⁵⁴

In the middle of Lucretia's joyous dance, in which the narrator hesitantly takes part, an old servant woman intervenes with directives from Lucretia's father to 'stop this ridiculous game at once' because Lucretia is 'not a child anymore'.⁵⁵ They are all taken to the father who is seated 'at the end of a long table, looking more like a geometric figure than anything else', and whose presence restrains everyone's speech. The father decides to punish Lucretia severely for breaking his rules, since she has ignored his edict several times before. He promises to burn Tartar, 'until there's nothing left of him'.[56] The narrator, now hiding behind a door, subsequently hears the neighing of a horse suffering intense agony. It is not entirely clear if it is only Tartar that is being burned, or if Lucretia's equine self also perishes in the flames. In the face of this terror, all the narrator can do is to cover her ears, 'for the most frightful neighing sounded from above, as if an animal were suffering extreme torture'.[57]

Lucretia clearly embodies aspects of Carrington's own self – the autobiographical clues to such a reading are overt. It is well known that the recurrent motif of the horse in her early work betrays Carrington's own close totemic identification with this animal. In 'The Oval Lady', Lucretia's horse alter ego might be seen to represent the author's own impulse to rebel against bourgeois ennui and decorum. Moreover, the rocking horse Tartar might be read as yet another aspect of the author's self, its reduplicated name alluding to Ernst's alter ego Loplop.[58] However, while Carrington's own rebellion against her family might ultimately be deemed as having been successful, that of Lucretia (and Tartar) is cruelly quelled, while the father, as an embodiment of bourgeois-patriarchal law, triumphs at the story's close. Meanwhile, the narrator – and by extension the reader – is forced to witness the agony of the burning horse in a completely powerless state, as if petrified.

Jonathan P. Eburne convincingly reads the story's abrupt ending and the narrator's passivity as an expression of Carrington's fear of complicity with patriarchal or proto-fascist ideologies.[59] In 'The Oval Lady', Eburne notes,

> power – however domesticated it may seem – becomes horrific at the point where its effects are downplayed rather than sensationalized, reproduced in and by the stories' protagonists rather than singled out as abhorrent. Lucretia's stern father may be the principal antagonist of 'The Oval Lady', but the story also outlines a ritual of complicity within which even the narrator becomes a participant.[60]

On this view, Carrington's representations of passivity thus have an overtly political resonance in the context of the imminent war. In addition to dramatising her anxiety about gendered subordination, then, the stasis of the protagonist at the story's close also registers Carrington's response to contemporary politics and her fear of unthinking complicity with fascist ideologies – an anxiety that is explored in greater detail in the memoir *Down Below*.[61]

The ending of the story in some ways parallels its beginning, which also featured the narrator observing a scene of simultaneous frenzy and stasis (the quivering feather in the still window frame). The narrator's initial curiosity and initiative, however, have turned to disquietude and paralysis. This state resembles both Ernst's concept of convulsive identity and his theory of collage. Like in 'The House of Fear', we might read the characters in 'The Oval Lady' as different aspects of a splintered self, which are in intense contradiction with one another. Yet the end of 'The Oval Lady' does not invoke the triumphant (and often erotic) insubordination that marks the convulsive identity represented or elicited by Ernst's collage novels. Indeed, the frenzied turmoil of the story's ending provokes not elation but a deadening passivity and desire to disappear. When Lucretia's self seems to merge with Tartar's in the perishing flames, the last remnants of the narrator's self expire too.

The anxiety provoked by the endings of both 'The House of Fear' and 'The Oval Lady' does not subdue their simultaneous deadpan humour, however, which works to further affiliate them with surrealism. J.H. Matthews suggests that the matter-of-factness of Carrington's short stories is inspired by a typically English tradition, 'so mysterious to the French that, in defeat, they refer to it helplessly as *l'humour anglais*'.[62] Several other critics, in addition to Carrington herself, have identified the strong influence of Lewis Carroll's work in these early stories.[63] Surely, though, the surrealists would not have felt helpless when confronted by Carrington's Carrollesque humour; indeed, Breton adopted both Carroll and Carrington for his project of creating an inventory of what he called 'black humour' – 'a partly macabre, partly ironic, often absurd turn of spirit that constitutes "the mortal enemy of sentimentality", and beyond that a "superior revolt of the mind"'.[64]

Carrington's black humour, inflected by the absurd anti-logic of *Alice's Adventures in Wonderland* (1865), characterises not only the curious game at the castle of Fear but also the violent plot of 'The Royal Summons', the third story in *The Oval Lady*. This story opens with the unnamed narrator revealing that she 'had received a royal summons to pay a call on the sovereigns of my country', but upon her arrival at the royal palace she is informed that '[t]he queen went mad yesterday'.[65] Cleopatra-like, the queen greets the narrator sitting in a bath of goat's milk filled with live sea sponges, with which she attempts to wash herself. Later she waters her flower-patterned carpet, as if the textile flowers were real. The intertextual echoes from *Alice* are overt. We immediately associate the mad queen's use of living creatures as a hygiene tool with the Queen of Hearts' croquet game with flamingos and hedgehogs.[66] Moreover, the confusion between representation and reality that makes the queen water her carpet evokes the many instances of wordplay and double meaning in *Alice* that serve to make signification impossible to pin down.

The narrator is persuaded by the queen to stand in for her in a meeting with the government later that day. In the government chamber it is decided that the mad queen must be dispatched by being thrown into a lion cage.

The assassin is to be elected in a game of draughts, which the narrator inadvertently wins. She finds herself 'rooted to the ground with horror', and when she tries to flee her fate a tall cypress tree '[tears] itself out of the earth by its roots' in order to stop the escape. The narrator has no choice but to go through with the gruesome deed; 'I would have liked to turn back', she confesses, 'but was afraid of the cypress and what it might be able to do with its hairy black branches'.[67]

The mere fact that the regicide is chosen in as seemingly banal a game as draughts is of course both surreal and Carrollesque. As the plot progresses, however, we come to the chilling realisation that this particular game of draughts is anything but banal; in fact, it extends beyond determining the queen's assassin into forming a structuring principle for the entire story. Both the narrator and the queen are the helpless pieces in this game, in which the one's coerced movements will lead to the annihilation of the other.[68] In Carrington's French original, this game is of course referred to by its French name, *jeu de dames*, which adds an overtly gendered dimension to the government's grotesque plot.[69] The game, I suggest, becomes a metaphor for the rigid rules of femininity in Carrington's contemporary social world; the only two options are to passively follow orders, like the narrator, or to be obliterated, like the queen/*dame*. Even nature itself, in the form of the cypress tree, joins the patriarchal forces that are bent on making women comply. As is typical of Carrington's narratives, this one too ends in mid-action, the terrified narrator arrested before the seemingly inevitable deadly conclusion: 'The more strongly I smelled the lion', she states, 'the more loudly I sang, to give myself courage'.[70]

The observation of the overarching metaphor of the *jeu de dames* in 'The Royal Summons' reveals an additional layer of meaning in several of the other stories in *The Oval Lady*. Indeed, the geometrical dimensions of the Oval Lady herself point to a possible reading of her as a chess piece; moreover, it seems significant that the original French renders her a *dame* rather than a *femme*. Her battle with her father, who 'look[s] more like a geometrical figure than anything else', might thus be read as a macabre strategy board game played out between the sexes.[71] The game metaphor is strengthened by Ernst's collage image for this story, which features a bust of a black horse positioned on a square base, seemingly frozen in mid-neigh and with a magpie stuck to its forehead; its statuesque look makes the viewer immediately associate the motif with the knight on a chess-board. Moreover, Carrington's own painting *Femme et oiseau* (1937), a visual companion to the 'The Oval Lady',[72] also depicts a horse-woman resembling a black chess piece (and also Carrington herself), caught in a frozen position in a window-like frame with a magpie perched on the windowsill (Figure 2.2). Here, the bottom of the window, which cuts the horse in half, performs the function of creating the bustlike look of the chess-board knight.[73] The chess-board knight is of course not identical to the chess-board queen, but, in the stories in *The Oval Lady*, images invoking chess and draughts all seem to reference a lack of female autonomy and control.

While horses in the Carrington bestiary have usually been interpreted by critics as embodiments of freedom and autonomy,[74] we begin to see a second set of connotations emerge around this figure. Viewed through the lens of the chess-board motif, the horse also, simultaneously, suggests rigid compliance. The robotic horses in 'The House of Fear' are a case in point, and perhaps Tartar, with his wooden legs screwed to the rockers, can too be interpreted in this light, signifying not only childhood play and freedom but also submission and regulation. And although horses in Carrington's visual work of this time are usually depicted in free gallop, we see in the 1942 painting *Green Tea* (also sometimes referred to as *The Oval Lady*) a rigidly stiff white horse chained to a tree. It would seem, then, as if the figure of the horse in Carrington's early work carries ambivalent meanings, simultaneously signifying freedom and the lack thereof.[75]

Carrington's references to chess must also be seen through the lens of surrealist representations of and fascination with chess more broadly. It is well known that many artists associated with the surrealist movement, including Ernst, harboured a strong interest in the game – a passion that culminated in 1944 in the exhibition *The Imagery of Chess*, conceived by Ernst, Marcel Duchamp, and the gallery owner Julien Levy, and which featured work by, among others, Dorothea Tanning, Kay Sage, Man Ray, and André Breton.[76] As Rebecca Munford has observed, for the surrealists, chess 'set in play a dynamic tension between passion and rational thought, and free play and deathly design, as well as dramatizing sexual and gender personifications and conflicts'.[77] Carrington's depiction of the game turns on precisely this tension, but, rather than foregrounding its alluring and erotic aspects, she seizes on its forced submission and logic of elimination. Moreover, as with her depiction of the simultaneous frenzy and stasis of surrealist convulsive identity, Carrington's references to chess emphasise the gendered stakes in the surrealist adulation of passivity – whilst psychic passivity and a hysterical sensibility might be generative modes for the male subject or artist, the female subject or artist, circumscribed by different social and cultural regulatory frames, risks losing any hope of effecting social change by giving up her claims to agency and subjectivity, instead becoming complicit in cementing cultural stereotypes about femininity.[78] The abrupt endings of all the stories in *The Oval Lady*, mediated by the often anguished and petrified first-person narrator, are key in understanding Carrington's ambivalence about surrealist passivity and convulsive identity.

2.2 Leonora Carrington, *Femme et oiseau*, 1937. Oil on canvas.

'Uncle Sam Carrington' too features both a horse and a game of draughts, played between the two Misses Cunningham-Jones, arbiters of bourgeois respectability and good taste. This story is told from a retrospective point-of-view, by a presumably adult narrator relating an anecdote from when she was eight years old. This absurd tale is a coming-of-age narrative, in which the young narrator-protagonist is confronted with the painful social and gendered rituals of the upper middle classes. Sam Carrington himself features only at the beginning of the story, as the social pariah of the Carrington family; together with Aunt Edgeworth he causes immense embarrassment to the family, and especially to the narrator's mother who 'had a certain social reputation to keep up', by laughing every time he sees the full moon. The mother confides in her daughter that she was ignored in the street by Lady Cholmondey-Bottom, which renders the narrator 'grief stricken'.[79] This particular episode has overt autobiographical roots; Joanna Moorhead, in her biography on Carrington, relates an almost identical event from Carrington's own childhood.[80]

Whilst it is hard to say anything conclusive about how Carrington herself felt about her mother's apparent misery in the face of social rejection, the narrator of 'Uncle Sam Carrington' is distraught and sets out on a late-night journey into the forest to find a solution to the family's 'sad state of affairs'.[81] There are deliberate fairy-tale resonances in the description of the narrator's night-time expedition.[82] Like Hansel and Gretel, she enters the forest anxious about getting lost; 'If I keep count of the trees until I reach the place I'm going to', she tells herself, 'I shan't get lost. I'll remember the number of trees on the return journey.'[83] This plan fails, however, since the narrator can count only to ten and soon goes astray. Suddenly she happens upon two cabbages locked in a deadly fight – this, we realise, foreshadows events to come.[84] These two cabbages 'were tearing each other's leaves off with such ferocity that soon there was nothing but torn leaves everywhere and no cabbages'.[85] A little later, the narrator is led by a horse she has met to the house of the Misses Cunningham-Jones, experts at 'the extermination of family shame'.[86] While the narrator is left to peruse a book from the Cunningham-Jones library, with the title *The Secrets of the Flowers of Refinement, or the Vulgarity of Food*, the two ladies set off for the kitchen garden to fetch for the narrator what she will need to supply her family with in order to alleviate their felings of shame. As the curious narrator soon finds out, the treatment consists of vegetables, which are not only harvested against their will but flagellated with a huge whip, while the ladies shout, 'One's got to suffer to go to Heaven. Those who do not wear corsets will never get there.' The horse whispers to the peeping narrator: 'It's always like this ... The vegetables have to suffer for the sake of society. You'll see that they'll soon catch one for you, and that it'll die for the cause.'[87] The ladies indeed manage to subdue a few rebellious vegetables, which they subsequently present to the narrator in a parcel as a cure for her family's social disgrace.

As indicated above, it is of course no coincidence that the Misses Cunningham-Jones are busy playing *une partie de dames* when the narrator and the horse arrive at their house. Indeed, their 'expertise' in resolving family problems seems to involve the subjugation not merely of vegetables but of women too. The vegetables that get whipped into submission are clearly gendered female, being forced into corsets in order to be considered socially respectable. The title of the book given to the narrator posits flowers as the pinnacle of refinement while food is the epitome of vulgarity; translated into interwar norms of upper-class femininity, we might say that women's social duty is to be aesthetically pleasing to look at; they should be corseted flowers bound for 'Heaven', which means quenching their vulgar desires for savoury (and possibly erotic) pleasure. Like the subdued vegetables after the Misses Cunningham-Jones's treatment, they are expected to be neatly packaged and contained, and subsequently played like pawns in a game aimed at maintaining, or perhaps gaining, social status. In the *jeu de dames* that is their social life, their movements are already predetermined.

While the narrator expresses horror at the sight of the cabbages attacking each other in the forest, hoping afterwards that it had only been a nightmare, she does not offer any clues to her emotional reaction to the violent treatment of the vegetables by the Misses Cunningham-Jones. The story ends with her impassively accepting the defeated parcel. Perhaps what we have witnessed is a successful first step in the gendered rite of passage that Carrington's interwar upper-class society imposed on young girls. The lesson presented by the whipped vegetables is that women must passively accept suffering 'for the sake of society'; this lesson is seemingly embodied by the compliant eight-year-old narrator at the end of the story.

Although placed before 'Uncle Sam Carrington' in the volume in which it was published, 'The Debutante' in many ways functions as its sequel. Revolving around another aristocratic initiation rite for young women – the debutante ball – it is also told in retrospect, opening with the reminiscent pronouncement 'When I was a debutante'.[88] 'The Debutante' is by far Carrington's most well-known literary work; on top of having been widely anthologised, it is the piece in her literary oeuvre that has received the most critical attention, and, as already indicated, the vast majority of these readings focus on the feminist rebellion the story seems to enact.[89] It is well known that the story has strong autobiographical origins; in 1935, Carrington was herself reluctantly presented as a debutante at George V's court.[90] 'It was the physical pain she remembered most about the night of her presentation', Joanna Moorhead tells us; Carrington related to her that she was 'wearing a tiara … And it was biting into [her] skull'.[91] Like the vegetables of 'Uncle Sam Carrington' she was required to suffer for the sake of social custom. Moorhead describes the event as 'the last time she ever does as she is told, or what [her parents] want her to do'. The year after, in 1936, Carrington chanced upon surrealism and the rest is, of course, history.

'The Debutante' is typically read as a re-enactment of Carrington's own ball, in which she, instead of reluctantly complying, lets her insurgence triumph. It tells the story of a young debutante who befriends a hyena at the local zoo, and together they hatch a plan that will allow the unwilling girl to escape her coming-out ball: the hyena will go in her stead, disguised by the torn-off face of the debutante's maid, whom the hyena will dispose of by eating her. The hyena indeed goes to the ball, but her animal identity is betrayed by her strong smell. The story ends with the enraged mother storming into the debutante's bedroom, recounting how the hyena suddenly stood up during dinner, tore off its mask and ate it in front of all the guests, and subsequently jumped out of the window.

It is not hard to see why this brilliant critique of what Moorhead aptly refers to as the upper-class 'cattle market' has been hailed by critics as one of the finest examples of Carrington's feminist-surrealist insubordination.[92] By construing an encaged animal as the narrator's alter ego, we realise, as Gabriele Griffin has pointed out, that both are 'trapped to be exhibited to a gaping public, the one in the zoo, the other in the confines of an upper-middle class home'.[93] But whereas the hyena escapes her imprisonment at the end of the story, the narrator remains trapped, cowering behind a chair in her bedroom. Despite the fact that the subversive plan is devised by both of them, it is thus only the hyena that embodies action at the story's close. I would therefore argue that the story does not enact quite as straightforward a rebellion as scholars have tended to suggest. Even though the closing image celebrates the transgressive hyena and mocks the conservative mother, it leaves the frightened narrator on the floor, petrified by fear. Eburne has aptly pointed out that the abrupt endings of Carrington's early stories seem 'more threatening than liberatory, populating Carrington's fictional universe with a menagerie of monsters and figures and imbuing it with an unsettling aura of anxiety'.[94] This observation also applies to 'The Debutante', whose black humour and anti-bourgeois insubordination do not neutralise the anxiety and tension between rebellion and compliance, or frenzy and stasis, which characterise all the stories in the *The Oval Lady*.[95]

If 'Uncle Sam Carrington' and 'The Debutante' can both be read as critiques of Carrington's contemporary society's initiation points into sanctioned femininity, the story 'A Man in Love' might fruitfully be interpreted as a statement on the next step in the trajectory of such gendered apprenticeship: motherhood. Here the narrator finds herself passively having to listen to a melodramatic greengrocer relating the story of how his wife Agnes faded away after their wedding night. Agnes's lifeless body now lies on a bed in the back room of his fruit and vegetable shop, and, although he 'water[s] her every day', the greengrocer has for the past forty years 'been quite unable to tell whether she is alive or dead'.[96] Even though she has kept completely still during this time, she has remained warm, and the greengrocer has subsequently used her hospitable body to hatch eggs. '[N]ext year', he tells the narrator, 'I shall plant some tomatoes. I'd be surprised if they didn't do very well in there'.[97] The image of woman has in this scenario been reduced to only a body; her body, in turn, has been reduced to one single function: a vessel for incubation.

The tension of the story is provided by the wistful greengrocer's apparently conflicting emotions regarding his wife's lifelessness. Even though he is 'blinded by his tears' as he reaches the climax of his story (which allows the narrator to slip out of the shop unnoticed), he has previously spoken with longing anticipation of the promise of Agnes's body to yield tomatoes, which he will presumably be able to sell in his shop.[98] This story is the only one in the collection in which the narrator is able to escape; moreover, unlike the other narrators, she is not fear-stricken at the end of the narrative. Instead, she leaves of her own free will, with a stolen melon to boot. The catatonic Agnes, on the other hand, remains trapped as the greengrocer's muse, functioning both as the object of his compulsive storytelling and the passive facilitator of his trade.

The stories in *The Oval Lady* all dramatise encounters between a passive, observing narrator and another female character: a rebellious daughter, a mad queen, a transgressive female hyena, subdued female-gendered vegetables and a maternal corpse. Most stories (with the exception of 'A Man in Love') end with portrayals of the state of paradoxical frenzy and stasis that both Breton and Ernst promote as 'convulsive', thus calling the idea of the autonomous self into question. In Carrington's work the narrator might be said to embody the rational ego, which is petrified into inaction by the irrational unconscious impulses that are represented by some of the other characters and events. As such, these stories contribute to the fundamental idea of surrealist thinking that, far from autonomous and rational, the self is ruled by a complex otherness within.

Moreover, the stories in *The Oval Lady* also clearly participate in the surrealist assault on bourgeois respectability, giving added insight into the specific ways in which these (often repressive) norms affected women of the time. At the same time, the way in which these stories connect a critique of gendered (and bourgeois) norms with the representation of a 'convulsed' passivity prompts a reading that goes beyond their alignment with surrealist ideas and ideals. Indeed, the anxiety and fear experienced by most of these narrators at the end of each story are not merely the unsettling, and putatively revolutionary, effect of Breton's convulsive beauty or Ernst's convulsive identity; it is also, I suggest, the crippling passivity of a 'femininity' confronted with patriarchal violence. Read in this way, the surrealist celebration of a 'feminine' passive sensibility, which would weaken the boundaries of the ego to allow unconscious impulses to surface, becomes complicit in the social disempowerment of actual women, for whom passivity and mystification were hardly liberatory conditions. The stories in *The Oval Lady* thus embody a schism: on the one hand they participate in the surrealist project of challenging the notion of a rational Cartesian self (which can be seen as a proto-feminist project), while on the other obliquely questioning the language and iconography with which surrealism advances this project.

Conclusion

This chapter has aimed to demonstrate how the stories in Leonora Carrington's *The House of Fear* and *The Oval Lady* actively contribute to surrealist theories of the self. Whereas 'The House of Fear', in my reading, appropriates the ideas and methods of André Breton and Max Ernst, the stories in *The Oval Lady*, by contrast, engage with these much more critically. By foregrounding the potentially harmful effects of passivity in general, and female passivity in particular, these narratives complicate the surrealist quest for irrational abandon and non-agency, epitomised by the *femme-enfant* figure. Carrington's active engagement with and extension of the theories and practices of Breton and Ernst prompt us to reconfigure the notion of 'surrealist theorising' as a male project. Indeed, *The House of Fear* and *The Oval Lady* teach us that surrealist theories of subjectivity should be seen as including an implicitly feminist facet.

Notes

I want to thank Kristoffer Noheden for his generous comments on an earlier draft of this chapter.

1 André Breton, *Nadja* (1928), trans. Richard Howard (London: Penguin, 1999), p. 11.
2 For an in-depth discussion on fragmented identity in the work of these artists, see e.g. David Lomas, *The Haunted Self* (New Haven: Yale University Press, 2000), and Elza Adamowicz, 'The Surrealist (Self-)Portrait: Convulsive Identities', in Sylvano Levi (ed.), *Surrealism: Surrealist Visuality* (New York: New York University Press, 1997), pp. 31–44.
3 This narrative perspective is not unique to the stories in *La Maison de la Peur* and *La Dame ovale*; we find a similar first-person narrator in, for example, 'Pigeon, Fly', 'The Three Hunters', 'Cast Down by Sadness', stories that were written (also in French), during the same time (1937–39). Notably, 'As They Rode along the Edge', 'The Skeleton's Holiday', 'Monsieur Cyril de Guindre', and 'The Sisters' are all told from a third-person perspective.
4 The novel *The Hearing Trumpet* (1974) stands out in Carrington's literary oeuvre for its definitive narrative resolution.
5 Whitney Chadwick, 'Leonora Carrington: Evolution of a Feminist Consciousness', *Women's Art Journal* 7:1 (Spring–Summer 1986), p. 37.
6 Breton famously proclaimed, in his speech to the Congress of Writers in Paris in 1935: '"Transform the world", Marx said; "change life", Rimbaud said. These two watchwords are one for us.' André Breton, *Manifestoes of Surrealism*, trans. Richard Seaver and Helen R. Lane (Ann Arbor: University of Michigan Press, 2004), p. 241.
7 See, e.g., J.H. Matthews (ed.), *The Custom-House of Desire: A Half-Century of Surrealist Stories* (Berkeley: University of California Press, 1975), Angela Carter (ed.), *Wayward Girls and Wicked Women* (London: Virago, 1986), and Jessica Amanda Salmonson (ed.), *What Did Miss Darrington See? An Anthology of Feminist Supernatural Fiction* (New York: The Feminist Press at CUNY, 1989).

8 Lomas, *The Haunted* Self, p. 1.
 9 André Breton, *Manifesto of Surrealism* (1924) in Breton, *Manifestoes of Surrealism*, p. 26, p. 29.
10 *Ibid.*, pp. 27–8.
11 Max Ernst, 'Beyond Painting' (1936), in Max Ernst, *Beyond Painting*, trans. Dorothea Tanning and Ralph Mannheim (1948; Washington, DC: Solar Books, 2009), p. 18.
12 Although collage-like techniques had been employed by for example Georges Braque and Pablo Picasso in their Cubist *papiers collés*, the emergence of collage is intimately associated with surrealism, and especially with the work of Ernst. See Elza Adamowicz, *Surrealist Collage in Text and Image: Dissecting the Exquisite Corpse* (Cambridge: Cambridge University Press, 1998), p. 4.
13 Comte de Lautréamont, *Maldoror and the Complete Works of Comte de Lautréamont*, trans. Alexis Lykiard (Cambridge: Exact Change, 1994), p. 193.
14 Ernst, 'Beyond Painting', pp. 22–3; italics in the original.
15 *Ibid.*, p. 23.
16 *Ibid.*, p. 33,
17 Breton, *Nadja*, p. 160.
18 Ernst, 'Beyond Painting', p. 33.
19 Breton, *Nadja*, pp. 159–60.
20 André Breton, *Mad Love* (1937), trans. Mary Ann Caws (Lincoln: University of Nebraska Press, 1987), p. 10. The first section of *Mad Love* was originally published as the essay 'La Beauté sera convulsive' in the fifth issue of the surrealist journal *Minotaure* in 1934.
21 Adamowicz, 'The Surrealist (Self-)Portrait', p. 42. Adamowicz is referring specifically to Loplop in this discussion, but the quotation has relevance for several other works by Ernst.
22 See Max Ernst, 'Data on the Youth of M.E.' (1942), in *Beyond Painting*, p. 50.
23 Lomas, *The Haunted Self*, p. 76.
24 *Ibid.*, p. 83.
25 Max Ernst, *A Little Girl Dreams of Taking the Veil* (1930), trans. Dorothea Tanning (Mineola, NY: Dover Publications, Inc., 1982), p. 9.
26 Simone de Beauvoir, *The Second Sex* (1949), trans. Constance Borde and Sheila Malovany-Chevallier (London: Vintage, 2011).
27 Amy Lyford, *Surrealist Masculinities: Gender Anxiety and the Aesthetics of Post-World War I Reconstruction in France* (Berkeley: University of California Press, 2007), p. 4.
28 Joanna Moorhead, *The Surreal Life of Leonora Carrington* (London: Virago, 2017), pp. 108–9.
29 Robert Belton, 'Speaking with Forked Tongues: "Male" Discourse in "Female" Surrealism', in Mary Ann Caws, Rudolf Kuenzli, and Gwen Raaberg (eds), *Surrealism and Women* (Cambridge, MA: The MIT Press, 1991), p. 54. Belton's analysis specifically concerns Carrington's painting *Self-Portrait: The Inn of the Dawn Horse* (1937–38).

30 See, for example, Renée Riese Hubert, 'Leonora Carrington and Max Ernst: Artistic Partnership and Feminist Liberation', *New Literary History* 22: 3 (Summer 1991), pp. 715–45; Whitney Chadwick, *Women Artists and the Surrealist Movement* (London: Thames & Hudson, 1985); and Whitney Chadwick, *The Militant Muse: Love, War and the Women of Surrealism* (London: Thames & Hudson, 2017).
31 Leonora Carrington, 'The House of Fear' (1938) in Leonora Carrington, *The House of Fear: Notes from Down Below*, ed. Marina Warner, trans. Kathrine Talbot and Marina Warner (London: Virago, 1989), p. 30.
32 *Ibid.*, p. 30.
33 *Ibid.*, pp. 31–2.
34 *Ibid.*, p. 32.
35 *Ibid.*, p. 32.
36 *Ibid.*, p. 32; ellipsis in the original.
37 Lomas, *The Haunted Self*, p. 80.
38 Carrington, 'The House of Fear', p. 30.
39 Like Loplop, the Bride of the Wind is a hybrid figure; although he does not directly describe her as a horse-woman, Ernst had in 1927 produced a series of *Bride of the Wind* paintings of two horses entwined in a convulsed embrace. It was presumably Carrington's own identification with horses (which can be seen throughout both 'The House of Fear' and the stories in *The Oval Lady*) that made Ernst cast her in the role of a horse figure from his own artistic repertoire; the 'Bride of the Wind' alter ego, however, does not seem to have been embraced by Carrington herself beyond the publication of *The House of Fear*.
40 Max Ernst, 'Preface, or Loplop Presents the Bride of the Wind', in *The House of Fear: Notes from Down Below*, p. 26.
41 *Ibid.*, p. 26.
42 Natalya Lusty, *Surrealism, Feminism, Psychoanalysis* (Farnham: Ashgate, 2007), p. 31.
43 Marina Warner, 'Introduction', p. 6.
44 André Breton, *Arcanum 17* (1944), trans. Zach Rogow (Los Angeles: Sun & Moon Press, 1994), p. 65.
45 Marina Warner, 'Introduction', p. 7.
46 Lusty aptly compares Ernst's introduction of Carrington into surrealism to her debutante presentation to upper-class society, underscoring the power dynamics inherent in both events. Lusty, *Surrealism, Feminism, Psychoanalysis*, p. 31.
47 *Ibid.*, p. 32.
48 The apparent lack of distance from the surrealist quest for passivity in 'The House of Fear', however, does not mean that Carrington was necessarily blind to its problems at this point. Indeed, the novella *Little Francis*, written in English in 1937, revolves around the frustration of a young English boy forced into a stiflingly passive position in relation to his beloved uncle. The autobiographical references to Carrington's relationship with Ernst are hard to miss; as Warner writes, '[b]y changing herself into a youth, [Carrington] uncovered a deeper truth about her relation to Max Ernst, revealing in the devotion and passivity of the boy Francis the tutelage in which Ernst and other masters held their *femme-enfants*, their brides of the wind'. Warner, 'Introduction', p. 10.

49 Quoted in Whitney Chadwick, *The Militant Muse: Love, War and the Women of Surrealism* (London: Thames & Hudson, 2017), p. 9.
50 See also 'Pigeon, Fly', Carrington's perhaps most poignant treatment of the problem of the muse cult in surrealism. 'Pigeon, Fly' is collected in *The Seventh Horse and Other Tales*, trans. Kathrine Talbot and Anthony Kerrigan (New York: E.P. Dutton, 1988).
51 Leonora Carrington, *The Oval Lady*, in *The House of Fear: Notes from Down Below*, p. 37.
52 Deborah B. Gaensbauer, 'Voyages of Discovery: Leonora Carrington's Magical Prose', *Women's Studies* 23 (1994), p. 273, p. 274.
53 Carrington, *The Oval Lady*, p. 41.
54 Whether intentional or nor, this scene too is very evocative of the way that Breton characterises convulsive beauty in *Nadja*: he says that surrealist beauty is 'subject to that wild gallop which can lead only to another wild gallop – that is, more frenzied than a snowflake in a blizzard – that is, resolved, for fear of being fettered, never to be embraced at all: neither dynamic nor static'. Breton, *Nadja*, p. 159. It is curious that both Carrington and Breton invoke horse imagery, snow, and, as we shall see, tension between the dynamic and the static.
55 Carrington, *The Oval Lady*, p. 41.
56 *Ibid.*, p. 42.
57 *Ibid.*, p. 43.
58 As Jonathan P. Eburne notes, while Tartar is Carrington's alter ego, the bird Matilda stands in for Ernst. Eburne, *Surrealism and the Art of Crime*, p. 238.
59 *Ibid.*, pp. 238–9.
60 *Ibid.*, p. 238.
61 *Down Below* was originally written in English, after which it was lost; it was subsequently orally narrated by Carrington to Jeanne Mégnen, in French. A portion of this oral account was translated back into English and published as 'Down Below' in the surrealist journal *VVV* in 1944. The entire text was finally published in English in 1972 and in French (*En bas*) in 1973.
62 J.H. Matthews, *Custom-House of Desire*, p. 33.
63 See, e.g., Gaensbauer, 'Voyages of Discovery', pp. 273–4; Natalya Lusty, *Surrealism, Feminism, Psychoanalysis*, pp. 26–7, 34; Marina Warner, 'Introduction', p. 14.
64 Mark Polizzotti, 'Introduction: Laughter in the Dark', in André Breton, *Anthology of Black Humor*, trans. Mark Polizzotti (1979; San Francisco: City Lights Books, 1997), p. vi. The quotations within the quotation are from Breton's 1939 introduction ('Lighting Rod') to the anthology.
65 Carrington, *The Oval Lady*, p. 49.
66 Lewis Carroll, *Alice's Adventures in Wonderland* (1865), in Lewis Carroll, *Alice in Wonderland* (Ware: Wordsworth Classics, 1995), p. 65.
67 Carrington, *The Oval Lady*, p. 54.
68 The reversed logic that renders the narrator rooted to the ground and the cypress tree mobile recalls Carroll's sequel to *Alice*, *Through the Looking Glass* (1871); so does the suggestion of chess pieces that are alive.
69 Leonora Carrington, *La Dame ovale* (Paris: GLM, 1939), n.p.
70 Carrington, *The Oval Lady*, p. 54.

71 *Ibid.*, p. 42.
72 Interestingly, the motif of *Femme et oiseau* appears much closer to the narrative of 'The Oval Lady' than the painting actually entitled *The Oval Lady* (1942; also known as *Green Tea*). Still, however, many aspects of the latter painting echo features of the volume *The Oval Lady* as a whole (such as the frozen immobility of the female character, the hyena, the white horse, the cypress trees, and the underground bat-cave).
73 Whether intentional or not, the visual effect of this painting invokes Breton's discussion of the phrase 'There is a man cut in two by the window' in the first *Manifesto of Surrealism*, pp. 21–2.
74 See, e.g., Warner, Introduction', and Georgina M.M. Colvile, 'Beauty and/ Is the Beast: Animal Symbology in the Work of Leonora Carrington, Remedios Varo and Leonor Fini', in Mary Ann Caws, Rudolf Kuenzli, and Gwen Raaberg (eds), *Surrealism and Women* (Cambridge, MA: The MIT Press, 1991), pp. 159–81.
75 See also *Little Francis*, in which the disempowered protagonist grows a horse's head, and subsequently perishes. Leonora Carrington, *Little Francis*, in *The House of Fear: Notes from Down Below*, pp. 69–148.
76 See Larry List, 'The Imagery of Chess: Revisited', pamphlet from *The Noguchi Museum*, www.kwabc.org/files/kwabc/news/2012/11/nyc_2012/larry_list/imagery_of_chess.pdf, accessed 18 June 2019.
77 Rebecca Munford, *Decadent Daughters and Monstrous Mothers: Angela Carter and European Gothic* (Manchester: Manchester University Press, 2013), p. 132.
78 As Chadwick aptly points out, the surrealist idealisation of woman 'turn[s] her into an abstract principle, a universal and an ideal. Passive and compliant, she waits for the world to be revealed to her'. Chadwick, *Women Artists and the Surrealist Movement*, p. 65.
79 Carrington, *The Oval Lady*, p. 61.
80 Moorhead, *The Surreal Life of Leonora Carrington*, p. 32.
81 Carrington, *The Oval Lady*, p. 61.
82 Griffin notes that '[t]he focus in Carrington's stories tends to be on a small number of individuals whose relations with each other become the subject of scrutiny … in the course of the story – a focus typical for fairy tales, with which Carrington's stories share some traits'. Gabriele Griffin, 'Becoming as Being: Leonora Carrington's Writings and Paintings 1937–1940', in Gabriele Griffin (ed.), *Difference in View: Women and Modernism* (London: Taylor and Francis, 1994), p. 96.
83 Carrington, *The Oval Lady*, p. 62.
84 In Carrington's later work, the cabbage takes on esoteric meanings and is used interchangeably with the alchemical white rose. In this story, however, the cabbage and vegetables generally seem to signify women.
85 Carrington, *The Oval Lady*, p. 62.
86 *Ibid.*, p. 63.
87 *Ibid.*, p. 65.
88 *Ibid.*, p. 44.

89 Particularly compelling readings of feminist rebellion in 'The Debutante' include Natalya Lusty's *Surrealism, Feminism, Psychoanalysis*; Alice Gambrell's *Women Intellectuals, Modernism and Difference: Transatlantic Culture, 1919–1945* (Cambridge: Cambridge University Press, 1997); and Susan Rubin Suleiman's *Subversive Intent: Gender, Politics, and the Avant-Garde* (Cambridge, MA: Harvard University Press, 1990).
90 See Moorhead, *The Surreal Life of Leonora Carrington*, p. 21.
91 *Ibid.*, p. 21.
92 *Ibid.*, p. 25.
93 Griffin, 'Becoming as Being', p. 96.
94 Eburne, *Surrealism and the Art of Crime*, p. 219.
95 Alice Gambrell has astutely pointed out that to interpret 'The Debutante' squarely as a 'wonderfully subversive performance' is to miss some of its more subtle meanings; 'I would argue', Gambrell writes, 'that the kinds of cultural critique embedded within Carrington's story are both somewhat less direct and somewhat more self-critical than this kind of reading might suggest'. Reading the hyena as a figure 'assembled from the body of a domesticated animal and the blood of a domestic worker', Gambrell notes that the story self-consciously demonstrates how the social rituals of the upper classes are predicated on the sacrifice of those belonging to the less fortunate ones. Thus, for Gambrell, Carrington's story 'references the deep ambiguities located in her heroine's (and by extension, her own) position: on one hand, both serve as pawns in the patriarchal game of the "marriage market"; on the other, however, both are privileged beneficiaries of the rigidly stratified British class system who play a crucial part in its maintenance'. See Gambrell, *Women Intellectuals, Modernism and Difference*, pp. 76–7. For a nuanced reading of the black and Carrollesque humour of 'The Debutante', see Lusty, *Surrealism, Feminism, Psychoanalysis*, pp. 26–7, p. 34.
96 Carrington, *The Oval Lady*, p. 57.
97 *Ibid.*, p. 57.
98 *Ibid.*, p. 59.

3

Recasting the human: Leonora Carrington's dark exilic imagination

Jeannette Baxter

In many ways, the history of Leonora Carrington's life and work is a history of exile. From an early age, Carrington displayed signs of being what Edward Said would go on to term an 'intellectual exile', with her spirited rebellion against any form of authority placing her 'outside the chatty, familiar world inhabited by natives ... Exile for the intellectual in this metaphysical sense is restlessness, movement, constantly being unsettled, and unsettling others.'[1] Her elopement to Paris with Max Ernst in the mid- to late 1930s at the tender age of nineteen was essentially an act of self-imposed exile, an opportunity to break free from the strict confines of her upper-class family, and to develop her artistic imagination without inhibition. Following a relatively peaceful and highly productive few years living and working with Ernst in Saint Martin d'Ardèche in southern France, however, Carrington was thrust into a condition of geopolitical exile by the brutality of the Second World War and the Nazi occupation of France. Ernst's multiple arrests – he was incarcerated first as an 'enemy alien' by the Vichy government in 1939, and then as a degenerate artist by the Nazis in 1940 – meant that Carrington had no choice but to flee fascist Europe. Displaced and alone, Carrington suffered a psychological breakdown and was committed by her family to Santander psychiatric hospital, another form of exile according to Michel Foucault,[2] where she was declared 'incurably insane'[3] and treated with the convulsion-inducing drug, Cardiazol. Upon her release, Carrington escaped Europe with Renato Leduc, the Mexican writer, poet and diplomat whom she married out of political convenience, and she joined a number of exiled surrealist artists (including Ernst) in New York, where she lived and worked until 1943. Unable to settle within the New York surrealist émigré community, though, Carrington moved with Leduc to Mexico, where they were welcomed into another community of surrealist exiles, centred this time on Benjamin Péret and Remedios Varo, Wolfgang Paalen, Kati Horna, and César Moro. When Carrington's and Leduc's marriage of convenience ended in the mid-1940s, Carrington met and married Emerico 'Chiki' Weisz, a photojournalist and Jewish Hungarian refugee who had walked across Europe with his friend, Robert Cappa, in order to escape Nazi persecution. Carrington and Weisz had two sons and she remained an artist in exile for the rest of her life, spending most of her time in Mexico and some of it in New York.

To date, critics working within, and across, literary and visual studies have approached Carrington's wartime experiences of geopolitical displacement as contextual platforms from which to launch vital, and revitalising, discussions into the ways in which exile experience enabled intellectual agency for the dislocated female artist. Even though Carrington's position within the New York émigré surrealist group remained marginal on the grounds of her sex, this short period of exile was, according to Martica Sawin, one of creative release in which the young avant-garde artist found the confidence to advance a creative vision that was in 'no way beholden to the claims of a modern tradition or to Surrealism other than for the license it gave to her own originality'.[4] Similarly, Whitney Chadwick characterises Carrington's exile in Mexico as a form of severance from the stranglehold of male-dominated European surrealism, one that delivered her, in turn, into the creative and critical possibilities of female artistic collaboration. In relation to Carrington's creative affiliation with Remedios Varo, for instance, Chadwick asserts: 'For the first time in the history of the collective movement called surrealism ... two women would collaborate in attempting to develop a new pictorial language that spoke more directly to their own needs.'[5] This story of exiled female surrealist alliance is one that Joanna Moorhead also foregrounds in her reading of the collaborations between Carrington, Varo, and Kati Horna. 'In a very real sense', Moorhead writes, 'they reinvented Surrealism in Colonia Roma, and this time around it was their own brand of equal-share and genuinely women-centred Surrealism'.[6]

Without doubt, feminist readings such as these have played an important part not just in recovering Carrington's extensive body of work from critical obscurity but in resituating it at the heart of key revisionist debates about the gender politics of visual modernism in general, and of wartime and postwar surrealism in particular. All of this is achieved, however, at the risk of underestimating the extent to which Carrington's surrealist imagination dares to engage in complex, and frequently disquieting, dialogues with the radical uncertainties of the modern exile experience. This chapter responds to that critical shortcoming by taking current thinking on Carrington's exile condition in a new and overtly political direction. Specifically, I focus on three short narratives written in, and about, exile: 'White Rabbits' (1941–42), which was first published in English in *View*, the New York-based surrealist journal set up by the poet and artist Charles Henri Ford to introduce surrealist thought and practice to America; *The Stone Door*, which was first completed in Mexico in the mid-1940s, but not published in its original

English until 1977; and, briefly, 'The Happy Corpse Story', another Mexican tale that, although composed in English in 1971, remains haunted by mid-twentieth-century history in startling ways. By opening these exile writings up to their historical and political contexts of production, this chapter makes the case for reading them as provocative fictional enquiries into one of the most urgent questions of the wartime and postwar eras: namely, what did it mean to be human in the face of barbaric acts of wartime cruelty and a Nazi genocidal policy that was recasting the human according to its own heinous ideology?

It is now well established that the 1940s saw the emergence of a wide range of philosophical, political and aesthetic enquiries into the shifting category of the human. Prominent amongst them were the exile writings of Hannah Arendt and Theodor W. Adorno, both of whom were forced to leave Nazi Germany on the grounds of their Jewish heritage, and both of whom were living and working as exiles in New York at the same time as Carrington: Arendt fled fascist Europe in 1941 for New York, where she remained for the rest of her life; Adorno sought sanctuary in New York before relocating to California at the end of 1941. Whilst there is no evidence to suggest that Carrington had contact with either Arendt or Adorno, her wartime and postwar exile narratives intersect nonetheless with certain aspects of their politico-philosophical analyses, including: the indeterminacies of the modern exile condition; the wartime transformation of the 'home' into a political and ethical question; and the human capacity for cruelty and violence. Moreover, they anticipate important strands of Said's influential postwar writings on exile, writings that have, in turn, emerged out of their own intellectual conversations with Adorno's and Arendt's wartime and postwar thinking. By foregrounding these points of intellectual connection, however, this chapter in no way claims equivalence between Carrington's exile experiences and those of Arendt, Adorno, or Said. On the contrary, a key aim is to tease out a dark and (still) critically neglected aspect of Carrington's personal and political history, which implicates her in the very discourses that her writings seek to challenge; namely, her familial connections with the British chemical company ICI, an international associate of the infamous German chemical industry conglomerate IG Farben.

Given the sensitivities of this chapter in Carrington's life, it is unsurprising that critics have focused their attention on other issues. But what matters is that neither Carrington nor her work shies away from this dark history. Rather, and as I have begun to indicate elsewhere, she develops a range of experimental literary aesthetics over the course of her career that seeks to confront and challenge its complex tensions.[7] Here, then, I shift my focus to Carrington's development of a dark exile aesthetic, one that, coming through from the counter-Enlightenment impulses of the gothic imagination, asks unsettling questions about what it means to be human in a world disfigured by the mass displacement of peoples and the extremities of wartime violence. As Neil Matheson observes in *Surrealism and the Gothic: Castles of the Interior* (2017), the gothic has always been a 'core aspect' of surrealist thought and practice, not only as a 'primary ingredient present at the origins of the movement and integral to its definition in the first Manifesto' but also as a recurring mode of cultural and political enquiry to which the surrealists turned at key moments in history.[8] Arguably, Carrington's work, both visual and literary, has always displayed a gothic sensibility, and, as Jonathan P. Eburne observes in *Surrealism and the Art of Crime* (2008), her haunting tales of bodily invasion produced across the mid- to late 1930s, such as 'The Debutante', 'The Oval Lady' and 'The House of Fear', explore the obscure territories of the gothic in the face of impending world war.[9] My concern, however, is with the way in which the gothic takes on a renewed intellectual, aesthetic, and political significance for Carrington in the wartime and immediate postwar periods, allowing her as it does not only to interrogate the deep unease of the modern exile condition but to bring the manifest and latent landscapes of contemporary history into dialogue so as to open up a troubling yet necessary trajectory of enquiry into the dark forces at work within humanity.

The dark indeterminacy of being: 'White Rabbits'

[H]ell is no longer a religious belief or a fantasy, but something as real as houses and stones and trees. Apparently nobody wants to know that contemporary history has created a new kinds [sic] of human beings – the kind that are put in concentration camps by their foes and internment camps by their friends.[10]

Hannah Arendt

Hannah Arendt's accusation that the atrocities of war and Nazi genocide have not only realised hell on earth but engendered new categories of the human finds fictional countenance across Carrington's exile writings. 'White Rabbits' opens on 'Pest St.', a conspicuous toponym that situates the story, and reader, not only in a landscape of implied infection but in a long tradition of katabatic writing, recalling as it does the large buglike 'pests' that plague the landscapes of 'Inferno', the first part of Dante Alighieri's *The Divine Comedy* (1314). Betraying a certain compulsion to bear witness to the 'recent events' of Pest Street, the unnamed narrator proceeds by describing an urban landscape of destruction and despair: 'The houses which were reddish black, looked as if they had survived mysteriously from the fire of London', she reveals, 'and the house in front of my window … was as black and empty looking as any plague-ridden residence subsequently licked by flames and saliva'd with smoke. This is not the way that I had imagined New York.'[11] What these opening lines suggest, but never articulate in any straightforward way, is that an organised attempt of some kind has been made to eradicate – by fire – an unidentified disease from this particular quarter of the city, reducing it to something of a ghost town. Little else about the conflagration, its perpetrators, or objective is explained; instead, this markedly claustrophobic tale unfolds through a dark poetics of indirection. The narrator tells us nothing directly about her own identity or background, for instance. Rather, we are left to infer from her comment about the shortcomings of present-day New York that she is a newcomer to the city; and that she might be of European, specifically British, heritage, is implied in the reference to the Great Fire which eradicated the bubonic plague – or Black Death – from the streets of London in 1666.

But these subtle references to other times and other places do not serve to keep the past at a safe distance, or to differentiate neatly between 'here' and 'there'; on the contrary, they work quietly to establish a tension-ridden relationship of temporal and spatial simultaneity. That is to say that the narrative perspective crafted so carefully and efficiently in 'White Rabbits' is a surrealist prototype of what Said terms the exile's 'double perspective': 'Because the exile sees things in terms both of what has been left behind and what is actual here and now, he or she has a double perspective, never seeing things in isolation.'[12] Said's reading of the exile perspective as plural and dynamic is anticipated throughout 'White Rabbits' by Carrington's conspicuous use of the epithet 'black': the fire-damaged homes in this isolated urban quarter are black; the 'ominously quiet' aeroplane in the sky is black; even the 'thick Pest street air' is polluted to the extent that the narrator suspects it 'must have blackened [her] lungs as dark as the houses'.[13] Clearly, the descriptor 'black' works accumulatively, on one level, to bring into view an external, hellish landscape that is damaged and damaging – the narrator suffers palpitations because of the extreme heat. At the same time, though, and as the narrator's reference to her poisoned body suggests, the ubiquitous term 'black' suggests deep corruption and decay at the heart of this gothic tale.

Carrington develops this line of enquiry in a series of strange, and increasingly horrific, encounters between the narrator and her enigmatic neighbour who lives in the house opposite, but whom she rarely sees. After several days spent 'watching for some kind of movement opposite', the narrator is pleased to observe her neighbour as she emerges on to the balcony with 'a large dish full of bones', which she proceeds to empty on to the floor and 'wipe out' using her 'very long black hair'.[14] This act of improvised domesticity is stomach-churning, yet it is the peculiarity of her subsequent request that truly disconcerts:

> 'Do you happen to have any bad meat over there that you don't need?' she called.
>
> 'Any what?' I called back, wondering if my ears had deceived me.
>
> 'Any stinking meat? Decomposed flesh meat?'
>
> 'Not at the moment', I replied, wondering if she was trying to be funny.
>
> 'Won't you have any towards the end of the week? If so, I would be very grateful if you would bring it over.'[15]

Published at a time when corpses were piling up all over war-torn Europe, and just a few months before the official implementation of Nazi policy for the systematised slaughter of European Jewry, the Final Solution, 'White Rabbits' sets up a haunting relationship of equivalence between the rotting victims of war and genocide, which Carrington witnessed on her escape across Occupied France and to which she would bear testimony in *Down Below* (1942), and the neighbour's repeated requests for fetid meat. As Said observes, within the exile's double perspective: 'Every scene or situation in the new country necessarily draws on its counterpart in the old country', so that 'both appear in a new and unpredictable light: from that juxtaposition one gets a better, perhaps even more universal idea of how to think, say, about a human-rights issue in one situation as compared to another'.[16] That issues of human rights are, indeed, at stake beneath the surface of this troubling neighbourly exchange ruptures through in the disturbing compound noun 'flesh meat'. Even though the term 'flesh' is not exclusive to the category of the human, it nevertheless connotes it. The horror of the term 'flesh meat' lies, therefore, both in its excess and in its indeterminacy: ontological boundaries between the animal and the human are blurred in such a way as to suggest that, in whatever kind of grotesque ritual of consumption the woman has planned, anything will do, even the decomposing remains of a dead or dying neighbour.

The reader's mounting suspicion that conventional codes of morality are absent from the world of 'White Rabbits' moves towards a horrific climax when the narrator, full of 'morbid curiosity', visits her neighbours a few days later with 'a large lump of meat', which she has allowed to fester for days. Unable at first to locate the 'house opposite' because it is concealed 'under a cascade of something', the intrepid visitor soon finds herself in a gothic setting that would not look out of place in the dark morality tales of Edgar Allan Poe. The door to the blackened house, we learn, is 'caving inwards' and 'no-one had been in and out of [it] for years'. Similarly, the 'dark' carved wooden interiors with their 'dark baroque furniture and red plush' are devoid of life. Instead, a floor 'littered with gnawed bones and animal skulls' clutters the narrator's vision, and this is overlaid by an all-pervading 'smell of putrid meat'.[17] Taken together, these gothic tropes bring into view an interior space that is simultaneously claustrophobic, excessive, and anachronistic. Appearing out of the darkness in an 'ancient beautiful dress of green silk', the ghoulish neighbour enters the narrative frame as if she has stepped out of another time and place, but the narrator's intrigue in her is momentarily displaced when, having handed over the rotten meat, she suddenly finds herself surrounded by a mass of carnivorous white rabbits: 'With a sensation of deep disgust I backed into a corner and saw her [the neighbour] throwing the carrion amongst the rabbits which fought like wolves for it.'[18] The force of the simile communicates a clear inversion in the natural order of things at number 40 Pest Street: the tame has become savage; herbivorous pets have become flesh-eating monstrosities; and an everyday act of domestic provision has become a stomach-churning spectacle of horror.

In 'We Refugees', Arendt writes of how world war and genocide have not only engendered a 'topsy-turvy' world but created a new category of the human, one that is displaced, dispossessed, and recast as an outsider – the refugee.[19] Even though Carrington's New York exile was underpinned by a very different set of politico-historical concerns and pressures, her work of the period is nevertheless acutely preoccupied with the radical uncertainties of what it meant to be an exile. Her participation in the *First Papers of Surrealism* exhibition (1942), which took its title from the American citizenship documents that her fellow surrealists were required to apply for (as Leduc's wife, Carrington was guaranteed passage into the USA), is indicative of how the early 1940s became a time of intense meditation on the physical, psychological, and political implications of displacement for Carrington.[20] And 'White Rabbits' is an important, early literary example of this. Beneath their gothic excess, for instance, the neighbour, 'Ethel', and her ghostly husband, Lazarus, embody a fiercely complex exile condition. This is signalled most forcefully in the indeterminate nature of their physical being: the neighbour's skin is 'dead white and glittered as though speckled with thousands of minute stars'; similarly, Lazarus, a gothic echo of the biblical character whom Jesus raised from the dead, cuts an uncertain figure with his 'identical glittering skin'.[21] Deathly and disintegrating – the neighbour's fingers fall off at the end of the tale – these gothic bodies, we glean, are riddled with leprosy, a highly contagious disease that, as Said notes, has become a metaphor for the modern-day exile: 'There has always been an association between the idea of exile and the terrors of being a leper, a social and moral untouchable.'²² The story's refusal to 'place' this anomalous, anachronistic couple in a clearly identifiable history damns them to remain in a state of perpetual displacement, an adept narrative strategy that not only reinforces the social isolation so inherent, as Arendt and Said variously observe, to the exile condition, but also indicts its deleterious impact on human life and experience.

At the same time, though, Carrington's dark surrealist poetics do not shy away from posing uncomfortable questions pertaining to the moral implications of the condition of displacement. After all, the neighbours' habit of feeding their rabbits rotten meat, and the closing insinuation that the narrator may provide the necessary 'flesh' in ways she had not envisaged, gives voice to a deeply uneasy morality. This is a particularly complex, not to mention sensitive, aspect of the exile condition that Arendt also starts to think through in 'We Refugees' when, having mapped out the pressures of assimilation with its interplay of optimism and guilt, and the crises of identity that arise from the forced adoption of designated categories – 'Our identity is changed so frequently that nobody can find out who we actually are' – she considers the potential consequences of cultural and social isolation:

> Man is a social animal and life is not easy for him when social ties are cut off. Moral standards are much easier kept in the texture of a society. Very few individuals have the strength to conserve their own integrity if their social, political and legal status is completely confused.²³

Carrington engages more directly, and extensively, with history's brutal assault on Jewish life, identity, and culture in the short novella *The Stone Door*, which reimagines the prewar and wartime experiences of her Jewish husband, Chiki Weisz. But the conspicuous naming of the exiled couple in 'White Rabbits' – Ethel and Lazarus are Hebraic names in origin – reaches out nevertheless to the Jewish experience, and it marks the beginning of a particularly difficult period of intellectual and ethical negotiation for Carrington as she attempts to work out, through fiction, the human consequences of a violent contemporary moment against which she is pressed up close, but within which she is also implicated.

The politics of restlessness in *The Stone Door*

> At the far end of this foul corridor through which contemporary man is making his way, it has become morally almost impossible to catch one's breath. This corridor represents the passage between the so-called universe of concentration camps, in a drunken rat's living memory, and a quite possible nonuniverse, for the advent of which a final perforated pattern is being perfected.²⁴
>
> André Breton

If Breton envisages contemporary history as a stinking corridor of death and corruption, *The Stone Door* extends this metaphor to a radically dark labyrinth out of which humankind must struggle to find its way. Indeed, critical readings of Carrington's first novel stand out for the ways in which they foreground the text's fierce conceptual and formal inaccessibility. According to Tobias Carroll, *The Stone Door* is 'unable to bear the weight of the accumulated history, myth and philosophy in its allusions'.[25] For Anna Watz, meanwhile, the novel 'repeatedly destabilises its own narrative framework by its many and sometimes overlapping narrative layers … its web of multiple narrative threads and perspectives and its convoluted symbolism sometimes confuse how the episodes of the novel belong together'.[26] At its very core, *The Stone Door* is a surrealist quest narrative about a young Hungarian Jew (Zacharias) and a nameless young woman in Mexico City who encounter each other in dreams and daydreams, but who can come together in actuality only by finding and opening the legendry stone door. Perhaps more than any other of Carrington's literary works, *The Stone Door* wears its biographical underpinnings heavily, so leading various feminist critics to interpret the text as a celebration of the union of the author and her second husband, the Jewish Hungarian-born photographer Weisz in Mexico.[27] Whilst such readings are perfectly reasonable, what is striking about the *The Stone Door*'s ending is that the union of the two protagonists is impending, but never actualised: instead of offering a story of settlement, then, Carrington's exile narrative remains unsettled; it 'ends' at the beginning of yet another exile story, namely, Zacharias's passage through the stone door as he follows the wind west.

It is the conceptual and formal restlessness of Carrington's dark exile novel that concerns the second part of this chapter. After all, *The Stone Door* is in many ways a narrative on the move: written in the mid-1940s in English, it was not published in its original language until 1977; the novel was then revised by the author and republished in a shorter and more accessible version for the 1988 collection *The Seventh Horse and Other Tales* (Carrington removed the densely symbolic narratives that frame the story of Zacharias and the unnamed woman in Mexico City). Working with the original text, I continue to focus in on the ways in which Carrington develops a dark surrealist exile aesthetic in order to pose necessarily difficult encounters with late wartime and postwar history. In so doing, Carrington's gothic 'turn' is much more politically motivated than critics have so far recognised. Even though Matheson's study on gothic surrealism mentions Carrington briefly, it does so only to assert how her modifications of motifs drawn from the gothic and its closely related phenomena – magic, alchemy, and the occult – are concerned to explore issues of female 'bodily experience'.[28] Such a reading not only fails to see that Carrington's gothic experiments are just as concerned with navigating the stinking passages of recent history as those produced by her male colleagues; it also ignores the complex exile dynamic that shapes and energises their production and, indeed, re-production. As Said observes, the exile, whether intellectual or actual, cannot 'go back to some earlier and perhaps more stable condition of being at home', and neither can they 'fully arrive, be at home with [their] new home or situation'.[29] *The Stone Door* enacts this modern exile condition conceptually and formally, composed as it is in full awareness that the exile state is never static, but interminably in process.

It is unsurprising, therefore, that the landscapes of *The Stone Door* are devoid of any sites of conventional refuge: the houses, buildings, and makeshift dwellings that we visit are spaces of unequivocal uncertainty. The novel opens in 'the middle of a deep forest, black and alive as an Aztec sacerdote's hair [where there] stood a big house. Victorian style, very sad neo-Gothic.'[30] Covered in thick, wet fungi, this rotting architecture is a temporary meeting place for three men – the Chinaman, the European, and the Jew – who act as overseers to what is called 'The Plan', a male-structured system of thought that determines how the world functions, but which has become 'stale and has been for many centuries now', and thus needs to be rethought and implemented anew.[31] Taken together, the gothic setting, the emblematic characters, and the failed 'Plan' form a rich, compound metaphor for a corrupt postwar, post-Holocaust reality. The European, a figure whose very being 'horrified' the other two men, makes this connection clear when he reports in a disarmingly matter-of-fact way how '"We have seen war ... Famine in Europe and uncountable bodies violently killed"'.[32] What is being established from the outset, then, is that the 'homeland' of Europe, that once seemingly secure house of Western civilisation, has been rendered fundamentally corrupt and unsafe by the barbarism of world war and the inhumane crimes of Nazi genocide.

Carrington advances this line of critique in the second chapter, which crosses temporal and spatial boundaries to an uncanny version of Mexico City and to a female character, Amagoya, who is an uncanny double of the author. Haunted by memories of Britain and the absent presence of an unnamed woman known only in the story as 'She' (and who is yet another uncanny version of Carrington), Amagoya cuts an uneasy figure. This manifests itself outwardly in the unquiet house that she now inhabits with its 'rickety hinges' that make 'small restless noises' in the eerie breeze.[33] Whilst the details of the troubled past of the house and its current and former inhabitants ('She') are never made clear, we glean from Amagoya's readings of She's diary entries that the diarist's life was also marked by tremendous agitation and isolation: 'I am always alone. That is what makes me suffer', She writes, 'I shriek with misery and rage ... alone and tortured in an empty apartment.'[34]

One source of She's agony is the absence of a man called 'Pedro', her presumed lover and a veiled reference to Renato Leduc who, according to Moorhead's biographical account of Carrington's exile in Mexico, was an absent presence, both physically and emotionally.[35] Yet, even at this early stage in the novel, its dark imagery and stagnant atmosphere suggest that its landscapes are haunted by a devastating collective history: 'The street is empty and foreign except at night. Outside, everything is tainted', writes She; 'I was bitterly alone in the land of the dead, on the wrong side of the great stone door.'[36]

Even though, like so many artists and intellectuals who benefited from Mexico's 'Open Door' policy on refugees from war-torn Europe, Carrington found political sanctuary with relative ease (her marriage to Leduc also meant that her 'place' in the country was guaranteed), the repeated depictions of unhomely spaces throughout *The Stone Door* pay testimony to a personal and collective exile condition characterised by metaphysical and actual 'out-of-placeness'. In this respect, Carrington's narrative resonates suggestively with Adorno's contemporaneous exile writings, such as *Minima Moralia: Reflections from Damaged Life* (1951). Fragment 18 – 'Refuge for the homeless' – which Adorno penned in 1944 has particular significance for this politicised reading of *The Stone Door*:

> Dwelling, in the proper sense, is now impossible. The traditional residences we have grown up in have grown intolerable: each trait of comfort in them is paid for with a betrayal of knowledge, each vestige of shelter with the musty pact of family interests ... The house is past. The bombing of European cities, as well as the labour and concentration camps, merely proceed as executors, with what the immanent fate of technology had long decided was to be the fate of houses ... It is part of morality not to be at home in one's home.[37]

In an age of 'homelessness' engendered by the mass displacement of war refugees, fascism's hideous appropriation and destruction of Jewish homes, and the industrialised killing of their inhabitants in concentration camps, any longing for the 'home' is, for the German Jewish exile, synonymous with a destructive nostalgia, moral irresponsibility, and deadly forgetfulness. Within a totally administered society, which found its most hideous expression in Nazism's systematised genocidal policies, there is no place of belonging, just organised systems of estrangement and control.

It is in Zacharias's exile tale that Carrington's interrogation of the politics of homelessness finds its fullest expression. Whilst never collapsing into pity, chapter four begins with the four-year old Zacharias, who is sent by his widowed mother (she can no longer afford to care for him) to an institution for boys far beyond the boundaries of Budapest. Before his journey North, however, the boy is subjected to a series of cleansing processes that invoke

Jewish Holocaust institutionalisation: he is 'disinfected', shaved, bathed, dressed, and given a numerical identity: 'Because he was only four, the youngest of all the children, Zacharias was dressed after the bath by the forlorn attendant', we learn; 'He was [then] put into long striped trousers of harsh material and a jacket buttoned up to the chin with the number 105 sewn on the left sleeve in the same place where people wear the black band of mourning.'[38] Given its immediate postwar moment of production, *The Stone Door* is remarkable for the way in which it dares to force disquieting encounters with Holocaust history, the full horrors of which were really only beginning to reveal themselves by the time the story was written. But even in this short passage, Carrington captures the terrible reality of the totally administered nature of Nazi genocide: the attendant may be 'forlorn', but he or she is nonetheless carrying out their role within a highly rational and structured system that dehumanises everyone within it.

In 'Looking Back on Surrealism' (1956), Adorno went on to identify the need for a form of modified postwar, post-Holocaust surrealism that does not merely strive to give shape and form to the unconscious but confronts instead the relationship between the conscious and unconscious landscapes of history. 'Surrealism's booty is images, to be sure, but not the invariant, ahistorical images of the unconscious subject to which the conventional view would like to neutralise them.'[39] Rather, Adorno insists, 'they are historical images in which the subject's innermost core becomes aware that it is something external, an imitation of something social and historical'.[40] Even though Adorno sells the surrealist political imagination short here – he overlooks surrealism's dedicated political 'turn' from the mid-1920s onwards, an intellectual and ethical response to French imperialist intervention in the 1925 Moroccan War – his comments have particular resonance for *The Stone Door*, which employs dreams, memories, and nightmares as serious forms of historical enquiry. Locked within a highly regulated and punitive institution, for instance, number 105 draws on his imagination in order to survive the physical and psychological cruelty that the teachers, managers, and administrators inflict on a daily basis, and it is in his dreams that he encounters (and falls in love with) 'She'. At the same time, though, number 105 is also known by his fellow inmates for his 'frequent nightmares', triggered as they are by the loss and loneliness of exile, and by a dark Jewish collective history that haunts him continuously: 'the horror was too near, it was inside him, all around and over his bed'.[41]

Indeed, the terrors of the Holocaust rupture the surface of the text when one of 105's memories of an illicit visit to the chambers of horrors at a local fair transforms from a recollection of sexual transgression (he encounters an 'orgy of horror', a wax model of a beautiful prostitute, images of syphilis victims, and a scene from the Spanish inquisition) into a realisation of humanity's limitless facility for cruelty:

> [The memory] usually began with a vaulted cellar furnished with a somewhat confused assembly of giant meat-mincers, iron armchairs with adjustable spikes in the seat and back, long man-shaped boxes, and a thing which looked like a monster sewing machine with a needle as long as a man's body and stained with clots of blood ... Eight pale-faced priests scampered lightly about the terrible vaulted chamber, pressing buttons and twirling handles; they were trying out the machines.[42]

What is arresting at this point in Carrington's development of a dark exilic aesthetic is that the haunted house motif of 'White Rabbits' has, by the late-1940s, evolved into a full-blown torture chamber. As Matheson points out, the writings of the Marquis de Sade assumed a new philosophical, political, and cultural relevance for surrealist writers and artists in the immediate postwar era when, with 'its tales of returning survivors and the accumulating evidence of the full extent of the Holocaust, the prevailing conception of human nature was radically shaken'.[43] Carrington's 1940s experiments in gothic surrealism fully deserve to be included in critical conversations like this, reaching out as they evidently do to Sade's provocative interrogations of the dark forces that reside within the human mind and, indeed, heart: the Priests' raw pleasure at imagining the pain they will be able to administer so efficiently with this new technology of torture is particularly unsettling.

Another aspect of *The Stone Door*'s enquiry into the late wartime and postwar human condition narrows in, however, to develop some of Carrington's earlier meditations on the perplexities of simply existing as a Jewish exile in the 1940s. At repeated points throughout the narrative, for instance, the young and older Zacharias is reminded of his outsider status: 'remember that we are Jews and our lot is hazardous and difficult', the institutional Director warns him, 'not only in Hungary but unhappily in many parts of the world'.[44] Whilst overt references to the Nazi persecution of European Jewry are absent from *The Stone Door*, conversations such as this ensure that discriminatory measures such as the racial laws, which were implemented in Hungary in the late 1930s following its political alliance with Nazi Germany, and under which Weisz would have lived before his flight from fascist Europe, are never far from the narrative surface. Furthermore, they also foreshadow the indeterminate nature of being that Jewish exiles would continue to experience even once sanctuary had ostensibly been achieved. This is Arendt:

> [B]eing a Jew does not give any legal status in this world. If we should start telling the truth that we are nothing but Jews it would mean that we expose

ourselves to the fate of human beings who, unprotected by any specific law or political convention, are nothing but human beings. I can hardly imagine an attitude more dangerous, since we actually live in a world in which human beings as such have ceased to exist for quite a while.[45]

As Lyndsey Stonebridge notes, Arendt's concern at this particular historical juncture has become 'the inability of the category of human rights to house the human in the face of totalitarianism'.[46] 'There is nothing', Arendt sees all too clearly, 'about being merely human, about simply existing, as a Jew or a refugee, that guarantees one any rights'.[47] *The Stone Door* engages with certain dimensions of this rapidly unfolding physical, psychological, and political reality through its depictions of Zacharias's increasingly precarious exile status: rootless, homeless, and unassimilated, he is the figure of the wandering Jew who simply does not know how to be in the world: 'If I lived on top of the highest tree in the world', he observes, 'I could not be more outside the lives of human beings. Though if anyone ever asked me where I am, I doubt I could reply … Let me in, let me in.'[48]

Even though Zacharias's appeals to cross through the stone door are eventually granted, it is inevitable that his 'final' stage of exile should end at the beginning of another journey. For exile is 'never the state of being satisfied, placid, secure'; it is 'nomadic, decentred, contrapuntal; but no sooner does one get accustomed to it than its unsettling force erupts anew'.[49] That Zacharias passes through the stone door on the tail end of a stampede of 'five hundred white sheep', all of which jump frantically into the sea and start swimming west, is doubly significant in light of Said's comments on the contrapuntal nature of the exile experience. On one level, that is, the sheep are haunting reminders of the shorn inmates of Zacharias's childhood institution, an image that is in turn redolent of the victims of the inhumane structures of the Holocaust. On another, the nervous cattle conjure up images of vulnerable wartime refugees on the move, 'large herds of innocent and bewildered people', as Said puts it, 'requiring urgent international assistance'.[50] Whilst a future undoubtedly lies ahead for Zacharias and his fellow travellers, then, it is an uncertain one, shaped and energised as it is by a devastating past of dislocation, loss, and the radical indeterminacy of being.

Undead histories: 'The Happy Corpse Story'

According to Said, the work of the intellectual exile operates 'by force of risk, experiment, innovation. Not the logic of the conventional but the audacity of the daring, and moving, moving, moving, representing change, not standing still.'[51] Written nearly three decades after *The Stone Door*, but published five or six years before it, 'The Happy Corpse Story' embodies precisely this kind of writing as risk-taking. Set in another hellish landscape, it brings together a young man, who attempts to conceal the physical scars of a brutal past (his elaborate wig hides 'a skull covered in black bristles'), and a female corpse that disintegrates and regenerates inexplicably.[52] In an echo of the quest romance of *The Stone Door*, the young boy is also cut off from, and in search of, his love, but the corpse is equally preoccupied by her own tale of woe, which she feels compelled to pass on. That the corpse will not be a teller of consoling stories, however, manifests itself clearly in her grotesque being: 'full of holes and dents, the corpse could talk out of any part of its body ... Think of listening to a story told straight into your face out of a hole in the back of the head with bad breath.'[53] The story, the corpse soon reveals, 'is all about my father', a businessman of evacuated personality whose blind commitment to the capitalist world's 'constant banquets, bazaars, meeting, and simple meatings where meat was eaten' meant that by an early age he had 'turned himself into a human wreckage'.[54] Whilst any reader would surely pause over the neologistic noun 'meating', it takes on all the more significance for the reader of 'White Rabbits' with its disquieting associations of the visceral horrors of wartime history.

Carrington dares to allow these associations to gain further unnerving force in the following part of the corpse's tale:

> As I was saying about my father ... he eventually became an executive for a firm. This meant that he actually executed persons with showers of legal documents proving that they owed him quantities of money which they did not have. 'Firm' actually means the manufacture of useless objects which people are foolish enough to buy. The firmer the firm the more senseless talk is needed to prevent anyone noticing the unsafe structure of the business. Sometimes these firms actually sell nothing at all for a lot of money, like 'Life Insurance', a pretense that it is a soothing and useful event to have a violent and painful death.[55]

This passage is striking initially for the ways in which it critiques the commodified, administered world of late capitalism, the very world, that is, that Adorno's and Max Horkheimer's exile work, *The Dialectic of Enlightenment* (1944), had linked so provocatively to the world of the concentration camps. But the corpse's conspicuous language choices – 'execute', 'shower', 'unsafe', 'violent and painful death' – allow that dark history to force its way into the narrative with troubling implications for its author. That is to say that this story, and indeed so much of Carrington's writing and art, is haunted by an obscure and critically obscured personal history: her father was a principal shareholder in Imperial Chemicals (ICI), which was part of an international wartime cartel with IG Farben, the notorious German chemical industry conglomerate that made spectacular capital (along with ICI) out of the production of Zyklon B gas; even though Carrington was exiled physically and emotionally from her father, she was nevertheless dependent upon his business connections to escape fascist Europe. Whilst no narrative should ever be reduced to its biographical contexts of production, 'The Happy Corpse Story' dares the reader to encounter it precisely on these terms. And these terms, of course, not only force into being disquieting images of systematised executions by gas showers, they implicate the author, no matter at what distance, in its horrifying history.

As I have observed elsewhere, Carrington's acts of writing and rewriting *Down Below* (1941–42; 1988), her haunting narrative of incarceration in a European asylum, are bound up with intricate and enduring feelings of guilt at her inadvertent wartime complicity.[56] 'The Happy Corpse Story' also exhibits these restless energies, but at the same time its dark aesthetic works more explicitly to force the bald recognition that the atrocious crimes committed against humanity throughout the wartime period were not perpetrated from outside the human frame. 'We are not simply the possible victims of executioners: the executioners are like us', wrote Georges Bataille in 1947: 'We should still ask ourselves: is there nothing in our nature that makes such horror impossible? And we really must reply: in fact, nothing. There are a thousand obstacles in us that oppose it', he continues; 'Nevertheless, it is not impossible. Our potential is thus not only for pain, it also extends to passion for torturing.'[57] From the haunted house of 'White Rabbits' to the torture chambers of *The Stone Door*, through to the unfolding horrors of 'The Happy Corpse Story', Carrington's dark exile narratives are so challenging to read and negotiate precisely because they insist, in different ways and to varying degrees, on the inalienable human quality of historical atrocity. And this is something of a sorrowful lesson that the corpse, who turns out to be the boy's dead mother (she has committed suicide out of guilt), insists that he pass on as she guides him away from hell (where her businessman father is in eternal damnation) and into an uncertain life and future: 'Now you must remember, and in order to remember you must return again, alone.'[58]

In the 'Prolegomena to a Third Surrealist Manifesto or Not' (1942), which Breton wrote whilst in exile in New York, he declared that Carrington figured 'among today's most lucid and daring' of surrealist minds, keeping company with the likes of Bataille, André Masson, Max Ernst, and Kurt Seligman.[59] With the full extent of the atrocities of war and the Holocaust still unfolding, Breton could not have been aware of the deep resonance that his comments would go on to have. What he clearly was aware of, however, was Carrington's formidable, developing potential to advance surrealism's wartime and postwar gothic project in aesthetically and intellectually provocative ways. As I have argued here, 'White Rabbits' and *The Stone Door* initiate disquieting lines of enquiry into the 'housing' of those new kinds of human beings – wartime refugees – who could not be accommodated by existing legal and political architectures (the Declaration of Human Rights in 1948 came after the writing of Carrington's texts). Coming some years later, 'The Happy Corpse Story' continues to be haunted by the horrific nature of mid-twentieth-century history, but it insists on keeping this human history up close in order to ask difficult questions about the very darkest of forces at work within it. It is for these reasons, then, that Carrington's dark exile narratives deserve not only to take up their proper place within international surrealist literary-political history; they deserve to be read as serious, and seriously disturbing, literary-political enquiries into the radical uncertainties of the modern human condition. If, as Adorno claimed towards the end of his time in exile, 'writing becomes a place to live' for the writer without a 'homeland', the fictions discussed throughout this chapter provide something of a temporary refuge for their displaced author.[60] But 'temporary' is the most important word in this sentence. Never one to fall for the illusion of stability, Carrington knew all too well that (in the same way that Adorno eventually conceded) even if exile writing could provide a potential place to live, to think, and take risks, it could only ever be an unhomely place – restless, precarious, and haunted interminably by the unquiet ghosts of history.

Notes

1. Edward W. Said, 'Intellectual Exile: Expatriates and Marginals', *Grand Street* 47 (Autumn 1993), p. 117. It is worth noting that the visual framing of Said's essay consists of two images, one by Max Ernst and the other by Marcel Duchamp, both of which were produced in exile in New York in 1942.
2. See Michel Foucault, *Madness and Civilisation: A History of Sanity in the Age of Reason*, trans. Richard Howard (New York: Vintage, 1988), p. 10.
3. Alice Gambrell, *Women Intellectuals, Modernism, and Difference: Transatlantic Culture, 1919–1945* (Cambridge: Cambridge University Press, 1997), p. 83.
4. Martica Sawin, *Surrealism in Exile and the Beginning of the New York School* (Cambridge, MA: MIT Press, 1995), p. 308.
5. Whitney Chadwick, *Women Artists and the Surrealist Movement* (London: Thames and Hudson, 1985), p. 194.
6. Joanna Moorhead, 'Surreal Friends in Mexico', in Stefan van Raay, Joanna Moorhead, Teresa Arcq, et al. (eds), *Surreal Friends: Leonora Carrington, Remedios Varo and Kati Horna* (Farnham: Lund Humphries, 2010), p. 78.

7   See Jeannette Baxter, 'Self-Translation and Holocaust Writing: Leonora Carrington's *Down Below*', in Jean Boase-Beier, Peter Davies, Andrea Hammel, and Marion Winters (eds), *Translating Holocaust Lives* (London: Bloomsbury, 2017), pp. 221–40.
8   Neil Matheson, *Surrealism and the Gothic: Castles of the Interior* (London: Routledge, 2017), p. 4.
9   See Jonathan P. Eburne, *Surrealism and the Art of Crime* (Ithaca: Cornell University Press, 2008), pp. 215–43.
10 Hannah Arendt, 'We Refugees' (1943), in Marc Robinson (ed.), *Altogether Elsewhere: Writers on Exile* (London: Faber and Faber, 1994), p. 111.
11 Leonora Carrington, 'White Rabbits', *View* 9–10 (1941–42), p. 7.
12 Said, 'Intellectual Exile', pp. 121–2.
13 Carrington, 'White Rabbits', p. 7.
14 *Ibid.*, p. 7.
15 *Ibid.*, p. 7.
16 Said, 'Intellectual Exile', p. 122.
17 Carrington, 'White Rabbits', p. 7.
18 *Ibid.*, p. 7.
19 Arendt, 'We Refugees', p. 119.
20 *First Papers of Surrealism* was held at Whitelaw Reid mansion on Madison Avenue at Fiftieth Street, from 14 October to 7 November 1942. Nearly fifty artists took part, drawn from France, Switzerland, Germany, Spain, and the US. Carrington exhibited two works: a line drawing, *Brothers and Sisters Have I None* (1942); and a painting that, given the contexts of its production, was aptly titled *La Chasse* (1942).
21 Carrington, 'White Rabbits', p. 7.
22 Said, 'Intellectual Exile', p. 113.
23 Arendt, 'We Refugees', p. 116.
24 André Breton, 'The Lamp in the Clock' (1948), in *Free Rein*, trans. Michael Parmentier and Jaqueline D'Amboise (Lincoln: University of Nebraska Press, 1995), p. 108.
25 Tobias Carroll, 'The Surreal Life', *The Paris Review* (14 August 2013), www.theparisreview.org/blog/2013/08/14/the-surreal-life/, accessed 2 July 2018.
26 Anna Watz, '"A Language Buried at the Back of Time": *The Stone Door* and Poststructuralist Feminism', in Jonathan P. Eburne and Catriona McAra (eds), *Leonora Carrington and the International Avant-Garde* (Manchester: Manchester University Press, 2017), p. 91.
27 See Marina Warner, 'Introduction', in Leonora Carrington, *The House of Fear: Notes from Down Below* (London: Virago, 1989), p. 20; and Watz, 'A Language Buried at the Back Of Time', p. 93.
28 Matheson, *Surrealism and the Gothic*, p. 196.
29 Said, 'Intellectual Exile', p. 117.
30 Leonora Carrington, *The Stone Door* (1977; London: Routledge & Kegan Paul, 1978), p. 1.
31 *Ibid.*, p. 33.

32 *Ibid.*, 3.
33 *Ibid.*, p. 6.
34 *Ibid.*, p. 10.
35 Joanna Moorhead, *The Surreal Life of Leonora Carrington* (London: Virago, 2017), pp. 174–5.
36 Carrington, *The Stone Door*, p. 28.
37 Theodor W. Adorno, *Minima Moralia: Reflections from Damaged Life* (1951. London: Verso, 2005), pp. 38–9.
38 Carrington, *The Stone Door*, p. 57.
39 Theodor W. Adorno, 'Looking Back on Surrealism', in Lawrence Rainey (ed.), *Modernism: An Anthology* (London: Blackwell, 2005), p. 1115.
40 *Ibid.*, p. 1115.
41 Carrington, *The Stone Door*, p. 59.
42 *Ibid.*, pp. 59–60.
43 Matheson, *Surrealism and the Gothic*, p. 211.
44 Carrington, *The Stone Door*, p. 71.
45 Arendt, 'We Refugees', p. 118.
46 Lyndsey Stonebridge, 'Refugee Style: Hannah Arendt and the Perplexities of Human Rights', *Textual Practice* 25:1 (2011), p. 72.
47 Stonebridge, 'Refugee Style', p. 76.
48 Carrington, *The Stone Door*, p. 83.
49 Edward W. Said, 'Reflections on Exile', in *Reflections on Exile and Other Literary and Cultural Essays* (London: Granta, 2001), p. 186.
50 Said, 'Reflections on Exile', p. 181.
51 Said, 'Intellectual Exile', p. 121.
52 Leonora Carrington, 'The Happy Corpse Story', in *The Seventh Horse and Other Tales* (1988; London: Virago, 1989), p. 177.
53 *Ibid.*, p. 177.
54 *Ibid.*, p. 178.
55 *Ibid.*, p. 178.
56 See Baxter, 'Self-Translation and Holocaust Writing', pp. 221–40.
57 Georges Bataille, *Œuvres complètes*, XI, 'Réflexions sur le bourreau et la victime: SS et déportés', p. 266. Quoted in Michael Surya, *Georges Bataille: An Intellectual Biography*, trans. Krzysztof Fijalkowski and Michael Richardson (London: Verso, 2002), p. 359.
58 Carrington, 'The Happy Corpse Story', p. 180.
59 André Breton, 'Prolegomena to a Third Surrealist Manifesto or Not', in *Manifestoes of Surrealism*, trans. Richard Seaver and Helen R. Lane (Ann Arbor: University of Michigan Press, 1972), p. 287.
60 Adorno, *Minima Moralia*, p. 87.

4

Colette Peignot: the purity of revolt

Michael Richardson

Early in 1923 André Breton wrote his 'Disdainful Confession', which would become one of the initiating documents of surrealism, setting out its fundamental moral position: 'Absolutely incapable of settling for the fate allotted to me, struck in my highest degree of awareness by the denial of justice that the notion of original sin, to my mind, in no way excuses, I refuse to adapt my existence to the pitiful conditions under which everyone *here below* must exist.'[1] This 'confession' given disdainfully and rejecting any idea of fault, has more in common with the ancient Egyptian 'negative confession' that the deceased supplicant made before Osiris in order to proceed to the next phase of the journey of the soul than with any Christian transcendence. Breton's is a complex text, one of several he wrote during this period in which he discusses Jacques Vaché, the avatar of revolt in his youth and now a dead man, whose impact on his early thinking was such that Vaché would be reborn as a surrealist in him (that is in Breton, as Breton expressed it in the *Manifesto of Surrealism*, 'Vaché is surrealist in me'),[2] and whose passing therefore has the feel of a death that is not a death. A confession thrown into the face of existence, the marker here might be the 'Death' card of the tarot pack that signifies transition and mutation. Breton approvingly cites Benjamin Constant's observation that all thinking is about death, and about one's own death, concluding that 'what truth can there be, if there is death'.[3]

We find numerous echoes of Breton's essay in the writings of Colette Peignot, who would undoubtedly have read it at the time it was published and whose work might be considered to constitute an extended 'disdainful confession'. Indeed, she seems to have taken up this very idea as a baton against which to measure the integrity of her own life, or more strictly her 'reason for living'. For instance, we find her writing this in a letter, probably in 1926, to Jean Bernier: 'My inconsistent life, *serving for nothing*, this absolute non-conformism seduced you. Was I not eternally inadaptable to all that surrounded me, irreducibly rebelling against *everything*?'[4] And unlike Breton, who reconciled himself with life as he grew older, Peignot would remain intransigently, if not on the side of death, at least against life, or against this life, and in favour of the quest for the 'real life' of which Breton speaks in the first sentence of the *Manifesto of Surrealism* of 1924.

Colette Peignot never participated in any direct way in surrealism, but she remained on its margins and its spirit permeated her adult life. Indeed we know from what Georges Bataille wrote about her after her actual death that surrealism 'seduced' her notwithstanding her apparent doubts about some of the people involved in it. In a fragment of a letter written to an unknown recipient (who may have been Paul Éluard), she spoke of a feeling of secret complicity that she experienced upon reading surrealist publications when she was fifteen years old, 'like a starving woman eating a piece of stolen bread'.[5] This sense of secrecy and withdrawal is central to an understanding of her work, which is one of the more searing, or rending and lacerating (*déchirant*), to use the term favoured by Bataille, of those connected to surrealism.

The name

Colette Peignot was born in Meudon, outside Paris, on 8 October 1903 into a well-connected and relatively wealthy self-made manufacturing family. Her father was the inventor of typographical characters and fonts that are still used today – he founded the company G. Peignot et Fils.

During her childhood she suffered two particularly traumatic events. The first was not simply the death of her father but, along with him, that of her three uncles, all killed during the First World War (this fact is still today commemorated by a Paris street named 'rue des quatres frères Peignot'). This cast a pall over the household. Her pious mother coped with the loss by devoting herself to obsessive housework and increasingly distancing herself from her four children, of whom Colette was the youngest. The second trauma was being sexually abused by the family priest, the effect of which was magnified when her allegations were dismissed. She was also in fragile health, suffering from a tuberculosis that would almost kill her as a child and would eventually be the cause of her actual death in 1938.

As an adult, her intellectual trajectory would be marked by successive love affairs with the journalist Jean Bernier, the Soviet writer Boris Pilnyak, the communist Boris Souvarine, and finally Georges Bataille. She would also have close intellectual friendships with Michel Leiris and Simone Weil. Politically committed, she stayed in the Soviet Union during 1930 and 1931, living with and sharing the lives of peasant families. Finding the atmosphere in the country 'stifling' as political repression became increasingly apparent, on her return to Paris she became active in anti-Stalinist groups, notably the Independent Communist Federation of the East and the Democratic Communist Circle animated by Souvarine, whose journal *La Critique sociale*, devoted to 'speaking the truth, no matter at what the cost, and taking into account the failures of the present so as to prepare the future's revenge', she would finance.[6] She wrote a few review articles for the journal and also contributed some short texts for another journal, *Le Travailleur communiste syndical et cooperatif*, over the course of 1933 and 1934. These (relatively ephemeral) texts would be the sum total of her work published during her lifetime. It was only after her death that Georges Bataille became aware of the mass of her writing and, together with Michel Leiris, published it privately in two small volumes, *The Sacred* in 1939 and *The Story of a Little Girl* in 1943. These two books were issued clandestinely in contravention of the stipulations of the Peignot family, which would not allow any legal publication of her work. Not until 1971 did her writings see the light of day, when Jérôme Peignot, her nephew, went against his family's (and specifically his father's) prohibition and made available a substantial body of her work under the title *Écrits*. In 1977 a revised and expanded edition was published. Since then other work (mostly correspondence) has come to light and been published separately. In 1995, the full text of the revised *Écrits* was published in English translation by City Lights.

Colette Peignot's writings are all published under the name 'Laure'. There is some contention about this name. Although Bataille and Leiris tell us that it was what she preferred to be called towards the end of her life they don't tell us why and in fact they rather contradict themselves. In their notes for *The Sacred* they write, 'a few months ago, the woman who called herself Laure died'.[7] Yet in the notes to *The Story of a Little Girl* they tell us that 'Among other handwritten corrections, the original typewritten copy bears "I saw" instead of "Laure saw". The woman we call Laure apparently considered representing herself under this name in a narrative distinct from *Story of a Little Girl*.'[8]

The displacement from 'the woman who called herself' to 'the woman we call' raises several questions, especially given the clandestine circumstances in which these two texts were originally published during the war and against the express stipulations of the Peignot family. Jérôme Peignot also tells us that his mother (Colette's sister-in-law) insisted that she should not be called Laure, as this was a designation created by Bataille and Leiris after her death.[9] The tale is tangled, however, because Colette's sister-in-law, Suzanne Peignot, may have had an interest in maintaining the family lineage in relation to Colette (who conversely may have assumed the name Laure in the last years of her life precisely to distance herself from that lineage – although even then it was not a complete break as Laure was one of her designated middle names).

Conversely again, since to have published the texts under her actual name would have been to have risked prosecution, Bataille and Leiris may have been using this name to disguise who the author actually was. This conjecture may be given credence by the fact that they justify this use by saying that she 'apparently' thought about using this name for another unwritten work. There are in fact some fragmentary erotic texts in which the character of Laure appears and which are perhaps the only remaining, or written, parts of what might have constituted this narrative.[10] These texts – more 'literary' (in a manner of speaking) than anything else within her oeuvre – recall Bataille's narrative style and give the impression that she was thinking about creating a work that followed in the same line of projective investigation (although they are far too fragmentary for us to be able to make any definite inference about her intentions). Bataille, of course, himself had a penchant for pseudonyms and for complicating the question of authorship, using the names Lord Auch, Pierre Angélique, Louis Trente, and Dianus to confuse or dissemble the authorship of his own writing.

We should however be careful not to fall into the mistake of regarding the formation of this character of 'Laure' as a kind of literary pseudonym or, even more insidiously, thinking that she was assuming this name to create herself as a separate, more literary, character who would be distinct from 'Colette Peignot'. Far more likely, given what we know of her fundamentally, and typically surrealist, anti-literary attitude, was that she was conceiving of this narrative – and the character of 'Laure' in general – as an exploration of an aspect of the 'otherness' inherent to her personality.

We do know that Peignot placed some significance on the nature of naming. Given her anthropological interests, we may speculate that she was well aware that many cultures treat names in ways that defy our modern 'common sense' idea that the name is merely a neutral designation serving to distinguish one thing from another and that may be arbitrarily applied (the Saussurian idea that there is no necessary relation between the signifier and the signified). In many cultures the name is considered to be a powerful living entity that must be treated with care and protected so that it cannot be misused by those who wish to harm us. The process of naming was often regarded as a magical act: the subject was given a name associated with their protective or totemic spirit. In ancient Egypt the name was one of the determining parts of the human personality that lived on after death and was an element essential to the integrality of the person. To assume a different name was therefore to assume a different personality, or to give a different emphasis to it, perhaps to play with the otherness of the person, even to become *other*. There is some indication that this may have played a part in the assumption of the name 'Laure' in relation to Colette Peignot (whether by herself or by Bataille and Leiris), for instance as a means of invoking an alchemical transmutation by means of homophonic association (Laure =

l'or). It also suggests a poetic association with the Marquis de Sade via his distant ancestor Laure de Sade, the legendary ethereal beloved of Petrarch's sonnets. For Leiris this name also represented 'a medieval emerald coupling her somewhat feline incandescence with a vaguely parochial sweetness like a stick of angelica'.[11]

In this sense, whether the adoption of the name was her choice or whether it was given to her by Bataille and Leiris is of little significance, because in the latter case we might say it was a 'gift' the two men offered to her after her death as a token of their love. We also know that Peignot had awareness of the power of the name by the one she certainly did assume: her published writings, the reviews she wrote for *La Critique sociale* and *Le Travailleur communiste syndical et cooperatif*, appeared under the name 'Claude Araxe'.

The reference here is to the river Arax, or Aras, south of the Caucasus, that flows into the Caspian Sea. Souvarine tells us that it was he who told her about this river, and that she was enchanted by its rebelliousness against human intention, being so fast-flowing that it would tolerate neither navigation nor bridges (Peignot includes a quotation from Virgil, *Pontum indignatus Araxes* – 'Arax indignant at bridges' – as an epigraph to one of her letters to Bataille). Souvarine's memory about the river was, however, somewhat at fault, since he says that it rises in Armenia and flows through Georgia.[12] In fact it rises in what is now Turkey and flows along the borders between Turkey and Armenia and then Azerbaijan and Iran. At the time it also constituted the boundary between the Soviet Union and Turkey and Iran, thus on the one hand separating communist and capitalist as well as Christian and Muslim worlds. It was also marked in the then recent memory as the locus of the Armenian genocide committed by the Turks. By assuming the name Araxe, she may also have been bringing attention to the problem of boundaries and the difficulty of crossing them, as she learned during her sojourn in the Soviet Union, which severely depleted her energies to the extent that, after she fell severely ill, her brother had to travel to Moscow to bring her back to Paris. She expressed her disillusionment with the failure of the Soviet experiment in an article published in 1933 entitled 'Le Mirage soviétique', describing the USSR as a 'land of workers and peasants which despises workers and peasants as nowhere else'.[13] All of her articles about the Soviet Union are written in a tone of indignation about the Stalinist repression that she had seen being imposed in what was supposed to be the home of the workers.

Communism

The 'cruel reality' behind this Soviet mirage nevertheless did not dampen her revolutionary zeal or determination. Recovering in Paris but always in fragile health she became the companion of Boris Souvarine, one of the founders of the French Communist Party but also one of the first to challenge Moscow's authority, having been expelled from the Comintern in 1924. Souvarine had founded an oppositional Democratic Communist Circle and Peignot would help him to establish the circle's journal that published eleven issues between March 1931 and November 1933 and included important essays by Karl Korsch, Simone Weil, Sigmund Freud, and, most significantly, 'The Notion of Expenditure' and 'The Psychological Structure of Fascism', the key works of Georges Bataille's early period. The publication was made possible only through Peignot's financial support; indeed, as Souvarine noted, the whole enterprise would not have been possible without her commitment to it.[14] But she was never motivated by ideology or idealism; she was rather attracted by a communism of the spirit, a shared communism, precisely the 'communism of genius' proclaimed by the surrealists in 1924. It was a communism irrevocably linked with her conception of the sacred.

4.1 Georges Bataille, Colette Peignot, and Georges Ambrosino, c. 1936. Photographer unknown.

The sacred

The notion of the sacred is the core around which Peignot's writing, and indeed the practice of her life, takes shape. Her conception of the sacred is singular, drawn both from anthropological research and from surrealist ideas of the marvellous, but above all from the experience of her own life. Her main notes on the theme comprise a short text she wrote in response to 'The Sacred in Everyday Life', the article Michel Leiris wrote as his contribution to the founding of the College of Sociology in 1936, although consideration of the sacred runs through everything she wrote.

Research into the sacred had been central to French sociological and anthropological research since the publication of Émile Durkheim's *The Elementary Forms of Religious Life* (1912) and has been further developed his students, notably by Robert Hertz in 'The Pre-eminence of the Right Hand' (actually first published in 1909, before Durkheim's own research appeared) and especially by Marcel Mauss in his *Essay on the Gift: The Form and Reason for Exchange in Archaic Societies* (1925). Leiris had been studying anthropology under Mauss and in his essay he applies notions about the sacred to events of his own life (doubtless influenced also by Freud's *Psychopathology of Everyday Life*). The essay was given first as a lecture at the College of Sociology in January 1937 and then published in July of the same year.

Peignot may have attended the lecture, or perhaps Leiris had given her a draft of the text to read (we know from his journal that he and Peignot had frequently met together during this period). Whatever the case, the text had a profound effect on her, impelling her to write the response that recounted her own experience in order to extend the discussion.

Leiris's text is set apart from most writing on the sacred in being situated in a personal response and largely unconcerned with any general theory. It initiates Leiris's great autobiographical project to 'acquire as exact and intense an understanding of [oneself] as possible'.[15]

Peignot responds directly to Leiris, applying the theoretical frame that his presentation lacks whilst also grounding her text in her own personal experience. She rejects his rather mundane examples of how the sacred becomes manifest in everyday life, denying that it is to be found in what is 'prestigious', 'extraordinary', 'dangerous', or 'forbidden' (as Leiris indicated), and applying to it notions that link it with the infinite, with life among other people, and, ultimately, with death. At its heart, however, the sacred is for her something apparently quite simple: it is 'communication', nothing more and nothing less. The complexity starts here, however: what does she mean by 'communication'?

Given the age in which we live today this may seem banal and easily misunderstood, for one of the ways in which the contemporary world is designated is that it is a 'communication age'. Does this mean that we now valorise what Colette Peignot saw as the locus of the sacred? Not at all: we might even say that 'communication' in its twenty-first-century sense is in many ways the polar opposite of her idea, even its very denial. This is because it has today become commoditised, serving as the vehicle for the transmission of information that is either devoid of content or, if it originally had any content at all, then it immediately becomes entrapped by the very means of its transmission. The consequence is that nothing is actually communicated at all: all distinction is lost as one thing becomes the equivalent of everything else. Yet, as the alchemists of old (and indeed all ancient forms of knowledge) recognised, a truth too widely disseminated loses its potency and becomes vulgarised and is ultimately valueless. The sort of communication that is at the heart of the sacred as Colette Peignot conceived it must therefore be placed at the opposite end of the spectrum from what is today valorised as 'communication'.

If we wish to understand what she meant by this idea, we should first recognise that it is fundamentally opposed to the transparency on which the contemporary world has placed its stake (which indeed Bataille, and no doubt Peignot herself, would have considered to be a denial of the sacred). To a greater or lesser extent the idea that modern society was irrevocably moving away from any conception of the sacred, much to society's own detriment, may also be said to be what united not only Peignot and Leiris as well as Bataille but all of their confrères, both within surrealist circles and on its margins. Against the positivist assumption of the ultimate knowability of the world, the sacred upholds the view that the world will always confound our attempts to understand it and can be approached only by indirect means.

The sacred was therefore seen as a vital issue at the time Peignot was writing and was of concern for some of the leading thinkers of the time. This led to a variety of different approaches raising diverse concerns, some of which conflicted with others. In particular the sacred was at the heart of the 'active sociology' that Bataille and Roger Caillois sought to initiate with their creation of the College of Sociology in 1936, and that Bataille wanted to take further with the secret society he formed called Acéphale. Despite a wealth of material having come to light, there is much that remains mysterious about both of these endeavours and we still know little about the actual functioning of Acéphale. The College of Sociology had been founded also with Leiris and Jules Monnerot (whose idea it may have been) but both men had serious reservations about its methodology – Monnerot soon withdrew altogether and Leiris participated in it only marginally. They had even more reservations about Acéphale, as did Caillois, although it seems that he may have played some part in it. Did Colette Peignot play any role in it?

Given her interests, and her relationship with Bataille over the period of the existence of these two groups, her involvement might be assumed, and it has often been conjectured that she may have been a key figure in both groupings behind the scenes in the same way she was with *La Critique sociale*. Yet nothing is less certain – there is no indication either in her own writing or in that of Bataille that she had any interest or involvement in either endeavour. Did she even know anything about it? One presumes she would have done since she was living with Bataille at the time. Yet the only reference to her in relation to Acéphale is a note by Bataille dated 8 March 1938 that she (or at least one 'C.P.') was among those proposed as a member in a memo dated 28 December 1938 (although the year must be a mistake and should be 1937).[16] Since the rules set out for acceptance into Acéphale[17] were quite involved and took several months to complete, it seems highly unlikely that she could ever have taken part in it since it was in March 1938 that her sickness entered its critical phase – she would be hospitalised and bedridden for the next eight months. Given Bataille's penchant for secrecy, imposed rigorously in relation to Acéphale, it would seem entirely possible that he never told her anything about it.

We can therefore only speculate at what she might have thought about these two endeavours. She certainly did have a decisive effect on the development of Bataille's own notion of the sacred, especially in relation to his recognition of its communicative aspects. But this influence really appears to have begun to be felt by him only after her death. Perhaps it wasn't until he read the writings she had left to him that he became aware that she was also thinking about the same issues. In fact, and despite what Bataille himself asserts, their ideas about these issues seem on many points to be quite divergent. This is especially so in one decisive respect that tends to give us reason to think that neither the College of Sociology nor Acéphale would have had a great interest for her. Bataille's interest in the sacred revolved around the idea of collective communion, which is what seems to have been the motivating factor in his determination to organise these groups. He conceived of Acéphale, and perhaps of the College of Sociology as well, as a 'sacred conspiracy' that would bind its adherents together and form a new community based on something comparable to what once united the affective communities that historically existed prior to the institution of contractual societies. In sociological terms it would represent a return to what Ferdinand Tönnies called a *gemeinschaft* society, an elective community opposed to the *gesellschaft* form that dominates the modern world and is based on the idea of a social contract. Yet nothing in the writings of Colette

Peignot gives any indication that this issue was of the slightest interest to her. Her overriding concern is tied to the relationship between the individual and what surrounds her or him, be it other people, the natural world, or the infinite.

We therefore need to consider the extent to which they were in accord on these questions, and even to wonder whether they discussed them at all. Bataille in fact tells us that

> [r]eading all her writings, entirely unknown to me, without a doubt provoked one of the most violent emotions of my life but nothing struck me and tore me more than the sentence ending the text in which she spoke of the Sacred. I was never able to express this paradoxical idea to her: that the sacred is *communication*. I had arrived at this idea only at the very moment I had expressed it, a few moments before noticing that Laure had entered into her agony. I can say in the most precise way that nothing that I had ever said to her could have approached this idea. The question was so important to me that I know exactly what it concerns. Moreover, we almost never had 'intellectual conversations' (she even reproached me for it at times; she was inclined to believe that this was contempt: in fact I only had contempt for the inevitable insolence of 'intellectual conversations').[18]

Even whilst coming to the conclusion that communication is at the heart of the sacred, though, Bataille's understanding of what this means is radically different from Peignot's. The definition he gives of the sacred as 'only a privileged moment of communal unity, a moment of the convulsive communion of what is ordinarily stifled' corresponds to nothing in the writing of Colette Peignot.[19] For her the communion is not convulsive; it is what 'is experienced by others, in communion with others'. The emphasis here is on the *with*. In other words, it is experienced *with* others and not as a moment of unity; indeed she often seems to fear such unity, being concerned to retain her own integral identity. This is emphasised by the equation she makes between the sacred and 'poetic work': 'The poetic work is sacred in that it is the creation of a topical event, "communication" experienced as *nakedness*. It is self-violation, baring, communication to others of a reason for living, and this reason for living "shifts."'[20]

Bataille says that this is close to his idea of communal unity, but for myself I find it expressing something very different. Far from a longed-for unity, there is a movement simultaneously towards other people *and away from them*. Peignot ends this definition of her conception of the sacred by saying that it is 'that which affirms me strongly enough to deny others'.[21] This seems fundamentally incompatible with the aims of Acéphale, which were largely determined by Bataille's own interests (we might even say that one of his objectives in Acéphale was to affirm himself *through* others) and they don't respond very much with the concerns expressed by Peignot in her writings.

We should remember too that, for all of its intensity and violence, the relationship between Colette Peignot and Georges Bataille appears to have been rather sporadic and not an especially intimate one. Their affair apparently begins in June 1934, but it wasn't until a year later that she actually definitively left Souvarine. Thereafter she and Bataille appear to have been together only intermittently. His refusal to be faithful, and her recurrent illnesses entailed that they would spend periods apart from one another. Moreover, their liaison seems to have been founded in an emotional and not intellectual attachment or complicity. Michel Surya speculates that Peignot was prepared to embrace Bataille's debauchery not out of predilection but from despair, as a will not to be afraid to experience the limits.[22] He may well be right: for her to share the proclivities of her lover was the price that had to be paid for love, for one of her characteristics was the need to give herself absolutely and unconditionally. There is even a sense that intellectually she felt closer to Leiris – as evidenced by the fact that they did apparently engage in the sort of intellectual conversations for which Bataille tells us he had contempt – and she may well have shared Leiris's reservations about the projects of both Acéphale and the College. At the same time her notion of the sacred also seems to be closer to the ideas about myth and the marvellous being developed within the surrealist group, especially by Breton and Pierre Mabille. In particular, Mabille's idea that the marvellous is all around us and often comes to us unbidden so as to bring our everyday perceptions into question and make us aware of the essential mystery of the universe is close to her perception.[23] And it is disorientation – a Bretonian term – rather than Bataille's laceration that constitutes the essence of the sacred as she conceives it.

She is also close to Breton in seeing in the sacred an intimation of that Rimbaudian 'real life' that is occluded by life as it is given to us by society. Seeking the sacred is for her a means by which to 'change life' and 'transform the world' in the sense that the surrealists gave to this double conjunction. But the movement of life is also Heraclitean, turning on itself like Nietzsche's eternal return: the prisoner escapes by jumping into the very place in which he must be executed. One of her characteristic poems is simply entitled '8', a number that seems to have had a special significance for her, an 'infernal' number that 'comes back to lasso me'.[24] It is as if she perceived existence as winding on itself, a consecration through fire that moves away only to lead back to where she already was: movement is stillness. But this is a journey leading to a rendezvous with oneself that offers the possibility of rediscovery. The only escape is into oneself, into the place where there is an intersection of life and death. In *The Story of a Little Girl* she imagines herself being transformed into various creatures (an eel, a dolphin, an earthworm) and then 'between the wall and the ivy [to become] a spider, a daddy-longlegs, a centipede, a hedgehog, everything one wants or perhaps even a ladybird'.²⁵ The latter perhaps had a meaning for her as a 'blessed' creature (as suggested by its strange French name that she uses, 'bête à bon dieu'). Once more there is no suggestion here of a desire for communal unity. Rather this desire of the child to seek refuge from the self in nature is closer to the sort of 'capture by the environment' described by Caillois in his notion of legendary psychasthenia. It was through her father that she became aware of the natural world and in writing about this experience and the memory she retains of it we get the sense that her transformation into natural forms also describes a will of reunification with those she has known who have died, and especially with her dead father. It is an experience of and through otherness (implying that our experience of the world is formed by the experience of others and the relationship we have with them) that forms a sense of self that is always open to the other in a way that is comparable with Breton's perception that who we are depends on whom we are pursuing. In the case of Colette Peignot what she was ultimately pursuing, or what was pursuing her, was death.

She makes it clear throughout her writing that death was always close to her. *The Story of a Little Girl*, a very short narrative, is filled with its presence, which clearly haunted her sensibility as it impinged directly on to her own childhood – not only the deaths of her father and uncles but also those of her godson and of Christiane, their housekeeper's daughter, who killed herself because her mother had been accused of stealing coal. Amidst all of this there was also the likelihood, and even perhaps desirability, of her own early death: 'I always believe in keeping poison close to me …' she would later write.²⁶ The very first words of *The Sacred* are 'I inhabited not life but death' as she perceives dead beings surrounding her and telling her that she 'belonged to their family'.²⁷ As a child she almost died from tuberculosis. In 1926 she attempted suicide (shooting herself in the heart, apparently at the break-up of her love affair with Bernier), and she seems to have come close to dying while in Russia. She was moreover constantly aware of the sickness that was eating her away internally and which she knew would eventually kill her. In the notes to *Guilty*, Bataille even writes, 'death took the name LAURE'.²⁸ And Leiris says that for years she 'had been on such a familiar footing with the angel of death that she seemed to have borrowed from it a little of its marble impenetrability'.²⁹

There is no sense of morbidity here though; she lived as if through death, which gave to life a greater sense of urgency and vigour. Leiris also notes that '[i]n comparison with me, C[olette] represented lucidity, energy and optimism'.³⁰ Her very sense of life came from this proximity of death, a determination to discover a reason for living, which was what founded her sense of the sacred: the communication at its heart was ultimately communication with the dead, or with death itself. Despite this, there is therefore also in her writing an overpowering desire to live, and even a recognition that attentiveness to the fragility of life is a necessary measure by which we establish and retain a sense of its vitality: 'Life for me can only be apprehension and it is this feeling alone that can help me to live and not vegetate', she writes.[31]

'No one has ever seemed to me as uncompromising and pure as she, or more decidedly "sovereign"', wrote Bataille.[32] This 'purity' extends to her attitude towards writing. Not only did she not publish anything during her lifetime, other than articles under the name 'Claude Araxe', she did not show anything she wrote to Bataille who, although he knew that she did write a lot, tells us that it was only on her deathbed that she showed him the file that contained the manuscript of 'The Sacred'. She says on the one hand that 'I need an audience', while on the other hand she laments 'the impossibility of true exchanges'.[33] Her life as much as her work exists between these two extremes, which is precisely the margin in which the sacred lies: the need to communicate on the one hand and the impossibility of communication on the other. But even as she longs for communication, at the same time she recoils from becoming too close to others, expressing relief that 'I am never where others think they can find me, and *seize* me'.[34] This fear of being 'seized', of being taken over by another power, is as great as her need to give of herself entirely and creates a tension that can never be resolved. We sense it in much of her correspondence with both Bernier and Bataille: a need for intimacy to be tempered by distance. As she expresses it in one of her last letters to Bataille, she had a need to go to the mountain alone, something which, she says, would 'save her life'.[35] Her 'purity' lies above all in her determination to live entirely on her own terms, to belong entirely to herself, and this links in again with what Breton wrote in his 'disdainful confession'.

The 'disdainful confession'

The notion of a 'disdainful confession' wasn't simply an early conceit on Breton's part. It became integral to surrealism and was pursued by the variants of the 'Truth Game', of which the 'Research into Sexuality' was the most notable example, and in various 'autobiographical' texts, among which we might include Breton's own narrative works, *Nadja*, *Communicating Vessels*, *L'Amour fou*, and *Arcane 17*. Other examples would include Michel Leiris's *L'Âge d'homme* and the four-volume *La Règle du jeu*, Unica Zürn's *Dark Spring*, and several of the works of Gherasim Luca and Joë Bousquet, to list only a few of the more notable examples. Within this rubric several of Bataille's works could also be situated, especially *Inner Experience* and *Guilty*, but also some of his 'fictional' texts, the distinction between 'fact' and 'fiction' being, in this context, entirely arbitrary.

These 'confessional' or 'autobiographical' writings really contain nothing either confessional or autobiographical and should more accurately be described as 'self-revelatory works' (revelatory in the sense that they do not necessarily reveal anything *about* the author but rather reveal something *to* him or her). Insofar as they are addressed to the reader, it is in a sense of complicity, seeking to involve the reader in this communicative sense of the revelation of 'being'; they were intended not so much to reveal the truth about the person as to lead towards what Antonin Artaud would express through the title of one of his books: a 'New Revelation of Being'. The double imperative Breton marked out at the beginning of *Nadja* in the question *qui suis je?*, in which the 'who am I?'[36] is irrevocably tied in with whom I am following, or whom I am related to, lies at the heart of this interrogation.

This interrogation is based on the assumption that the self is not an entity existing in itself. Rather it subsists only in relation to what surrounds it: we come into existence only by acknowledging the presence of the other. In some ways these surrealist texts may be seen as the opposite of an *auto-biography*, which very definitely assumes the existence of a self that may be projected on to the world (the very fact of presuming to write a conventional autobiography generally tends to suggest that the person is confident about their self-identity). In contrast, doubt about the very existence of the self lies at the heart of these surrealist narratives. Instead of aggrandising self-identity, they explore their own sensibility in relation to what surrounds it. This is based on a view of the fundamental otherness of the world, as well as the fundamental otherness of other people (and ultimately of oneself); we are implicated in an adventure we haven't chosen and from which we cannot escape. The idea of a 'disdainful confession' is a way of responding to this condition without accepting it as inevitable: we can seek out the 'real life' that lies behind it. It is a protest against the condition of the world – and of one's position within it – at the same time as it is an attempt to come to terms with that condition. Colette Peignot's quest lies fully within this surrealist questioning and doubt.

Notes

1 André Breton, 'The Disdainful Confession', in *The Lost Steps* (1924), trans. Mark Polizzotti (Lincoln: University of Nebraska Press, 1996), p. 1.

2 André Breton, *Manifesto of Surrealism* (1924), in *Manifestoes of Surrealism*, trans. Richard Seaver and Helen R. Lane (Ann Arbor: University of Michigan Press, 2004), p. 27.
3 Breton, 'The Disdainful Confession', p. 1.
4 See Jean Bernier, *L'Amour de Laure*, ed. Dominique Rabourdin (Paris: Flammarion, 1978), p. 89.
5 Laure, *Collected Writings*, trans. Janine Herman (San Francisco: City Lights, 1995), p. 131.
6 Boris Souvarine, 'Sombre jours', *La Critique sociale* 6 (1932), p. 242; translation mine.
7 Georges Bataille and Michel Leiris, 'Notes', in Laure, *Collected Writings*, p. 86.
8 *Ibid.*, p. 32.
9 See Bernier, *L'Amour de Laure*, p. 180.
10 See Laure, *Collected Writings*, pp. 64–70.
11 Michel Leiris, *Scraps: The Rules of the Game*, vol. 2 (1955), trans. Lydia Davis (Baltimore: Johns Hopkins University Press, 1997), p. 215.
12 Boris Souvarine, 'Prologue' to the republication of *La Critique sociale* (Paris: Éditions de la différence, 1983), p. 25.
13 Laure, *Écrits retrouvés* (Paris: Les Cahiers des Brisants, 1987), p. 19; translation mine.
14 Souvarine 'Prologue', p. 24.
15 Michel Leiris, 'The Sacred in Everyday Life' (1938), in Denis Hollier (ed.), *The College of Sociology*, trans. Betsy Wing (Minneapolis: University of Minnesota Press, 1988), p. 31
16 See Georges Bataille, *The Sacred Conspiracy: The Internal Papers of the Secret Society of Acéphale and Lectures to the College of Sociology*, ed. Marina Galletti and Alastair Brotchie (London: Atlas Press, 2017), p. 268.
17 See Bataille, *The Sacred Conspiracy*, pp. 242–3.
18 Georges Bataille, *Guilty*, trans. Stuart Kendall (New York: SUNY Press, 2011), p. 177.
19 *Ibid.*, p. 176.
20 Laure, *Collected Writings*, p. 45.
21 *Ibid.*, p. 45.
22 Michael Surya, *Georges Bataille, an Intellectual Biography*, trans. Krzysztof Fijalkowski and Michael Richardson (London: Verso, 2001), pp. 198–9.
23 Pierre Mabille, *The Mirror of the Marvelous*, trans. Jody Gladding (Rochester, VT: Inner Traditions, 1998), p. 14.
24 Laure, *Collected Writings*, p. 48.
25 Laure, *Collected Writings*, p. 15; translation modified.
26 See Bernier *L'Amour de Laure*, p. 90.
27 Laure, *Collected Writings*, p. 78.
28 Bataille, *Guilty*, p. 201.
29 Michel Leiris, *Journal 1922–1989* (Paris: Gallimard, 1992), p. 214.
30 Leiris, *Journal 1922–1989*, p. 316.

31 Laure, *Les Cris de Laure* (Strasbourg: Éditions les Cahiers, 2014), p. 32; translation mine.
32 In Laure, *Collected Writings*, p. 237.
33 *Ibid.*, p. 45, p. 83.
34 *Ibid.*, p. 83.
35 *Ibid.*, p. 151.
36 André Breton, *Nadja*, trans. Richard Howard (1928; London: Penguin, 1999), p. 11.

5

Suzanne Césaire's surrealism: tightrope of hope[1]

Kara M. Rabbitt

In 1943, Suzanne Roussi Césaire, wife of the poet-politician Aimé Césaire and co-founder with him, René Ménil, and Astride Maugée of the influential 1940s Martinican cultural review *Tropiques*, eulogised, resurrected, and reinvented surrealism for a Caribbean context in an essay titled '1943: Le Surréalisme et nous':

> Beaucoup ont cru que le Surréalisme était mort. Beaucoup l'ont écrit: Puérilité: son activité s'étend aujourd'hui au monde entier et le surréalisme demeure, plus vivace, plus hardi, que jamais. André Breton peut considérer avec orgueil l'entre deux guerres et affirmer qu'au mode d'expression créé par lui depuis plus de 20 ans s'ouvre en 'au delà' de plus en plus vaste, immense.[2]

> (Many believed surrealism to be dead. Many wrote as much. Childish nonsense: its vitality today extends across the globe. Surrealism lives on, more vibrant, more tenacious than ever. André Breton can consider with pride the interwar period and note that the mode of expression he created more than twenty years ago has expanded into an ever-growing and immense 'beyond'.)

In this work, Suzanne Césaire defines surrealism's 'living presence: young, ardent, and revolutionary' in an active phase of evolution, though she adds, 'It would be more accurate to say it has blossomed'.[3] This blossoming, she claims, was taking place in the challenging soil of a Caribbean island fighting against the 'injustice and hypocrisy' of a colonial system, selected by its new practitioners as a weapon of war: 'Et parmi les puissantes machines de guerre que le monde moderne met à notre disposition "leddites et cheddites" notre audace a choisi le surréalisme' ('And from among the powerful machines of war, "the bombs and explosives", that the modern world places at our disposal, our audacity chooses surrealism').[4] The essay concludes that this choice of cultural weapon is not simply a gift from the French intellectuals and artists who inspire these Martinican writers, but rather a resurrection and a transformation of their surrealism towards a new one, one yet to be built by the 'us' of her Martinican readership:

> Des millions de mains noires, à travers les ciels rageurs de la guerre mondiale vont dresser leur épouvante. Délivré dun [sic] long engourdissement, le plus deshérité [sic] de tous les peoples se lèvera, sur les plaines de cendre.
>
> Notre surréalisme lui livrera alors le pain de ses profondeurs. Il s'agira de transcender enfin les sordides antinomies actuelles: blancs-noirs, européens-africains, civilisés-sauvages: Retrouvée enfin la puissance magique des mahoulis, puisée à même les sources vives. Purifiées à la flamme bleue des soudures autogènes les niaiseries coloniales. Retrouvée notre valeur de métal, notre tranchant d'acier, nos communions insolites.
>
> Surréalisme, corde raide de notre espoir.[5]

> (Millions of black hands will hoist their terror across the livid skies of the world war. Delivered from a long state of numbness, the most disadvantaged of all peoples will rise up above the plains of ashes.
>
> Our realism will then offer them the bread of its depths. We will finally transcend the current sordid antinomies of White/Black, European/African, civilised/savage. We will rediscover the powerful magic of the mahoulis, drawn from the living wells of the lifeforce. We will purify the idiocies of colonialism in the welder's blue flame. We will regain our metal worth, our cutting edge, our surprising communions.
>
> Surrealism – the tightrope of our hope.)

The writer of these powerful words, Suzanne Césaire remains a figure of conjecture and fascination decades after her early death in 1966. One of the island's most ardent advocates of the power of surrealism as a literary, cultural, and political tool, she served during a pivotal moment as a catalyst of cultural change and transnational engagement for Martinican literature, and then – textually – disappeared, publishing nothing after 1945. Her lingering legacy speaks to the impact not only of her few published essays, seven in all through the years of *Tropiques*'s short wartime life in Martinique, but also of her influence on a generation of intellectuals through her advocacy, her teaching, and her parenting of six highly influential children.[6] By all accounts a passionate teacher and an equally passionate socialist, Suzanne Césaire sculpted through the pages of the journal *Tropiques* – those she wrote, edited, or worked to bring to print – a vision of the force of language to change lives.

Suzanne Césaire's relation to surrealism is often either lauded or ignored in studies of her work, depending on the critic's focus. It is clear in her writing that she celebrated the release from the constraints of description offered by surrealist texts. The scathing indictment of realist novels detailed in André Breton's 1924 manifesto, for example, appears to have provided in her imaginary a powerful mechanism to move beyond the trap of the tropical that she so powerfully refuted in her writings about Martinique. And Suzanne Césaire's essays, filled with parataxic leaps and the pirouettes of an active mind freeing its thoughts from argumentative forms, demonstrate as much as or more than many of the journal's poetic texts the power of surrealism's liberatory possibilities. Including this mid-century Caribbean essayist in a collection on surrealist women could be viewed, however, as ceding her fully to the surrealist camp, as Tracy Sharpley-Whiting warned against in her 2002 study of *Negritude Women*.[7] In her passionate explorations of poetics as means for cultural and cognitive liberation, Suzanne Césaire applied nevertheless the most dynamic uses of the tools of surrealism in *Tropiques*'s pages. This brief biographical and bibliographic overview will explore Césaire's engagement with surrealism as a poetic and political weapon as well as some of the complexities of her lingering symbolic significance as an emerging Caribbean cultural force.

After decades of virtual silence about this intriguing figure in twentieth-century studies of Caribbean writers, scholars began in recent decades to mine carefully Césaire's few published works to better appreciate the key means they craft for embracing a distinctly West Indian cultural identity and for advancing an emerging Martinican surrealist poetics.[8] For, despite her status as co-founder of *Tropiques* and the lyrical beauty of the seven short essays she wrote for its pages, Césaire's separation from her famous husband – which remains an unstoried part of his biography to this day – and her departure from the island before her death seem to have assured her cultural obscurity for the following two to three decades: there is almost no reference to her in works on Aimé Césaire or on Martinique until relatively recently.[9] The voice of Maryse Condé offered one major exception as early as 1978: in her critical introduction to Aimé Césaire's *Cahier d'un retour au pays natal*, Condé termed Suzanne Césaire the theoretician of the *Tropiques* revue.[10] Condé would, in fact, become by the 1990s one of the most influential forces leading to the reopening of Suzanne Césaire's pages. Daniel Maximin's literary dialogue with the writers of *Tropiques* and *Légitime défense* in his 1981 novel *L'Isolé Soleil* likewise invited a new appreciation of Césaire's significance. In the 1980s and 1990s the few critics who studied her did so through the inspiration of one or both of these influential Guadeloupean writers.[11] Condé's special edition of the journal *Callaloo* in 1992, for example, dedicated to the literature of Guadeloupe and Martinique, provided a wealth of new perspectives on Césaire's essays.[12]

Interpellations of Suzanne Césaire's essays by these later writers led to subsequent studies of her influence. In a significant 1994 article, entitled 'Suzanne Césaire et *Tropiques*: de la poésie cannibale à une poétique créole', Marie-Agnès Sourieau recuperates Césaire as a precursor of *créolité* and explores how she shifts the vital question of origin to one of a relation to place. In so doing, Sourieau implicitly evokes both Césaire and the feminised land of Martinique as a maternal-like figure providing, paradoxically, not a single origin but what Sourieau terms 'the process of collective relationships that create Caribbean identity' ('le processus de relations collectives qui façonnent l'identité antillaise').[13] In the Caribbean, the USA, and Europe, Césaire's essays have more recently provided new inspiration to critics exploring this intriguing figure whom Jennifer Wilks has termed the 'Madonna' of francophone modernism.[14] A firm believer in the fertility and vitality of the Caribbean, Césaire provides a critical point of origin for theoretical examinations of the cross-pollination of cultures and voices she celebrated in her essays. Daniel Maximin's re-edition of Suzanne Césaire's extant works under her own name for the first time in his 2009 edition *Le Grand Camouflage: Écrits de dissidence (1941–1945)*, and their translation into English by Keith Walker in 2012 as *The Great Camouflage: Writings of Dissent (1941–1945)*, have provided new generations of readers direct access to her words. More than half a century after her death, Suzanne Césaire's writings thus render anew a present and vital Martinique and offer still-fresh views of what surrealism can mean in this distinct realm.

Born Jeanne Aimée Marie Suzanne Roussi, on 11 August 1915, Césaire followed an early journey similar to that of many of her generation. In the early 1930s, as was typical of bright young colonials, she left Martinique to complete her education in France, studying literature at the University of Toulouse. A classmate of Aimé Césaire's sister, she met her future husband through this connection and moved to Paris, where the two married in 1937. Like many of her contemporaries, after her studies in France Césaire brought back to Martinique a solid grounding in European intellectual history, a firm belief in French leftist politics, a new awareness of the richness of African cultures, and an expansionist vision of surrealism's radical poetics. Crucially, she also embraced fully the cultural diversity and vitality of the Black Americas at a time when many Martinican intellectuals were turning away from Europe only to focus almost exclusively on Africa.

A mother and a scholar, Césaire is a compelling figure not least in the balancing of the many roles she played. Shortly after her 1937 marriage to Aimé Césaire, she gave birth in Paris to their first son, Jacques. The couple returned to Martinique in 1939 and had another son, Jean-Paul, that year. Césaire then appears to have briefly taught, along with her husband, at the Lycée Schoelcher in Fort-de-France. The two, along with René Ménil and Aristide Maugée, founded the cultural revue *Tropiques* in 1941. Césaire wrote three essays that year as well as producing another son, Francis. During the period of 1942 to 1945, she gave birth to her daughter Ina, wrote four more essays for *Tropiques*, and joined her co-editors in the battle for its continued publication. Author of seven short essays in all for *Tropiques*

5.1 Suzanne Césaire. Date and photographer unknown.

between 1941 and 1945 and co-editor of this vital cultural review, Césaire influenced her native land as much by her efforts in support of the journal's existence and content – as editor, paper-procurer, protestor against censorship – as she did by her published works within it.

In fact, Césaire's efforts were key to the journal's very existence as well as for its content. Arguably her eighth published text, and one of the most overtly political pieces of writing from the *Tropiques* collective, is the letter Césaire appears to have drafted and that all signed in 1943,[15] rejecting censorship and rebuking the inherent racism of the Vichy puppet government in Martinique following an interdiction of the journal's publication by Lieutenant Bayle, the propaganda chief of Admiral Robert. In this text, which reappropriates his insults of their work into battle cries, the heretofore hidden agenda of the collective[16] is roared out in what very much sounds like Césaire's powerful voice:

> Nous avons reçu votre réquisitoire contre *Tropiques*.
> 'Racistes', 'sectaires', 'révolutionnaires', 'ingrats et traîtres à la Patrie', 'empoisonneurs d'âmes', aucune de ces épithètes ne nous répugne essentiellement.

'Empoisonneurs d'âmes' comme Racine, au dire des Messieurs de Port-Royal.
'Ingrats et traîtres à notre si bonne patrie' comme Zola, au dire de la presse réactionnaire.
'Révolutionnaires' comme l'Hugo des 'Châtiments'.
'Sectaires', passionnément comme Rimbaud et Lautréamont.
'Racistes', oui. Du racisme de Toussaint Louverture, de Claude Mac Kay et de Langston Hugues – contre celui de Drumont et de Hitler.
Pour ce qui est du reste, n'attendez de nous ni plaidoyer, ni vaines récriminations ni discussion même.
Nous ne parlons pas le même langage.[17]

(We have received your indictment of *Tropiques*.
'Racists', 'sectarians', 'revolutionaries', 'ungrateful traitors to our good Fatherland', 'poisoners of souls', none of these epithets really bothers us.
'Poisoners of souls' like Racine, according to the gentlemen of Port-Royal.
'Ungrateful traitors to our good fatherland', like Zola, according to the reactionary press.
'Revolutionary' like the Hugo of *Châtiments*.
Passionately 'sectarian' like Rimbaud and Lautréamont.
'Racists', yes, of the sort of racism of Toussaint Louverture, of Claude McKay and of Langston Hughes – against that of Drumont and of Hitler.
As for the rest, do not expect from us pleas, vain recriminations, or even discussion.
We do not speak the same language.)

As one of the main editors, as a primary force procuring material support during a time of rationing and shortages, and in her powerful protest against censorship, Césaire served as a key figure in bringing forth the key cultural resource that was *Tropiques* for wartime Martinique. Like those of numerous women in intellectual or political movements, her contributions as an unsung facilitator of work bearing the names of others undoubtedly precluded her having time to publish more of her own writing. One wonders, as well, how many of the journal's unsigned pages may have come from her pen.

After the war the Césaires moved to Paris when Aimé Césaire was elected assemblyman for the newly created French department of Martinique. They had two more children, Marc, born in Paris in 1948, and Michèle, born in Fort-de-France in 1951. By Michel Leiris's account, Césaire spent her Sundays selling communist newspapers for the cause in Paris, even with then five young children at home.[18] She seems to have returned with her husband to Martinique after he left the Communist Party in 1956, but separated from him in April of 1963 and returned to Paris to teach. She died three short years later, at the age of fifty, on 16 May 1966. Though we have not a single printed word from her after 1945, Césaire did write a play loosely adapted from an 1890 novel written by Lafcadio Hearn about the 1848 slave revolt in Martinique, *Youma, The Story of a West-Indian*

Slave. This theatrical adaptation, titled *Aurore de la liberté* ('The Dawn of Liberty'), was performed by an amateur group in 1952 but never published.[19]

In many cultural histories of the period and of her island, however, Césaire remains more concept than woman or writer. As Annette Joseph-Gabriel aptly summarises in her essay 'Beyond the Great Camouflage: Haiti in Suzanne Césaire's Politics and Poetics of Liberation', 'Suzanne Césaire's legacy in Caribbean literature is characterized by an uneasy combination of homage and erasure'.[20] Jennifer Wilks notes in her chapter on Suzanne Césaire in *Race, Gender, & Comparative Black Modernism*: 'The challenge of reading Suzanne Césaire comes not from a dearth of biographical information, ... but from a scarcity of creative output.'[21] The biographic and the bibliographic appear, however, linked in both erasure and homage. Césaire's creative output is evident in the seven published essays, the one published letter, and her editing of *Tropiques*. Her very symbolic significance, however – as cultural figure, as surrealist theorist, as Martinican matriarch – stems at least partially from the very lacunae that surround her few published texts and the outline of her life detailed above. We would wish to know more about Césaire's personal passions, her political dissent, the creative force she dedicated to her teaching, the unpublished and now lost play, the letters tossed by recipients, the unsigned missives and unacknowledged editorial voice threaded throughout and yet invisible within the pages of *Tropiques*.

Suzanne Césaire's complex identity as a surrealist is founded, as well, on both the biographic and the bibliographic. The Césaires were 'discovered' by André Breton in Martinique in 1941 (an encounter detailed in Breton's essay 'A Great Black Poet: Aimé Césaire'), and engaged with him after the war in New York in 1945. If Aimé Césaire in an interview with Jacqueline Leiner that opens the 1978 re-edition of *Tropiques* seems to distance himself from a direct surrealist influence by stating that he 'shared the same ancestors as them ... Rimbaud, of course, Mallarmé, the symbolists, Claudel, Lautréamont',[22] Suzanne Césaire appears to have more directly and enthusiastically embraced surrealism's possibilities and poetics. Her essays, which focus above all on the varied means of constructing a distinctly Martinican cultural identity, advance surrealism as a tool toward this goal.[23] These essays – in the fullest sense of the term as explorations, ruminations, and attempts – sought out a distinct rhetorical engagement with her readers, inviting them as 'us' to become participants in an enunciative moment of action being created within the act of reading.[24]

Inclusion of Césaire's essays in multiple surrealist anthologies[25] both in French and in English translation speaks to her importance, particularly during the war, for the evolution, expansion, and indeed survival of the surrealist movement. Her symbolic surrealist influence has also been explored in such recent works as *Invisible Surrealists*, a 2014 exhibition by artist Sam Durant at the Paula Cooper Gallery in New York, which featured several paintings and sculptures inspired by her words and her image.[26] This surrealist reinvestigation of Césaire has led to some very fruitful dialogues – by Robin D.G. Kelly and others – with her writings for European and North American contexts. There is a certain danger, however, of reducing Césaire's essays to any one theoretical or poetic system, even if that system is as antisystematic as surrealism aspires to be.

Césaire's evolving relation to surrealism and increasing embrace of its potential for her own distinct purpose plays itself out in her seven essays. One of her earlier works in *Tropiques* studies the influence of Alain, the critic/philosopher Émile-Auguste Chartier, whose work reflected a theory of art as a call to action and of criticism as response to that call, to the shock generated in us by art. Césaire explores this function of art as a fundamental force that moves through and surpasses the individual, that calls to both the artist and the reader to succumb to its power, in relation to which humanity is dependent and not dominant:

> Il s'agit maintenant de saisir et d'admirer un art nouveau, qui tout en gardant l'homme à sa vraie place, fragile et dépendante, ouvre cependant à l'artiste des possibilités insoupçonnées, dans le spectacle même des choses ignorées ou tues.
> Et nous voilà dans le domaine de l'étrange, du merveilleux et du fantastique ...[27]

(Now we must seize upon and admire a new art, which both keeps humanity in its true place – fragile and dependent – and opens up unsuspected possibilities to the artist through the surprising spectacle of forgotten, silenced things.

And here we land in the realm of the strange, the marvellous, and the fantastic ...)

> À une nouvelle conscience du monde, à une nouvelle conscience de l'humain répond un jeu nouveau, splendide.
> Et déjà de troublants chefs d'œuvre sont le signe de cette reconnaissance et voici se lever sur ce monde transfiguré et retrouvé les promesses d'un art qui sera expression totale de la vie.
> Et ici, il convient de citer le nom d'André Breton, ses poèmes, son livre admirable: 'l'Amour fou'.[28]

(A new and splendid game answers this emerging consciousness of the world and of humankind.

Troubling masterpieces already mark this awakening, and above this transformed and rediscovered world rises up the promises of an art that will be the total expression of life.

And here, we must cite the name of André Breton, his poems, his amazing book *Mad Love*.)

Suzanne Césaire's view of a new art in this early essay is clearly inspired by the surrealism already explored by her peers in Paris (such as the *Légitime défense* collective), and one can read in this passionate call for a new poetics a well-versed student of the work of Rimbaud, Lautréamont, Breton, among others. But Césaire's urgency in her discussion of these questions is hardly academic: she is driving towards a transformative relation to place, and specifically towards a Martinique emerging as a vital force that pulses through her children's blood. Her use of the deictic 'maintenant' ('now') and of the enunciatively marked present and future tenses of spoken discourse engage her readers in the creation of this vision, as do the deictic 'voici' and 'ici' ('here'): here and now are the driving moments of her text, pulling us into its present and towards what will be. This early essay on Alain thus serves, in many ways, as a precursor of Césaire's later more explicit explorations of surrealism.

Rhetorically, Césaire also begins developing in her early work what becomes a consistent call to her readers to engage this 'emerging consciousness of the world', drawing them into the moment of the text's creation and challenging them to join forces with the text and with the possibilities of art to transform. She speaks to the fertile possibility of Martinique, calling upon her compatriots to rise up and to recognise their place in the world, reminding them in her 1941 essay 'Léo Frobenius' that 'Ici, aussi, des hommes naissent, vivent et meurent; Ici aussi, se joue le drame entier' ('Here, too, people are born, live, and die; here, too, the whole drama plays itself out').[29] This 'here', this present and presence gain an urgency in her writing that grows through her essays, culminating in the compelling call for a new Martinican literature of her final essay, 'Le Grand Camouflage' (1945).

In each of her essays, in fact, Césaire categorically refuses and textually rejects any distance from the Caribbean space her writing evokes. In 'Misère d'une poésie', her 1942 essay on John Antoine-Nau, she critiques colonial representations of Martinique as an exoticised and eroticised feminine space as examples of 'touristic' literature. For Césaire, the island is not an object but a subject, whose inclusive subjectivity embraces and expands that of her readers whom, again, she draws in by use of a repeated first-person plural pronoun that pulls us into the movement and moment of the text.

One could also read in this insistence a mild rebuke of the writers from whom she draws inspiration in her emphasis of an Antillean agency. In direct contrast to the French predecessors she echoes above and even to certain contemporary poets of the Negritude movement,[30] Suzanne Césaire refuses – absolutely – any textual distance from the Caribbean space. In the two essays in which she directly engages surrealism, Césaire challenges a lingering exoticism or eroticism in stereotypical depictions of the Caribbean space as a feminised object of conquest or desire. In addition to the 1943 text 'Le Surréalisme et nous' cited above, Césaire's 1941 essay 'André Breton, poète' explores in Breton's writing his nameless feminine muse: 'Femme sans nom,' she quotes from his work, 'qui brise en mille éclats le bijou du jour' ('Nameless woman who breaks the day's jewel into a thousand beams of light').[31] In her reading, however, this woman sees more accurately the signifying forces at play than does, perhaps, the poet himself: 'Pour la femme cet hymne étrange, ce convulsif appel aux puissances du monde et du désir où l'amour prend sa signification totale qui est d'intégrer l'homme au cosmos, de le mettre en liaison directe avec les éléments' ('For woman this strange hymn serves as a convulsive call to the power of the world and of desire, where love gains its full significance: that of integrating man with the cosmos, of putting him in direct contact with the elements').[32] In this essay, which explicitly celebrates 'le plus authentique poète français d'aujourd'hui' ('the most authentic French poet of our times'), Césaire begins to carve, nevertheless, a distinct use of Breton's work for her own purposes.[33]

Drawing on this early challenging of the use of woman as object, Césaire builds through her essays to an increasingly explicit critique of any representation of Martinique as an exoticised or eroticised feminine topography, such as that she condemned in her critique of Antoine-Nau: 'nuit des madras multicolores / Sur les tiges des beaux corps balances' ('night of multicoloured madras / Around the legs of beautiful balanced bodies'). She castigates the view of any poet who 'looks but does not see' and urges her readers to remember that 'la vraie poésie est ailleurs … zut à l'hibiscus, à la frangipane, aux bougainvilliers. La poésie martiniquaise sera cannibal ou ne sera pas' ('true poetry is elsewhere … forget about the hibiscus, plumeria, or bougainvillea. Martinican poetry will be cannibalistic or it will not be').[34] In contrast to poetic depictions of the island's beauty, Césaire's relation to place is grounded in geography, anthropology, history, meteorology, and ethnography. Martinique is not the exotic woman of the colonial dream, nor the sterile and silent land of her co-editors' fears, but a lush if harsh site of upheaval, energy, vitality. It is a land of mixing, and of repression, and of possibility. And, as she concludes in her 1945 'Grand Camouflage', if the blinding beauty of her island turns the heads of poets, 'c'est qu'il fait certes trop beau, ce jour-là, pour y voir' ('it must be too beautiful that day to see').[35]

Césaire posits in her writing that it is rather the job of the reader and of the writer both to open their eyes ('ouvrez les yeux')[36] and to look within. In her 1941 essay 'Leo Frobenius and the Problem of Civilisations' she asserts that 'Il est maintenant urgent d'oser se connaître soi-même, d'oser s'avouer ce qu'on est, d'oser se demander ce qu'on veut être' ('It is now urgent to dare to know ourselves, to dare to admit to ourselves who we are, to dare to ask ourselves what we wish to be').[37] In her 1942 'Malaise d'une civilisation' she argues for a collective identity – 'ourselves' – that will place Martinicans in fertile relationship with their land:

> Il est exaltant d'imaginer sur ces terres tropicales, rendues enfin à leur vérité interne, l'accord durable et fécond de l'homme et du sol ... Nous voici appelés à nous connaître enfin nous-mêmes, et voici devant nous les splendeurs et les espoirs ... Il s'agit ... d'une mobilisation de toutes les forces vives mêlées sur cette terre où la race est le résultat du brassage le plus continu; il s'agit de prendre conscience du formidable amas d'énergies diverses que avons jusqu'ici enfermées en nous-mêmes. Nous devons maintenant les employer dans leur plénitude, sans déviation et sans falsification. Tant pis pour ceux qui nous croient des rêveurs. La plus troublante réalité est nôtre. Nous agirons. Cette terre, la nôtre, ne peut être que ce que vous voulons qu'elle soit.[38]

> (It is exhilarating to imagine in these tropical lands, finally returned to their internal truth, a long-term and fruitful covenant between people and earth ... We are called to finally know ourselves and find in front of us our splendours and our hopes ... It is a question of mobilizing all the living strength of this land where race is the result of constant mixing; it is a question of becoming aware of the incredible mass of diverse energies the we have until now bottled up inside. We must now employ them fully, without hesitation or falseness. Too bad for those who think us dreamers. We will act. This land, our land, can only be what we want it to be.)

Césaire's 'living land', filled with dynamic and diverse people, opens a space hitherto unfound in Martinican literature and occupies it with the active subjects her readers become: present with her in the repeated first-person plural of the text, 'We will act'.

Her writing – an idiosyncratic and aggressive assault on rationalist prose, riddled with parataxis – delves further in each essay into the possibilities beyond the dogmatic essay style of even the more innovative of some of her contemporaries. One need only compare the occasionally surprisingly prosaic essays of Breton[39] with Césaire's more lyric evocations to witness the power of her forms, culminating in the call to being of a new Martinican literature in 'Le Grand Camouflage', to be found, again, 'here':

> Cependant les balisiers d'Absalon saignent sur les gouffres et la beauté du paysage tropical monte à la tête des poètes qui passent. À travers les réseaux mouvants des palmes ils voient l'incendie antillais rouler sur la Caraïbe qui est une tranquille mer de laves. Ici la vie s'allume à un feu végétal. Ici, sur ces terres chaudes qui gardent vivantes les espèces géologiques, la plante fixe, passion et sang, dans son architecture primitive, l'inquiétante sonnerie surgie des reins chaotiques des danseuses. Ici les lianes balancées de vertige prennent

pour charmer les précipices des allures aériennes, elle [sic] s'accrochent de leurs mains tremblantes à l'insaisissable trépidation cosmique qui monte tout le long des nuits habitées de tambours. Ici les poètes sentent chavirer leur tête, et humant les odeurs fraîches des ravins, ils s'emparent de la gerbe des îles, ils écoutent le bruit de l'eau autour d'elles, ils voient s'aviver les flammes tropicales non plus aux balisiers, aux gerberas, aux hibiscus, aux bougainvilliers, aux flamboyants, mais aux faims, aux peurs, aux haines, à la férocité qui brûlent dans les creux des mornes.[40]

(But the cannas of Absalon bleed into the depths, and the beauty of the tropical landscape intoxicates passing poets. Through the shifting network of palms they see the Antillean conflagration rolling into the Caribbean, a tranquil sea of lava. Here, life ignites into a vegetal fire. Here, in these hot lands that keep alive geological species, the plant holds – within its primitive architecture – the passion and blood and disquieting noise of the dancers' chaotic movements. Here, the lianas swinging vertiginously take on aerial allures to charm the precipices, grasping with their trembling hands the elusive cosmic trepidation that builds through the nights inhabited by drums. Here, poets feel their heads reeling as they drink in the fresh odours of the ravines, they seize upon the collection of islands, they listen to the sound of the surrounding water, they watch the rising tropical flames not of canna, of gerberas, of hibiscus, of bougainvilleas, of flamboyants, but of hunger, of fear, of hatred, of the ferocity burning in the hollows of the hills.)

'Here', 'here', 'here': Suzanne Césaire calls her readers into the presence of place. She grounds her work in the hills and ravines of her ravaged if beautiful native land, in depictions not just of the island's flora but also of its socio-cultural realities. The text's deictic markers force us into a now, a here, an urgency of the immediate. There is no distance or disdain possible for the reader: we are called to see, to share in the presence of this place her prose brings vividly before our eyes. Césaire's essay refuses both the prosaic style of the intellectual essay and the prosody of a poem. Her readers slide into the text 'vertiginously'; her words pull us into her world and thrust us against its rough and unsettling beauty.

It is not, then, surprising that 'Le Grand Camouflage' is Suzanne Césaire's most widely cited essay. This 1945 study of Martinique, the closing document of the last published edition of *Tropiques*, offers the richest example of the political force of the poetic for this writer in its idiosyncratic assault on rationalist prose. Its urgent phrases embed lyrical evocations of place while challenging her readers to alter their relationship to it. In an interactive exploration of a highly complex and diverse island, which evokes its multiple influences and origins, its problematic histories, and its powerful meteorological, geological, and cultural forces, the text calls into being a new Martinican literature that renders the island and its people fully present and places us within its fierce power.

'Le Grand Camouflage' also explores the poetic power of two distinct spaces – the Black Americas as a whole and Haiti in particular – in relation to Martinique. While Aimé Césaire and their Francophone colleagues and compatriots of the period were exploring a Negritude poetics inspired by the Africa that had inspired the French surrealists, Suzanne Césaire focused forcefully on the cultural diversity and vitality of the Caribbean region. Annette Joseph-Gabriel, in a recent overview of the function of Haiti in and for the writings of Suzanne Césaire, draws heavily from unpublished archives of personal letters and Césaire's work with students at the College Saint Estienne (which Joseph-Gabriel was able to access through the generosity of Marc Césaire) to argue for her prescient Antilleanity, as also detailed by Sharpley-Whiting.[41] Focusing on the Césaires' five-month sojourn in Haiti in 1944, Joseph-Gabriel conjectures on the significance of this visit for both the future politics of Césaire and those of Martinique, as well as on the theorist's poetic vision, which was political in its very conception: 'For Césaire, surrealism was not solely a literary aesthetic. It was also a politically engaged movement that condemned imperialism worldwide.'[42] In light of the fact that André Breton and Pierre Mabille, too, experienced time in Haiti as a turning point, it is perhaps no accident that Suzanne Césaire's most ardent and best-known essay postdates this 1944 visit to Haiti and references – in both its opening and its closing passages – that island's symbolic landscape. 'Le Grand Camouflage', her only published work after this sojourn in Haiti, 'confirms Haiti to have been a pivotal experience because it reveals an expanded focus from her initial work centered on Martinique to a larger vision of the Caribbean'.[43] Recalling the necessity of evading censorship during the Vichy regime, and citing a letter Césaire wrote to the French Writer Yassu Gauclère from Haiti, Joseph-Gabriel notes that '"The Great Camouflage" is apt both as the title of her final essay and as a description of her entire body of work'.[44] In this view of Suzanne Césaire's surrealism, as also shared by Michael Richardson in his introduction to *Refusal of the Shadow: Surrealism and the Caribbean*,[45] 'Césaire rejects the top-down model of political and artistic representation and advocates instead a collective, communal deployment of surrealism to counter wartime oppression'.[46]

If 'Le Grand Camouflage' marks the climax of her voice in *Tropiques*, Césaire's theoretical anchoring of the journal in radical cultural production is manifest throughout its pages. In an exploration of Césaire's essays occasioned by Daniel Maximin's 2009 edition of her writings, Gilles Bounoure speaks to her incendiary standing in the mid-century imaginary. He examines how her essays, when finally collected in one volume, reveal her as a prophetic if neglected figure.[47] Specifically speaking of the encounter with André Breton in April 1941 as detailed in his *Martinique charmeuse de serpents* (1948), Bounoure underscores that subsequent essays by Suzanne Césaire in *Tropiques*

– 'André Breton, poète' (October 1941) and '1943: Le Surréalisme et nous' (October 1943), in particular – served as 'les plus directs, les plus clairs et les plus profonds qu'ait publiés cette revue sur ce sujet, mieux appropriés et inspirés même que ceux, déjà remarquables, de René Ménil et d'Aimé Césaire' ('the most direct, the clearest, and the most profound that would be published by this journal on this subject – more appropriate and inspired than even the also remarkable essays of René Ménil and Aimé Césaire').[48] Citing the political and cultural contexts of *Tropiques*'s production, Bounoure names Césaire a great figure of intellectual resistance, as significant in the journal's ultimate cultural force as her more widely known male co-editors, whose work was all the more significant given her concurrent roles as teacher, wife, and mother.[49] He also correctly underscores the critical importance of the letter discussed above that Suzanne Césaire drafted and all of the co-editors signed in 1943, which addresses the question of Martinican culture and the political and poetic tools the *Tropiques* collective were exploiting, including surrealism.[50] In sum, Suzanne Césaire's work for *Tropiques* was both practical and theoretical, assuring the journal's production as well as its purpose.

Suzanne Césaire brought *Tropiques*'s readers back to the land in which they lived and invited them to consider their interrelationship with it and with each other. Her essays based the originality and legitimacy of the Martinican people on their relationship to the place that had sculpted them for over three centuries and which offered them a unique sense of generational continuity. Her importance for the very existence of *Tropiques*, for the vitality of its pages, and for the influence on subsequent generations through the theoretical framework she laid out for a new Caribbean literature cannot be overstated. And in these efforts, her use of surrealist poetics was neither arbitrary nor idolatrous. As Michèle Praeger argues in her work on Suzanne Césaire and André Breton in *The Imaginary Caribbean and the Caribbean Imaginary*, Césaire provided an important challenge to 'a certain frivolity of arbitrariness' in surrealist discourse and proved a significant ability to make use of surrealism to 'reunit[e] ethics and aesthetics in her metaphor'.[51]

The revolutionary use of surrealism as a cultural tool of liberation within *Tropiques*'s pages is clearest in the writings of Suzanne Césaire. From her earlier studies of European writers, to her 1941 exploration of the poetics of André Breton, to her Caribbean surrealist manifesto '1943: Surrealism and Us', to her and the journal's concluding essay 'The Great Camouflage', Césaire offers one of the most audacious views of surrealism's salvation not of but by its Caribbean practitioners. As sculptors of language, she invites writers to wield the power of poetry to forge a new identity through its use: 'We will purify the idiocies of colonialism in the welder's blue flame.

We will regain our metal worth, our cutting edge, our surprising communions. / Surrealism – the tightrope of our hope.'

Notes

1. Portions of this study were previously published in a 2013 essay, 'In Search of the Missing Mother: Suzanne Césaire, Martiniquaise', *Research in African Literatures* 41:1 (Spring 2013), pp. 36–54, and are reprinted with the permission of Indiana University Press.
2. Susanne Césaire, '1943: Le Surréalisme et nous', *Tropiques* VIII–IX (1943), p. 14. Unless otherwise noted, references to Suzanne Césaire's essays refer to the 1978 facsimile edition of *Tropiques* (Paris: Jean-Michel Place). All translations of the French in this chapter are the author's.
3. Césaire, '1943: Le Surréalisme et nous', p. 15.
4. *Ibid.*, p, 17.
5. *Ibid.*, p. 18.
6. For a full rundown of their accomplishments, see Patrice Louis, *A, B, Césaire: Aimé Césaire de A à Z* (Matoury, Guyane: Ibis Rouge, 2003), pp. 45–6.
7. Tracy Denean Sharpley-Whiting, *Negritude Women* (Minneapolis: University of Minnesota Press, 2002), p. 17.
8. See, for example, the collection of essays of the special edition of *Research in African Literatures* published in Spring 2010 (41:1).
9. Examples of the missing story of Suzanne Césaire's significance can be found in such works as Renée Larrier's *Francophone Women Writers of Africa and the Caribbean* (Gainesville: University Press of Florida, 2000), which devotes exactly one-quarter of a sentence to her, or in Clarisse Zimra's earlier 'W/Righting His/tory: Versions of Things Past in Contemporary Caribbean Women Writers', in Makoto Ueda (ed.), *Explorations: Essays in Comparative Literature* (Lanham: University Press of America, 1986), which makes but passing reference to the theorist, p. 231.
10. In fact, the direct quotation is more circumspect: 'Il est intéressant de constater que sa femme Suzanne se fait en quelque sorte le théoricien du groupe' ('It is interesting to note that his wife Suzanne became in some sense the group's theoretician'). Maryse Condé, *Cahier d'un retour au pays natal: Analyse critique* (Paris: Hatier, 1978), p. 12.
11. Michèle Praeger, for example, specifically thanks Maximin for 'attract[ing] his readers' attention to this beautiful and lucid little-known text'. Michèle Praeger, *The Imaginary Caribbean and the Caribbean Imaginary* (Lincoln: University of Nebraska Press, 2003), p. 180n5 (in reference to 'Le Grand Camouflage').
12. Ann Armstrong Scarboro, for example, offers therein her view of 'Le Grand Camouflage' as 'a blueprint for a literature of liberation', claiming that the writers Zobel, Schwarz-Bart, Glissant, and Maximin are in their works 'respond[ing] to Suzanne Césaire's call to action'. Ann Armstrong Scarboro, 'A Shift toward

13 Marie-Agnès Sourieau, 'Suzanne Césaire et *Tropiques*: De la poésie cannibale à une poétique créole', *The French Review* 68:1 (1994), p. 77.
14 Jennifer M. Wilks, *Race, Gender, & Comparative Black Modernism: Suzanne Lacascade, Marita Bonner, Suzanne Césaire, Dorothy West* (Baton Rouge: Louisana State University Press, 2008), p. 109.
15 Though this letter was signed by 'Aimé Césaire, Suzanne Césaire, Georges Gratiant, Aristide Maugée, René Ménil, Lucie Thésée', it directly responded to an appeal by Césaire for materials permitting the journal's publication. Gilles Bounoure presumes her to be the author, and Anny Dominique Curtius cites an interview with the Martinican historian Roland Suvélor, in which the latter noted that Suzanne Césaire 'embodied the critical and dissident vision of the journal'. Gilles Bounoure, 'Suzanne Césaire et la question de la civilisation', *ContreTemps* 6 (2010), p. 130; Anny Dominique Curtius, 'Cannibalizing Doudouisme, Conceptualizing The Morne: Suzanne Césaire's Caribbean Ecopoetics', *South Atlantic Quarterly* 115 (2016), p. 516.
16 See Katerina Gonzalez Seligmann's 'Poetic Productions of Cultural Combat in *Tropiques*', *South Atlantic Quarterly* 115:3 (2016), pp. 498–9, for a more in-depth discussion of the ways the readers needed to 'read between the lines' in the early editions of *Tropiques* to capture the metaphors missed by the censors.
17 Suzanne Césaire, 'Réponse de *Tropiques*', 12 May 1942; bold font in the original. Included in unnumbered pages of the 'Documents-Annexes' in facsimile edition of *Tropiques* (Paris: Jean-Michel Place, 1978).
18 Michel Leiris, *Journal de Michel Leiris (1922–1989)* (Paris: Gallimard, 1992), pp. 473–4.
19 Georgiana Colvile dates the play from 1955. Georgiana M.M. Colvile, *Scandaleusement d'elles: 34 Femmes surréalistes* (Paris: Jean-Michel Place, 1999), p. 74. Michel Leiris gives a date of 1952 (*ibid.*, p. 88). I follow this date since his text appears to be an eye-witness account and was published shortly thereafter. For a study of the source and contexts of this play, see Kara M. Rabbitt, 'History into Story: Suzanne Césaire, Lafcadio Hearn, and Representations of the 1848 Martinique Slave Revolts', *Anthurium: A Caribbean Studies Journal* 12:2, Article 3 (2015).
20 Annette Joseph-Gabriel, 'Beyond the Great Camouflage: Haiti in Suzanne Césaire's Politics and Poetics of Liberation', *Small Axe* 20:2 (2016), p. 1.
21 Wilks, *Race, Gender, & Comparative Black Modernism*, p. 108.
22 'Entretien avec Aimé Césaire par Jacqueline Leiner', *Tropiques* VI, pp. v–xxiv.
23 In *The Black Surrealists*, which primarily speaks to Aimé Césaire's complex relationship with surrealism but does address in a few pages Suzanne Césaire's contributions in *Tropiques*, Jean-Claude Michel notes that 'Surrealism was above all a stepping-stone for the black Francophone poets in their quest for a lost personality. This specific racial awareness differentiated more over the black surrealists from their European counterparts, and conferred a new dimension to the movement' (p. 175). He concludes that 'Surrealism exerted a deep influence on French-speaking black writers because it was suitable to their revolutionary

impulse, to their intense desire for a New World free from racism and exploitation, and to their dissension against a language which was not their native dialect'. Jean-Claude Michel, *The Black Surrealists* (New York: Peter Lang, 2000), p. 176.

24 Curtius offers an intriguing interpretation of this process in what she terms '*Tropiques*-poétique'. Anny Dominique Curtius, 'Suzanne Césaire et la *Tropiques*-poétiques du morne: de *Tropiques* aux patrimoines immatériels des nœuds de mémoire', *Revue de littérature comparée* 364 (October–December 2017), pp. 408–11.

25 See, for example, anthologies edited by Mary Ann Caws, *Manifesto: A Century of isms* (Lincoln: University of Nebraska Press, 2001), Penelope Rosemont, *Surrealist Women: An International Anthology* (Austin: University of Texas Press, 1998), or Georgiana Colvile, *Scandaleusement d'elles: 34 Femmes surréalistes* (Paris: Jean-Michel Place, 1999).

26 Images from and a review of this exhibit can be found in Hrag Vartanian, 'The Revolutionary Postcolonial Imagination of Surrealism', *Hyperallergic* (17 October 2014), https://hyperallergic.com/154167/the-revolutionary-postcolonial-imagination-of-surrealism/, accessed 25 September 2019.

27 Suzanne Césaire, 'Alain et l'esthétique', *Tropiques* II (1941), p. 59.

28 *Ibid.*, p. 61.

29 Suzanne Césaire, 'Léo Frobenius et le problème des civilisations', *Tropiques* I (1941), p. 36. In translating Césaire's use of 'Man' I have, where appropriate, adopted current acceptable avoidances of the gendered term in English, maintaining the neutral sense of humanity I interpret as her meaning. In fact, 'Homme' often reads in her pages as the most non-gendered form of humanity, even as she maintains the gender-ridden standards of academic discourse of her day. When, as below, she contrasts 'woman' to 'man' I have left the distinction. Though outside the scope of this chapter, it should be noted that Césaire's use of Fobenius's ethnological theories has been harshly criticised by some, including Romuald Fonkoua in his work on Edouard Glissant. Though Fonkoua does not take enough into account the ways in which Césaire's perceptions of cultural identities evolve dramatically through her essays in *Tropiques*, he does show the theoretical limitations of at least her early forays into the questions she raises regarding Martinican identity. Even Fonkoua, however, stresses that ultimately Césaire's work reveals, in his words, 'the Antillean's quasi-obsessive quest for an adequate expression of self' ('la préoccupation presque obsédante des Antillais en quête d'une expression adéquate du moi'), the vital component later writers sought from her interrogations. Romuald Fonkoua, *Essai sur une mesure du monde au XXe siècle: Edouard Glissant* (Paris: Honoré Champion, 2002), p. 137. For additional consideration of Césaire's use of European sources in her earlier essays see Kara M. Rabbitt, 'Suzanne Césaire and the Forging of a New Caribbean Literature', *The French Review* 79:3 (2006), pp. 538–48.

30 Léopold Sédar Senghor's evocative 'Femme noire' (1945), for example, while loving and laudatory, focuses on the place of the male poet in relation to the woman/land, rather than on her/its agency.

31 Suzanne Césaire, 'André Breton, poète', *Tropiques* III (1941), p. 32.

32 *Ibid.*, pp. 32–3.
33 This may explain why, in her own life, Suzanne Roussi Césaire appears to have turned away from any figurehead function. If her writing categorically refused exoticised visions of place, her biography likewise demonstrates an apparent refusal to embrace the roles and interpretations thrust upon her, including glowing literary portraits of her by such contemporaries as Breton or Leiris. Her move away from the public status owned by her husband and towards the more direct interaction of the classroom, activist politics, public theatre, are choices that may partially account for Césaire's subsequent erasure in contemporary histories.
34 Suzanne Césaire, 'Misère d'une poésie: John Antoine-Nau', *Tropiques* IV (1942), pp. 49–50. Césaire here clearly invokes Breton, who famously closes his novel *Nadja* with the words: 'La beauté sera CONVULSIVE ou ne sera pas'. André Breton, *Nadja* (1928), in *Œuvres complètes*, vol. 1, ed. Marguerite Bonnet with Philippe Bernier (Paris: Gallimard, 1992), p. 753.
35 Suzanne Césaire, 'Le Grand Camouflage', *Tropiques* XIII–XIV (1945), p. 273.
36 Suzanne Césaire, 'Malaise d'une civilisation', *Tropiques* V (1942), p. 45.
37 Suzanne Césaire, 'Léo Frobenius et le problème des civilisations', p. 36. I have opted to translate the impersonal 'on' and 'se' ('one' and 'oneself') of the original as 'we' and 'ourselves' in recognition of the rhetorical drive of the text and of the common replacement of the first person plural in French by the third person singular (as exemplified by the phrase 'On y va' for 'Let's go'). Césaire's phrase here recalls René Ménil's postulation in 'Généralités sur l'écrivain de couleur antillais' in the 1930s predecessor of *Tropiques*, *Légitime défense*: '[P]uisque l'Antillais de couleur exprime les sentiments d'un autre ... il convient donc au noir antillais de reconnaître d'abord ses passions propres et de n'exprimer que lui-même, de prendre, en sens inverse de l'utile, le chemin du rêve et de la poésie' ('Since the Caribbean writer of colour expresses the feelings of an other ... he should first recognise his own passions and express only himself. Moving away from usefulness, he should take the path of dreams and of poetry'). René Ménil, 'Généralités sur l'écrivain de couleur antillais', in *Légitime défense* (Nendeln, Liechtenstein: Kraus, 1970), p. 9.
38 Suzanne Césaire, 'Malaise d'une civilisation', *Tropiques* V (1942), pp. 48–9.
39 An example can be found in the first *Manifesto of Surrealism*, wherein Breton defines his terms thus: 'Surrealism is founded on the belief in the superior reality of certain forms of association heretofore neglected, in the omnipotence of the dream, and in the disinterested play of thought. It attempts to eradicate all other psychic mechanisms and to substitute itself for them in the resolution of life's principal problems'. André Breton, *Manifestes du surréalisme* (Paris: Gallimard, 1977), p. 37; translation mine.
40 Suzanne Césaire, 'Le Grand Camouflage', p. 273.
41 Sharpley-Whiting, *Negritude Women*, p. 97, p. 102.
42 Joseph-Gabriel, 'Beyond the Great Camouflage', p. 6.
43 *Ibid.*, p. 10.
44 *Ibid.*, p. 4.

45 Michael Richardson, ed., *Refusal of the Shadow: Surrealism and the Caribbean* (London: Verso, 1997), p. 14.
46 Joseph-Gabriel, 'Beyond the Great Camouflage', p. 8.
47 Gilles Bounoure, 'Suzanne Césaire et la question de la civilisation', *ContreTemps* 6 (2010), p. 127.
48 *Ibid.*, p. 128.
49 *Ibid.*, p. 129.
50 *Ibid.*, p. 130.
51 Michèle Praeger, *The Imaginary Caribbean and the Caribbean Imaginary* (Lincoln: University of Nebraska Press, 2003), p. 80.

6

Kay Sage alive in the world

Katharine Conley

Smiling figures resembling children stand as though perched like birds on a large tree branch in the frontispiece that Jean Dubuffet made for Kay Sage's first published book of poetry in French, *Demain, Monsieur Silber* ('Tomorrow, Mister Silber'; 1957). The children have knowing looks and an adult air to their noses. Except for their size, they could be old men. This image containing human beings initially contradicts the solitary portrait of Sage that emerges from her better-known paintings as well as other poems in this and her three other volumes of poetry in French and English published between 1957 and 1962: *The More I Wonder* (1957), *Faut dire c'qui est* ('Tell It Like It Is', 1959), and *Mordicus* ('Bite It', 'Through the Bit', or 'Obstinately', 1962).[1] Dubuffet's frontispiece also specifically illustrates the collection's title poem, 'Demain, Monsieur Silber', written in dialogue and featuring children. That she entitles her entire collection after this poem and that Dubuffet's single drawing for the volume illustrates it indicates its importance.[2] Also of importance is the connection between humans and birds signalled by Dubuffet's image.

Born Katherine Linn Sage near Albany, New York, in 1898, Kay Sage discovered surrealism in Paris after seeing surrealist paintings at the Galerie Charpentier in 1935, including *Je vous attends* ('I Am Waiting for You') by Yves Tanguy.[3] This discovery led her to separate from the Italian prince she had married in Rome in 1925 and move to Paris, where she met Tanguy in 1938.[4] They married and moved to the United States in 1940, where they lived first in Manhattan and then in two different houses in Woodbury, Connecticut, which became a centre for gatherings of surrealist friends during and after the Second World War. Sage's biographer, Judith D. Suther, explains her commitment to surrealism as a voluntary expression of 'loyalty' to the surrealists' 'artistic ideals', to which she remained true for the rest of her life.[5] Sage's poetry is notable for her command of slang, the colloquial French she shared with Tanguy, despite having learned formal French as a child in school and while travelling with nannies and her mother between the United States and Europe.[6] Her three volumes written in the intimate, personal French she shared with Tanguy were triggered by the shock of his sudden and unexpected death by cerebral haemorrhage on 15 January 1955. Sage herself died by suicide almost exactly eight years later, on 8 January 1963, from a shot through the heart. She was sixty-four years of age.

Many who know her paintings are surprised to learn that Sage was also a poet, the author of poems she released to the public through publication starting only in 1957, two years after Tanguy's death. She wrote poetry throughout her life, from childhood onwards. Her first 'published' poem in her high-school yearbook was about a bird, 'A Bird Set Free From His Cage' (1915–16).[7] She also published an illustrated volume of poems for children in Italian in 1937.[8] Of the two volumes published in 1957, the one in English, *The More I Wonder*, was a collection of poems written between 1925 and 1955.[9] The other volume from the same year, *Demain, Monsieur Silber*, was the first of three books written in French and published in France. All three books published in France were at least partially subsidised by her. Her correspondence and the subsidies for publication she provided demonstrate how urgently she wished this work to be known. In addition to these volumes, 250 other poems remain unpublished.[10]

At first look, Sage's poems appear deceptively simple. Often short, colloquial, and apparently inconsequential, they seem unlikely to sustain close reading. Initially, an admirer of the paintings might consider them primarily of biographical interest. Indeed, autobiography mixed with poetry, art, and politics constitutes the primary mode of surrealist expression, beginning with André Breton's *Nadja* (1928), initially published serially, starting in 1926. Sage's poems are of biographical interest to those curious about the individual who created such hermetic paintings of empty dreamscapes, mostly devoid of living beings.[11] Many of the poems express despair and loneliness. They appear to track her growing frailty, her deteriorating eyesight, and her sense of irredeemable loss in the face of Tanguy's absence. As she explained in a letter to a friend, with Tanguy she had experienced 'total and devastating love … It was simply an amalgamation of two beings into one blinding totality.'[12] Nonetheless, many of her poems reveal a wry, self-aware sense of humour and a purposeful sense of self, determined to mark her experience, despite her awareness of how unfashionable the expression of grief and feeling by a widow in her late fifties may have been at the time. The poems also reveal a person well-established in her world, interconnected with others, including individuals in her town, which could have been references to Woodbury, Connecticut, where she lived from 1941 until her death, or her husband's native Brittany, where their ashes were left on a beach to be washed out to sea by the incoming tide in July 1963.[13] A surprising number of Sage's poems show a deep, personal connection with animals, as well, who are completely absent from her paintings. In the four volumes she published in the last five years of her life, cats, squirrels, cows, an occasional horse, and, primarily, birds appear as slang references, companions, and avatars, sometimes, for herself.

My goal in this chapter is to show the deceptive power of Sage's poems, partly derived from wordplay linked to her bilingual mastery of both French and English. I focus particularly on those poems that refer to animals because they reveal a largely unknown aspect of Sage's identity as a human being and as an artist who connected more with others than her paintings devoid of living beings would suggest. Dubuffet, for example, was an important friend to Sage. He first met Sage and Tanguy through mutual friends, and then reconnected with her personally in Connecticut in 1961, after having been in correspondence with her concerning the illustrations he had agreed to contribute to her work, stating that her poems 'truly impressed' him 'for their striking elliptical brevity, their tacit violence, and above all their radically anti-intellectual, anti-intelligence position'.[14] His praise for Sage echoes his own artistic commitment to outsider art, as expressed in his essay 'Art Brut in Preference to the Cultural Arts', published in conjunction with his 1949 exhibition of *art brut* in Paris, in which he proclaimed unfettered admiration for art produced by those 'unscathed by artistic culture', who 'derive everything ... from their own depths'.[15] He saw in Sage's 'anti-intellectual, anti-intelligence position' a reflection of the pure expression of inner being he admired in the work of self-taught artists, while at the same time understanding perfectly well how Sage's sophistication mirrored his own. He found her work 'curiously in accord with' his own 'outlook and positions'.[16] Their shared search for modes of expression that were unfiltered, one could say uncontaminated, by their equally shared high culture was clearly a source of mutual appreciation. Sage's neighbour Friedl Richter reports her pleasure with her collaboration with Dubuffet: 'The only time I ever saw Kay Sage really happy in her later years – as happy as she had been when Yves Tanguy was alive – was when she was doing that book with Jean Dubuffet [*Mordicus*]. She behaved just like a little girl in her excitement for that book.'[17]

Dubuffet's emphasis on Sage's 'elliptical brevity' is apt, as is his admiration for her mastery of 'all the subtle shadings of the informal spoken idiom' of French.[18] Every word in a poem by Sage is chosen carefully in a way that has particular resonance for bilingual readers, for whom the crossover effect of some of her word choices, between French and English, initially inspires a double-take, and then lands with a moment of recognition. This crossover effect occurs repeatedly across the poems, revealing that the happy accident of the way Sage uses slang unlocks precise and intentional double meanings whereby one language, one meaning, overlaps with and haunts the other.[19] Her approach to poetry poses a complement to her approach to painting. As she told a *Time* magazine reporter for the 1950 profile of her, 'Serene Surrealist', with her paintings she strove for 'a sort of showing what's inside'.[20]

Sage's life spanned the early to mid-twentieth century and, whilst she lived through tremendous social change and two world wars, she died before the women's movement had made a widespread impact in the late 1960s and 1970s. She nonetheless embodied the goal sought by many women of the generation that followed hers to assert themselves as the equal of men in their professional and personal lives and to claim recognition for their individuality. In her most personal poems, she reveals despair born of loss and trauma stemming from childhood that is more visible to us today, especially considering how she was perceived by her contemporaries: as a refined, even 'patrician' person with very good manners.[21]

Surrealism attracted women partly because women were acknowledged within the group, starting with the titular character in Breton's *Nadja* and his recognition in writing of the work of women such as Valentine Hugo, Leonora Carrington, and Claude Cahun. Dorothea Tanning, in her first autobiography *Birthday*, described her experience of participating in the surrealist movement as 'a banquet' – 'You needn't make excuses for putting on a banquet and inviting one and all.'[22] Her analogy compares the group's interactions to a festive dinner party, a philosophical symposium, within which her perspective was welcome. Sage hosted many social occasions for the surrealists, including dinner parties, 'always [with] a most original menu and exquisitely prepared', according to a friend, both in Paris and the United States.[23] James Thrall Soby of the Museum of Modern Art recalls how in Paris in 1939 she had 'a lot of close, personal friends. And they used to congregate at her apartment.'[24] Before Tanguy's death in 1955, their house in Connecticut was 'a pivotal center' for surrealist gatherings.[25] Breton included Sage in his 1941 assessment of the movement and credits automatism for presiding over her 'tender, stripped-down vision'.[26] This description of her paintings also applies to her poems.

In the poems studied here, Sage embraces the surrealist tradition of identifying with animals, starting with Breton's self-identification with his astrological sign of Pisces in *Soluble Fish*, his first volume of automatic writing published in tandem with the first *Manifesto of Surrealism* in 1924. Max Ernst identified himself with Loplop, the Bird Superior, as an alter ego, and Leonora Carrington identified herself with the white horse that appears in her 1937–38 self-portrait, *Inn at the Dawn Horse*. Tanning, who considered Sage to be a friend, included her dog Kachina in both her painting and her writing.[27] Tanning's photomontage *The Artist as a Dog* (1967), published in *Birthday*, shows herself with her dog's face superimposed over her own. For those familiar with Sage's paintings, her turn towards animals comes as a surprise. She identifies explicitly with a bird in the final poem of her final volume of poetry, *Mordicus*. In other poems, however, animals serve more as intermediaries with the world, vehicles for acerbic social commentary, and also companions. Read together, these poems reveal a voice connected to nature, to the humour embedded in everyday life, a poet very much alive in the world.

Sage's paintings convey what Stephen Robeson Miller has characterised as an 'ominous stillness'.[28] Whitney Chadwick posits her 'clarity of form' as a deceptive means 'of obscuring content'.[29] She sees Sage's 'vision [as] striving for absoluteness of feeling'.[30] Gloria Feman Orenstein has a more political view of Sage's work as showing an 'annihilation of the powerful female principle from all forms of contemporary civilization' as a commentary on the experience of being an unrecognised woman artist in the mid-twentieth century.[31] The *Time* magazine profile, which constitutes a form of recognition, nonetheless identifies her work as a 'private cloudland'.[32] In an exhibition brochure, Soby perceives in her 'pavilions of dreaming' 'a setting which is neither park nor garden but somewhere, deep in memory, their like'.[33]

Sage dwells less on exterior space than on inner feeling in the poems. With humour, she expresses a preference for animals over people. There are eight references to birds in her poems (including ducks), three to cats, three to cows, two to squirrels, an incidental horse or donkey, and a dog, as in *mal de chien*, slang for having a hard time. The squirrels tend to be stand-ins for everybody or anybody; the cows are usually ironical stand-ins for humans, and the cats are friends. Only the birds come close to acting as avatars for herself, starting with the first poem she published at the age of seventeen, as well as her moods, feelings, and her sense of her own identity. Only birds come close to serving as the totemic animals recognisable in works by Breton, Ernst, Carrington, or Tanning.

It is through the intermediary of birds that Sage reveals details about her life that are more readily recognisable today as signs that she may have received unwanted sexual attention from family friends as a child, signs that might have gone unremarked at the time of the poems' publication. It is through birds that these poems help the contemporary reader situate Sage fully in her time, decades before the women's movement when frank discussions of ageing, sexual history, desire, identity, and feelings became acceptable for women. Despite sensitivity to the opinions of others that may be found in her journal and letters, Sage forges ahead in her insistence that these poems find their way into publication, that her voice be heard in France as well as the United States.

This connection to others in the animal world corrects the impression many familiar with Sage's paintings have of her as different from other surrealists because of her isolation within a movement founded on collective creativity, partnership, and collaboration, starting with the blurred identities of Breton and Philippe Soupault as co-authors of the first automatic text published in 1920, *The Magnetic Fields*.[34] Sage's poems involving animals vindicate her as a surrealist who was involved with others and was less remote than she may have seemed from her paintings. In the poems in French, in particular, there is often a companion to whom the poet speaks, there are townspeople, and, most of all, there are the animals themselves. The portrait of an artist living within a community emerges and makes sense of Sage's attraction to a movement grounded in collective activity and interpersonal exchange of ideas and ideals.

Both of the squirrel poems appear in *Demain, Monsieur Silber*. 'L'Autre côté' ('The Other Side'), written conversationally, as though telling a story to a confidant, posits a squirrel setting an example for why it is advisable to avoid exposing oneself to others, outside of one's inner circle. 'Un écureuil traverse la route / Pourquoi?' ('A squirrel crosses the road / Why?'), the poem begins.[35] As a result of crossing 'to the other side', the squirrel was bound to get hit by a car and reduced to a 'smudge'. Although Sage herself may have followed this advice in her everyday life as a widow, keeping to herself more often than not, in her professional life as a painter and poet she exposed her most private visions and feelings. Her paintings were well received in the 1950s, as the *Time* magazine profile confirms. Her books of poetry, however, earned almost no response; they received no reviews or public comment. In other words, she clearly did not follow the implicit advice in 'L'Autre côté' but regularly emerged from her private domain to cross over the imaginary road into the world. An earlier poem, 'L'Insomnie', refers to the 'inquiétudes des écureuils' (the anxieties of squirrels'), which kept her up at night when she couldn't sleep, along with concern for 'l'inutilité des feuilles, / aux cris des fleurs quand on les cueille' ('the uselessness of leaves, / the cries of flowers when they are picked'). Sleeplessness at night is 'drôlement vache, la nuit' ('pretty awful') she concludes in French slang, which plays on the opposites embedded in the literal meaning of the French phrase, 'drôlement vache' ('funnily awful') to convey the irony of a state of anxiety that is the opposite of funny.[36] Moreover, 'vache' as the slang for 'awful', doubles as the proper noun for 'cow'. And while it may be argued that this doubling could be coincidental, there is nothing in Sage's practice that points to her settling for coincidence except in the surrealist sense that chance can provide deeper understanding through surprise. In this case, that deeper understanding springs from her articulation of how it feels to be wakefully anxious in the night, in a way that connects the poem's speaker more fully with the animal world because what stimulates her worry springs from empathy with others, specifically, empathy for animals with whom she shares a sense of fellowship.

Actual cows appear in two poems about the life cycle that put humans in their place. One appears in her English-language book of poems, *The More I Wonder* (1957). These poems are less immediate and conversational, less spontaneous in their flow than those in her three French volumes. Despite its more expository style, 'Funeral in Milan' displays Sage's acerbic humour. She contrasts a formal funeral procession heading towards the 'tall Gothic church' in the first line with the sudden appearance of a 'butcher's cart' 'behind the procession' at the poem's conclusion, from which a boy descends wearing a blood-stained apron and dragging 'the stumpy remains of half-amputated legs, / the pale peeled body / of a cow'.[37] Humans and cows both die and are carried in carts after their death, these parallel images suggest, one species encased in coffins, the other not. The appearance of the butcher's assistant reminds the reader that, in life, humans feed on cows. Within this comical scene, the human life cycle is manifest in a way that could be summed up succinctly as: we are born, we eat, we die; we consume and are consumed by the natural world around us. Decades before animal studies prompted humanistic philosophers to consider animals as fellow creatures to animal-humans, Sage was humorously placing both animals and humans within the same broad category of sentient beings. What is human life worth, she appears to be asking, within the larger scheme of a human being's experience of the world?

Sage slyly reverses the assumption in 'Funeral in Milan' – that the purpose of cows is to feed humans – in her nursery-rhyme-like 'Vive la vache' ('Long Live the Cow'), from her final volume *Mordicus* (1962), illustrated by Dubuffet and hand-set and published by his friend Pierre-André Benoît, in which she once again ties together the life cycles of animals and humans. The title of this collection, *Mordicus*, an adverb meaning 'obstinately', plays on the French verb meaning 'to bite', 'mordre', and on the French nouns for death, 'mort', and horse bit, 'mors', as a reminder that animals and humans both bite and may be comparably harnessed, if not outright controlled, by human assumptions about appropriate behaviour.[38] Embedded in this poem and in the wordplay of the collection's title lies confirmation of Sage's view of sentient human life as less self-determined, less hierarchically superior to animals, than many humans tend to think. Her poems serve an equalising function, cutting humans who pride themselves on philosophical acuity and self-control down to size, reminding them of the levelling factor of mortality, of which humans like herself are acutely aware.

Dedicated 'with friendship and affection' to Dubuffet, no doubt in a nod to his own 'anti-intellectual, anti-intelligence position', Sage's poem gleefully contrasts man's ability to think, 'le mécanisme / de la pensée / de l'homme' ('the mechanism of man's thought'), which she scorns as 'bougement faux' ('damn faulty'), with the usefulness of his buried corpse to hungry cows.[39]

The pages facing the poem show a hominid figure by Dubuffet that has a head resembling a cow's. How different are the two species, really, Sage seems to ask? Whereas 'l'absurdité / de ses idées / déborde de son / chapeau' ('the absurdities of man's ideas overflow his hat'), his corpse 'l'est bon / sous terre / pour faire / pousser les coquelicots' ('is good / beneath the earth / for helping / poppies to grow').[40] Decomposed human corpses can fertilise fields in which poppies flower – delicacies for cows. 'Vive la vache / vive la vache et le crapaud' ('Long live the cow / long live the cow and the toad'), this biting indictment of human intelligence concludes. The coupling of 'cow' and 'toad' to a bilingual ear brings to mind the unflattering uses of these words in English as designations for women as 'cows', on the one hand, and for flattering fools, as in 'toady', on the other. Furthermore, the American slang word 'crap' for excrement or as an exclamation of frustration hovers tauntingly over/under the French 'crapaud', for a reader familiar with Sage's own love of slang.

Cats are the most familiar animals in Sage's poems (in French, an 'animal familier'). Visitors to her Connecticut house commented on the two Siamese cats who lived with her and Tanguy.[41] 'Accent grave' plays ironically on the English meanings of 'grave' as an adjective, a synonym for solemn, and as a noun, indicating a burial plot. Sage pokes fun at her own solitariness with a French colloquialism for how she laughs at herself, 'je ris aux anges' ('I roar with laughter'), in a way that intersects with the double entendre of the title, since to laugh with angels literally would mean to be already dead. She concludes the short poem with another colloquialism for talking to oneself – 'je parle aux chats' ('I talk to cats'), which was also, most likely, literally true in her personal life.

In another poem involving a cat, 'Mon ami', the cat she identifies as her friend responds with a purr to her confession that she has had too much to drink: '– j'suis saoul... j'déconne... [*sic*]' ('I'm drunk, I'm talking crap...').[42] The cat's purr strikes a double entendre as well, since, although ostensibly companionable for those who know cats, this cat's purr also expresses lack of interest in her human predicament: '– J'm'en fous, qu'y ronronne, -ça me rrrrregarrrrrde / ab-so-lu-ment / pas' ('I don't care, he purrrrs, / to me it means ab-so-lu-te-ly / nothing'), this cat responds. This 'nothing' at the poem's conclusion distinctly conveys the loneliness embedded in this exchange with her 'poor friend', as she addresses 'my cat'.[43] In 'Hommage aux chats' from *Faut dire c'qui est*, she openly admits to getting along better with cats than people. The poem expresses the poet's opinion that cats are more honest than humans since, unlike humans, 'ils ont des griffes, / ils ont des dents, / mais ils s'en servent qu'à la rigueur' ('they only use their teeth and claws in a pinch') whereas with people, it's hit or miss, 'tandis que chez les gens / c'est au p'tit bonheur'.[44] These poems, like 'L'Autre côté', in which the squirrel gets crushed for daring to leave home, reveal a person scarred by her interactions with others, who suffers when she goes out.

In real life, Sage was viewed by some as 'awkward' and she was not always served well by her formal title of princess from her first marriage.[45] She counted amongst her friends Tanguy's former housemate from Paris, Marcel Duhamel, who helped her publish her poems in France, and Dubuffet.[46] She maintained a lifelong friendship with Flora Whitney, whom she knew since boarding school, and the Sobys.[47] She was friends with Tanning, although not close, and friendly with her neighbours Friedl Richter and Régine Tessier Krieger, to whom she dedicated a copy of *Mordicus* and a collage from *Your Move*, her final exhibition of objects at the Catherine Viviano Gallery, and to whose husband David she left her easel and painting materials.[48] Another neighbour, who did not know her well, described her as 'elegant' yet perceived her to be 'a remote and private person' who had 'a quite unexpected flash of humor'.[49] The poems show how she also funnelled her wit into writing and her yen for interaction into observations of animals and mental dialogues with Tanguy as a way of keeping alive their lost intimacy.[50]

Birds were the most significant animals in Sage's poems, whose mention reveals the most about the poet's view of the self as an individual. In 'Menu', for example, the first poem to mention birds (and a horse), in her first volume, *Demain, Monsieur Silber*, the reference to 'un cheval, une alouette' ('a horse, a lark'), provides a superficially light-hearted answer to the weighty question of the riddle of life: namely, to live is to eat: 'Au jour le jour au plat du jour / un p'tit pâté chouette; / la vie c'est ça, c'est ça tout court, / un cheval, une alouette' ('From day to day, to the dish of the day / a nice little pâté; / life is this, it's simply this, / a horse, a lark').[51] For a bilingual person like Sage, this four-line poem turns on the double meaning of owl or 'chouette'. Used as an adjective, in slang it translates as 'nice', as in 'a nice little pâté'. In its noun form, however, 'chouette' translates as 'owl', a bird. Moreover, horsemeat was commonly consumed in France until recently. 'Alouette', the final word of the poem, refers to a bird served as a delicacy in pre-Second World War France.

'Lark' in English also refers to a bird and it, too, has a double meaning, in slang, as 'fun', as in 'a lark'. 'Chouette' and 'alouette', as a result, resolve into slang forms that turn on Sage's bilingual sensibility and sense of humour. These words cross between French and English and transform birds into 'nice' and 'fun', thus conflating the answers to the implicit questions buried in the poem, namely, 'what is life' with 'what is on the menu' of the day. The single reference to a donkey, in 'Amorce' ('Bait') from *Faut dire c'qui est*, is also linked to food, but this time as a play on words that resolves into Sage's opinion that it's best to mind one's own business. 'Amorce' compares men with donkeys in the sense that both need a 'carrot' to motivate them: 'L'homme, comme l'âne, / a besoin d'une carotte'. She concludes the poem by stating that she grows her own carrots and basically minds her own business: 'j'les cultive, moi, / mes propres carottes'.[52] The largest question a human being can pose is reduced to the mundane question of what to eat. With typical humour, Sage seems to be asking what difference it makes. As with 'Vive la vache', Sage displays a hearty appreciation of food as the essence of life and shows herself to be rooted in the everyday as a complement to the more guarded, abstract, and distant paintings of her 'cloudlands' and 'pavilions of dreaming', apparently devoid of natural life.

The second poem to refer to birds also turns on the double meanings embedded in slang. This untitled poem from *Demain, Monsieur Silber* implicitly contrasts city and country mice and opens in the first stanza with questions posed to a friend about 'des drôles d'oiseaux' ('strange birds'): 'Qu'est-que tu fais, là-bas à Paris? / Tu sors le soir? Y a des souris? / Des drôles d'oiseaux? Des merles? Des pies? / Des maquereaux et des poules farcies?' ('What are you up to in Paris? / Do you go out at night? Are there mice? / Strange birds? Blackbirds? Magpies? / Mackerels and stuffed hens?').[53] The noun for blackbird, 'merle', can translate into 'nasty customer' in slang whereas a 'pie' or magpie in English can serve as a reference to 'gossip' in either language. A 'mackerel' can be a fish, but 'maquereau' is also a familiar term for 'pimp'. Finally, a 'stuffed hen', as in 'poule farcie', could refer to dinner or a plump prostitute. In contrast, the poet's voice in the poem sounds like the narrative voice of a person who lives in the country, like Sage, whose only worry is if a bird will fall from its nest and have to be put back:

> Pour nous autres, c'est pas pareil;
> On s'abrutit, on a sommeil.
> Y a pas de drames, pas de délits
> à moins qu'un oiseau tombe du nid —
> Et encore, faut-y le dégotter...[54]

> (It's different for us;
> We vegetate, we're sleepy.
> There's no drama, there are no crimes and misdemeanours
> Unless a bird falls from its nest
> And we have to pick it up...)

Birds are the only creatures in this poem for whom the poet expresses tenderness, despite the suggestion of obligation in the phrase 'faut-y le dégotter...' ('we have to pick it up...'). Only the bird will be rescued, the poet seems to warn her young friend, as she warns her to beware of the untrustworthy nonsense of 'des gros matous et des fines chipies' (fat cats and clever bitches) when she goes out in Paris at night. The poem concludes: 'T'as de la chance d'être à Paris / Mais, c'est pas sûr que c'est pire ici' ('You're lucky to be in Paris, / But it's not at all certain that life is worse here [in the country]').[55]

Birds conclude the third poem of the first volume, 'Finis Coronat Opus' ('The Crowning Work'). 'Ma vie est à sa fin' ('My life is at its end'), the poem begins. There seems to be no point to anything as 'le bateau prend l'eau' ('the [poet's] boat is sinking'). The poem closes on a morose note: 'J'ai rien à faire sauf observer / les erreurs des oiseaux' ('I have nothing to do except observe / the errors of birds').[56] Superstition has it that a bird in the house presages death and, indeed, a wild bird flew into their house shortly before Tanguy developed a severe headache, was taken to the hospital by ambulance, and died. The painting Sage completed in the months after his death, *Bird in the Room* (1955), depicts this presage fulfilled. It shows a forbiddingly empty room, whose dark grey tones convey emptiness and absence.[57]

The poem 'Demain, Monsieur Silber' reveals its importance and link to Dubuffet's frontispiece when it becomes clear that it refers to sexual predators of the sort that have become familiar figures in news stories of the latter twentieth and the early twenty-first centuries but were mostly not recognised or held to account in the mid-twentieth century. It seems significant that Sage entitles the poem with the phrase used by the clever children in the poem whom she depicts as successfully fending off an unsavoury sexual predator. 'Demain, Monsieur Silber' ('Tomorrow, Mr Silber'), they repeat, suggesting that they intuitively know better than to accept his invitations to stay any length of time in his house.[58] She suggests that they instinctively recognise bribes when they hear his offer of treats and sweets and have the presence of mind to avoid this man's so-called friendship. The poem in essence unmasks the town paedophile and implicitly praises the children for their instinct to flee under the guise of polite refusal, avoiding unnecessary attention or reprobation.

The adult in the poem addresses the children colloquially as 'les p'tits enfants, les p'tits copains' ('little children, little friends') in his attempts to induce them to visit him. 'Demain, Monsieur Silber / demain', they reply ('Tomorrow, Mr Silber / we'll come tomorrow'). These knowing children likely provided the source for Dubuffet's cheerful yet disturbing image. They wisely rebuff Monsieur Silber's offerings of cakes and wine: 'J'ai des bonnes galettes / et j'ai même un peu de vin' ('I have tasty cakes / and I even have a little wine').[59] Their refrain echoes nursery rhymes or fairy tales in which children escape monsters disguised as caregivers, like the grandmother-wolf in 'Little Red Riding Hood'. That the poet adopts the title of this poem about children resisting a possible predator for the title of her first book invites readers to conclude, that she, like the children, had first-hand experience of the Messieurs Silbers of this world.

The fourth of Sage's bird poems, 'Souvenirs d'enfance' ('Memories of Childhood') echoes the title poem, 'Demain, Monsieur Silber', in its depiction of a man whom clever children should avoid.[60] This is the saddest of the poems to depict individuals who prey on children. She crosses two famous children's songs, 'Au clair de la lune' and 'Alouette', as a way of portraying how insidious a predator's technique can be – using lullabies familiar to children as comforting tunes with which their caretakers lull them to sleep. The poem opens with the first line of 'Au clair de la lune' but then identifies the familiar friend Pierrot from the song, 'mon ami Pierrot', as 'ton ami Pierrot', *your* friend, not the poet's. For readers familiar with Sage's post-humously published memoir, *China Eggs*, the 'you' immediately conjures Sage's irresponsible mother, whom she describes in the first paragraph as a parent for whom ten-year-old Sage felt responsible. She had to remove the bullets from a revolver, 'which she had put, loaded, on her dressing table', Sage remembers. She continues: 'I think I was ten the first time she made me give her a hypodermic of morphine.'[61] This parent, this 'you' to the child who thinks in terms of familiar lullabies, could have had friends like the one in this poem and not have noticed the inappropriate attention such 'friends' were paying to her daughter, who, by all accounts, was considered beautiful.

Following the introduction of the scenario in the familiar child's song 'Au clair de la lune', the plucked lark from 'Alouette', appears. 'Alouette' turns on the refrain, 'je te plumerai' ('I will pluck you'): 'Alouette, gentille alouette / Alouette, je te plumerai.' In Sage's poem, this 'alouette' is male and has already lost his feathers, like the emperor without his clothes from a different children's story. He is nothing but 'un sale oiseau' ('a dirty bird') to the poet, the kind of adult family friend who preys on children. With this retrospective view of an unpleasant memory, possibly a childhood trauma, Sage suggests spent sexuality with the bird's 'candle' going out, his 'chandelle est morte', and the conclusion in which she begs for the dirty bird to be thrown out – 'Fous-le à la porte/ pour l'amour de Dieu' – an appeal she would have been helpless to enforce as a child.[62]

The fifth poem to refer to birds, 'Corbeaux' ('Crows') from *Faut dire c'qui est*, similarly links a bird to a disposable animal.[63] This four-line poem begins with the poet's admission of having killed a crow. She expresses no regret over the act, stating in the final two lines, 'mais y en a des milliers / juste autour du coin' ('but there are thousands of them / just around the corner'). In the sixth poem to refer to birds, 'Répétition' from *Faut dire c'qui est*, Sage refers to birds as examples of the repetitions in everyday life that weary her. 'J'suis fatiguée de faire / sans arrêt / les mêmes choses' ('I am tired of doing / ceaselessly / the same things') the poem begins.[64] She is tired of wearing the same rose-scented perfume and of 'cet oiseau / qui, tous les jours, se pose / exactement là / sur la branche du chêne / criant de plus belle / à tour de bras / sa même rengaine' ('that bird / who, every day, lands / precisely there / on the oak branch / crying out loud / relentlessly / the same tune'). She is tired of the daily sunrise, the patter of pundits, tears, even laughter. The most sustained part of the poem is devoted to the bird. The French slang for 'relentlessly' that Sage uses to describe the bird's song, 'à tour de bras', visually evokes the image of arms or wings spinning, which conjures the mental image of a bird turning to land on a branch in a way that converges with the image of a human being, arms spinning, turning in circles. With this double image, poet and bird converge – the repeated behaviour of the creature that annoys her is simultaneously a projection of the frustration she feels within, and that metaphor of turning ultimately turns against herself.

In the seventh poem with a bird reference, 'Deux canards et moi' ('Two Ducks and Me'), from *Faut dire c'qui est*, the bird-fowl are more sympathetic.[65] They are companions. In real life, Sage even named one of her ducks after Lucy Lippard, who, at the start of her distinguished career, was hired by Pierre Matisse at the Museum of Modern Art to assist Sage with the catalogue raisonné of Tanguy's work Sage completed before her death. Lippard reports liking Sage 'very much' and thinking Sage 'was fond' of her, as well, 'for the brief period we knew each other. (She named a duck in her pond after me!)'.[66] Lippard perceived Sage to be 'a lonely, courageous woman with a cutting sense of humour'.[67] In the poem Sage compares herself to the ducks:

> ils montent sur une pierre,
> ils redescendent,
> ils nettoient,
> ils regardent dans le vide
> tout comme moi. [68]
>
> (they climb on a rock
> they climb back down
> they wash
> they look into the void
> just like me.)

The last strophe begins with the sentence: 'Le monde / l'est pas beaucoup plus grand / qu'un étang, / et d'une' ('The world / isn't much bigger / than a pond / and of one'), by which she suggests that her world is self-contained and isolated from others. She concludes the poem by directly addressing an unknown interlocutor, indicating she is not completely enclosed within her own world, at least not yet: 'Vous sauriez pas me dire, vous, / par hasard, / si dans la lune / y aurait pas un petit trou / pour moi et mes canards?' ('Could you tell me, you there / by chance', she asks: 'if in the moon / there might not be a small corner / for my ducks and me?'). This 'petit trou' or small hole colloquially suggests a small place on the moon, which plays on the literal sense of the colloquial expression for 'in one's own world' in French, 'dans la lune', which translates literally into 'in the moon'. She triangulates her interaction with an unnamed person using the ducks as intermediaries. She further links herself and the moon with the rhyme that occurs between the odd grammatical construction 'd'une', 'of one', with 'lune' or moon. She also interjects another odd, ungrammatical pronoun, 'le', to separate subject from verb – 'le monde / l'est pas beaucoup plus grand / qu'un étang' ('the world / it isn't much bigger/ than a pond').[69] Grammatically, this phrase should read 'le monde / n'est pas beaucoup plus grand / qu'un étang' (the world isn't much bigger than a pond). Her slang adjustment through the interposition of the unnecessary pronoun 'le' or 'it' grammatically distances the speaker from the world, rhetorically underscoring the disenchantment she feels and projects on to the ducks.

Sage's last bird poem was the final poem she published, situated at the conclusion of *Mordicus* and entitled 'Mon oiseau et moi' ('My bird and me'). In this mournful poem the bird not only belongs to her, he *is* her. The link between herself and the bird is no longer by intermediary as in 'Répétition', or comparison, as in 'Deux canards et moi', it is explicit. Because of her concluding statement, 'cet oiseau / c'est moi' ('this bird, / is myself'), the portrait she makes of the bird may be understood as a self-portrait:

> j'ai un oiseau
> qui vient se poser
> au bord de mon étang.
> cet oiseau est à moi,
> c'est évident.
> il est triste
> il est silencieux
> il est grand
> et haut sur pattes.
> il ne fait strictement rien.
> il ne bouge pas
> il est noir et mat
> il est en deuil.
> il observe le monde
> tranquillement
> du coin de l'œil.
> c'est pas un oiseau ordinaire
> non, c'est pas du tout ça...

n'en soufflez pas un mot
mais je crois,
en fin de compte,
que cet oiseau
c'est moi.[70]

(i have a bird
who alights
at the edge of my pond
this bird is mine,
clearly.
he is sad
he is silent
he is big
and tall on his feet.
he does absolutely nothing
he does not move
he is black and matte
he is in mourning.
he observes the world
calmly
out of the corner of his eye.
he's not an ordinary bird
no, that's not at all what I mean...
don't tell anyone
but I think,
ultimately,
that this bird
is myself.)

The poem reads like a harbinger of death. Sage first describes the bird as belonging to her but not herself. Rather it is a creature she observes with interest since he alights at the edge of her pond. She sympathises with him because he seems to be solitary and quiet, like herself. But as the poem progresses she describes the bird in increasingly human terms. The bird's stillness moves inward as she moves from describing him from the outside, as standing very still, to describing his inner emotions with her explanation that he is 'en deuil' ('in mourning'), like herself, as though the dull blackness of his feathers and stillness of his pose were the direct result of the loss and sadness he feels and she felt after Tanguy's death. The following line confirms this movement from the outer to the inner bird when she qualifies his gaze as calm observation, as though he were a human being like herself.

Once again playing on slang as it slides from English to French and back, Sage's indirect reference to the bird not being 'un oiseau ordinaire' ('no ordinary bird') refers back to herself, since in English 'birds' are women and Sage knew she was anything but ordinary. (She was also described as 'big', like the bird.)[71] She ends with the explicit identification of the bird with herself and she does so in the shape of a secret shared with an otherwise invisible and unnamed interlocutor. This poem is a monologue addressed to a sympathetic but possibly absent listener. It seems as though she saw herself disappearing into the bird at a time when she was thinking regularly about disappearance from the world, especially in the French sense of 'disparu' as a euphemism for death.

Sage's poems, which frequently express frustration with life, may be understood as expressing frustration with her deteriorating health and failing eyesight, when read biographically. She attempted suicide by overdose in April 1959 and was successful four years later, almost exactly eight years following Tanguy's loss.[72] She had slowly been losing her sight for seven years at that point. Although she suffered from 'an irregular heartbeat, chronic indigestion, and respiratory difficulties', she continued to drink and smoke and was prodigiously productive with her publication of four books of poems and completion of two major exhibitions at the Catherine Viviano Gallery in 1960, her well-reviewed 'full scale retrospective of 59 oil paintings from 1937 through 1958', and, in November 1961, a show of three-dimensional objects linked by an extended poem, *Your Move*, because collage and object-making became easier to produce with her failing eyesight.[73] She inscribed at least two copies of *Mordicus* before she died, one to Régine Tessier Krieger.[74] She never saw the catalogue of Tanguy's work that had been completed at the time of her death, although she knew that its publication was assured.[75]

One of the last notes Sage made in her journal before her suicide attempt in 1959 expresses her wish to join Tanguy in another life – 'The first painting by Yves that I saw, before I knew him, was called *I'm Waiting for You* – I've come. Now, he's waiting for me again – I'm on my way' (27 April 1959).[76] Her exhibitions and publications show how firmly Sage remained alive in the world until the end, despite her infirmities and grief, when she finally chose to take the definitive step to join the life companion she had once described as the 'only friend who understood everything'.[77] Increasingly deprived of sight, she wrote her suicide note in red pencil in French, 'L'extinction des lumières inutiles, Kay Sage Tanguy, jan. 1963' ('The extinction of useless lights'), paying final tribute to the importance of light and the impossibility of living without it.[78]

Notes

1 Sage published a volume of poetry in Italian, *Piove in giardino* ('It's raining in the garden') under her married name, K. di San Faustino, in Milan in 1937

(email with Stephen Robeson Miller, 5 July 2018). Unless otherwise noted, all the translations of poems from French are mine.
2. Sage also entitled a painting in 1949 *Tomorrow, Mr. Silber*. See Stephen Robeson Miller, *Kay Sage, Catalogue Raisonné* (Munich, London, New York: Mark Kelman and Hollis Taggart and Delmonico Books-Prestel Publishing, 2018), pp. 226–7.
3. Stephen Robeson Miller, email, 3 July 2018.
4. As the marriage was a 'noble' one, it required a papal annulment, which came through on 8 June 1939. Stephen Robeson Miller, *Kay Sage: The Biographical Chronology and Four Surrealist One-Act Plays* (New York: Gallery of Surrealism, 2011), p. 33.
5. Judith D. Suther, *A House of Her Own: Kay Sage, Solitary Surrealist* (Lincoln: University of Nebraska Press, 1997), p. 101.
6. In his definitive chronology of Sage's life and work, Stephen Robeson Miller cites an interview with Sage's childhood friend, Flora Payne Whitney: 'Katherine's French was very good from her European experiences and so was my French, so we stood out in a way and also fell in with each other.' Miller, *The Biographical Chronology*, p. 17.
7. *The Stephen Robeson Miller Research Papers about Kay Sage*, 1898–1983; microfilmed by the Archive of American Art, Smithsonian Institution, microfilm roll 2886, frame 12.
8. See note 1. Flora Whitney Miller, Sage's best friend at Foxcroft School in Middleburg, Virginia, notes that Sage 'wrote poems and was involved with her art even at Foxcroft'. Quoted in Miller, *The Biographical Chronology*, p. 17.
9. Suther argues persuasively that 'internal evidence suggests that the collection [of 73 undated poems] spans about thirty years, from ca. 1925 to 1955'. Suther, *A House of Her Own*, p. 247n9.
10. I thank Miller for this fact.
11. *The Passage* from 1956 constitutes a notable exception.
12. Letter to Heinz Henghes from 6 November 1959, quoted in Miller, *The Biographical Chronology*, p. 73.
13. From a letter by Pierre Matisse to James Thrall Soby on 7 July 1963, quoted in Miller, *The Biographical Chronology*, p. 78.
14. I thank Miller for clarification on the friendship between Sage and Dubuffet in an email from 11 July 2018. Also, see Miller, *The Biographical Chronology*, p. 76.
15. Jean Dubuffet, 'Art Brut in Preference to the Cultural Arts', trans. Paul Foss and Allen S. Weiss, in *Art Brut: Madness and Marginalia*, special issue of *Art & Text* 27 (December 1987–February 1988), p. 31.
16. Miller, *The Biographical Chronology*, p. 76.
17. My thanks to Miller (email correspondence 11 April 2018 and 24 July 2018). Friedl (Mrs Hans) Richter is inaccurately referred to as Frieda Richter in the *The Biographical Chronology*, p. 76, but corrected to Friedl by email.
18. Miller, *The Biographical Chronology*, p. 76.
19. See Katharine Conley, *Surrealist Ghostliness* (Lincoln: University of Nebraska Press, 2013).

20 'Serene Surrealist', *Time* 55:11 (13 March 1950), p. 49.
21 Roz Jacobs, quoted in Miller, *The Biographical Chronology*, p. 68.
22 Dorothea Tanning, *Birthday* (San Francisco: Lapis Press, 1986), p. 11.
23 Miriam Gabo, quoted in Miller, *The Biographical Chronology*, p. 52.
24 James Thrall Soby, quoted in Miller, *The Biographical Chronology*, p. 31.
25 Nicolas Calas, quoted in Miller, *The Biographical Chronology*, p. 51.
26 André Breton, 'Artistic Genesis and Perspective of Surrealism', in *Surrealism and Painting*, trans. Simon Watson Taylor (Boston: MFA Publications, 1972), p. 82.
27 Tanning told me she had been friends with Sage in a conversation at her apartment in New York on 17 March 2005. Miller lists Tanning and Ernst among the house guests to stay with Sage and Tanguy in the house they moved into in 1946, Town Farm. Miller, *The Biographical Chronology*, p. 48. There is also a record – and a photograph – of a trip Sage and Tanguy made to Sedona, Arizona, to visit Tanning and Ernst, in 1951, based on an interview from July 1979. *Ibid.*, pp 58–9.
28 Stephen Robeson Miller, 'The Surrealist Imagery of Kay Sage', *Art International* (September–October 1983), pp. 32–47.
29 Whitney Chadwick, *Women Artists and the Surrealist Movement* (London: Thames & Hudson, 1985), pp. 168–9.
30 Chadwick, *Women Artists*, p. 168. Chadwick cites Sage as she is quoted in 'Serene Surrealist', p. 49; see Chadwick, *Women Artists*, p. 239n27.
31 Gloria Feman Orenstein, 'Reclaiming the Great Mother: A Feminist Journey to Madness and Back in Search of a Goddess Heritage', *Symposium* 36:1 (1982), p. 55.
32 'Serene Surrealist', p. 49.
33 James Thrall Soby, *Kay Sage*, Exhibition brochure (Rome: Galleria dell-Obelisco, 1953), unpag., in Jonathan Stuhlman, 'Double Solitaire: Kay Sage's Influence on Yves Tanguy', in Nancy Wallach (ed.), *Double Solitaire, the Surreal Worlds of Kay Sage and Yves Tanguy* (Katonah, NY: Katonah Museum of Art, 2011), p. 45.
34 Most readers discovered which poet had written which section only from their handwriting with the publication of first facsimile edition in 1988.
35 Kay Sage, *Demain, Monsieur Silber* (Paris: Seghers, 1957), p. 43. Sage's lawyer John Monagan, in his 'Preface' to her posthumously published memoir, *China Eggs* (Charlotte and Seattle: Starbooks, 1996), provides a translation for 'L'autre côté' (p. vi).
36 Sage, *Demain, Monsieur Silber*, p. 30.
37 Kay Sage, *The More I Wonder* (New York: Bookman Associates, 1957), p. 49.
38 I thank Fabrice Flahutez for a helpful conversation about possible etymologies for *Mordicus*, June 2018.
39 Kay Sage, *Mordicus* (Alès: PAB [P.A. Benoît], 1962), unpag.
40 Sage, *Mordicus*, unpag.
41 See Miller, *The Biographical Chronology*, p. 51.
42 Sage, *Demain, Monsieur Silber*, p. 59; ellipsis in the original.
43 *Ibid.*, p. 59.

44 Kay Sage, *Faut dire c'qui est* (Paris: Debresse, 1959), p. 69.
45 Matthew Josephson, quoted in Miller, *The Biographical Chronology*, p. 44.
46 Suther reports that in the winter of 1961–62 Dubuffet requested that 'she send him some new poems, which he would combine with his drawings to make *Mordicus*', an offer that 'lifted Sage's spirits'. Suther, *A House of Her Own*, p. 220.
47 Miller, *The Biographical Chronology*, p. 17, pp. 77–8, and *The Stephen Robeson Miller Research Papers about Kay Sage* (microfilm reel numbers 2886–2888).
48 Suther, *A House of Her Own*, p. 205. In the 1990s, Régine Tessier (formerly Régine Tessier Krieger) was a Lecturer in French at Dartmouth College and came to speak to students in my first-year seminar on women artists and writers in the surrealist movement. She was my neighbour in Vermont in the 2000s. One of the collages in the catalogue for *Your Move* is dedicated to Régine and David Krieger. Kay Sage, *Your Move: Exhibition of Objects and Collages* (6–25 November 1961), unpag.
49 Audrey Skaling, quoted in Miller, *The Biographical Chronology*, p. 56.
50 Miller cites a letter he received from Roberto Matta in 1977 in which Matta explains how he 'always ended up for a cocktail at the Tanguys' when he visited the Calders in Connecticut. Stephen Robeson Miller, 'The Intersection of Art and Fate in the Lives of Kay Sage and Yves Tanguy', in Wallach (ed.), *Double Solitaire, the Surreal Worlds of Kay Sage and Yves Tanguy*, p. 22. In her first autobiography, *Birthday*, Tanning adopted a similar dialogue structure for her writing, in which she evoked her husband Max Ernst through the writing, which she began after his death in 1976.
51 Sage, *Demain, Monsieur Silber*, p. 16.
52 Sage, *Faut dire c'qui est*, p. 34.
53 Sage, *Demain, Monsieur Silber*, p. 26.
54 Ibid., pp. 26–7; ellipsis in the original.
55 Ibid., p. 27.
56 Ibid., p. 28.
57 Tessier Krieger explains: 'In 1955 she became very disturbed when a bird flew in the house in Woodbury, Connecticut, where she lived with her husband, Yves Tanguy, because, according to her superstition, a wild bird in the house meant a death in the family. A few days later, Yves was rushed to the Waterbury hospital, where he died shortly thereafter.' Régine Tessier Krieger and Thomas W. Leavitt Krieger (eds), *Kay Sage, 1898–1969*, Exhibition catalogue (Ithaca: Herbert F. Johnson Museum, 1977), unpag. Also in Suther, *A House of Her Own*, p. 167.
58 Sage, *Demain, Monsieur Silber*, p. 31.
59 Ibid., p. 31.
60 Ibid., p. 40.
61 Kay Sage, *China Eggs*, ed. Judith Suther (Charlotte and Seattle: Starbooks, 1996), p. 28.
62 Sage, *Demain, Monsieur Silber*, p. 40. Sage published two other poems with 'Souvenirs d'enfance' in the title, both in *Faut dire c'qui est* (1959). The first one,

'Souvenirs d'enfance II' (p. 42), begins with a reference to another children's song, 'Frère Jacques, / frère Jacques', yet it ends with an echo of the first 'Souvenirs d'enfance', 'OU ETES-VOUS', indicating that the rescue she may have hoped for was not forthcoming. The second one, 'Souvenirs d'enfance panaches' (p. 66), constitutes another echo of the first one, since it imagines she has been given a husband, but he turns out to be a street man on the Pont Neuf 'qui brosse, qui frotte' ('who brushes, who rubs'), presumably not in a good way.

63 Sage, *Faut dire c'qui est*, p. 21.
64 Ibid., p. 29.
65 Ibid., p. 40.
66 Lucy R. Lippard, quoted in Miller, *The Biographical Chronology*, p. 74.
67 Ibid., p. 74.
68 Sage, *Faut dire c'qui est*, p. 40.
69 Ibid., p. 40.
70 Sage, *Mordicus*, unpag.; ellipsis in the original.
71 Matthew Josephson wrote in a letter to Stephen Robeson Miller: 'My encounters with her paintings were much more favorable than with her person. You know she was a large woman of imposing figure and a strong heavy physiognomy, lined and interesting looking (rather than pretty).' *The Stephen Robeson Miller Research Papers about Kay Sage*, microfilm roll 2886, frame 374. David Krieger gives a similar assessment of Sage's physical presence at the end of her life: 'She was "5'8"" rather strongly built'; 'She was "fleshy" "not fat"'; 'The total impression was one of *power*'; 'She had "large hands"'. Ibid., frames 663–4.
72 Suther relates the details of this suicide attempt and cites from Sage's journal (206–7). As early as May 1955, four months after Tanguy's death, she wrote: 'I understand now why people say you have to be made to kill yourself. It's unbelievably hard to make the decision, if you're not (9 May 1955).' Tessier Krieger describes the day: 'On that cold morning of January 8, I called to inquire about her health and later learned from the state trooper who had answered the phone that she had shot herself'. Tessier Krieger and Leavitt Krieger (eds), *Kay Sage*, unpag.
73 Suther, *A House of Her Own*, pp. 113–14.
74 My thanks to Miller for this verification, based on information from the Galerie 1900–2000 run by Marcel Fleiss, email 11 July 2018.
75 Suther, *A House of Her Own*, p. 222.
76 Ibid., p. 207.
77 Suther cites a letter Sage wrote on 3 February 1955, shortly after Tanguy's sudden death: 'Yves was my only friend who understood everything.' Suther, *A House of Her Own*, pp. 161–2.
78 Miller, *Kay Sage, Catalogue Raisonné*, p. 25.

7

Outside-in: translating Unica Zürn

Patricia Allmer

As many critics have noted, and as their titles suggest, Unica Zürn's (1916–70) writings are deeply concerned with disease and disorders both mental and physical. Illnesses are suffered by their protagonists and by the figures populating their worlds, like the father at the beginning of 1969's *Dunkler Frühling* (*Dark Spring*), whose initial paternal authority dissolves as we quickly learn that 'er sieht krank aus' ('he looks ill'), 'dass er fast am Typhus gestorben wäre, in der Zeit, als sie so nach ihm geschrien hatte' ('because he had almost died from typhus during that time she cried so much for him').[1] In Zürn's texts disease signifies at physical, psychological, and ideological levels. Conventional orders of perception become disordered, bleeding disturbingly into each other; fantasies collapse into flights of disconcerting, corporeal reality, and corporeal reality becomes itself bizarrely disordered, as body-parts become synecdochal containers of misplaced organs, like the narrators' eyes at the start of *Das Haus der Krankheiten* (*The House of Illnesses*), which (her Doctor tells her) have 'hearts' which 'have been shot right through the chest' ('die beiden Herzen in Ihren Augen sind mitten durch die Brust geschossen').[2] Organs are in turn figured as elements of a symbolic domestic space – 'es handelt sich um den Raum der Herzen und um das Zimmer der Augen' ('the suite of the heart and the room of eyes') – evoking a feminised domestic space reminiscent of Salvador Dalí's 1935 portrait of Mae West.[3] Imaginary figures populate ostensibly real spaces and vice versa; and the very structures of grammar and syntax crumble and blur, effacing distinctions between narrator and protagonist, actant and auteur, and constantly calling into question the very notion of a telling and showing narrative self, or indeed of any self distinct from the other selves produced by and contained in its fevered imagination. Add to this the complex hieroglyphic interdependence of writing and image across Zürn's oeuvre, and we begin to see how her texts present a critical problem of definition that calls into question the relations between historically grounded biographical narratives and imaginary discursive formations, and the ways each intersects with the other to undermine and destabilise their respective effects.

Critics tend to search for fundamental autobiographical significances in Zürn's writings, and thus to bind them to the biographical narratives defined, in particular, by the author's own histories of mental illness (possibly triggered by experimentation with mescaline), her relations with Hans Bellmer and Henri Michaux and with surrealism, and her suicide in 1970. The writings themselves tirelessly evade such categorisations. Instead they invite allegorical, fantastic, or other generic comparisons that both reinforce and subtly subvert any simple correspondence with (auto-)biographical histories. Critics have conventionally used these features of her works to locate Zürn problematically within the broad category of 'outsider art', and to perform feminist and psychoanalytic readings, like that offered in Luce Irigaray's controversial short essay 'Une Lacune natale (pour Unica Zürn)' ('A Natal Lacuna', 1985). Irigaray attempts to read Zürn's work as an aesthetic protest, thereby reducing it to a simple tension between 'a question about art' and its production by a Laingian 'divided self', and that cliché of postwar existentialism, 'a search for identity'.[4] Caroline Rupprecht, in contrast, appeals to both biography and critical rumour when she writes of *Der Mann im Jasmin: Eindrücke aus einer Geisteskrankheit* (*The Man of Jasmine: Impressions of a Mental Illness*) (published in 1970, the year Zürn committed suicide) that 'its images are no longer fictitious but said to represent real hallucinations'.[5] Gary Indiana asserts that Zürn left 'an unnervingly precise record of her time on earth in her writings, drawings and paintings', but continues: 'The writings for which she is best known reflect an excruciating mental state, relieved solely by fantasies and hallucinations; reality, in her description, is unbearably harsh and punitive, a realm of grotesquerie.'[6] And Renée Riese Hubert, describing the writings as 'poems and autobiographical texts',[7] argues that, in *Das Haus der Krankheiten* (written over ten days' illness with jaundice fever across April and May 1958), 'fictionalization frequently surfaces: dreams, intermittent recollections, views from unknown perspectives, echoes from fairy tales and black magic'.[8]

This chapter will explore a series of questions around currently available English translations of Unica Zürn's German works. I would like in particular to consider how translators and scholars have tended to construct their versions of Zürn's texts in accordance with autobiographical narratives (a connection which also, of course, binds her work to her relations with male artists like Bellmer and Antonin Artaud). A recent review essay of *The Trumpets of Jericho*, on the website vice.com, exemplifies this tendency: 'The German author's most recently translated novella, "The Trumpets of Jericho", bears direct resemblance to her life', declares the headline.[9] Zürn's works become in these analyses reflections of her life, elaborated in autobiographical readings that tend to ignore or gloss over her more abstract, philosophical themes, and particularly her allusions to works from

German-language literature and their adaptations into different media. Translations, in turn, tend both to make lexical and syntactic choices that restrict interpretation of Zürn to these familiar critical narratives, and to suppress or omit her allusions to other works – her situating herself within traditions other than those that affirm the autobiographical imperative. This leads furthermore to particular constructions of Zürn that emphasise her apparent conformity to a critical convention of what we might call the autobiographically focused woman artist (a common construction in critical work on women artists and writers connected to surrealism), and correspondingly underplay the complexity of her work, and thus its significance beyond this conventional reading.

My starting hypothesis is that Zürn's works already express conscious and unconscious anxieties about (their own, but also the wider implications of) untranslatability – specifically the impossibility of translation's adequacy to the experiences represented in the works, which, I would argue, strip away the autobiographical surfaces of linguistic and pictorial representation to insist, instead, that writing-pictorialism necessarily fails to fulfil any adequate autobiographical function. This impossibility of translation manifests itself at a variety of levels, from the difficulty of word-to-word equivalence signalled in Zürn's anagrammatology of psycholinguistic trauma, to the ekphrastic failures of her pictorial plans and diagrams to correspond adequately to the psychic spaces and dramas she tries to represent. These failures are implicit in questions of supplementarity and circular reference that preoccupy Zürn – we can never be sure whether the pictures are meant to illustrate the writing, or whether the writing elaborates on the illustrations, and neither can be understood to represent the life, in any simple sense.

Zürn's texts, with their abrasive relations to questions of translatability, correspond in interesting ways to the theory of the Moroccan critic Abdelkebir Khatibi (1938–2009), who, Emily Apter writes, 'defines untranslatability as a layered forgetting associated with traumatic memory sequences, erotic fantasies, and intimations of mortality that are unexpectedly triggered by the bilingual unconscious'.[10] All these elements – traumatic memory, eroticism, mortality – are integral to Zürn's fictional universe, suggesting a central concern with the question of the untranslatable experience which is reified insistently in the linguistic and pictorial spaces Zürn constructs. The general critical version of Zürn has led to the introflexive aspect of her work being understood as a 'symptom' of a necessary link between 'creativity and pathology', as João Ribas puts it.[11] Ribas's own version of this understanding translates Zürn's schizophrenia into surrealist terms, reading it as a '"staged" or "performed" madness'.[12] Her obsession with anagrams (a crucial, highly constrained form of intra-oeuvre translation, 'the ground of our language, and not its rupture', as Foucault claimed of Artaud)[13] becomes an 'intense fixation on phenomena' which is 'paranoid' but, Ribas insists, 'must not be entirely pathological'.[14] And this has been, effectively, how Zürn's works have been interpreted – as written and pictorial translations of her experiences of mental illness.

This chapter focuses on three connected aspects of translations of these works – some of the lexical choices made in their rendering into English, and how their idiosyncratic transmediality and intertextuality have been incorporated into this rendering. The first concerns decisions about equivalence between the written and the pictorial. The second engages one kind of politics of translation – the choices, conscious or otherwise, of the translator to equate terms via selection, inclusion, and omission, from the variety of options available. The third concerns the non-German reader's access to intertextual borrowings or allusions – the preservation (or otherwise) of the relations of Zürn's works to intertextual matrices specific to German linguistic and literary fields. In practice these distinct aspects of translation overlap significantly, as will be shown.

The relationships between image and text within Zürn's oeuvre are complex – several of her writings exist in manuscript form, and many of them contain illustrations, often plans and maps of imaginary buildings and psychological spaces which are diagrammatically annotated to signify within the narrative frame. Much of Zürn's work incorporates images alongside, or within, or containing, writing in German, her mother-tongue. These works exist as a specific form of intra-oeuvre transmedial translation, and have generated in turn a variety of explanatory appendages, as they have been translated into other languages. Translations of these works need to make several decisions about whether and how to interpret and render these different elements, and how to relate the elements to each other in producing a readable text in the target language. These issues impinge in turn on the question of translatability itself, as several substantial elements of Zürn's works present the appearance of hieroglyphics and thus may effectively be, as Apter argues (of Eugene Jolas's science-fiction languages), '*beyond* translation, beyond Babel'.[15] The diagrammatic elements in particular require, for effective translation, some ingenuity and the suspension of simple correspondence, and questions of equivalence constantly impinge upon any simple rendering of them into another language. These questions relate also to the critically convenient but problematic reading of the works as fundamentally autobiographical – a process of analytical translation (very familiar in the analysis of work by women artists!) that transforms the idiosyncratic elements of a given work in relation to a specific context, that of narratives of the artist's life.

Pierre Joris, a translator-commentator on Zürn's works, makes some pertinent points here. He discusses the 'dilemma' posed to the translator by her 'extremely formal yet playful' works, which present problems of procedure – do we render the translation according to the formal procedure employed (for example, anagrammatisation), or to the 'semantic construct' that results from the procedure?[16] This dilemma hints at what Gayatri Spivak means when she writes that the translator should 'pray to be haunted by the project of the original'[17] – Joris suggests that, to be adequate, translations of Zürn's work need to compromise, to accommodate its 'hauntedness' at the levels of form and content. The question of 'haunting' is, of course, profoundly pertinent in relation to a postwar German-language writer whose works are themselves haunted by, and offer subtle allusions to and translations of, other literary works, and histories both personal and geopolitical – suggesting another kind of compromise, between the rendering of the individual work in another language, and sustaining fidelity to its 'original' socio-cultural context.

Zürn's *Das Haus der Krankheiten* provides a good illustration of these issues. A beautiful facsimile of Zürn's text was published in 1986 by Brinkman & Bose und Lilith of Berlin, so we can see the complexity of interconnections between handwritten text and image, and that in many cases the images clearly constitute maps of imaginary spaces. The image three pages into the facsimile offers a complex network of symbolic forms (Figure 7.1). Zürn's characteristic obsession with excessive specularity mutating into hapticity is signified by a large open eye in the centre, and a series of smaller eyes – evoking Dalí's dream-sequence sets for Alfred Hitchcock's 1945 film *Spellbound*. On the top right is what looks like a feather pattern, an organic plant-like form rising from bottom centre, a table of letters and hieroglyphic symbols that resemble musical notations to the right decorated with a starfish and an ass's head, the word 'Mittwoch' (which Zürn has spelt 'Mitwoch') bottom left, and so on – all with 'Das Haus der Krankheiten' written across and up the page from lower left.[18]

The interlinking of image, tabular form, and inscription is complex, organic, and multi-medial – text and image, pictorial and tabular, ink and pencil, organic and artificial (the transmission tower, bottom right) – all demand and resist simple decoding as visual precursor to the text that follows. Zürn's dense pictorial symbolism creates a sense of enmeshment within weblike, constantly developing forms that sprout sinister observing eyes and transmit betraying signals. Everything suggests a threateningly organic-technological entrapment that prepares us for the claustrophobic constriction of the dense, wavy, slightly irregularly spaced lines of cursive prose of the narrative and its circular syntax and restricted anagrammatic repetition. Malcolm Green's English translation for Atlas Books in 1993 renders these lines of cursive text as blocks of typeset prose, complying with what Chelsea Jennings calls 'a commonsense understanding of textuality

7.1 Unica Zürn, *Das Haus der Krankheiten*, n.p., from Unica Zürn, *Das Haus der Krankheiten*.

that allows linguistic code to be reinscribed and reprinted'.[19] Green's translation reproduces Zürn's illustrations, presenting them in sequence, before offering English versions of the (handwritten) German texts accompanying them, followed in a separate section (titled *Translation Of The Texts In The Pictures*) by transliterations of the writings incorporated into the texts themselves (Figure 7.2). What results is a translated text that presents its source text in three dismembered but sequentially logical sections. A further complexity is evident in Green's decision to provide 'plans of the illustrations where necessary', so that the translated illustration text can be mapped spatially on to the original illustration.[20] The illustration page described above is presented in Green's translation as following the title page, which it does in the original (which, however, actually has two title pages) – and as being followed by another illustration, 'The Plan of the House of Illnesses' (Figure 7.3).

This latter illustration actually occurs, in the German facsimile, eight pages from the end of the text. Zürn has written its title across the top – 'Plan

148 Patricia Allmer

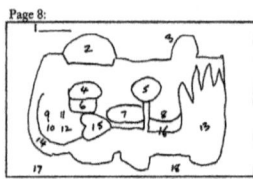

Translation Of The Texts In The Pictures
(A plan of the illustrations has been provided where necessary)

Page 6: Title page
THE HOUSE OF
from the end of April till the beginning of May 58
noted and drawn in Ermenonville/Oise
ILLNESSES
Stories and pictures from a case of jaundice
Manuscript No.2 à H.M. (Herman Melville)

Page 7:
The House of Illnesses; Wednesday;

Page 8:

1) Plan of the House of Illnesses; 2) Cabinet of the solar plexuses; 3) Dr. Mortimer's watch-tower; 4) The room of eyes; 5) The shooting range for the enemy; 6) The enemy's hiding places; 7) The hall of bellies; 8) The bosom room; 9) Smell; 10) Word; 11) Sound; 12) Image; 13) The chambers of hands; 14) The vaults of the head; 15) The suite of the hearts; 16) The enemy's secret path; 17) Wednesday; 18) Thursday

Page 10:
An ace shot

55

7.2 Unica Zürn, *The House of Illnesses*, trans. Malcolm Green, p. 55.

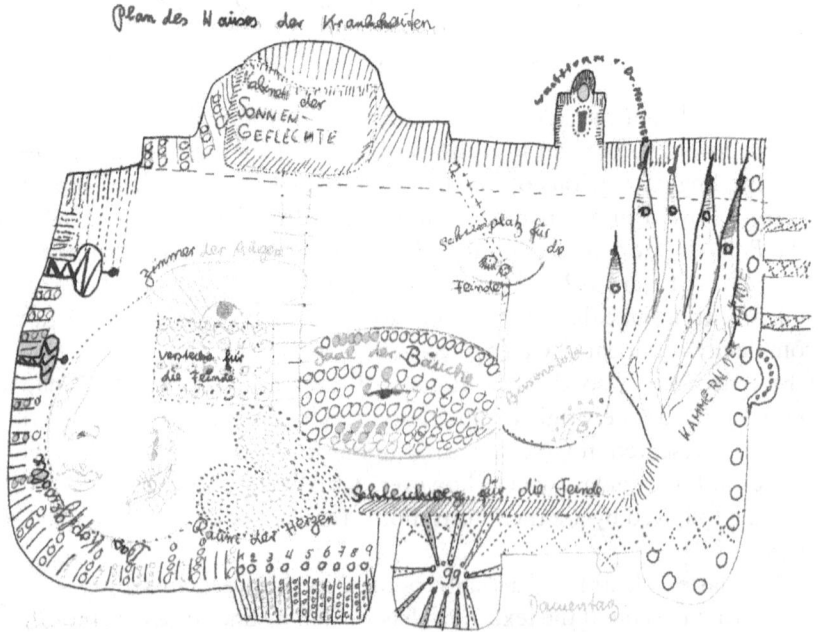

7.3 Unica Zürn, *Plan des Hauses der Krankheiten*, n.p., from Unica Zürn, *Das Haus der Krankheiten*.

des H auses der Krankheiten' with a visible gap isolating the H of 'Hauses', drawing attention to the presence of the word 'aus' in 'Haus', and thus foregrounding a crucial German pun throughout *Das Haus der Krankheiten*. The pun, and its emphasis here, is erased in Green's translation of it as 'Plan of the House of Illnesses'. Furthermore, moving this image to the front of the translation resituates it as a plan of a textual space to come, rather than a concluding, pictorial summary version of a text drawing to its conclusion. Zürn's placement of it near the end implies a plan of a textual space now mapped out by the experiences recorded in the preceding text. Green relocates the plan to offer the reader an opening guide to the text, while its original placement suggests the text as guide to produce the plan. Green's translation of *Das Haus der Krankheiten* is thus also a *transformation* of the text, a dismembering and reconstruction of its elements (similar, at a textual level, to Zürn's use of anagrams) that remains (in Spivak's word) 'haunted' by the deliberate formal dislocations of its original.

There's also the question of verbal translation, the issue of ambiguity within verbal correspondence across languages, and how this influences the reading of *Das Haus der Krankheiten*, in which confusions of domestic, bodily, and carceral space abound. Esra Plumer argues that these confusions result in 'a monadic space with no gaze outward', in which Zürn 'conspicuously expresses the state of illness as magical, visionary and pleasurable'.[21] The 'outward gaze' that Plumer misses is, however, an integral element of the cryptographic punning that Zürn employs in this text, and, indeed, a key element of the narrator's apperception – part, in effect, of the secret narrative of the text – literally, in German, an insistent gaze *aus*. It is embedded in the textual surface of puns and repetitions so that, as Derrida argues of literature itself, *Das Haus der Krankheiten* becomes a 'place of all these secrets without secrecy, of all these crypts without depth'.[22] *Das Haus der Krankheiten* deploys extensive cryptographic or cryptonomic overdetermination, demanding we read its (German) text with eyes alert to its punning.

The concept of 'outside' structures the entire text like an absent centre, returning insistently within the discursive frames Zürn deploys. The embedding of *aus* in the word *Haus* suggests the problematic confusion of inside and outside, containment and escape, that Zürn's text exploits – *Haus* and *aus* echo each other across the text as simultaneous and contradictory figures of institutional containment and potential escape to the 'outside'. Tracing forms of 'outside', like *aus* or *draussen*, through the text and hearing it always as an echo of *Haus*, we find the narrator's desire to escape constantly figured by perceptions of a world beyond the geographical and psychological confines of her illness – a world that exists intertextually, beyond the textual confines of Zürn's own writing. Towards the end of the first section, 'Mitwoch [sic] bis Freitag: Ein Meisterschuss', she tells us: 'hörte ich draussen die erste Nachtigall' ('I heard the first nightingale outside') – a reference generally evoking the importance of the nightingale in German folk mythology, for example in the 1843 Hans Christian Andersen tale translated into German as *Die chinesische Nachtigall*. Zürn's allusion spreads to include the themes of Anderson's tale, which centre on tensions between being inside and outside, and the boundaries between which are fragile yet also absolute: the emperor's castle is made of porcelain, but the narrative makes clear that he barely leaves, nor is much allowed (be it news or people) to penetrate the inside. One strand of the narrative evolves around the tension between the nightingale's desire to come and go as she feels and her being held against her will inside the castle.

Drawing on John Keats's Romantic poem 'Ode to a Nightingale' (1819), Andersen's tale is usually interpreted as a tribute to the Swedish opera singer Jenny Lind (1820–87), who nearly married Frédéric Chopin in 1849. Its extensive influence on modernist art includes Lotte Reiniger's silhouette-animation production in 1927, which Zürn may well have seen, and whose visual semiotics strikingly resembles that of Zürn's pictorial style in its evocation of ornamental silhouettes. Zürn would have been familiar with Reiniger's films as, during the Third Reich, she worked in Berlin for Universum Film AG, first as a shorthand typist and then writing commercials (from 1936 to 1942), which produced and distributed German films, including a number of Reiniger's (who also made several commercials), from 1917 until the end of the Second World War. This chain of allusions is deeply embedded in Zürn's prose – more is connoted by her German prose but lost in its English translation. Green translates 'hörte ich draussen die erste Nachtigall' as 'I heard a nightingale outside', dropping the word '*erste*', 'first'.[23] In doing so he erases the lexically specific and deliberate allusion to a late Romantic nature poem, *Erste Nachtigall*, by the German priest and librettist Franz Alfred Muth (1839–90).

Through this allusion, Zürn figures the outward gaze as auditory experience via an intertextual reference that momentarily takes us outside the confines of her narrative, into another formalised textual space, that of Muth's highly conventional poem, with its strict tetrameters, quatrains, and AABB rhyme-scheme, and into the textual space of romantic religiosity more broadly connoted by Muth's writings. The nightingale, a deeply symbolic bird in cultural traditions, conventionally connotes the fragile freedoms of music and poetry. The allusion in the context of *Das Haus der Krankheiten* suggests, perhaps, the possibility of aesthetic expression outside the experience of illness; it certainly embeds in Zürn's writing a reference to German poetic tradition, lost in the English translation, that subtly shifts the focus of her work, making it more overtly writerly than simply autobiographical-confessional.

Later in *Das Haus der Krankheiten*, the narrator asserts 'obwohl man weiss, dass ich ausserhalb dieses Hauses keine Zuflucht habe' ('it is well known that I have no refuge outside of this house').[24] *Zuflucht* (literally 'fleeing towards') is translated by Green as 'refuge', but also suggests its synonyms 'sanctuary' or 'asylum', indicating the ambiguities exploited by Zürn's German. Whatever 'refuge' might lie 'outside' may also be merely a repetition in another form of the institutional space, the 'asylum' that constitutes the 'house of illnesses', and thus effectively not be an 'outside' at all. Whatever is 'outside' is, implicitly, a translated version of the 'inside'. Zürn's text thus incorporates within its structure the possibilities and hazards of its own intra-linguistic translation. The puns on 'Haus' and 'aus' – an extended *aus-witz*, of course – echo each other in a binding, closed, circuit of linguistic parallelism, exemplifying what Emily Apter calls 'the gulfs of untranslatability at the heart of every language'[25] – quite apart from those between languages.

Zürn wrote *Dunkler Frühling (Dark Spring)* in 1969, a year before her suicide. The text echoes Frank Wedekind's *Frühlings Erwachen* (1890–91) in both title and its exploration of adolescent sexuality. Drawing on classic cinematic and literary adventure stories from her youth and childhood, Zürn translates into her narrative 'innocent' (and socially conventional) allusions to violence. Melodramatic lines from (for example) caption frames in Douglas Fairbanks's *The Black Pirate* (1926) such as 'It was the custom of THESE PIRATES to SUBDUE their *prey*, LOOT the *ship*, BIND their *captives* and BLOW THEM UP'[26] (typography original) are reworked through this process of intermedial translation into narratives of masochistic erotic acts. Through this, Zürn traces and magnifies the obscenity of the social in its normalisations of abusive acts. Her transformations in this text of the Oedipal narrative across genres generate ambiguities around questions of blame and guilt that have profound historical resonances. After a man sexually exposes himself to Elisa and her friends on their way home from school, one girlfriend confides to Elisa: 'Ich wollte, er wäre jetzt draussen. Ich würde hingehen und das Ding anfassen ... Nicht der Mörder, sondern das Opfer ist schuld'. Caroline Rupprecht translates this as: 'I wish he was out there now, I'd go and touch the thing. Not the killer but the victim must be blamed.'[27]

'Schuld' is here translated as 'blamed', shifting from adjective (guilty) to passive verb. The translation adds the modal imperative 'must be', not present in Zürn's German text, which further situates the action of 'blaming' outside the object to be blamed. But 'Schuld' is cognate with Old English *shild*, meaning debt, fault, or guilt. As Nietzsche reminds us in *Zur Genealogie der Moral* of 1887, it signifies 'debt', 'fault', 'blame', 'liability', as well as 'guilt' – 'Ich bin schuldig' means 'I am guilty'. Nietzsche notes that the moral concept ('guilt') derives from the material one ('debt'); 'One word evokes the other', wrote Günter Grass in Peeling the Onion (2007) – '*Schulden, Schuld* – Debts, Guilt'.[28] The difference between 'blame' (something imposed upon or assumed by someone) and 'guilt' (the moral feeling of responsibility for an event) is crucial in comprehending the specifically German philosophical and historical contexts of the ethical and political universe of Zürn's writings, as the efforts of the Nuremberg Trials (1945–49) to weigh guilt and place blame clearly demonstrate.

The narrative attributes this moral position on murderers and guilty victims to a historical event: 'Diesen Satz prägte ein bekannter Berliner Strafverteidiger in einem berühmten Sittlichkeits-Prozess der zwanziger Jahre' ('The phrase was coined by a well-known Berlin defense attorney as part of a famous sex-crime trial during the twenties').[29] But Zürn is also translating intertextually across genres here – her actual source is probably a 1920 novella by the Austrian-Bohemian writer Franz Werfel (1890–1945) titled *Nicht der Mörder, der Ermordete ist schuldig* (*Not the Murderer, but the Murdered, Is Guilty*; and here the 'schuldig' form emphasises the legal dimension of 'being guilty'). This is a narrative of patricidal guilt and father–son conflict, itself based (its author claimed) on 'a crime which was a nine-days-wonder in Vienna' and whose title comes, its central character points out (in a further translation), from 'an old Albanian proverb: "Not the murderer but the murdered is the guilty one."'[30] Born in Prague, Franz Werfel was a lifelong friend of Max Brod and Franz Kafka, and, in 1929, married Alma Mahler, after she divorced Walter Gropius; they escaped Nazi-occupied France via Spain and Portugal, fleeing to the USA in 1941. Werfel's novella *Nicht der Mörder* is a conservative analysis of the dangers of generational conflict – the central character Karl desires, but fails, to kill his father, the anarchist group he joins is no threat to society but a muddle of disorderly misfits, and he eventually renounces his childhood hatred of his father and devotes himself instead to family life and 'the freed, limitless earth, that she may absolve us of all our murders'.[31] Zürn's allusion to Werfel's novella, a product of early Weimar cultural anxiety with its overt themes of anarchist subversion of the patriarchal order, momentarily relocates her work in terms of 1920s German-language fiction, and particularly expressionist literature of the 1920s, rather than the outsider-art genres with which she is conventionally associated.

A final exemplary embedded knot of mythical and literary allusions that is elided in translation can be found early in *Die Trompeten von Jericho* (published in 1968, and translated into English in 2015 by Christina Svendsen). Zürn's narrative, a grim and darkly humorous meditation on the last stages of a pregnancy, uses the symbolism of the raven to signify a kind of voracious, brooding mortality: 'Meine Freunde sind die schwarzen Raben ... Ein Rabe ist durch das Fenster hineingeflogen und pickt in dem Teller Brocken von Fleisch' ('My friends are the black ravens ... A raven flew into the window and is picking at chunks of meat on the plate').[32] A few lines later she writes of her newborn son: 'Und seine zerfetzen, blutigen Reste, werde ich zeremoniell in sieben verschiedene Pakete verpacken und an meine letzten sieben Liebhaber verschicken' ('And I will ceremonially package his tattered, bloody remains in seven different packages and send them to my last seven lovers').[33]

The translation faithfully records the text's obsession with the *schauerlicher* ('gruesome') physicality of birth and its visceral proximity to death, but leaves implicit Zürn's references to the well-known Grimm fairy tale *The Seven Ravens*. Given Zürn's work for Universum Film AG, she would almost certainly have known of the cinematic adaptation of this tale made by the brothers Diehl in Gräfelfing who, from 1929 to 1970, ran the most important German puppet animation film studio in Germany. The first evening theatrical presentation of an animated puppet movie in Germany was of their 1937 film *Die sieben Raben*. Zürn's allusion again embeds her work into German folk and cinematic traditions in ways that translation, adhering to critical narratives of autobiographical reference, tends to elide.

These questions of translation permeate the ways Zürn's works have been received by English-speaking readers and critical audiences. Closer analysis of the choices made by translators, and of the ways Zürn's writings draw on literary and other traditions, enables us to resituate her in different, potentially enlightening contexts. These include the importance of references to works of German literature in her works, the influence on her texts and images of her experience of working in the German film industry, and the ways her linguistic creativity extends from anagrams and overt forms of play to more subtle kinds of ambiguity across written and pictorial media. These polysemic linguistic features, exploiting etymology and the links that 'haunt' German linguistic and literary traditions, generate alternative possible translations, and thus alternative potential readings of her works as unbound from the narratives of autobiographical reference and male influence that have dominated her critical reception so far.

Notes

1 Unica Zürn, *Dunkler Frühlung* (Gifkendorf: Merlin Verlag, 2008), p. 7; *Dark Spring*, trans. Caroline Rupprecht (1970. Cambridge: Exact Change, 2010), p. 38.

2 Unica Zürn, *Das Haus der Krankheiten* (Berlin: Brinkman & Bose & Lilith, 1986), p. 53; *The House of Illnesses*, trans. Malcolm Green (1958. London: Atlas Press, 1993), p. 9.
3 Zürn, *Das Haus der Krankheiten*, 61; *The House of Illnesses*, 33.
4 Luce Irigaray, 'A Natal Lacuna' (1985), trans. Margaret Whitford, *Women's Art Magazine* 58 (1994), pp. 12–13.
5 Caroline Rupprecht, 'The Violence of Merging: Unica Zürn's Writing (on) The Body', in *Subject to Delusions* (Evanston: Northwestern University Press, 2006), p. 132.
6 Gary Indiana, 'A Stone for Unica Zürn', *Art in America* (June–July 2009), p. 71.
7 Renée Riese Hubert, 'Unica Zürn and Hans Bellmer', *Sulfur* 29 (1991), p. 98.
8 *Ibid.*, p. 103.
9 Blake Butler, 'The Hallucinatory Terror of Unica Zürn', *Vice* (2015), www.vice.com/en_us/article/yvxkmk/the-hallucinatory-terror-of-unica-zrn, accessed 16 April 2018.
10 Emily Apter, *The Translation Zone – A New Comparative Literature* (Princeton: Princeton University Press, 2006), p. 105.
11 João Ribas, 'Unica Zürn – Oracles and Spectacles', in Mary Ann Caws and João Ribas, *Unica Zürn: Dark Spring* (New York: The Drawing Centre, 2009), pp. 11–12.
12 *Ibid.*, p. 22.
13 Cited in Gilles Deleuze and Félix Guttari, *Anti-Oedipus: Capitalism and Schizophrenia*, trans. Robert Hurley, Mark Seem, and Helen Lane (London: Athlone Press, 1985), p. 132.
14 Ribas, 'Unica Zürn – Oracles and Spectacles', p. 23.
15 Apter, *The Translation Zone*, p. 119.
16 Pierre Joris, 'A Note on Translating Unica Zürn's Anagrammatic Poems', *Sulfur* 29 (1991), p. 87.
17 Gayatri Chakravorty Spivak, 'Translating into English', in *An Aesthetic Education in the Era of Globalisation* (Cambridge, MA: Harvard University Press, 2012), p. 253.
18 Unica Zürn, *Das Haus der Krankheiten* (Berlin: Ullstein Verlag, 1986), n.p. Subsequent references are to the unpaginated facsimiles reproduced in this edition.
19 Chelsea Jennings, 'Susan Howe's Facsimile Aesthetic', *Contemporary Literature* 56:4 (2015), p. 664.
20 Zürn, *The House of Illnesses*, trans. Green, p. 55.
21 Esra Plumer, *Unica Zürn – Art, Writing, and Postwar Surrealism* (London: I.B. Tauris, 2016), pp. 168–9.
22 Jacques Derrida, 'Literature in Secret: An Impossible Filiation', in *The Gift of Death & Literature in Secret*, trans. David Wills (Chicago: University of Chicago Press, 1999), p. 157.
23 Zürn, *The House of Illnesses*, p. 15; *Das Haus der Krankheiten*, p. 55.
24 Zürn, *Das Haus der Krankheiten*, p. 58; *The House of Illnesses*, p. 25.
25 Apter, *The Translation Zone*, p. 126.

26 Caption frame, *The Black Pirate* (directed by Albert Parker, 1926).
27 Zürn, *Dunkler Frühling*, pp. 28–9; *Dark Spring*, p. 69.
28 Günter Grass, *Peeling the Onion*, trans. Michael Henry Heim (London: Harvill Secker, 2007), p. 28.
29 Zürn, *Dunkler Frühling*, p. 29; *Dark Spring*, p. 69.
30 Hans Wagener, *Understanding Franz Werfel* (Columbia: University of South Caolina Press, 1993), pp. 73–4.
31 *Ibid.*, p. 76.
32 Unica Zürn, *Die Trompeten von Jericho*, in *Das Weiss emit dem Roten Punkt: Texte und Zeichnungen*, ed. Inge Morgenroth (Frankfurt and Berlin: Ullstein Taschenbuch, 1988), pp. 118–19; *The Trumpets of Jericho*, trans. Christina Svendsen (Cambridge, MA: Wakefield Press, 2015), pp. 2–3.
33 Zürn, *Die Trompeten von Jericho*, p. 119; *The Trumpets of Jericho*, p. 3.

8

Ithell Colquhoun's experimental poetry: surrealism, occultism, and postwar poetry

Mark S. Morrisson

Ithell Colquhoun (1906–88) has primarily been known to scholars of surrealism for her paintings and her brief involvement in the London Surrealist Group in the late 1930s and early 1940s. To a largely different set of scholars – those researching Western esotericism and neo-paganism in Britain – she is known primarily for her involvement in several hermetic and ritual magic groups and in neo-pagan circles, and for her 1975 book *The Sword of Wisdom: MacGregor Mathers and 'The Golden Dawn'*.[1] Only relatively recently has the significant relationship between Colquhoun's surrealism and her occultism been explored seriously.[2] Much of that reassessment has focused on her paintings and her occult surrealist novella *Goose of Hermogenes* (1961). Yet Colquhoun wrote poetry from the 1930s into the final decade of her life, and some of it is significantly more accessible today than at any point since her death.[3]

Scholarly assessment of Colquhoun's poetry is long overdue. Indeed, the history of surrealist poetry in England has received relatively little scholarly attention – let alone English surrealist poetry after the 1930s. And surrealist poetry written by English women has received virtually none. In one of the only monographs on English surrealist poetry across the twentieth century, Rob Jackaman mentions only two female poets – Sylvia Plath, whom he discusses briefly, and Edith Rimmington, whose prose poem 'The Growth at the Break' he offers as evidence of 'a weakening of efficacy in Surrealism's transforming vision'.[4] In 1978, a decade before Ithell Colquhoun's death but well into the second decade of the British Poetry Revival, the complete absence of English women from Edward B. Germain's Penguin paperback *English and American Surrealist Poetry* (1978) suggests how little their work was known by the reading public.[5]

Though women were a minority among surrealist artists and writers both in the UK and internationally, those associated with the surrealist group in London in the 1930s and 1940s did indeed write poetry. David Gascoyne, perhaps the founding figure for English surrealist poetry, still receives more scholarly attention than any other English-language surrealist poet of the early period, but other poets are coming back into print. Of the twenty-one writers represented in Michel Remy's recent anthology, *On the Thirteenth Stroke of Midnight: Surrealist Poetry in Britain* (2013), almost a quarter are women associated with the early surrealist group: Emmy Bridgwater, Sheila Legge, Grace Pailthorpe, Edith Rimmington, and Ithell Colquhoun.

Though Colquhoun published only two volumes of poetry during her lifetime, her poetry appeared in literary magazines and other journals throughout her adult life. But what can the poetry and literary career of a minor surrealist poet show us that would merit more than a footnote in histories of surrealism and of the British Poetry Revival? Colquhoun's literary career reveals a continuous engagement with surrealist practices in her writing across a period that literary historians often characterise as a lacuna in experimental poetics at mid-century. More significantly, it shows us ways in which surrealism was disseminated into domains of British culture, maintaining a subversive agenda of transformation but one whose meanings, cultural affiliations, and resonances shifted as it moved at times away from the domains of the art world or literary culture and into the realms of neo-paganism, ecocriticism, and ecofeminism.

Accounts of surrealism, modernism, and post-Second World War British poetry

To understand the unusual path Colquhoun's poetry travelled after the war, we must first look at the common accounts against which it might be understood. A commonplace about British modernist poetry – and, in particular, British surrealism's trajectory in post-Second World War experimental poetics – is that it had essentially run its course well before the British Poetry Revival of the 1960s and 1970s. From this perspective, surrealism had its moment in England, but that moment was essentially over by the late 1940s. The heyday was perhaps marked by the 1936 *International Surrealist Exhibition* at the New Burlington Galleries in London, the coalescence of the London Surrealist Group, and the publication of the *London Bulletin* from 1938 to 1940 by E.L.T. Mesens.

Whilst much of the historiography of British surrealism focuses on its visual art and its manifestos, events, and exhibitions, the movement was also producing literature and exerting some influence on poetry. In the October 1933 issue of *New Verse*, David Gascoyne published what is likely the first intentionally surrealist poem by an English writer, 'And the Seventh Dream Is the Dream of Isis'. He then served as an early explicator of the French movement to English audiences in the 1930s, publishing his *Short Survey of Surrealism* in 1935. But the Second World War took its toll, with the *London Bulletin* ceasing publication in 1940, the London Surrealist Group disbanding in 1947, and the London Gallery itself finally closing in 1951. Gascoyne left for France. He did not return to the UK until the 1960s, and he resisted being called a 'surrealist poet' because he had 'had stopped writing automatically'.[6]

In the prevailing account, it was not just surrealism that waned in England in the 1940s and 1950s but the experimental linguistic and formal impulses of modernist poetry more generally. Noting the exhaustion of T.S. Eliot's poetry after the *Four Quartets* (1943), the isolation of David Jones, the fact that Basil Bunting's continuity with Ezra Pound was not noticeable until the publication of *Briggflatts* in 1966, and the time lag before the 1978 appearance of Hugh MacDiarmaid's most ambitious postwar writing, Drew Milne argues that

> modernism in Britain never made it out of the bunkers of the war. Writers who might have become the focus for new avant-garde groupings were scattered amid scarce resources, with few institutions on which to lean ... Amid Britain's retreat from its former imperial and colonial powers, and up against various anti-modernist entrenchments among little Englanders, the continuity and development of modernist poetry in English seemed exhausted or in exile.[7]

The 'little Englanders' of Milne's account, as in many others, are, of course, the Movement poets coming into prominence in the 1950s and 1960s. Account after account of the British Poetry Revival of the 1960s and 1970s positions the Movement as the symptom or cause of an unambitious orthodoxy and tepid little Englandism. But it is important to note that the Movement's grip on poetry was in part accomplished by a successful periodical strategy, as Peter Barry and Robert Hampson explain: 'where the modernist movement (and the British Poetry Revival later) forged its identity through "little magazines", "the Movement" concentrated on the weekly periodicals – the *Spectator,* the *Listener,* the *New Statesman* – which immediately gave access to a larger audience'.[8] But that particular postwar poetic orthodoxy was, by the mid-1960s, already under assault as the British Poetry Revival took root.

Energised in part by the influence of postwar American poetry, the British Poetry Revival saw affinities with modernist and avant-garde practice in the re-emergence of little magazines as a primary vehicle of experimental poetry, especially in London and Cambridge. Tim Longville's *Grosseteste Review* (1968–84), Robert Hampson, Ken Edwards, and Peter Barry's *Alembic* (1973–79), and later magazines, such as Stephen Pereira's *Angel Exhaust* and Ken Edwards's *Reality Studios* in the 1980s, serve as strong examples. Perhaps the most thrilling, if failed, insurrection was the brief move into the venerable Poetry Society of many of the young avant-garde poets, and the takeover by Eric Mottram in the early 1970s of the society's moribund journal, *Poetry Review*, initially founded as a journal of modernist poetry by Harold Monro in 1912. But in 1974, Charles Osborne of the Arts Council swept in to take control of the Poetry Society, and he turned off most Arts Council funding of little magazines, a trend that continued until the mid-1980s.[9] That, then, was the periodical environment facing efforts to revive surrealism in the 1970s and 1980s.

Nevertheless, surrealism was of interest to some of the poets of the British Poetry Revival – perhaps most notably Tom Raworth, one of only six British poets anthologised in Germain's Penguin collection. Yet there seems to have been little sense of a continuing surrealist literary practice in Britain after the Second World War. For the most part, surrealism was portrayed as a bold but incomplete project: something to revive or rediscover, often with inspirations from abroad. In 'Surrealist Poetry Today',[10] a talk given at the Poetry Society, the poet Lee Harwood finds that sense of unrealised potential in surrealism even in the 1930s.

Harwood is not unusual in understanding the 1970s as a moment for initiating a surrealist project that was largely discontinuous with earlier efforts:

> It's still 'early days' in our digestion of the essential surrealist lesson, its techniques, and approaches to the creative act, process. The awkwardness, and failure, of the earlier British Surrealists of the 1930s and 1940s, David Gascoyne and others, is only too obvious. If anything, our appreciation of surrealist approaches has come not direct from Paris, but from New York.[11]

But he notes that the 'essence of surrealism goes far beyond a French literary coterie or a reveling in the fantastical', and that its features can be found in contemporary British poetry.[12] For Harwood in 1974, surrealist poetry engages ideals of art as social action, collaborative authorship with other writers and with readers, and found objects like Duchamp's, as well as a set of techniques – 'collage, fragmentation, the cinematic technique of co-existing realities, and reality in speech and the silence/noise around it'.[13]

Colquhoun's persistent surrealism: before the British Poetry Revival

Despite the validity of narratives coming from key figures in the British Poetry Revival or those of later literary historians, surrealist poetry had not disappeared in post-Second World War Britain before the revival. Nor were the little magazines we most associate with the revival the only venues in which to find surrealism. Ithell Colquhoun's career as a poet offers a counter to the narratives I have presented above.

An early British participant in surrealism who had attended the 1936 *International Surrealist Exhibition* in London, Colquhoun left behind her fairly traditional Slade School training of the late 1920s to begin exhibiting as a surrealist under E.L.T. Mesens's auspices in 1939 and publishing prose poems in the *London Bulletin*. That connection with organised surrealist activity in London ended quickly, though. Colquhoun was purged from the group by Mesens in early 1940 for refusing to comply with his requirement that she should not publish or exhibit in non-surrealist venues or hold membership in secret societies.[14] Refusing to give up her already serious commitments to occultism, she soon made things worse for herself with Mesens, Jacques Brunius, and Roland Penrose by siding with Toni del Renzio (to whom she was briefly married) in a power struggle within British surrealism between Mesens and del Renzio.[15] Though she exhibited and published with a number of dissident surrealist groups in later years, her ties to the London group were never restored.

As I have argued elsewhere, this marginalisation and her brief fellow-travelling with the 1940s New Apocalypse group, as well as her temporary removal to Cornwall during the Blitz and her permanent move there in the late 1950s, have, until recently, kept Colquhoun a minor presence in the scholarship on British surrealism.[16] Yet the path Colquhoun followed for her writing after her ostracisation from the London Surrealist Group demonstrates more of a survival of surrealist and modernist poetry in post-Second World War Britain than the standard accounts acknowledge and also offers an example of a formally challenging female poet publishing outside the periodical circuits of the British Poetry Revival.

At the heart of Colquhoun's project as a writer and artist during this period was her exploration of the productive tensions between the individual consciousness and processes that could transcend it: essentially, between the personal and transpersonal. Though not all of Colquhoun's poetry was grounded in automatism – whether that of group composition, such as in the chain poem, using dream material as the basis of her writing, as in her novels; found objects; objective hazard; or hermetic procedures – it was, nevertheless, as important to her writing as it was to her painting. Rehearsing the history of arguments about automatism within British surrealism is beyond the scope of this chapter, but a central tension in the 1940s was identified by Nicolas Calas in a 1942 publication edited by Toni del Renzo: '[a] turning-point in the life of modern poetry has led up to a crisis within surrealism, which can be felt in both poetry and painting. It is what I have called the *crisis of automatism*.' While praising the power of automatism to release images from the unconscious, Calas argued that 'we have to take up an attitude which cannot be dictated solely by the laws of the unconscious.

Once he has discovered a new reality, the painter can no longer be content to work purely automatically.'[17] This concern that surrealism had ceased to make an impact because it had abandoned the idea of the artist's conscious manipulation of materials can be seen in the emergence of Henry Treece and J.F. Hendry's New Apocalypse movement, with which Colquhoun briefly flirted during the war (and we shall see this issue emerge again in the neo-surrealist journals of the 1970s and 1980s). Whilst Treece was included in Germain's surrealist poetry anthology years later, neither he nor the other Apocalyptic writers saw themselves as surrealists, and the main point of rupture was automatism. The New Apocalypse circle advocated conscious control by the writer of his or her materials. Though their common ground was not large in the early 1940s, both Colquhoun and Hendry were critiquing a vision of surrealism as emerging from the individual unconscious. Hendry argued that 'Apocalyptic work is "successful" surrealism, successful in the sense of being an expression not of the individual vision alone but of the social vision'.[18]

Colquhoun came to understand her surrealist practices in her painting, her writing, and her occultism as participating in a kind of transpersonalism.[19] As Richard Shillitoe has argued,

> One of the reasons why automatism became central to Colquhoun's work was because it provided her with methods that linked the surreal with the hermetic both philosophically and technically ... The act of painting ... becomes an act of divination that connects the artist to natural and spiritual forces. Automatic paintings reveal the interconnectedness of the inner and outer worlds, the subject and the object, the I and the Other.[20]

Indeed, while Colquhoun had earlier made few claims for automatism and her surrealist art that moved significantly beyond a psychological interpretation of automatic processes, with both the London Surrealist Group and the Apocalypse group behind her, she increasingly explored the possibility that the materials received through automatism were coming from other minds or occult forces beyond the individual human mind.[21]

Such claims to authorship by an entity or force outside the author can vex even the most impressed literary critics. For example, downplaying the seriousness of Yeats's occult investments, Richard Ellmann did his best to speak of Yeats's *A Vision* – a text composed from automatic writings undertaken by Yeats and his young bride, Georgie Hyde-Lees – as an imaginative key to the poet's symbolism. Similarly, in the 1970s, both James Merrill and his partner David Jackson insisted that the transcribed materials in Merrill's *The Changing Light at Sandover*, obtained through Ouija board sessions, had come from sources beyond themselves. Yet, as Devin Johnston notes,

Helen Vendler 'quickly passed over the poem's occultism by suggesting that the "machinery" of spirits can be "accepted as a mode of imagination"'.[22]

So, during the period in the 1940s when common accounts see modernism and surrealism foundering in England, Colquhoun would publish in literary periodicals invested in surrealism but from outside the circle. A selection of her poetry appeared, for instance, in Alex Comfort and John Bayliss's *New Road 1943*, in a controversial 'Surrealist Section' edited by del Renzio, which includes work by Leonora Carrington, Charles Henri Ford, Conroy Maddox, Robert Melville, and many others, as well as by André Breton, Max Ernst, André Masson, and Benjamin Péret. By the 1950s, however, Colquhoun's work was appearing in literary little magazines that had no direct relationship to the English surrealists of the 1930s at all – such as Antony Borrow's *The Glass* (1948–54), which he hand printed on his hundred-year-old press.

Periodicals such as *The Glass* demonstrate the persistence of surrealism even after its group activities had ended. Without invoking surrealism or any other avant-garde group of the pre-Second World War years, Borrow eschewed the rhetoric of the avant-garde by calling his opening editorial an 'apology' rather than a 'manifesto' and steered clear of the group dynamics of the prewar avant-garde entirely, but then went on to call for something quite subversive and not unlike a surrealist project of challenging a reality that is 'largely a matter of habit – the accretion of acquired beliefs'.[23] In a revolutionary mode reminiscent of the historical avant-garde, Borrow exclaimed that

> It is for us to remodel desire by remodelling the concept of the possible. Laws, natural or judicial, exist only so long as we choose to obey them. For the writer there lie open two methods of dislocating the ordinary. The first is the elimination of all inherited or conditioned supposition; the splitting of the accepted patterns of consciousness back into their component parts. Second is the rearrangement of the patterns themselves into a new landscape.[24]

Such a rearrangement 'results in fantasy', and he continues, it 'is our purpose to assert a belief in the impossible, the supernormal, those demons of the air that are both grotesque and marvellous'.[25]

The tour de force of this first issue of *The Glass* was Ithell Colquhoun's prose poem 'The Myth of Santa Warna', which signalled the powerful synthesis of Cornish regionalism, neo-paganism, mythology, landscape, and hermeticism that would mark Colquhoun's best work for the remainder of her life. The poem engages a Christian myth that may itself relate to an earlier Celtic one. The obscure early Christian Santa Warna drifts from Ireland in a coracle to what is now St Agnes in the Scilly Isles off Cornwall and sanctifies a natural well that may have had earlier Celtic significance:

'The skin-stretched basket is drawn to an inlet, moors itself in the yielding sand; cries of the toweellies awaken its passenger'.[26] In paintings from the period (for example, *Santa Warna's Wishing Well*, *Linked Islands I*, and *Linked Islands II*), Colquhoun had been exploring not just the Santa Warna myth but also the specific geography of the Scillies that gave it form: Santa Warna's well and the Neolithic standing stone, known as the Old Man of Gugh, that is separated from St Agnes at high tide and joined by a sandbar only at low tide. The crux of the poem lies in this linkage:

> Only a channel divides the west and east, the near and far; a bar bared at low-tide connects them for half the day. When the sea is flowing, the way over is dangerous – a few feet of water and one is swept away by the undertow to drown.
> Santa Warna takes root in the west, recognizing on the eastward semi-isle a presence older than her own. There on a ferny incline stands the Old Man of Gugh, his roots ringed by bell-heather.
> Voice of the clashing sea! Spray and whirlpools, currents and rocks, jaws, teeth and tendrils, a sucking tongue. Ramparts of hurtling water, bastions of wave! She is defended but imprisoned.[27]

Whilst the poem includes some narrative elements, describing Santa Warna's arrival, for instance, it also demonstrates the use of parataxis that would drive much of Colquhoun's most successful poetry and give it a surrealist or modernist feel even when it might otherwise seem fairly conventional. For example, the channel formed at high tide separating Santa Warna's well from the Old Man of Gugh is described in terms of seemingly antithetical natural forces – 'Spray and whirlpools, currents and rocks' – but also of physiological components of a jarringly personified sea and botanically and geologically rich island – 'jaws, teeth and tendrils, a sucking tongue'. Shillitoe perceptively interprets Colquhoun's project using the myth in the poem and its accompanying gouaches as an exploration of 'the alchemical fusion of sexual differences', as the phallic menhir side joins the female well, both joined and separated by the sea, an exploration of a gendered female creativity and power linked to nature and to the earth.[28] This fusion of antithetical elements thrives in the paratactical syntax.

The example of *The Glass* and the presence of Colquhoun's remarkable 'Myth of Santa Warna' in its inaugural issue show both that surrealism was still very much alive, even if not as group action, twenty years before it would see a resurgence in the British Poetry Revival, and that the animus against myth in the verse of the ascendant Movement poets in the 1950s did not preclude a strain of modernist poetry invested in myth from finding a home in the little magazines the Movement eschewed. In a remarkable issue that featured Colquhoun's 'Little Poems on the Theme of the Way' and an essay by Ross Nichols, the Cambridge academic who would, in 1964, go on to found the Order of Bards, Ovates, and Druids and write prolifically on Druidry, Borrow and his new co-editor Madge Hales published the answers to a questionnaire from the previous issue that had asked such questions about myth, symbols, and Jungian archetypes as 'Do you consider that such symbols originate in the human psyche, by which they are projected as myth; or that they arise elsewhere', 'Why are the dark gods considered obscene?' and 'Do you accept, on any level, the doctrine of alchemical correspondence: "as above, so below"?' The respondents to the survey all affirmed the importance of myth in society, and many were drawn to Freudian and Jungian interpretations. Borrow and Hales also threw in a question they must have known Colquhoun would want to answer: 'Do you consider surrealism to have failed, and if so, what were the elements in it that led to such failure?'[29] Asserting 'that the dark gods are considered obscene is the result of dualistic thinking', and proclaiming, 'I accept the aphorisms of the Smaragdine Tablet: "as above, so below" is one method of affirming a non-dualistic outlook – a Western summary of Advaitin philosophy', Colquhoun then took up the question about surrealism: 'Though surrealism as a movement is not suffering more than a temporary eclipse, one cannot deny that throughout its history it has been hindered by two main weaknesses.' Those were its failed and destructive efforts at political agitation: 'Surrealism once beyond its earliest Dada phase was essentially an introverted movement, and should have developed subjectively rather than assume the "false mask" of the social reformer.' As Colquhoun saw it, the other problem for a surrealist movement that 'has been engaged in "psychical research"' from its inception was that 'the movement's approach to esoteric study and experiment was too diffuse and sporadic to impress a naturally sceptical world ... However, much valuable work on subjects such as Objective Hazard, Unconscious Communication, Humour Noir and Alienation of Sensation has been done; and as an instance of "creative occultism" the Surrealist Tarot, devised by a group which met in the early days of the war is most remarkable.'[30] Other responses ranged from those of Ross Nichols, who dismissed surrealism as 'not the dim fructifying mystery of the cave womb, but the sinister subconscious of sophisticated modern man',[31] to the surrealist Simon Watson-Taylor, who averred that 'Surrealism has been the only concerted movement between the two world wars to attack seriously and fundamentally the problem of the tragic division of man's resources, to attempt to resolve the seemingly implacable antinomy between the "real" and the "imaginary"'.[32] Colquhoun saw no disjunction between surrealism and the neo-druidry of her friend Ross Nichols, and she would later associate herself with his Order of Bards, Ovates, and Druids.

But *The Glass* was not about to make an effort to resuscitate surrealism. Rather than publishing an explicitly surrealist periodical, Borrow drew together interests in myth, the occult, and poetry and positioned Colquhoun's work in a way that gestured forward to the spiritualities and syncretism we might now identify with the New Age in the 1960s, 1970s, and 1980s. Borrow, himself a Fortean, turned his new little magazine, the *London Broadsheet* (December 1954 to June 1955), increasingly to occult topics as well as poetry, and he published poetry and essays by Colquhoun on topics such as divination and Aleister Crowley's Thelemic Aeonics. And writing by Colquhoun was by then appearing widely in non-literary magazines. She frequently placed articles on occult topics in *Prediction* magazine while publishing fairly conventional poetry in the Catholic *Aylesford Review*, for instance. During this period, Colquhoun's follow-up to her deeply personal travel book about Ireland, *The Crying of the Wind* (1955), was the even more innovative travel book about her home county, *The Living Stones, Cornwall* (1957). That book blended surrealist-style drawings with writings about earth energies, stone circles, and Colquhoun's fascination with prehistoric religions and a kind of pan-celticism. Both books would now fit nicely into genres of creative non-fiction that did not exist when they were published.

Colquhoun's and Borrow's investments in myth in modern culture and in poetry ran counter to the rejection of modernism and its 'myth kitty' by some poets associated with the Movement in the 1950s. In perhaps the most quoted statement of this sensibility, Philip Larkin wrote in 1955: 'As a guiding principle I believe that every poem must be its own sole freshly created universe, and therefore have no belief in "tradition" or a common myth-kitty or casual allusions in poems to other poems or poets, which last I find unpleasantly like the talk of literary understrappers letting you see they know the right people.'[33] This from Larkin was a dig at the allusiveness and 'tradition' invoked by Eliot, Pound, and modernist poetry in general, but the rejection of the 'myth-kitty' was a shared gesture of many of the poets whom Robert Conquest would publish in his *New Lines* anthologies, in which he argued, 'If one had briefly to distinguish this poetry of the fifties from its predecessors, I believe the most important general point would be that it submits to no great systems of theoretical constructs nor agglomerations of unconscious commands'. Conquest thus called for an 'empirical' poetry 'free from both mystical and logical compulsions'[34] and from the modernist prosody and 'pastiche' that Conquest would later associate with an unwanted influence from American modernist poetry.[35]

Whilst the British Poetry Revival would reject the little Englandism and narrow conventionality of the Movement and find inspiration in pre-Second World War modernist and avant-garde practices, Colquhoun had never ceased mining those veins. Within a decade, as Matthew Sterenberg has compellingly documented, Frank Kermode and other literary critics would be extolling the role of myth in modern literature and culture. Kermode cautioned against Larkin's and Amis's rejection of mythology: 'The myth-kitty is inexhaustible; the ancient gods survive.'[36]

Domaining, periodical communities, and the circulation of surrealism

As the British Poetry Revival was achieving momentum in a number of new little magazines and institutions in the 1960s and 1970s, Colquhoun's poetry yet again followed a different path – one that would lead her to audiences far outside those for the new periodicals spawned by the revival. This trajectory shows that Colquhoun successfully disseminated her surrealism across a wider range of British culture than can be styled as the 'art world' within which surrealism, despite its revolutionary aspirations, had largely travelled before the war. But the meanings of her poetry changed as it travelled and its recognisability as surrealism became less relevant. As the anthropologist Marilyn Strathern explains,

> In cultural life, in those habits of thought about which for most of the time we are very much unaware, the ideas that reproduce themselves in our communications *never reproduce themselves exactly*. They are always found in environments or contexts that have their own properties or characteristics ... moreover, insofar as each is a domain, each imposes its own logic of 'natural' association. Natural association *means* that ideas are always enunciated in an environment of other ideas, in contexts already occupied by other thoughts and images. Finding a place for new thoughts becomes an act of displacement.[37]

One might consider, for instance, the domaining effect in the uses and understandings of automatic writing. In the mid-nineteenth-century spiritualist contexts, automatic writing (and séances in general) were understood to impart spiritual or personal information about lost personal connections, the afterlife, and mysterious or secret events. In the later nineteenth and early twentieth centuries, automatic writing was used in hermetic and theosophical circles as a form of revelation of hidden wisdom (much as Yeats and Georgie's Communicators were thought to be imparting to them). In 1920s and 1930s surrealism, automatism was valued for, as Breton put it, expressing 'the actual functioning of thought ... in the absence of any control exercised by reason, exempt from any aesthetic or moral concern'.[38] (By the 1970s and 1980s, as Michael Richardson lamented, the domain of consumer advertising had co-opted surrealist imagery, threatening the integrity of surrealism itself.)[39]

The subversive agenda of automatism in surrealism and its use in esoteric practices, both of which informed the production of much of Colquhoun's writing and paintings, changed forms as they travelled into different domains late in Colquhoun's life, and they took on different meanings that might be unrecognisable to those who worried that surrealism was being taken up by consumer culture. Take, for example, the publication history of Colquhoun's short poem 'Uath' (from the old Irish word for hawthorn). The short and formally conventional poem was one of the twenty-two poems Colquhoun wrote for her first published volume of poetry, *Grimoire of the Entangled Thicket* (1973) – a collection of surreal images and poems written for the Celtic tree alphabet that drew the Celtic lunar months into a synthesis with the Kabbala. (The number twenty-two was derived, as Colquhoun explained, from 'the thirteen months and the nine yearly festivals'.)[40] Linking the publication to Robert Graves's *The White Goddess*, Colquhoun claimed that 'one can find more than a hint of a Celtic *qabalah* in this close link between letters and numbers: Einigan, the First Man of *Barddas*, is equivalent to Adam Qadmon, and either Tree-Alphabet can aptly be placed on the "paths" of the Tree of Life diagram'. But she also explicitly tied the collection's poems and images to modern goddess paganism, to her surrealist automatism, and to the environmental movement in which she was becoming increasingly invested: '1972 was an important year to devotees of the Silver Crescent, for the thirteen months of the Calendar coincided exactly with their New Moons ... I made a number of drawings based on the automatic process known as decalcomania, which evoke the spirit of various trees.' Making the connection to environmental explicity, she continues: 'Some of these, and the poetic sequence, I offer to the White Goddess at a time when wasteful technology is threatening the plant-life (and with it all organic life) of earth and the waters.'[41]

UATH
(Hawthorn, May 13–June 10)

Hawthorn, bringer of cleansing vision
Dark bush that pushes away
All that mars chaos-creation
All that is not earth-play!

Dew rises at first warm sunset
Spring into summer, the Stag and the Hound
Not from above descending
But subtle smoke from the ground

> Ivory buds and opening petals
> On cold of a burnished sky –
> Thorns against gold that changes to twilight
> Of lapis lazuli.

'Uath' was intended for publication in *Grimoire of the Entangled Thicket* but could not be included due to page constraints. Had the poem appeared in that collection, 'Uath' would have been positioned at the intersection of the art world of surrealism (Colquhoun exhaustively listed her recent gallery exhibitions in the volume), neo-paganism in Cornwall, and esotericism. In the context of the semi-abstract and surreal images and the modernist syncretism of the work, the insertion of the natural world celebrated in the poem into esoteric systems of meaning via the Kabbalistic resonances, the hint at a mythology of the seasonal change, and even the hermetic implications of the colours and gemstone all stand out.

Whilst Colquhoun placed her poetry in neo-surrealist little magazines, such as John Lyle's *TRANSFORMAcTION* (1967–79) – which promoted itself as 'founded by Jacques Brunius, E.L.T. Mesens, and John Lyle in

8.1 Ithell Colquhoun, cover of *Grimoire of the Entangled Thicket*, 1973.

1967 to provide a forum for the Surrealist movement in Britain' – she was also publishing in journals of British neo-paganism. 'Uath' was published in three different magazines: *Ore* (1981), *New Celtic Review* (1982), and *Wood and Water* (1983).[42] Whilst Eric Ratcliffe's long-running *Ore* (1954–95) engaged frequently with neo-druidry and other elements of New Age Britain, it was, at its heart, a poetry little magazine. Stripped of its initial surrealist and modernist contexts in the *Grimoire* project, the subversive and epistemological aspects of 'Uath' did not travel with it into its publication in *Ore*. But when it appeared next in Colin Hazelwand's *New Celtic Review*, the beautifully hand-painted little magazine of the druidic Golden Section Order, its Celtic spiritual connections would have again returned to the poem, but without any overt connection to its surrealist or modernist roots.

The publication of 'Uath' in the goddess religion ecofeminist periodical *Wood and Water* exposes a different set of meanings for the poem. Here, 'Uath' was published with an image, but not one of Colquhoun's; rather, the image was a more visually conventional decoration (Figure 8.2). Nevertheless, in *Wood and Water*, Colquhoun's authorship line at the bottom of the poem also lists her as a resident of Penzance, and a brief note mentions the availability by mail order of 'A poetic sequence, based on the Beth-Luis-Nion together with Ithell's own illustrations evoking the spirits of various trees'. The assumptions that readers would know what the Beth-Luis-Nion was, that they would be drawn to evocations of the spirits of trees, and that they could be on a first-name basis with 'Ithell', even if many would not have known her personally, signify a very different periodical community, to use Lucy Delap's term.[43]

The copious list of exchange advertisements from almost two dozen magazines at the back of the *Wood and Water* issue illuminates a network of magazines devoted to neo-pagan causes (including the 'druidic revivalism' of the *New Celtic Review*), earth mysteries, geomancy, and witchcraft around Britain and in California and Oregon, as well as radical feminist journals and radical environmentalist or pagan collaborations, such as *P.A.N.*, 'Pagans Against Nukes'.[44] A poem whose genesis in Colquhoun's occult surrealism no longer needed to be asserted (nothing of surrealism was mentioned in the note advertising the *Grimoire*) could transfer to the entirely different domain of these later periodicals and be taken up as contributions to group spiritual dynamics that had no perceived connection at all to surrealism or the avant-garde. Nevertheless, the poem's appearance in *Wood and Water* should not be read as a loss of subversive meaning in this new domain; rather, its subversiveness here was no longer based in surrealism but instead in the radical political and spiritual agendas of eco-paganism in Cornwall. The spiritual life of the trees spoke to the environmentalist imperatives of

8.2 From *Wood and Water*, vol. 2, no. 7, 1983.

goddess religion in Cornwall, and those imperatives led Colquhoun into contact with environmental and anti-nuclear activists.

My point here is that this trajectory of Colquhoun's literary output across several different types of publications shows not that she abandoned surrealist automatism to participate in the broader culture of New Age spiritual publications but rather that her career as a surrealist poet, though making no discernible impact on the history of the British Poetry Revival, demonstrates ways in which surrealism's impact had spread into arenas of culture that the London group could scarcely have imagined in 1940, as Mesens expelled Colquhoun from the circle. In Colquhoun's work a pagan-informed ecocritical consciousness about location and history came into contact with a surrealist practice that sought the depths as well as esoteric resources to generate new knowledge, rather than a narrow psychological self-knowledge. Her poetry did not seem out of place either in *Melmoth* or in *Wood and Water* and demonstrates that experimental writing existed comfortably far outside the circuits of British literary culture.

Osmazone: bringing hermeticism back to readers of surrealist poetry

All of these strands of Colquhoun's thought and writing came briefly together late in her life in her second published volume of poetry. Her crowning achievement as a poet was the publication by Tony Pusey, an expatriate British surrealist by then living in Sweden and part of the Dunganon group, of a book of Colquhoun's poetry entitled *Osmazone*. Whilst there was certainly something of a revival of surrealist efforts in Britain in the 1970s and 1980s, Tony Pusey's letters to Colquhoun in her Tate archive reveal how precarious the efforts were.[45] These letters illustrate both Pusey's concern that much of the poetry had no connection with surrealism[46] and his efforts to make connections with some of the 1940s London group (such as Edith Rimmington, Emmy Bridgwater, and Eileen Agar).[47] He floated the idea of Colquhoun's publishing a volume of her poetry with his group for around £130 for two hundred copies.[48] Further correspondence showed that while the audience for surrealist revival efforts might be small, there was clearly an apparatus emerging through which to distribute the volume that became *Osmazone* and a periodical network to publicise the volume.[49] Despite Pusey's sober warnings of the small amount of money sales would likely bring in, Colquhoun went ahead with the plan. She clearly viewed the volume as a much bigger, chronologically arranged collection than Pusey was able to publish, but with his design work and typing, and Colquhoun's £150, the volume was brought to completion. Years in the making and significantly scaled back from Colquhoun's initial conception of it, the volume featured prose poems dating as far back as a 1940s poem about menstruation, a surrealist chain poem, a poem about the anus, a number of prose poems, and poems composed from found objects, such as 'Confidential Service', comprising names of condom brands. Shillitoe notes that, '[i]f there is a theme that recurs throughout the collection, it is that of the personal made public: the celebration of private parts and bodily functions'.[50]

Colquhoun's synthesis of surrealism, modernism, and hermeticism reveals itself most strikingly and originally in her most distinctive contributions to twentieth-century poetry – poems that involve surrealist automatisms in intricate oneiric collages or the incantatory offerings in *Osmazone*, such as 'Ode to the Philosophical Mercury' and 'Hypnagogic Interior'. As Shillitoe notes, the 'Ode'

> is the final poem from a series of eleven that together make up the *Anthology of Incantations* ... Philosophical mercury is a standard name in alchemy for the female principle. Many of the names of alchemical substances listed in the

sequence are taken from Dom Antoine-Joseph Pernety's Treatise on the Great Art, sometimes quoted verbatim. Other names are from the writings of Eugenius Philalethes.[51]

'Ode to the Philosophical Mercury' recalls the wordplay and alchemical imagery in Ezra Pound's 1912 poem 'The Alchemist, Chant for the Transmutation of Metals'. Pound's poem reads, in part,

> Saîl of Claustra, Aelis, Azalais,
> Raimona, Tibors, Berangèrë,
> 'Neath the dark gleam of the sky;
> Under the night, the peacock-throated,
> Bring the saffron-coloured shell,
> Bring the red gold of the maple,
> Bring the light of the birch tree in autumn
> Mirals, Cembelins, Audiarda,
>   Remember this fire.[52]

Pound achieves an incantatory power using anaphora and weaving alchemical imagery and allusions into this stanza (such as the 'peacock' – an allusion to the 'cauda pavonis' phase of the alchemical operation), and he uses the women's names as he understood medieval alchemists to use them in charms and equations. But Pound roots his poem in the classical and the courtly past of troubadours back to which so many of his poems reach.[53] In short, the alchemy is a vehicle for a larger project of cultural renewal.

Colquhoun's 'Ode', by contrast, demonstrates a very different project. Her collage of alchemical names and substances invokes alchemy as an esoteric practice of value in the present. Among the poem's many evocations of philosophical mercury:

> Mercury is white wind
> mercury is aqua-coelestis fire
> mercury is phlegma ros water of clouds
> vessel of nature vessel of Hermes
> green vessel of Saturn.[54]

With its repetitive invocation of Mercury and of the 'vessel' and its play of alliteration, Colquhoun's incantation creates a rich and vital verbal texture, as does Pound's. But Colquhoun's is essentially evoking alchemical knowledge *as knowledge*, richer for those for whom alchemy and hermeticism are living projects, and not in the service of a more general invocation of aesthetic creativity. Incantation, in Colquhoun's poem, is a technique for the living esoteric poet and reader. The words from which Colquhoun assembles this collage-like poem are themselves already metaphorical – 'vessel of nature vessel of Hermes / green vessel of Saturn' – and laden with the same classical and medieval resonances that Pound found so thrilling. But the parataxis of the poem works as an accumulation of adjacent phrases in different languages and esoteric traditions that are there not to contribute atmospherics but rather to build on for a specific purpose. As Shillitoe explains of Colquhoun's magical and esoteric poetry, using examples from poems referencing the Kabbala, '[p]oems such as these would be unintelligible to anyone not familiar with the Qabalah, but, to an occultist, they would be of value in building up a magical image during ceremonial or meditative workings'.

A similarly powerful synthesis of modernist collage technique, surrealist automatism, and Colquhoun's intimations of a dream world achievable through incantation can be found in 'Hypnagogic Interior'. Whilst the poem sounds in many ways like one of the several incantatory poems on alchemical images derived from Colquhoun's ritual occult practices, it is not. It is a verbal collage made entirely from found text: the words were cut out from a list of names of moths. 'Hypnagogic Interior' included a note from Colquhoun listing the poem's automatisms as 'découpage, collage, objective hazards', suggesting that she found it important for the reader to understand that automatism was at the heart of the poem.[55]

As was typical of Colquhoun's use of automatism in her writing, the poet's conscious efforts to assemble a poem from found content produce a powerful and deliberate effect of sound, rhythm, and image. The first stanza reads:

> Silvery arches
> Small angle shades
> Scarce burnished brass
> Small argent-and-sable.[56]

The sibilant alliteration throughout the stanza, and repetition of falling dactyls and trochees, provides a verbal texture to metallic imagery whose colours are invoked by common ('silvery' and 'brass') as well as deliberately antique diction ('argent', 'sable'), in what is a tactile, almost architectural, synthesis ('arches', 'angle', 'burnished brass').

The aurally rich and visually evocative antique blend of the first stanza gives way to a second stanza that thrives on a different organising logic:

> Water-ermine
> Narrow five-spot burnet
> Brown argus
> Barred chestnut[57]

Heavily trochaic and almost clipped, coming after the flowing first stanza, this stanza's surreal first line is itself the name of a white moth, but one that combines the luxurious white fur associated with royalty and pageantry with water in a hyphenated accretion that, like many surrealist images, combines elements seemingly incongruous – wetness and royal fur spawning combination images as disjunct as bedraggled royalty or a royal pageant on a river. The stanza's alliterative insistence on all things brown ('burnet', 'brown argus', and 'barred chestnut') immediately undercuts the images of white with which it began and creates incongruous associations between the lofty diction of Greek mythos in the latinised 'argus' and the American slang (whether Colquhoun knew this or not) of low monetary exchange, the 'five spot' being a name for a five-dollar bill.

'Hypnagogic Interior' then ends with even more seemingly unrelated combinations:

> Great brocade
> (Hidden wolf-light?)
> Pale shining brown[58]

The ostentatious splendor of 'great brocade' immediately elicits an antithesis, 'Hidden wolf-light', with intimations of lurking danger somehow tied to illumination. This contrast to the first line seems somehow to suggest a question, and a parenthetical question at that. The poem then ends on an image hardly imaginable to the conscious mind of a colour that simply does not, in our normal world, shine: 'Pale shining brown'. The poem, then, in its assemblage of real moth names cut from a found page, gives the reader exactly what it promises in its title: a visual, aural, and imagistic blend of the incongruous that evokes the surreal interiority of the mind falling asleep.

In the poetry of *Osmazone*, Colquhoun gave expression to her lifelong commitment to the surrealist project and its dissemination across the different domains of knowledge through which she attempted to understand her life and the natural, physical, and spiritual world in which she felt she sought a place by moving past an ideal of creation as a personal act of the artist's self. As has been said elsewhere of the affinities between surrealism and a strand of contemporary American avant-garde poetry, 'Both Surrealism and Language poetry are attempts to decenter the idea of the self as creator'.[59] Ultimately, Colquhoun's oeuvre eludes any personal interpretation. Perhaps it is fitting that she ended the collection with 'Dance of the Figure Cousins', a numerical concrete poem that she understood as 'inadvertent surrealism' and that resists textual interpretation entirely. As a minor poet, Colquhoun's poetry scarcely registers in histories of surrealist literature. But her dissemination of surrealism into many corners of post-Second World War British culture and her determined efforts to make art and poetry through automatisms that undermined the ideal of a personal self as creator are feats worthy of further exploration.

Notes

1 See Dawn Ades, 'Notes on Two Women Surrealist Painters: Eileen Agar and Ithell Colquhoun', *Oxford Art Journal* 3:1 (1980), pp. 36–42; Whitney Chadwick, *Women Artists and the Surrealist Movement* (London: Thames & Hudson, 1985); Michel Remy, *Surrealism in Britain* (Aldershot: Ashgate, 1999); Eric Ratcliffe, *Ithell Colquhoun: Pioneer Surrealist Artist, Occultist, Writer, and Poet* (Oxford: Mandrake, 2007); and Steve Nichols (ed.), *The Magical Writings of Ithell Colquhoun* (Morrisville, NC: Lulu, 2007).
2 See Richard Shillitoe, *Ithell Colquhoun: Magician Born of Nature*, rev. ed. (Morrisville, NC: Lulu, 2010); Mark S. Morrisson, 'Ithell Colquhoun and Occult Surrealism in Mid-Twentieth-Century Britain and Ireland', *Modernism / Modernity* 21:3 (2014), pp. 587–616; and Amy Hale, *Ithell Colquhoun: Genius of the Fern Loved Gully* (Cambridge, MA: MIT Press, 2020).
3 In addition to the poetry published in Michel Remy (ed.), *On the Thirteenth Stroke of Midnight: Surrealist Poetry in England* (Manchester: Carcanet, 2013), new selections are now available in *I Saw Water: An Occult Novel and Other Selected Writings by Ithell Colquhoun*, ed. Richard Shillitoe and Mark S. Morrisson (University Park, PA: Penn State University Press, 2014); Fulgur Press has recently brought out her previously unpublished volume, *The Decad of Intelligence* (Lopen, Somerset: Fulgur, 2017). And Shillitoe has edited a new selection of Colquhoun's writings including poetry, recently published as *Medea's Charms: Selected Shorter Writing* (London: Peter Owen, 2019).
4 Rob Jackaman, *The Course of English Surrealist Poetry Since the 1930s* (Lewiston: Edwin Mellen, 1989), p. 142.
5 Edward B. Germain (ed.), *English and American Surrealist Poetry* (New York and Harmondsworth: Penguin Books, 1978).
6 Quoted in Peter Nicholls, 'Surrealism in England', in Laura Marcus and Peter Nicholls (eds), *The Cambridge History of Twentieth-Century English Literature* (Cambridge: Cambridge University Press, 2005), p. 399.
7 Drew Milne, 'Neo-Modernism and Avant-Garde Orientations', in Nigel Alderman and C.D. Blanton (eds), *A Concise Companion to Postwar British and Irish Poetry* (Chichester: Wiley-Blackwell, 2009), pp. 156–7.
8 Peter Barry and Robert Hampson, 'Introduction: The Scope of the Possible', in Robert Hampson and Peter Barry (eds), *New British Poetries: The Scope of the Possible* (Manchester: Manchester University Press, 1993), p. 6.
9 R.J. [Dick] Ellis, 'Mapping the UK Little Magazine Field', in Robert Hampson and Peter Barry (eds), *New British Poetries: The Scope of the Possible* (Manchester: Manchester University Press, 1993), p. 84.
10 Lee Harwood, 'Surrealist Poetry Today', *Alembic* 3 (Spring 1975), pp. 49–54.
11 *Ibid.*, p. 53.
12 *Ibid.*, p. 49.

13 *Ibid.*, pp. 51–3.
14 Remy, *Surrealism in Britain*, p. 210.
15 Silvano Levy, 'The del Renzio Affair: A Leadership Struggle in Wartime Surrealism', *Papers of Surrealism* 3 (Spring 2005), p. 13.
16 Morrisson, 'Ithell Colquhoun and Occult Surrealism', pp. 587–616.
17 Nicholas Calas, 'The Light of Words', *Arson: An Ardent Review, Part One of a Surrealist Manifestation* (March 1942), p. 15.
18 James Findlay Hendry, letter to Ithell Colquhoun (ALS), 31 August 1941, Tate Gallery Archive TGA 929/1/865.
19 As I have argued in 'Colquhoun and Occult Surrealism'.
20 Shillitoe, *Ithell Colquhoun*, p. 58.
21 See, for example, Colquhoun's discussion of the possible transpersonal origin of a dream that inspired one of her paintings, in Ithell Colquhoun, 'The Order of the Sun and Moon, Nicaragua', typescript, 1979, Tate Gallery Archive TGA 929/2/1/43.
22 Devin Johnston, *Precipitations: Contemporary American Poetry as Occult Practice* (Middletown, CT: Wesleyan University Press, 2002), pp. 100–1.
23 Antony Borrow, 'Apology', *The Glass* 1 (Summer 1948), pp. 1–2.
24 *Ibid.*, p. 1.
25 Johnston, *Precipitations*, p. 2.
26 Ithell Colquhoun, 'The Myth of Santa Warna', *The Glass* 1 (Summer 1948), p. 21.
27 *Ibid.*, p. 22.
28 Shillitoe, *Ithell Colquhoun*, pp. 94–7.
29 Antony Borrow and Madge Hales, 'The Questionnaire', *The Glass* 9 (1953), n.p.
30 'Replies', *The Glass* 9 (1953), pp. 25–6.
31 *Ibid.*, p. 29.
32 *Ibid.*, p. 33.
33 Philip Larkin, 'Statement', in *Required Writing: Miscellaneous Pieces 1955–1982* (London: Faber and Faber, 1983), p. 79.
34 Robert Conquest, 'Introduction', in Robert Conquest (ed.), *New Lines: An Anthology* (London: Macmillan, 1956), p. xv.
35 Robert Conquest, 'Introduction', in Robert Conquest (ed.), *New Lines – II: An Anthology* (London: Macmillan, 1963), p. xxv.
36 Frank Kermode, quoted in Matthew Sterenberg, *Mythic Thinking in Twentieth-Century Britain: Meaning for Modernity* (New York: Palgrave Macmillan, 2013), p. 168.
37 Marilyn Strathern, *Reproducing the Future: Essays on Anthropology, Kinship and the New Reproductive Technologies* (Manchester: Manchester University Press, 1992), 6; italics in the original.
38 André Breton, *Manifesto of Surrealism*, in *Manifestoes of Surrealism*, trans. Richard Seaver and Helen R. Lane (Ann Arbor: University of Michigan Press, 1989), p. 26.

39 Michael Richardson lamented in *Melmoth*'s inaugural issue in 1980, 'We should also bear in mind that today the so-called "surreal" which never had much to do with surrealism anyway, is commonplace – c/f cigarette advertising which has certainly learned from surrealist imagery'. Ultimately, Richardson worried, the current crisis 'threatens to tear surrealism apart and give it back in pieces for recuperation into bourgeois society'. Michael Richardson, 'Whither Surrealism?', *Melmoth* 1 (1980), p. 26.
40 Ithell Colquhoun, *Grimoire of the Entangled Thicket* (Stevenage: Ore Publications, 1973), p. 3.
41 *Ibid.*, p. 3.
42 Ithell Colquhoun, 'Uath', *Ore* 27 (1981), p. 6; as 'Uathe' in *New Celtic Review* (Beltane, 1982), p. 5; *Wood and Water* 2:7 (1983), p. 3.
43 Delap explains that 'The term "periodical community" refers to the material, cultural, and intellectual milieu of a periodical or group of related periodicals'. Lucy Delap, 'The *Freewoman*, Periodical Communities, and the Feminist Reading Public', *The Princeton University Library Chronicle* 61:2 (2000), p. 234.
44 In the exchange advertisement page, Pagans Against Nukes described themselves as 'a pagan/occult alliance to resist nuclear weapons and power, on both political/activist levels and psychic/magical'.
45 See Tony Pusey, ALS to Ithell Colquhoun (n.d.), Tate Gallery Archive TGA 929/1/1814.
46 Tony Pusey, ALS to Ithell Colquhoun (n.d.), Tate Gallery Archive TGA 929/1/1816.
47 Tony Pusey, ALS to Ithell Colquhoun (n.d.), Tate Gallery Archive TGA 929/1/1817.
48 Tony Pusey, ALS to Ithell Colquhoun (n.d.), Tate Gallery Archive TGA 929/1/1819.
49 Tony Pusey, ALS to Ithell Colquhoun (n.d.), Tate Gallery Archive TGA 929/1/1820 and TGA 929/1/1822.
50 Richard Shillitoe, from his website *ithell colquhoun: magician born of nature*. www.ithellcolquhoun.co.uk/osmazone.htm, accessed 10 June 2018.
51 Shillitoe, www.ithellcolquhoun.co.uk/osmazone.htm.
52 Ezra Pound, 'The Alchemist', in *Personae: The Collected Shorter Poems of Ezra Pound* (New York: New Directions, 1971), p. 75.
53 Pound refers to the ladies using the Provençal 'midonz' and sets the poem 'under the larches of Paradise' that Tim Materer sees resonating long into Pound's later cantos. Tim Materer, *Modernist Alchemy: Poetry and the Occult* (Ithaca: Cornell University Press, 1995), pp. 57–8.
54 Ithell Colquhoun, 'Ode to the Philosophical Mercury', in *Osmazone* (Örkeljunga: Dunganon, 1983), p. 11.
55 In a follow-up to Michael Richardson's *Melmoth* essay on automatism and surrealist poetic practice, Colquhoun provided her own 'Notes on Automatism' in the magazine's second issue. Citing her own chain poem in TRANSFORMAcTION 5 as an example, she advocates for collage and found objects as automatisms in poetry, explaining that she had 'found poems in a Gaelic Grammar and in entomological lists'. This latter refers directly to 'Hypnagogic Interior'. Ithell Colquhoun, 'Notes on Automatism', *Melmoth* 2 (1980), pp. 31–2.

56 Ithell Colquhoun, 'Hypnagogic Interior', in *Osmazone*, p. 20.
57 *Ibid.*, p. 20.
58 *Ibid.*, p. 20.
59 Charles Borkhuis, 'Writing from Inside Language: Late Surrealism and Textual Poetry in France and the U.S.', in Mark Wallace and Steven Marks (eds), *Telling It Slant: Avant-Garde Poetics of the 1990s* (Tuscaloosa: University of Alabama Press, 2002), p. 244.

9

Leonor Fini's abhuman family

Jonathan P. Eburne

Je pense à l'extrême indigence et extrême richesse de notre vie, à ma possibilité de pousser les choses toujours plus loin, à vivre tout avec l'acharnement d'une morsure à la sauvagerie, cruauté, vengeance, consommation des choses, possibilité de se reconstituer, comme s'imaginaient ceux qui ont inventé la résurrection de la chair. Je prendrais plutôt l'exemple du Phoenix barbare, sauvage, que je me sens parfois.[1]

(I consider the extreme indigence and extreme richness of our lives; of my ability always to push things further and to live with the harsh bite-marks of savagery, cruelty, vengeance; of the consummation of all things and the possibility of reconstituting oneself, much like what those who invented the resurrection of the flesh had in mind. I would rather take the example of the barbarous, wild Phoenix, whom I sometimes feel myself to be.)

Leonor Fini

'Si le surréalisme a été quelque chose', the literary historian and critic Xavière Gauthier wrote in 1971, 'c'est bien au niveau des perversions promues par ses peintres et quelques-uns de ses écrivains' ('If surrealism amounted to anything, it is on account of the perversions promoted by its painters and certain of its writers').[2] According to Gauthier, the much-vaunted idea of a 'surrealist revolution' was conceivable only through the movement's capacity for perversion. Such perversion referred less to a repertory of psycho-sexual gymnastics, however, than to the redirection or subversion of the normative patriarchal law to whose hegemony Hélène Cixous famously referred as 'L'Empire du propre': an empire of the selfsame (*propre*), but also an empire of the clean (*propre*), signifying patriarchy's imperial recourse to transparency and self-evidence.[3] Surrealism's promise lay in its capacity for both twisting and sullying such a law, for introducing within its functioning the resistances of deviation, errantry, and opacity.[4] But is it possible to pervert an empire?

Gauthier's appeal to surrealist perversion was tempered by her overall charge that surrealism promised but seldom delivered such perversion, save in a small number of the most radical, even pornographic, of its works. Her 1971 book *Surréalisme et sexualité* challenged the prevailing notion that the surrealist movement was – or, rather, had once been – a 'revolutionary' synthesis of Marxism and psychoanalysis that aspired at once to a political programme of social revolution and a liberatory cultural programme of freedom and love. According to Gauthier the movement's ambitions were crippled by its regressive ideas about women, who were either treated as objects of violent desire or idealised as muses, sirens, *'femmes-enfants'*, or other mythologised fantasies. Surrealism's true emancipatory potential lay instead in the group's (often failed) deployment of sexuality as a sovereign imperative against which normative social structures stood as an impediment; sexuality thus functioned as a force of social dissolution rather than either an idealised condition or, for that matter, a tactical instrument. This meant privileging the more sinister iterations of desire in surrealist art and literature – sadism, compulsion, obsession, and violent fantasy – over the more apparently salutary surrealist ideas of 'mad love'. Thus downplaying the surrealism of poets such as André Breton, Paul Éluard, and Louis Aragon in favour of a surrealism articulated through the work of Hans Bellmer, Antonin Artaud, Toyen, Pierre Molinier, and Joyce Mansour, Gauthier's polemic upheld an artistic practice for which, as in any revolution, it was the human body that was at stake. 'Le risque', Gauthier writes, 'est total: il y va du corps' ('The risk is total: the body is at stake').[5]

Something akin to this notion of 'perversion' would be fundamental to the militant feminist discourses in France during the 1970s to which Gauthier contributed both as an author and as the founder and editor of the journal *Sorcières*. Levying an analogously polemical investment in the corporeal stakes of artistic and political practice, the Mouvement de libération des femmes (MLF) was – much like the surrealist movement – internally fractured not only along tactical and theoretical lines (with regard to social policy, legal autonomy, and attention to the 'third world', for instance) but also along the lines of what might be called the administration of risk. What, in the end, did it mean to risk everything? Did the political demands of feminism stop at nothing less than a fundamental overturning of structural injustices, or could the terms of revolutionary change be disarticulated as a set of rhetorical flourishes that were, in the end, not so far out of step with the values and institutions of the neoliberal state?[6] In *Surréalisme et sexualité* Gauthier interrogates the surrealist movement on precisely this front. Two years later, she responded with a short monograph on the painter Leonor Fini, who figures briefly in the earlier study as an artist whose work, for all its delicate beauty, bore a capacity to shatter assurances that she would later attribute to other feminist authors such as Marguerite Duras, Cixous, and the nineteenth-century Communard Louise Michel.[7]

The choice of Leonor Fini as the monographic focus of a book on avant-garde feminism might seem curious, given that by the 1970s Fini – by her own admission – had largely fallen out of contemporary debates about the status of avant-garde art and had little bearing on debates about the politics of feminism.[8] Born in Argentina in 1907 and raised in Trieste, Fini had emigrated to Paris in 1931; she befriended a number of the artists and writers affiliated with the surrealist movement but never formally participated in the Parisian group around André Breton, even though her paintings were often included in major surrealism-focused exhibitions such as Alfred Barr's *Fantastic Art, Dada, and Surrealism* show in 1936. In the decades after the Second World War Fini had become a media celebrity on account of her well-documented appearances at society costume balls and her work as a designer of sets and costumes for the stage and screen, as much as for the collectability of her art. I nonetheless consider Gauthier's monograph on Fini to be a continuation of her attention to 'perversion' as a political imperative, in spite of Fini's own distance from the sphere of political engagement, militancy, or even rhetoric. In Fini's work, sentiments were far from politically neutral. Herself a close friend of numerous surrealist poets and writers who fiercely guarded her independence from the organised movement, Fini likewise articulated a position toward 'la condition de la femme' that Gauthier finds fascinating for its refusal of liberal feminism: whereas Fini claimed 'depuis toujours … que la femme est mal traitée, considérée avec injustice' ('since time immemorial … women have been treated poorly, unfairly judged') and thus revolted against this condition, she nonetheless distanced herself from the affirmation or rights-oriented projects of organised feminist movements. She detested, for instance, 'le mot *égalité*. Cela n'existe pas. Les femmes ne sont pas *égales*' ('the word *equality*. That does not exist. Women are not *equal*').[9] Fini was hardly the only twentieth-century artist to reject – as well as misrepresent – the politics of organised feminism. Yet her work appealed to Gauthier, I propose, on account of the specificity with which it opens up a powerful set of alternative myths and figurations of sexual and social relations, outlining a living praxis of disalienation: the dissolution of social hierarchies through artistic, ritual, and erotic integration.

'I don't believe in "the death of painting"', Fini writes in 1975, commenting on the exigency of her work as fuelled by something other than contemporary demands. 'I believe it to be an activity linked to ancient sources, which go back to gardener birds, to the courtship rituals of animals, which have been handed down to us through the discovery of play and magic by the first men.'[10] Fini's appeal for Gauthier lay in the literalness with which the artist pursued this claim. Beyond the declaratory gesture of devoting a book-length study to a woman artist, that is, Fini's work was significant to Gauthier for its investment in something akin to a biopolitics modelled on the intimacies of the animal, vegetable, and mineral worlds. As Fini herself put it, 'la peinture est pour moi une démarche biologique, en cela abhumaine, en dépit des figures humaines que je peins' ('for me, painting is a biological process and thus abhuman, despite the human figures I paint').[11] In the earlier study Gauthier attributes this 'démarche biologique' to the feminine power of the prenatal, a powerful and disquieting sphere of maternal creation for which, she writes, 'Christian paradise is but a projection'.[12] In the later study, Gauthier forgoes the maternal imagery implicit in this formulation, heeding the artist's own emphasis on non-reproductive sexuality to designate instead a more ecologically expansive set of 'abhuman' co-ordinates within the artist's figural universe. In Fini's artwork, Gauthier writes, 'Les règnes animal, végétal, minéral et humain s'imbriquent, s'accolent, sans jamais se confondre, fusionner dans un temps mort, mais en se heurtant toujours. Ce mélange n'est pas réconciliation béate, mais tension' ('The animal, vegetable, mineral, and human kingdoms intertwine, intermingle – without ever becoming conflated or fusing in dead time, but instead always colliding. This mixture is not a beatific reconciliation, but a tension').[13] The regulation of life itself in Fini's painting – at once *bios*, *zoe*, and *psyche* – is subject to the mutability and interpenetration of all things, a process of 'molting' (*mue*) and transformation that left the world of strict human definition. Such mutability is depicted in characteristic paintings of the 1940s such as *Sphinx Philagria* (1945) (Figure 9.1). Its title alluding to a genus of tropical moth, the painting's tangle of stumps and vines, skulls and insects, which both surround and appear to comprise the lower body of the titular figure, outline a condition of vital fluctuation that fascinated many of the artist's friends and critics for its 'intimate, macabre theater' of life, death, and fecundity.[14]

The abhuman 'intimate theater' of Fini's painting extended, moreover, to the artist's very praxis of life, from her public face to her most intimate associations; at a distinct remove from militancy, Fini's practice of 'total risk' took the form of a transformation in the expectations of intimacy and the rituals of communal domestic life. Certainly, Fini's art proceeded from the 'disalienation of women', which Gauthier considered to be the necessary condition for any revolutionary sexuality.[15] Yet for Fini, such disalienation had less to do with political solidarity or collective belonging than with the profoundly *integrating* functions of the practices she aligned with art: ritual transformation, erotic intimacy, and animal kinship. What Gauthier describes as 'le mouvement de vagues et les méandres troublées et troublantes de la genèse finienne' ('the wavelike movement and the troubled and troubling meanderings of Finian genesis') constituted itself as a set of artistic and experiential processes through which 'la misérable barrière entre le réel et l'imaginaire, le passé et le futur, est balayée, comment s'élève en spirales, en volutes, une exigence qui fait naître, ordonne et métamorphose' ('the miserable barrier between the real and the imaginary, the past and the

9.1 Leonor Fini, *Sphinx Philagria*, 1945. Oil on canvas.

future, is swept away in the spiralling plume of an exigency that gives rise to birth, order, and metamorphosis').[16] Here Gauthier paraphrases André Breton's language for describing the epistemological and political project of surrealism; in doing so Gauthier portrays the artist and her work as a movement in themselves: actants in a process of world-making in which 'there is no preconceived idea, thus no intellectualism; it [the idea] *is* and imposes itself like a reality'.[17] This reality, as Gauthier describes it, is ultimately a world in which the dissolution of bourgeois social constraints has already taken place, and in which the very contours of human existence are also likewise in flux, yielding a universe charged with sexual ambiguity and the proliferation of hybrid beings.[18] Fini describes this abhuman process in terms similar to Gauthier's: her paintings do not solicit interpretation so much as they call for participation, a 'complicity' in the sensorium to which they beckoned. 'Les tableaux', she writes, 's'expliquent d'eux-mêmes. Ils proposent un monde où l'on n'a qu'à se plonger ... Il est difficile de comprendre une oeuvre. Il faut la laisser agir, fasciner ou répugner. Le spectateur doit se laisser aller à contempler, à subir si on veut et, s'il est attiré, appelé par un tableau, c'est que là, il y a un élément qui existe en lui (une sensation, une présence, un souvenir), peut-être *intraduisible* en mots' ('The paintings explain themselves. They propose a world into which one has only to dive ... It is difficult to understand a work. It must be left to act on its own, whether to fascinate or to disgust. The spectator must allow himself to contemplate, to submit, if you like, and, if he is attracted, called by a painting, it is because there is an element that exists in him (a sensation, a presence, a remembrance), that remains untranslatable into words').[19]

Though she considered this process of being 'called' or compelled to submit to the world-making capacities of her artwork to be untranslatable into words, this certainly did not mean that Fini did not write. On the contrary, Fini not only participated actively in the literary milieu as a prolific theatrical designer and book illustrator in the decades after the Second World War, but she also began publishing a number of books of her own in the wake of Gauthier's 1973 study. The remainder of this chapter approaches the three novels Fini published in the late 1970s – *Mourmour* (1976), *L'Oneiropompe* (1978), and *Rogomelec* (1979) – as autofictions that mythologise the intimacies of Fini's artistic life and which, in doing so, offer narrative extensions of her artistic and conceptual system. Fini's published fictions appeared in rapid succession during the second half of the 1970s, in a period that saw numerous career retrospectives of Fini's artistic work, in the form of exhibitions as well as films and critical studies, as well as a number of additional albums and artists' books featuring hitherto-unpublished samples of Fini's prose.[20] This included Gauthier's own 1973 study of the artist, which, as Gauthier stressed, consisted largely of Fini's own words; it also included a number of other career-spanning books published around the same time, including *Le Livre de Leonor Fini* (1975), and, perhaps most tellingly, an annotated photography album *Miroir des chats* (1977) that documented and meditated on the lives and habits of Fini's menagerie of seventeen cats. As relatively late-career works that began appearing as the artist neared seventy years of age, Fini's writings deploy many of the stylistic motifs for which she had become famous: mysterious dreamlike settings, erotic adventures, nocturnal ceremonies, and a dramatis personae of hybrid creatures, including sphinxes and sentient cats. Read in tandem with *Miroir des chats* and *Le Livre de Leonor Fini*, the fictions disclose how closely the iconography of Fini's paintings draws upon the particulars – even the peculiarities – of the artist's life, which were likewise well documented in the popular press. Fini had long become a household name on account of the inventiveness of her costumes and costume designs. Yet this new wave of materials revealed Fini's home life to be no less artistically saturated – and, perhaps, no less outlandish – than her public persona.

Fini's published writing emerged in concert – and in conversation – with the queer anti-humanism of her postwar friends and associates, a group that included Jean Genet, Jean Cocteau, Hector Bianciotti (who lived and worked as Fini's secretary for eight years), and the less well known playwright and novelist Juan Baptista Piñero, among others. Yet foremost in her attentions were her long-term human companions Stanislao Lepri and Constantin Jelinski, as well as her cats, who had grown number to seventeen by the early 1970s. Largely dedicated to her 'family' of sexually polymorphous human and animal companions, with whom Fini took up residence in the ruins of a Franciscan monastery in Nunzio, Corsica, each summer, Fini's written work veers away from the recognisably political, even the recognisably anti-humanist tendencies in European thought of the 1970s (and today) in its fantastic iterations of a kind of sovereign, quasi-aristocratic *practice of life*.

What is 'perverted' in Fini's work, I propose, are the presuppositions of liberatory discourse itself, the media and definitions of political subjectivity and, in particular, of political kinship that Fini's writing and art both frustrate and redirect. Not only did Fini's work contribute to postwar French discourses on 'perversion' that accompanied the publication of erotic fiction such as Pauline Réage's (Anne Desclos's) *Histoire d'O* (1954) and the complete works of Sade, both of which Fini illustrated; it also challenged the implicit humanism of feminist discourse in the 1970s, even Gauthier's, insofar as the antisexist struggle to dismantle oppressive social structures as well as 's'attaqu[er] en chacun de nous à ce qui nous est le plus intime et qui nous paraissent le plus sûr' ('to attack in each of us that which is the most intimate and which seems to be the most certain to us'), as Simone de Beauvoir put it, still presumed a human subject.[21] In turn, Fini's synoptic work of the 1970s subjects contemporary iterations of such 'perturbation' to an abhuman practice and discourse of queer kinship and multi-species world-making that both anticipates and, to a certain extent, also challenges the political exigency of establishing new conditions of possibility for non-normative sexuality and counter-hegemonic love. The interrogation of cherished concepts thus extends, in Fini's writing, art, and domestic life alike, to the abhumanism she described in 1972 as a 'démarche biologique' that dissolved the singularity of the human form in favour of polymorphous intimacies that incorporated the animal, the vegetal, and the mineral.

For this very reason, Fini's most 'perverse' work might also seem to be the most frivolous and ancillary to her painting, a set of late career writings that dwell on her interest in costumes, her domestic living arrangements, her summer vacations, and her cats; such books are written, moreover, in a spirit of both play, and, as she notes in an interview, 'complicity'.[22] Yet to underestimate such practices – or Fini herself – would be a mistake, as Gauthier notes in *Surréalisme et sexualité*, revealing more about the viewer than about the work itself. 'Penser qu'une telle toile, ou quelque autre de Léonor Fini est décorative', Gauthier notes, 'est un mouvement de défense contre un sentiment de malaise et d'angoisse' ('To consider any one painting by Léonor Fini as decorative is to yield to a movement of self-defence against a feeling of uneasiness and anguish').[23] Such 'complicity', a gesture of incorporation, denotes an abiding lifelong practice of calibrating the possibilities of and thresholds between love and friendship, as well as the very species-being of the human. It is for this reason, I propose, that the total, bodily 'enjeu' to which Gauthier gestured plays out in the books Fini wrote about *and for* her enormous menagerie of cats.

Ivre de joie: *Mourmour*

Fini's first extended foray into fiction is the novel *Mourmour, conte pour enfants velus,* published by Éditions de la différence in 1976, a publishing house founded that same year and for which she worked on illustrated editions of Marcel Schwob's *Livre de Monelle* and her friend Gilbert Lély's *Oeuvres poétiques*; the same press also published *Miroir de chats* the following year. Episodes from the novel had appeared earlier in other contemporary works by or about the artist: *Le Livre de Leonor Fini* featured an episode from the novel entitled 'Visite à la grotte' ('A Visit to the Cave'), and Gauthier's 1973 monograph published excerpts alongside other of the artist's unpublished writings.

Mourmour is a novel about an island refuge for cats and various feline hybrids, including the eponymous protagonist, who, we learn on the novel's first page, is the child of a feline mother and an unknown human father. Mourmour has been raised to pass – though not without the occasional raised eyebrow – as human; his mother trims the fur short on his paws so that he can attend the local school with the other village children. He has learned to laugh off astonished remarks and jibes from human children about 'why his ears are so pointy and why his pupils become tiny slivers around midday'.[24] The novel opens as Mourmour and his mother, Belinda – a large, white, long-haired cat – are preparing to leave the village under cover of night, in order to emigrate to an island sanctuary where they can finally live among their own. Mourmour's departure from a life of camouflage and secrecy bears undertones of Fini's own childhood drama of escape, during which the artist's mother fled with her daughter from Buenos Aires to her native Trieste in order to escape her domineering husband. According to Fini's biographer Peter Webb, her estranged father published a self-justifying pamphlet appealing for custody, *Por la tenencia di mi hija*, and once tried to have Leonor kidnapped.[25] Fini later recalled having to dress up as a boy as a safety measure, a gesture of physical transformation echoed in Mourmour's own habits of inter-species passing.

As the novel's title suggests, however, the story of Mourmour is less a fictionalised account of Fini's childhood than a tale about and for cats: a 'conte pour enfants velus' ('a tale for furry children'). Though it bears strong autobiographical undertones, the novel's principal conceit involves mythologising the journey Fini and her household – her human companions Lepri and Jelinski, as well as her seventeen cats – took each summer to Corsica, where they took up in a ruined Franciscan monastery Fini first visited in 1954 and purchased three years later. After the brief opening narrative of departure, therefore, the novel luxuriates in the splendours and mysteries of the monastery and the escapades that unfold therein. The site likewise figures in each of Fini's principal fictions of the 1970s as the centripetal setting and motif of each narrative: as in *Mourmour*, *Rogomelec* (1979) narrates a curative journey to an island monastery; so too does *L'Oneiropompe* (1978), an oneiric fantasy about the search for a missing cat, which winds up in a similarly isolated setting, concluding with a ceremony of restitution on a mysterious island. *Mourmour* is unique, however, insofar as the island retreat is populated entirely by cats. Early in the novel Mourmour's magisterial and overtly sexualised mother, Belinda, describes the monastery as a picturesque – and human-free – haven: 'les ruines, les plantes grimpantes, les anges sculptés qui s'émiettaient, la foule de roses trémières, les rochers en forme de temple et l'église en forme de rocher' ('the ruins, the climbing plants, the crumbling angel statues, the throngs of hollyhocks, the temple-shaped rocks and the rock-shaped church').[26] Such an interpenetration of stone and plant, built and natural forms, already signals the erotic possibilities afforded therein. In a 1976 interview, Fini jokes that *Mourmour* represents the real-life Corsican monastery with such accuracy that she was anxious about showing it to any of the residents of the village, lest they think that the plot described what they were up to there.[27]

Indeed, the plot details of *Mourmour* are unmistakably racy, in spite of the novel's titular claim to be a story for 'enfants velus'. As Fini notes in a 1976 interview, what is infantile about the tale is the paradisiacal, partly feral environment of polymorphous perversity that suffuses it: the feline analogue, perhaps, to Freud's golden age of infantile eroticism.[28] As one of Fini's contemporary sketches makes clear (Figure 9.2) what unfolds on the novel's Boccacian island of cats and feline hybrids is a story of erotic sexual awakening based on an oneiric yet anatomically specific attunement to the habits and anatomies of cats: prowling, nuzzling, napping, licking, grooming, and wrestling – a spectrum of sensory contact that extends, in Fini's novel, to sexual penetration. Indeed, lest the specificity of such practices remain uninterrogated for the novel's 'furry' readers, Mourmour recounts a scene of erotic intimacy with his mother, Belinda, early in his island residency. The scene of maternal incest unfolds as a sensory incorporation of the

9.2 Leonor Fini, *Étude pour* Mourmour, 1976. Ink, watercolour, and wash.

narrator within the feline body of his mother, who seems to have grown to an enormous size, resplendent with jewels in her bedroom:

> Dès qu'elle me prit dans ses bras, je me suis trouvé nu et très enivré et exalté, car ma mère avait mis des parfums différents sur chaque parti de son corps. La cannelle à l'héliotrope de sa chevelure me rendit si fou que j'oubliais ma petite taille, je commençais par mordre sa bouche, mettre ma langue dans ses jolis trous de nez arqués; elle riait et me disait: 'Tu es vraiment en enfant.' ... Belinda me saisit par le bras et posa mon ventre contre sa bouche, j'étais ivre de joie, je nageais sur ma mère et en ma mère, car elle était pour moi l'air et l'eau – miauler était trop peu pour exprimer ce que je ressentais –. Le prodige ne se fit pas attendre: au lieu de devenir très petite comme la fée, elle fit devenir mon sexe très grand, presque aussi grand que moi-même et elle l'enfila dans son corps avec un rugissement de triomphe. La chambre, autour de nous, se mit alors à tourner.[29]

> (As soon as she took me in her arms, I found myself naked and deeply intoxicated and exhilarated, for my mother had put various perfumes on each part of her body. The cinnamon on the heliotrope of her hair made me so crazy that I forgot all about my small size; I began by biting her mouth, putting my tongue

into her pretty, arched nostrils; she laughed and said to me, 'You really are a child.' ... Belinda grabbed me by the arm and placed my stomach against her mouth; I was drunk with joy, I swam on my mother and in my mother, because she was air and water to me – meowing was not enough to express how I felt –. The most wondrous thing soon followed: instead of becoming very small like the fairies, she made my sex very large, almost as big as I was, and she slid it into her body with a roar of triumph. Then the room around us began to spin.)

Whilst borrowing from the lubricious archive of French erotic writing to which Fini had been contributing illustrated editions since the war, this scene of feline incest also articulates Fini's abhumanism on a more conceptual level, presenting not only a calculated flouting of heteronormative, bourgeois sexual mores but also an allegory for Fini's claim to have abdicated from the human species altogether. *Mourmour* is as much a novel about what the island refuge excludes, I propose, as about the licence it permits: there are, after all, no humans on the island. As Fini herself put it in an autobiographical text published in 1973, 'Je me suis donc volontaerement exilée de l'espèce [humain], et les compagnons que je préfère et que j'ai choisi ont fait de même – il en résulte des relations incestueuses: les meilleurs' ('So I voluntarily exiled myself from the [human] species, and the companions I prefer and whom I've chosen have done the same – this results in incestuous relationships: which are the best').[30] In the face of compulsory heterosexuality and the presumption of reproductive sexuality, Fini chose 'incest', an index for the polyamorous, queer, and multi-species intimacies she cultivated.

'I have never lived with just one person', Fini notes in an interview published in 1978. 'Since I was eighteen, I have preferred to be in a sort of community – a big house with my atelier and animals, cats, and friends, and with one man who was rather a lover and another who was rather a friend. And it has always worked.'[31] *Mourmour*'s ecstatic sensuality figures this 'work' as a process which, as the publisher Patrick Mauriès has noted in the context of an earlier period in the artist's life, constituted a sustained project of 'recherche de la juste distance, de l'équilibre entre indépendance et partage, amour et amitié, fidélité et aventure, cette tension vers le phalanstère, ou du moins la communauté de valeurs' (a 'search for the right distance, for the balance between independence and sharing, love and friendship, fidelity and adventure, this tension toward phalanstery, or at least a community of values').[32] What Fini described – and, I maintain, allegorised – as non-human incest voiced the artist's abiding commitment to sustaining a practice of artistic and amorous life, which she cultivated in the name of the 'abhuman' intimacy and inter-species commingling her mid-century painting depicted in figural form.

Not all responses to Fini's domestic living conditions were necessarily sanguine. As Sylwia Zientek has written, accounts of visits to Leonor, Stanislao Lepri, and Constantin (Kot) Jelinsky in Fini's Paris apartment tend to reflect on the unusual atmosphere that prevailed there – much in the manner of Mourmour's human classmates. 'They were', Zientek writes, 'a separate world, whispering and giggling, communicating with each other through semi-words, a metalanguage or code referring to their experiences and anecdotes that no one outside their circle could understand'.[33] José Alvarez, for instance, with whom Fini collaborated on *Le Livre de Leonor Fini*, described this 'incestuous' atmosphere in less than glowing terms: 'I loved her but I was not part of the "family". The atmosphere was stifling there, and she was like a boa constrictor, devouring her closest friends. I loved Stanislao and Kot [Jelinsky] even more, and I used to take them out to dinner so that they could escape from her for a while. But she needed a "family" like them to protect and adore her.'[34] As her depiction of the island refuge in *Mourmour* suggests, Fini was hardly oblivious to such criticisms – indeed, given that her artwork teems with mythological femmes fatales who likewise present amalgamations of love, care, need, and predatory suffocation, such characterisations of Fini's lifestyle might be considered a constitutive element of its construction. Anticipating Alvarez's criticism by nearly thirty years, Lepri's 1949 painting *Les Voyeurs* (Figure 9.3) is telling for its inversion of the spectacle of polyamory it both naturalises and seeks to protect against a gawking public. In its autobiographical portrait of the 'family', Fini – posed in what appears to be a half-hearted display of seductiveness – may figure as the painting's dominant spectacle, but its drama of attention centres on the exchange of gazes between her 'incestuous' household and the penned-up onlookers whom they observe in turn. Crouched over as if to peer through cracks in the wooden crate that separates them, Lepri and Jelinsky seem to derive voyeuristic pleasure from the small horde of no less voyeuristic onlookers crowded into the crate. Fini's 'family' was less a private idiosyncrasy to be shielded against the prying eyes of the public, the image suggests, than a carefully constructed world set at a deliberate remove from the ideological and 'species'-bound practices of the contemporary public.

The scene of maternal feline incest in *Mourmour* begins to illuminate the sensory contours of this constructed world. Most fundamentally, such scenes offer a tongue-in-cheek parody of the daily lives and habits of the artist's own menagerie of cats. The white, long-haired Belinda, for instance, was one of the cats documented in *Miroir des chats* (1977), a lavishly illustrated photo-book that both playfully narrates the habits of Fini's seventeen cats and, more subtly, meditates on the sensory and epistemological repercussions of a life spent among them. The sensory register extends directly from the

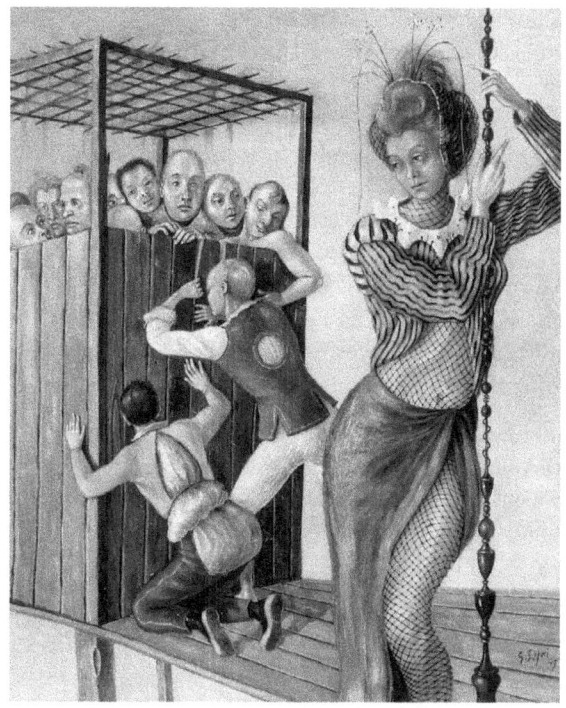

9.3 Stanislao Lepri, *Les Voyeurs*, 1949. Oil on canvas.

empirical: in *Miroir des chats* Fini describes a scene during breakfast in bed one morning in which a number of the cats envelop themselves in the bedsheets while Belinda scratches the artist and knocks over the powdered milk, rendering the bedclothes gritty. Another cat, Mignapouf, has a turd tangled in his long fur, which rubs against the sheets. 'I carefully remove it from him', Fini notes almost casually, turning to describe how other cats chew on her ear and lick her left cheek with their scratchy tongues.[35] Fini's sensorium may be joyful, but the intimacies she describes incorporate discomfort and disgust as much as pleasure. Cats, she later notes, are fluid. Yet they also retain – as a matter of prestige – a wild animal's ability to incite fear.[36] This barrage of stimuli extends to the indiscriminate polyamory of the feline and hybrid creatures in Fini's novel, whose abiding practices of licking, nuzzling, grooming, and exploring incorporate aggressive play and, of course, the ability to hunt, torture, and kill other animals. Reciprocally, such practices also multiply the fields of erotic and bodily intimacy beyond even the combinatory perversions of, say, Sade, Pauline Réage, or Hans Bellmer, insofar as they proceed from non- or extra-human forms of embodiment.

Mourmour explores the contours of such intimacies; the novel unfolds as a picaresque series of charged encounters, which alternately concern Mourmour's sexual education and, in his exploration of the ruined monastery, his sensory education as well. Entering the grotto beneath the monastery, for instance, Mourmour witnesses the island's 'collections' in their Roussellian assortment of automated *tableaux vivants*. In harmony with the fantastic eroticism of the novel's animate creatures, the tableaux further rehearse the recombinatory sensory and corporeal assemblages encountered elsewhere on the island. One tableau in the collection, for instance, features an ornate bed on which reposes a woman with bovine abdominal breasts, whose reclining odalisque figure is draped in empty jam jars, discarded candy wrappers, and other detritus:

> Sa chemise se révélait, on voyait alors qu'en bas du ventre elle avait des seins. Oui, des seins inguinaux, comme une véritable vache, c'étaient des pis de vache dodelinant, mous et pleins. Elle se mettait à les traire doucement... puis, juste à ce moment, une ombre noire envahissait tout.[37]

> (Her shirt was revealing, and through it we could see that she had breasts at the base of her stomach. Yes, inguinal breasts, just like a cow's: a cow's udder, nodding, soft and full. She began to milk them gently... then, at that very moment, a dark shadow fell over everything.)

As in the scene with Belinda, Mourmour's wide-eyed account lingers on the hyperbolic sensuality of the reclining figure, who seems to luxuriate in a perpetual flux between feeding and lactating, sleeping and waking. Beyond the spectacularised eroticism of such tableaux, the novel's episodes – much like the fantastic mechanisms described in Raymond Roussel's *Locus Solus* (1914) – present constructions that intercalate bodies and machines, animate and inanimate forms, with a realism and affective charge that belies the often playful or even arbitrary linguistic basis of their construction. The mysteries and secrets of the island open up to hybrid creations and creatures that, by contrast, utterly naturalise the sentient cats who populate the island monastery.

Further episodes in the novel introduce a series of hybrid mythological creatures drawn from the fantastic bestiary of Fini's paintings and indicating the extent to which such hybrids remained in circulation within her figural and conceptual universe. Like the career-spanning studies in which excerpts from the novel first appeared, *Mourmour* is synoptic in its incorporation of figures from and allusions to the painter's extensive body of artistic work. Its scenes gesture towards the subjects of paintings from the previous quarter-century; this includes the characteristic sphinxes that feature in some of the artist's most well known work, such as *Sphinx Amalbourga* (1942) and *Les Stryges Amaouri* (1947) (Figures 9.4 and 9.5). In the novel, the sphinxes

Leonor Fini's abhuman family 193

9.4 Leonor Fini, *Sphinx Amalbourga*, 1942.

9.5 Leonor Fini, *Les Stryges Amaouri*, 1947. Oil on canvas.

circulate among the island's other inhabitants both as further marvels of the ruined monastery and as participants in the ritual life of the sanctuary. The young narrator is enamoured of the gender ambiguity and, in particular, the unknown desires of the 'belle et musculeuse' ('beautiful and muscular') Amaouri;[38] the sphinx Amalbourga recites a poem in German and sings 'Casta diva' at a ceremony for the moon. In the earlier paintings, the hybrid mythological creatures, each modelled on Fini herself, tend to a young, nude, sleeping male figure, modelled after Sforzino Sforza, one of the artist's lovers of the period. Such figures appear resolutely allegorical, as their names suggest: the name 'Amalbourga' signifies a figure of salvation, a 'soccorritrice' or rescuer, according to the nineteenth-century almanac Fini used as a resource.[39] 'Amaouri', in turn, homonymically evokes 'love' (Amori/Amour), but it also alludes to the notorious Inquisitor of the Albigensian Crusade who coined the phrase 'Kill them. For the Lord knows who are His'; in the same almanac, 'Amauri' signifies simply 'Oscuro'.[40] Notably, in translating the figures from the 1947 painting into *Mourmour*, Fini changed the Amaouri from a pair of strixes (birdlike, vampiric creatures of classical myth) to a single, hermaphroditic sphinx: 'vous, males-femelles, êtes-vous donc trop parfaits – trop complètes pour desirer?' ('Are you, male-female, too perfect – too complete – for desire?').[41]

Such mythological creatures are fundamental features within Fini's abhuman world-making, I propose, insofar as they serve to demarcate the conceptual as well as spatial and temporal contours of the familial universe to which Fini's written and painted work beckons. Certainly, in figural terms the paintings highlight the salutary function of such refuges, in emphasising 'the regenerative power of the sphinx and her ability to return the individual to his/her primordial nature', as Alyce Mahon has proposed.[42] Much has been made of Fini's interest in and persistent figuration of sphinxes, as well as other mythological figures, particularly insofar as they invoke the world-making affordances of care and indulgence within the artist's figural universe of animal, vegetal, and mineral commingling and transformation.[43] For the sake of my purposes here, however, I propose that the inclusion of such creatures in Fini's fiction is less allegorical – as an embodiment of feminine power, for instance – than architectural.[44] In the context of *Mourmour*, that is, such figures invoke the material rather than purely mythological function of sphinxes in order to mark the thresholds of the novel's abhuman sanctuary, with its closed universe of open feline sensuality. As architectural features, such mythological creatures define the 'zone of equivocation and ambiguity' that characterises Fini's abhuman intimacies and transformation, where 'one side passes into another'.[45] In this regard the 'power' of figures such as Fini's sphinxes lies in the extent to which they earmark the world-making capacity of the literary and artistic works in which they appear; in doing so, they also serve as the threshold between Fini's figural universe and the lifestyle she had spent half a century developing: a style of living, but also a style of living understood as a carefully designed praxis – a form, perhaps, of theatre.

A pestilential smell: *L'Oneiropompe*

The world-making capacities of Fini's paintings had long fascinated her intellectual friends and collaborators, who were attuned to both the sensuality and the extravagance of her figural repertoire.[46] The surrealist artist Victor Brauner, for instance, observed Fini at work in her studio in 1958, concluding that the painting she created was 'l'histoire de la matière et de la vie, au-delà du présent et du passé' ('the history of matter and life, beyond the present and the past'). The painting he witnessed was *Vespertilia*, an oil composition based, presumably, on the poem of the same title published in 1895 by Rosamund Marriott Watson (under the pseudonym Graham R. Tomson), which recounts a fateful meeting with a mysterious, veiled, living-dead woman: 'Her fair face glimmering like a white wood-flower / That gleams through withered leaves'.[47] In his avid account of Fini's painterly process, Brauner describes how the figural 'personage royal, tragique' ('royal, tragic character') emerges from the 'chaos frétillant de couleurs à caractère chimico-minéral en movement vertigineux' ('writhing chaos of chemico-mineral colours in vertiginous movement') of Fini's spontaneous, unsketched canvas, which he describes as 'chaos primordial d'où viendra la vie' ('the primordial chaos from which life emerges').[48] This life-giving (yet also tragic, mortal) primordial chaos characterised the figural iconography of Fini's adaptation of Marriott's decadent poem of love and death; more significantly for Brauner, it described the process and evolution of Fini's canvases. A few years earlier, the novelist and playwright Jean Genet offered a sustained account of the 'primordial chaos' Brauner described; in his published *Lettre à Leonor Fini* (1950), Genet meditated on the artist's 'démarche biologique' with an analytical precision that both praised Fini's sensory universe for its imbrication of animal, vegetable, and mineral while also criticising his friend for the limits of her political aspirations.

Genet's account of Fini was, above all, a laudatory gesture of reciprocity from the author to the artist; Fini had illustrated several of Genet's published works (such as *Galère* in 1947) and would later create the set designs for his plays (such as *Les Bonnes* in 1961 and *Le Balcon* in 1969).[49] She notably created two iconic portraits of Genet in 1950, the first featuring the author's direct gaze, looking slightly pained as if contemplating the fate of the world; the second is a beatific, a three-quarter profile of the author elevating his gaze towards the heavens, as if to anticipate Jean-Paul Sartre's *Saint Genet*, which was published two years later. Genet's letter is no less striking a portrait of Fini in turn, articulating what she would herself later refer to as her abhumanism.

In his approach to Fini's mid-century paintings Genet begins by describing the 'pestilential' smell they conjure, 'exquisite and poisonous'. Genet's striking synaesthesia is notable not only for its olfactory rather than ocular orientation towards works such as *Sphinx Philagria* (Figure 9.1) but also for the accumulation of organic forms it delineates: 'this [smell]', Genet writes, 'can be recognized, by a wide-open nostril, as being composed of a thousand scents, interwoven, yet distinct according to each level and layer, in which you might find ferns, mud, the corpses of pink flamingos, salamanders, marsh reeds, a population of heavy scents, at once salubrious and harmful'.[50] Genet's approach to comprehending Fini's artworks subtly reconciles their sensory extravagance with the imperatives of postwar existentialism; that is, rather than framing their figural economy or creative process in surrealist terms, as evidence for the interruptive, transformative function of material phenomena, Genet presents Fini's work as evidence of a struggle to wrest meaning from a chaotic universe.

Genet's account of the ways in which such 'pestilential' odours find their 'hesitant, though precisely distinct' visual form in Fini's paintings and drawing is offered less as a description of their content or sensory effects alone, Genet explains, than as a testament to their 'complexity and their architecture' which are 'comparable to the complex architecture of swamp odors'.[51] For Genet, Fini's project bears ontological rather than formal or procedural significance, analogous to the 'vertiginous movement' and 'chaos frétillant' described by Brauner, a movement in and of *being*. In his *Lettre à Leonor Fini*, first published in pamphlet form in 1950, Genet outlines a 'dazzling universe' of flora and fauna, vegetable and animal, that both proliferates and breeds and yet nonetheless 'bears witness to an intimate, macabre theater'.[52] It is an elemental world that Genet likens to that of fable on behalf of its commingling of cruelty and creation, death and generation alike.

In a manner no less perspicacious, Genet's *Lettre* also introduces a nuanced, albeit strident, political critique of the artist in the form of an exhortation for Fini to 'complete the drama' her work imagines: to pursue its abhuman trajectory with the full intensity and 'cruel goodness' he saw immanent within it. In his letter, that is, Genet urges Fini towards a more explicit political engagement:

> if you tolerate any advice at all, I will advise you to stay not so long in the human world, in order to return to those dreams in which you call your sisters,

the ivy-imprisoned nymphs. Do not think, Leonor, that I am joking: Stop the game of appearances: appear ... the whole mystery of vegetable-animal conspiracy seeks to be resolved in a purified countenance, in a face.[53]

The 'purified countenance' Genet describes here refers to the ethical confrontation her images demand: the imperative of taking the 'difficult path' of abhumanism itself, which Genet likens both to crime and to the necessity of embodied political commitment. Though it remains veiled in the *Lettre*, Genet's imperative echoes the postwar critiques of surrealism by existentialist philosophers such as Beauvoir and Sartre, for whom the surrealist movement's tendency to formalise its own disruptive engagements as a set of prescribed rules, turning the 'difficult path' into a royal road: 'unruliness', as Beauvoir puts it in *The Ethics of Ambiguity* (1948), 'has become a rule'.[54]

Genet's *Lettre* is ultimately both a critique and an appeal to the artist to resist such routinisation in favour of participation, engagement in the active, mortal struggle for ethical, historical, and political meaning: a struggle, as Gauthier would later put it, with mortal stakes. Thereby nudging Fini away from a belated affiliation with the surrealist movement – before and during the war Fini's work was, and would continue to be, included in major exhibitions dedicated to surrealism – Genet's depiction of Fini's art asserts the degree to which its world-making designates a living ecosystem, at once moral and mortal, rather than a purely imaginary sphere. 'Till now', Genet asks at his most polemical,

> what have you been doing? On canvases, sometimes the world of your daydreams, sometimes that of your dreams, you have offered us a representation of them. If such an occupation allowed you to perfect your artistic gifts, it is only as you bring yourself up to date about a desperate world that we will understand your poetry. There exists a moral realm. It is absolutely the only one where it matters that the artist discover it by means of form. But it is the most perilous and noblest moral domain that interests us – as to its nobility, no preexistent law instructs us, we must invent it. And it is our entire life that we must conform – make conform – to this invention.[55]

My point in citing Genet's assessment of – and hortatory response to – Fini's work at mid-century is to highlight the extent to which Fini's later work responds to it. Fini's late fictional work discloses the extent to which the artist heeded Genet's injunction to invent a moral 'law' to which 'our entire life' must be made to conform. For in spite of Fini's stark divergence from Genet's ideas about political militancy, Fini did, I maintain, invent her own 'law' for the moral realm to which her life and work alike conformed. During the 1960s Genet famously dedicated himself to supporting the work of militant groups such as the Black Panthers and the Palestinian *fayadeen*, definitively upholding the notion that 'revolution' was a term that applied to violent political action, not to writing or art. As he put it in an oft-excerpted 1975 interview, 'What are referred to as poetic or artistic revolutions are not exactly revolutions'. He explains: 'In revolutionary action, you put your body at risk; in the artwork, and in whatever recognition it receives elsewhere, you put your reputation at risk, perhaps, but your body is not in danger ... When you're involved in revolution, your body is exactly what's in danger, and the whole revolutionary adventure is in danger at the same time.'[56] Fini's work makes no such appeal to either revolution or to the singularity of political violence; indeed, in a late interview with her biographer Peter Webb, Fini describes the last time she saw Genet: 'He was so pleased to see me, but he had a gigolo with him and all they did was talk about politics. It was all very boring.'[57] Nonetheless, Fini's fictional writings resolutely distinguish the 'vegetal-animal conspiracy' of her abhumanism from a mere game of appearances: it was theatre, perhaps, but a living theatre, a theatre of faces rather than masks.

Published only a few years after her final collaboration with Genet in 1969 but over a quarter of a century after his *Lettre*, Fini's second novel, *L'Oneiropompe* (1978), offers a belated response to Genet's assessment of her 'moral realm'. The story of a love triangle between a nameless male narrator, a cat, and a young boy, *L'Oneiropompe* begins with a meditation on odour and conducts what we might consider to be an allegorical survey of the artist's career, recounted through overlapping narratives of loss and retrieval. The novel's title translates roughly to 'The Dream Conductor', a neologism derived from the mythological figure of the psychopomp, a guide for souls who escorts them into the afterlife. Like *Mourmour* the novel is set in a synoptic universe comprised of motifs from across Fini's extensive artistic career, from mysterious train rides to dreamlike theatrical spectacles and nocturnal ceremonies. The novel opens as the narrator arrives in a nameless city in the middle of the night; the narrative proceeds from an atmosphere of urban mystery reminiscent of the psychological fantasies of Wilhelm Jensen or E.T.A. Hoffmann, shifting to the island enclave only towards the climactic final scene of the novel. Entering a nearly deserted hotel, the narrator finds the night porter who conducts him to his room, only to find that the room smells powerfully of a stable or rabbit-hutch. The narrator is comforted rather than disgusted by the strong animal odour: 'Rabbits?' he wonders, adding that 'The idea that the smell of those graceful animals came all the way up to me [from the courtyard below] brought me happiness'.[58] The odour returns periodically until, on the second morning at the hotel, the narrator hears animal sounds – mooing, neighing, a roar – that seem to be coming from the adjoining bedroom. In a manner that echoes – and perhaps parodies – Genet's description of the 'luxurious, burgeoning, invading universe' to which Fini's mid-century painting beckons, the barnyard odour turns out to be a perfume, 'Moment Suprême', sprayed by neighbouring hotel guests engaged in nightly sex acts dressed as animals. Genet's account of the 'pestilential smell' conjured by Fini's paintings is, here, neither pestilential nor authentic.

This comic revelation of the neighbours' rather banal indulgence in quasi-bestial 'perversion' is offset, however, by the erotic charge of the narrator's own encounter with the titular oneiropomp, a large cat whom the narrator initially spots in the street one evening and whom he later finds lying on his hotel bed. Upon hearing the neighbours' nightly antics the cat proceeds to urinate on the adjoining door, to the outrage and consternation of the neighbouring guests, who complain that the hotel has 'gone down'.[59] Having roused the neighbours from their nocturnal activities, the narrator finds that he and the cat have started kissing. Whereas the neighbours in their bestial masquerade engage in a 'game of appearances', as Genet might put it, the narrator encounters a real 'face', the face of a cat. Of course, the encounter remains a fictional one – unlike, say, the artist Carolee Schneemann's documentary films and images of herself kissing her cats.[60] Yet the novel's framework for pursuing this encounter is generic rather than erotic, whereby the theatricality of gestures and scenes takes on ritual significance.

L'Oneiropompe is, I propose, a quest narrative, a romance: it recounts a mystical journey to retrieve the oneiropomp once he begins to show preference for the young boy who lives in the apartment opposite that of the narrator. The quest is compounded by a series of other returns and restorations, including the theft and return of a basalt statuary head, a seemingly arbitrary set of operations nonetheless vested with sacred intensity. The novel is ultimately a story about the trials and tribulations of finding the lost cat, which culminates with the narrator's virtually penitential voyage to a mysterious island, whereby he must swim across a bay and fight through thorns in search of the missing beloved; the tale ends with a climactic ritual feast where the cat majestically reappears, like the return of the Harvest King in pagan ceremonies. The novel's generic framework as a quest romance highlights the ceremonies of transformation that proliferate throughout the novel, from the retrieval of the basalt statuary head to a series of oneiric, theatrical encounters that parse out the narrator's pursuit of the oneiropomp as a series of ritual acts, however incomprehensible their content might remain to both narrator and reader.

Such rituals, I propose, suture Fini's fictions to her domestic life in a manner that stresses their consistency with the costumes, games, and erotic intensities of the artist's 'moral realm'. Far from mere diversions or the exercise of a 'private language', the practices of masquerade and ceremony were fundamental to Fini's ideas about the laws of mutability according to which she and her 'family' of friends, lovers, and companion species organised their intimacy. As Fini writes in *Le Livre de Leonor Fini*, 'se costumer, c'est l'instrument pour avoir la sensation de changer de dimension, d'espèce, d'espace' ('dressing up is a tool for creating the sensation of changing dimensions, species, spaces').[61] Such a 'sensation' of changing species was, for Fini, both a concrete sensory experience and, as I have been arguing, a moral and biopolitical commitment. To the extent that ceremonial rituals of dressing up and transforming oneself constituted a form of theatrical play rather than, say, a set of explicit political tactics, *L'Oneiropompe* nonetheless dramatises the intensity of feeling and bodily commitment with which Fini's nameless male narrator – and Fini herself – acted out the ritual steps of her 'théâtre amoureux'. Such commitment amounts not, perhaps, to a politics of militancy or engagement but instead to a biopolitics founded on engineering practices of bodily and erotic life and the formation of communities according to principles other than those of liberal humanism. Ontological but not necessarily existentialist in its orientation to the demands of being, Fini's ceremonial imagination outlined a set of procedures that were at once aesthetically and socially demanding, even totalising, precisely on account of their manifest luxury and retreat from the sphere of human intercourse.

Primordial chaos: *Rogomelec*

'Puis tous levèrent la tête et regardèrent devant eux, vers le trône en forme de barque, où se tenait calme et rayonnant, le Chat' ('Then all raised their heads and looked in front of them, towards the throne in the form of a boat, where, calm and radiant, stood the Cat').[62] The return of the resplendent cat-king on the final page of *L'Oneiropompe* is at once a *coup de théâtre* – the spectators literally applaud – and a ritual act of restoration. *L'Oneiropompe*, a novel fraught with anxiety and uncertainty, though not without Fini's characteristic humour, closes in triumph. The following year, however, Fini published *Rogomelec*, a novel that largely inverts this conclusion: whereas *L'Oneiropompe* concludes with the narrator terminating his quest on a mysterious island, *Rogomelec* ends with the narrator's definitive departure; whereas *L'Oneiropompe* concludes with the ceremonial return of the feline 'king', the very name *Rogomelec* refers to 'he who stones the king', as we learn late in the 1979 novel. A far more haunted narrative than the two previous novels, *Rogomelec* casts an uneasy shadow over the phalanstery of Fini's island refuges. As an allegory, the novel seems to meditate on the finitude of the artist's invented worlds. And indeed, Fini's polyamorous family would change irrevocably in number the following year: Lepri died of prostate cancer in December 1980, the year after *Rogomelec* was published. The world may have been finite, bounded by mortality, but it was no less dedicated to the abhuman practices of Fini's sensorium.

The ruined monastery in which *Rogomelec* takes place becomes, in this iteration of Fini's mythos, a sanitorium run by monks. The narrator arrives by boat seeking a 'cure' for an unnamed condition or ailment; the ritual forms of treatment proffered by the monks involve a series of elaborate, practically Huysmanesque corporeal stimulations, including the ingestion of various tinctures, the nude caresses of a monk named Calpournio, and the application of live octopi to the skin. Yet the novel's monastic sensorium is undergirded by a deeper sense of threat than Fini's two earlier fictions, which culminates in the gripping final scenes of the novel: having witnessed a ritual for the 'return of the king' – the narrator explores the ruins of the monastery to hear screaming whereupon, in terror, he finds hanging the corpse of a crowned figure: the king has not been 'stoned' but, as one of the monks anticipated, has instead been sacrificed, or murdered, otherwise.

The novel's shroud of anxiety sets in when, during a ceremony for celebrating the arrival of the (unnamed) king, the (likewise unnamed) narrator finds he is the only one among the monks and other island inhabitants and guests who cannot see him:

> Je vis le trône traverser le portail en or.
>
> J'entendis des cris bestiaux, des chants solennels, des paroles récitées, scandées, hurlées. Des feux d'artifice, des feux de Bengale, des torches éclairaient violemment les Chemins que chacun fixait avec des regards fous. 'Le Roi, le Roi, le Roi!' Et les moines se jetaient à la terre, se roulaient l'un sur l'autre. Certains montraient leur derrière nu où un soleil phosphorescent était peint.
>
> Mais moi, je n'arrivais pas à voir le Roi.[63]

> (I saw the throne cross the golden gate.
>
> I heard brute yelling, solemn singing, words recited, chanted, shouted. Fireworks, roman candles, and torches lit up the Paths, toward which everyone stared with mad expressions. 'The King, the King, the King!' And the monks threw themselves on the ground, rolling over one other. Some showed their bare bottoms, on which a phosphorescent sun had been painted.
>
> But I could not see the King.)

When the narrator finally does encounter the king, he does so, it seems, too late: while exploring the scorched ruins of an ancient monastery, the narrator, as previously mentioned, hears a series of horrific screams emanating from within. When he arrives at the source of the screams, he finds a corpse hanging from the rafters, clad in gleaming armour. The king, it seems, has been murdered – although, true to the monk's prediction, not by stoning. It remains unclear throughout the second half of the novel as to whether the king is the island's sole sacrifice, or whether the narrator, the only witness to the corpse, is also to be its casualty – or whether, for that matter, his experience of terror and subsequent departure constitutes the 'cure' that enables him to leave. Such a radical shift in tenor indicates that the transformations named by Fini's abhumanism extend to sacrifice; though haunted by the spectre of death – even violent death – *Rogomelec* nonetheless incorporates this latter mode of transformation within its conceptual framework, even at the expense of the mythos of an island sanctuary.

Fini's fictions outline an abhumanism articulated through an eroticised kinship among friends and 'companion species', animal and plant, living and dead, mythological and corporeal – a kinship that extends through comedy and tragedy alike. Fini's sensorium is not limited to humanistic presumptions about the constraints of embodied life. Rather, as the scholar Janet Lyon has suggested in an essay on Fini's friend Leonora Carrington, 'the continua between life and death, whether they are liberatory or ominous, are portrayed as flows'. Lyon argues that the latter writer-artist's work persistently flouts both species and gender in ways that 'redirect us beyond humanist presumption, while as a matter of course also registering their narrowness'. Fini, like Carrington, demonstrates 'the transience of any distinction among states of life, death, time, embodiment'. Yet, in a telling distinction, her work does so without the affective neutrality, the matter-of-factness, of Carrington's work.[64] Rather, as she dramatises in the breathless conclusion to *Rogomelec*, Fini's work demonstrates an emphatic, even defiant theatricality characteristic of her practices and depictions of inter-species transience. Even when individual characters remain affectless, as exemplified in the painting, likewise titled *Rogomelec*, that graces the cover of the novel (Figure 9.6), Fini stages their neutrality as a *coup de théâtre* in its own right, as part of a ceremonial mise-en-scène that bears all the powers of ritual transformation to which Fini appealed as the source and wellspring for her art, a metaphorical as well as sensory appeal to the 'transience among states' Lyon describes. In this regard the *Rogomelec* painting recalls the striking self-presentation of Fini's well-known 1949 painting *The Angel of Anatomy* (Figure 9.7), whose paradoxically animate and anatomically exposed figuration finds its echo in the uncertain status of the crowned figure in *Rogomelec*. Does the title refer to the figure – 'he who stones the king' – or does it intimate that the regal figure portrayed in the image is about to be sacrificed?

In the 1949 painting, the angel's (non-binary, gender-indeterminate) expression of affectlessness belies, I propose, the baroque gestural economy of the figure itself; it does so, however, largely in extending the characteristic folds and ornamentation of figural surfaces – the powdered wig, the decorative toile – to the anatomical structure of the figure's own body. This conflation

9.6 Leonor Fini, *Rogomelec*, 1978. Oil on canvas.

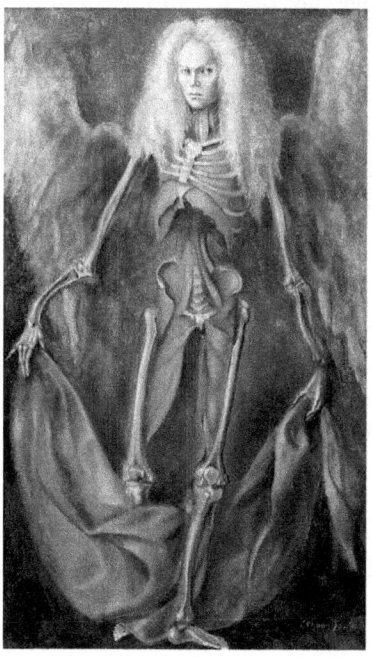

9.7 Leonor Fini, *The Angel of Anatomy*, 1949. Oil on canvas.

of inner structure and exterior affect is repeated in the abstract chiaroscuro of the painterly background in which one can discern a pair of wings, as a kind of supplement to the Angel's baroque displacements. Inverting the aesthetic gesture typical of early modern medical illustration to figure dissected human anatomical specimens as animate subjects, *The Angel of Anatomy* incorporates the dissected body within the figural logic of portraiture. At once flayed and living, the Angel's theatrical impassivity is not only capable of subjectivity but is also somewhat more-than-human.

So too does Fini's *Rogomelec* painting, with its regal figure meeting the spectator's gaze with a mixture of defiance and, perhaps, unrest, present an analogously baroque theatre of affectlessness: rather than showing its skeleton, however, the titular figure bears a massive, magisterial cloak of feathers that drape around the figure's feet like a folded set of wings; the cloak bears ostrich feathers on one side and peacock feathers on the other.[65] As I have suggested, the ambiguity of the portraiture suggests the underlying disquiet, even horror, invoked in the novel and indicates the extent to which Fini's abhumanism was not restricted to erotic satisfaction or pleasure alone, but involved discouragement, sacrifice, and death as well.

What distinguishes Fini's work from contemporary discourses of posthumanism has to do with the effects to which Fini mobilises this theatricality – the affective and especially erotic charges her writing and painting both figure and perform. Cruelty, sadism, masochism, longing, jealousy, and playful excess challenge the ethical priorities of much posthuman discourse, undergirding (or perhaps overlaying) the ecological imbrication of human and non-human, animate and inanimate, with polymorphous desire as well as fear, cruelty as well as kindness, intimacy as well as despair and disgust. At an explicit remove from the sphere of political engagement, Fini's worldmaking fictions seek to enact 'the transformation of one's sensorial and perceptual coordinates in order to acknowledge the collective nature and outward-bound direction of what we call the self', as Rosi Braidotti has written. Yet they do not so much do this for the sake of public attachments or even for a solidarity that might predictably extend beyond the intimacies of Fini's 'family'.[66] Fini's sensorium is dedicated not to the posthuman but to the abhuman: that is, a movement away from the human, yet always in reference to its terms. It names a threshold condition that confronts the sovereign subject with its mortality, which traverses the Cartesian mind/body divide, and which passes vertiginously between nature and culture, animal and human. These categories are less eradicated altogether than perpetually folded over, unveiled, traversed; and in doing so Fini seems less to be making a 'political' statement than invoking ceremonial acts of intimate transformation, the crossing of thresholds.

Fini's work attends to the transformations among states, species, and modes of existence that designate modes of existence alternative to the anthropocentrism of European late modernity. Her abhumanism stages a biopolitical intervention on the order of intimacies rather than rights: on the affordances of queer kinship and even domesticity rather than class struggle or collective mobilisation. As we have seen, Fini's biopolitics – or, to cite Donna Haraway's recent neologism, her symbiopolitics – emerges not only on the order of representation (in the narrative and figural attention to polyamory, inter-species love, animal–human hybridity) but also on the order of an amorous and artistic life predicated on their communicability as discourses and sensory experiences to be shared among intimates in private and published form. Such an intervention proceeds, ironically, even perversely, from a frustration of the ready instrumentality of political communication. In spite of the teleological connotations of her very surname, Fini's artistic performance (ritual, fictional, and image production) does not presuppose a political telos, but, perhaps most significantly, in theatrically refusing a 'politics', whether through affiliation with surrealism or other political positionings, her work *perverts* any such instrumental teleology.

It is possible to reconcile Fini's 'perverse' biopolitics with feminist politics insofar as they mutually implicate heteronormative sexuality and the bourgeois family as apparatuses for reproducing pliable bodies and subjects of capitalist labour. Fini's work certainly affords this, particularly in her claim to have 'refusé de procréer, refuser "l'utile"' ('refused to procreate, refused the "useful"').[67] Yet insofar as her biopolitical turn explicitly veers away from organised politics, it would be disingenuous to reconcile Fini's abhumanism with political militancy or claims to revolutionary political action, whether feminist, surrealist, anticolonial, Marxist, or otherwise. What I propose instead is to consider Fini's biopolitical, familial world-making as a function of her very distance from organised politics; just as her notion of abhumanism signifies a biological 'démarche' ('trajectory') away from the species-being and normative ideologies of humanism, so too does it signify a redirection of the struggles for sovereignty or empowerment: a perversion of, rather than substitute for, political intentionality. Just as Gauthier proposed to evaluate the metaphenomenon of surrealism on behalf of its perversions, Fini's work is significant for its perversion of the political intensities of surrealism and feminism alike, from which it veers – but from within which it nonetheless derives its meaning and upon which it impresses an interrogation of its utopian horizon and sense of risk alike. Is it possible to pervert an empire? Perhaps not; but it is not an empire – the patriarchal 'law' of domination – that Fini's work seeks to pervert. Rather, it is the grounding notion of direct militant action from which her abhumanism distances itself; the result, I maintain, is an expanded field of existence within which 'human exceptionalism and the utilitarian individualism of classical political economics becomes unthinkable', as Donna Haraway puts it. In Fini's work, such instrumental logics become 'Seriously unthinkable: not available to think with'.[68] What happens when humanism ceases to function as a noun, as a tool? As Fini's work teaches us, it opens up instead to a praxis: a field of continual transformation and generative possibility – primordial chaos.

Notes

1 Leonor Fini, quoted in Xavière Gauthier, *Leonor Fini* (Paris: Musée de poche, 1973), pp. 71–2. All translations are the author's unless otherwise noted.
2 Xavière Gauthier, *Surréalisme et sexualité* (Paris: Gallimard, 1971), p. 357.
3 Hélène Cixous, 'Sorties', in Cixous and Cathérine Clément, *La Jeune née* (Paris: UGF, 1975), p. 144.
4 On errantry and the 'right to opacity', see Edouard Glissant, *The Poetics of Relation*, trans. Betsy Wing (Ann Arbor: University of Michigan Press, 1997), p. 189.
5 Gauthier, *Surréalisme et sexualité*, p. 58.
6 In her manifesto-like essay 'Lâchez tout' (1977), the surrealist critic Annie Le Brun later upbraided the 'néo-féminisme' of Gauthier, Cixous, Marguerite Duras, Julia Kristeva, Luce Irigaray, and other poststructuralist feminists on the very same grounds, demonstrating how far the radical feminist statements of the early 1970s became increasingly amenable to the bourgeois family and the state. See Le Brun, *Vagit-Prop, Lâchez tout et autres textes* (Paris: Jean-Jacques Pauvert, 1990).
7 See, especially, Marguerite Duras and Xavière Gauthier, *Les Parleuses* (Paris: Éditions de Minuit, 1974).
8 See Peter Webb, *Sphinx: The Life and Art of Leonor Fini* (New York: Vendome Press, 2009), pp. 209–15.
9 Leonor Fini, quoted in *La Création étouffée*, eds Suzanne Horer and Jeanne Socquet (Paris: Pierre Horay, 1973), pp. 190–1. Also quoted in Gauthier, *Leonor Fini*, pp. 75–6.
10 Leonor Fini, *Le Livre de Leonor Fini*, quoted in translation in Webb, *Sphinx*, p. 215.
11 Leonor Fini, text for a 1972 exhibition catalogue, quoted in Gauthier, *Leonor Fini*, pp. 13–16.
12 Gauthier, *Surréalisme et sexualité*, p. 335.
13 *Ibid.*, p. 43.
14 Jean Genet, *Lettre à Léonor Fini* (1950), in *Fragments of the Artwork*, trans. Charlotte Mandell (Stanford: Stanford University Press, 2003), p. 9. Webb mentions that the title 'Philagria' comes from Mazzonni's *Almanacco perpetuo*

martiro-etimologico and means 'someone who loves plants and nature', but the Almanac does not contain a listing for this term. See Webb, *Sphinx*, p. 113.
15 Gauthier, *Surréalisme et sexualité*, p. 276.
16 Gauthier, *Leonor Fini*, p. 13.
17 *Ibid.*, p. 8.
18 *Ibid.*, p. 67.
19 Leonor Fini, quoted in Gauthier, *Leonor Fini*, p. 5. The term 'complicity' comes from an interview with Fini anticipating the publication of her first novel, *Mourmour*. Pierre Boncennes, 'Leonor Fini s'explique', *Lire* (Décembre 1976), p. 31.
20 Fini's artist's books from this period include *Histoire de Vibrissa* (1973), *Histoires and legends du chat* (1973), *Le Temps de la Mue* (1973), and the unpublished *Minsky Follies* (1980). These books were all published in limited editions and, like *Mourmour and Miroir des chats*, largely concerned cats. For a complete bibliography, including the books Fini illustrated, see Richard Overstreet's bibliography in Webb, *Sphinx*, pp. 285–96.
21 Simone de Beauvoir, 'Présentation', in *Les Femmes s'entêtent* (Paris: Gallimard, 1975), p. 13.
22 Cf. Boncennes, 'Leonor Fini s'explique', p. 31.
23 Gauthier, *Surréalisme et sexualité*, p. 341.
24 Leonor Fini, *Mourmour, conte pour enfants vélus* (Paris: Éditions de la différence, 1976), p. 9.
25 Webb, *Sphinx*, p. 8. See also Fini's own account in Nina Winter, *Interview with the Muse: Remarkable Women Speak on Creativity and Power* (Berkeley, CA: Moon Books, 1978).
26 Fini, *Mourmour*, p. 12.
27 Boncennes, 'Leonor Fini s'explique', p. 25. See also Webb, *Sphinx*, p. 251.
28 Boncennes, 'Leonor Fini s'explique', p. 29.
29 Fini, *Mourmour*, p. 26.
30 Fini, in *Création étouffée*, p. 191.
31 Leonor Fini, in Winter, *Interview with the Muse*, p. 58.
32 Patrick Mauriès, 'Note de l'éditeur', in Leonor Fini and André Pieyre de Mandiargues, *L'ombre portée: Correspondance 1932–1945*, trans. Nathalie Bauer (Paris: Gallimard, 2010), p. 8.
33 Sylwia Zientek, 'Kot Jeleński, Leonor Fini i Stanislao Lepri : Ménage à trois', *Niezla Sztuka* (10 November 2015), https://niezlasztuka.net/strona-glowna/kot-jelenski-leonor-fini-i-stanislao-lepri-porozumienie-dusz-czy-wybryk-nieobyczajny/, acccessed 19 September 2019.
34 José Alvarez, quoted in Webb, *Sphinx*, p. 259.
35 Fini, *Miroir des chats*, p. 39.
36 *Ibid.*, p. 152.
37 Fini, *Mourmour*, p. 44; ellipsis in the original.
38 *Ibid.*, pp. 102–3.
39 Raffaello Mazzonni, *Almanacco perpetuo martiro-etimologico* (Rome, 1839). See also Alyce Mahon, 'La Feminité triomphante: Surrealism, Leonor Fini,

and the Sphinx', *Dada/Surrealism* 19 (2013), p. 13, https://doi.org/10.17077/0084-9537.1274, accessed 19 September 2019.
40. Mazzonni, *Almanacco perpetuo martiro-etimologico*, p. 70.
41. Fini, *Mourmour*, p. 103.
42. Mahon, 'La Feminité triomphante', p. 5.
43. Rachael Grew, in an essay on Fini's sphinxes and female 'monstrosity', describes an exploration of inter-species hybridity that involves the fusion not only of different animal species (feline and human) and animate and inanimate parts but in particular of the *powers or capacities of these figures*. The kinds of sphinxes that appear in Fini's paintings from the 1940s and 1950s, as well as in her later writings, combine life-giving powers of creation with the capacity for cruelty and destruction. For Fini, the sphinx can be viewed not only as the ambivalent Great Mother goddess but also as a parthenogenic creator. Yet beyond seeking to 'trouble' or subvert or otherwise recast the binary logic of many feminine archetypes that so often figure in surrealist and second-wave feminist discourses alike – as well as much subsequent scholarship – these 'powers' are capacities that Fini's work plays out *in themselves*. Rachael Grew, 'Sphinxes, Witches and Little Girls: Reconsidering the Female Monster in the Art of Leonor Fini', in Elizabeth Nelson, Hannah Priest, and Jillian Burcar (eds), *Creating Humanity, Discovering Monstrosity: Myths and Metaphors of Enduring Evil* (Oxford: Inter-Disciplinary Press, 2010), pp. 97–106.
44. In one of the early pages of *Le Livre de Leonor Fini* the artist includes an image of herself as a child, sitting astride an ornamental sphinx at the chateau de Miramar in highlighting the architectural features of Trieste.
45. See Almut-Barbara Renger, *Oedipus and the Sphinx: The Threshold Myth from Sophocles through Freud to Cocteau*, trans. Duncan Alexander Smart (Chicago: University of Chicago Press, 2013), p. 27. In distinguishing thresholds from borders as the 'zone' marked by the presence of a sphinx, Renger writes: 'Whereas every border seeks to distinguish or discriminate, and hence establish absolute definitions and binary structures, the threshold, through its "in between" positioning, marks out an area shared by both sides. Situated in between, the threshold constitutes a zone of equivocation and ambiguity, a place where boundaries are dissolved, where one side passes into another.' Renger, *Oedipus and the Sphinx*, p. 27.
46. See, for instance, the limited-edition book of prints and short texts published in 1950 as *Portraits de famille* (Paris: Georges Visat), which includes texts by Jean Cocteau, Francis Ponge, Jacques Audibertiu, Marcel Bealu André Pièyre de Mandiarges, and Lise Deharme.
47. Graham R. Tomson, 'Vespertilia', in *The Yellow Book* 4 (January 1895), pp. 49–52. *The Yellow Nineties Online*, ed. Dennis Denisoff and Lorraine Janzen Kooistra (Ryerson University, 2011), www.1890s.ca/HTML.aspx?s=YBV4_tomson_vespertilia.html, accessed 19 September 2019.
48. Brauner witnessed Fini creating *Vespertilia* in 1958 and described the process in admiring detail; see Webb, *Sphinx*, pp. 200–1. See also *Minsky Follies*, p. 129.

49 On Fini's relations and collaborations with Genet, see, especially, Thierry Dufrêne, 'Jean Genet et Léonor Fini: qu'est-ce que la vérité en art?', in Agnès Vannouvong (ed.), *Genet et les arts* (Paris: Les presses du reel, 2016), pp. 161–71.
50 Jean Genet, *Lettre à Leonor Fini* (1950), in *Fragments of the Artwork*, p. 8.
51 Ibid., p. 8.
52 Ibid., p. 9.
53 Ibid., p. 10.
54 Simone de Beauvoir, *The Ethics of Ambiguity*, trans. Bernard Frechtman (New York: Citadel Press, 1976), p. 54.
55 Genet, *Fragments of the Artwork*, p. 14.
56 Jean Genet, 'Interview with Hubert Fichte' (1975), in *Fragments of the Artwork*, p. 125, p. 120.
57 Quoted in Webb, *Sphinx*, p. 177.
58 Leonor Fini, *L'Oneiropompe* (Paris: Éditions de la différence, 1978), p. 12.
59 Ibid., p. 45.
60 See, for instance, Schneemann's video piece *Fuses* (1964–67), as well as the images in *Infinity Kisses I* (1980–87) and *II* (1990–98). On Schneeman and cats, see, especially, Thyrza Nichols Goodeve, '"The Cat Is My Medium": Notes on the Writing and Art of Carolee Schneemann', *Art Journal* 74:1 (2015), pp. 5–22.
61 Fini, *Le Livre de Leonor Fini*, p. 41.
62 Fini, *L'Oneiropompe*, p. 164.
63 Leonor Fini, *Rogomelec* (Paris: Stock, 1979), p. 84.
64 Janet Lyon, 'Carrington's Sensorium', in Jonathan P. Eburne and Catriona McAra (eds), *Leonora Carrington and the International Avant-Garde* (Manchester: University of Manchester Press, 2017), p. 173, p. 166.
65 See also Fini's 1977 painting *Extrême nuit*, which translates to 'extreme night' but also invokes the maxim 'tout extrême nuit', meaning: all extremes are harmful. Such reversibility, and the threat that the earlier painting figures in its implied, if unknown, discourse between the bird-man and the female figure likewise characterises *Rogomelec*.
66 Rosi Braidotti, *The Posthuman* (Cambridge: Polity, 2013), p. 193.
67 Leonor Fini, in *Creation étouffée*, p. 191.
68 Donna Haraway, *Staying with the Trouble: Making Kin in the Chthulucene* (Durham, NC: Duke University Press, 2016), p. 30.

10

'Open sesame': Dorothea Tanning's critical writing

Catriona McAra

Could I, a dreamer, argue that history and literature are bedfellows?[1]
Dorothea Tanning

Alongside her better-known visual oeuvre as a painter and sculptor, Dorothea Tanning (1910–2012) also produced a smaller, although by no means less interesting, literary output. Indeed, her writings could be said to inform her visual art and vice versa. She worked on her one novel (or, more accurately, novella), *Chasm: A Weekend*, from 1947 to 2004, almost the span of her entire career.[2] Set in the desert of the South-West, it is tempting to read the novella as a fictive biography of its author who lived in Arizona sporadically between 1943 and 1957, as well as a micro-history of western women's struggles since the Salem witch trials of 1692. The spectre of twentieth-century wartime fascism looms large, endowing her novella with historical authenticity, and representing a real-life patriarchal force which her protagonist, Destina, must overcome. Tanning's fiction writing extended to short stories such as 'Blind Date' (1943) and 'Dream It or Leave It' (1947), a draft narrative for a ballet on the theme of William Wordsworth's literary character Lucy Gray (c. 1947), as well as biographies of fellow artists Max Ernst (1949; 1983) and Bill Copley (1951).[3] Her own autobiographies, *Birthday* (1986) and *Between Lives: An Artist and Her World* (2001), occupy a gap between fiction and non-fiction; crammed with poetic language, anecdotes, and self-reflective inner monologues. As the cultural theorist Mieke Bal argues, all biographical writing is fiction to some extent, whilst Tanning herself reminds us that 'everything we do is an autobiography'.[4] These autobiographies have come to function as indispensable primary histories and memoirs of the avant-garde cultures she lived and worked through, and are often cited as sources for scholarship on other artists she was connected to. Indeed, given her longevity, Tanning became a reluctant spokesperson for several artistic and literary movements.

Yet Tanning's writing does more, revealing a sharp critical thinker as well as an important contributor to experimental literary forms. For example, through her niece Mimi Johnson, Tanning became a supporter of the conceptual writer and performer Constance DeJong who set up Standard Editions, financed by Tanning, in order to self-publish DeJong's *Modern Love* (1977) and an earlier version of Tanning's *Chasm* manuscript entitled *Abyss* (1977).[5] Later, in the mid-1990s, Tanning was considered one of the 'oldest living, emerging poet[s]', attending readings and associating with literary circles around New York, ushered by a younger generation of writers such as Brenda Shaughnessy.[6] Although Tanning was no stranger to poetry, having spent time collaborating with the surrealists in the 1940s and 1950s and having experimented with poetry herself since at least the 1970s, this medium gradually became her focus. As her physical investment in painting waned, poetry became her primary expressive vehicle, with some critics even referring to this late flowering as her 'second career'.[7] Figures such as James Merrill, Richard Howard, and Harry Mathews supported this later practice, and by the millennium she was publishing in several high-profile poetry magazines.[8] Tanning's commitment to this field is evidenced by her substantial donation to the Academy of American Poets, setting up what would become the annual Wallace Stevens Award (1994) which leading literary figures like Adrienne Rich would win (1996) and Susan Stewart would judge (2006–10). Tanning describes the poetry scene as an 'enchanting world ... like the stile in the fairy tale that Blunder did not recognize as the wishing gate he had sought all day'.[9] This notion of her text/image intersection as a turnstile or gateway would become a recurrent metaphor, a portal that could yield and enable the artist to traverse her medial domains.

What is lesser known at present is Tanning's attention to non-fiction. Far from wishing to segregate her fictional writing (much of which, as I have suggested, contains illuminating material pertaining to the history of the twentieth century and the surrealist movement), the focus here will be on writing by Tanning which critiques intellectual history and/or comments directly on artists and movements. This chapter seeks to position such writing (especially her self-reflexive artist's statements) in the context of her broader oeuvre, as well as within the discursive framework of revisionary feminist perspectives on surrealism, and to explore how Tanning both shores up and splinters away from such thinking. Significantly, much of this material by Tanning was drafted and/or published in the 1970s, 1980s, and 1990s concurrently with major shifts in revisionary scholarly pursuits. In what follows, I reconsider select writing through a historiographical approach. In particular, I focus on two texts by Tanning from the late twentieth century: 'Statement' (1991) and 'Some Parallels in Words and Pictures' (1989). I will also consider one example of her artist's books, *Ouvre-Toi* (*Open Sesame*) (1971), which I believe could hold the keys to understanding the intermedial overlap in her broader practice. My aim is to recontextualise Tanning within a transitional late modernist and feminist milieu when surrealism was becoming historicised. Combining factors that delayed her receipt of wider critical acclaim were no doubt stylistic (as well as gender-orientated), namely her visual narratives coupled with her self-confessed penchant for purple prose, as 'floral' language is sometimes described, and the narrative excesses of the gothic, fantasy, and western genres. By realigning Tanning's writings with her imagery, and by retrospectively drawing both parallels and contrasts with revisionary histories, I argue for a rereading of Tanning's critical writings as an undisclosed manifestation of the feminist cause in surrealism studies and beyond.

Making a statement

It is often pointed out that Tanning did not personally consider herself a 'feminist' and found the term misleading.[10] However, it is also true that her work has had a sizeable effect on subsequent generations, particularly in terms of clarifying an investment in surrealist techniques which also sought for gender equality.[11] Whitney Chadwick reflects on the discomfort faced by certain surrealists in her foundational, if, at times, problematic, *Women Artists and the Surrealist Movement* (1985): '[t]hat the very existence of such a book creates philosophical problems for some of the women involved', she notes, 'seems to me regrettable, if unavoidable'.[12] An intersection between living surrealist figures and revisionary perspectives is notable at this moment in history, and not without tension. On the one hand, work by surrealist-associated figures like Tanning was finally celebrated and brought to critical attention. On the other, these living and, by and large, still practising artists/writers were categorised and historicised. Tanning explicitly rejected such limitations. A second (or third) generation of feminist revisionary history is now attempting to nuance these position statements, map the genealogies, and reprise the vitality of these politics while acknowledging that historiographies are never neutral.[13]

Writing on Angela Carter's intertextual appropriation of surrealist legacies, Anna Watz has explored the overlap that has occurred between the primary histories of surrealism and the secondary historiography of its feminist critiques: 'Carter's feminist-surrealist aesthetic can arguably be seen as contributing to a revisionary history of the avant-garde, one that considers certain strands of 1970s experimental feminist writing as a continuation and an elaboration of what we have come to think of as the historical avant-garde.'[14] The founding of the Virago feminist publishing house by Carmen Callil in 1973 can be seen as symptomatic of this intersection (Virago would publish *Chasm* in 2004). Expanding with a political force since the 1970s, an extensive history of revisionary scholarship now exists, much of which, in turn and for better or worse, would conversely fold back on to shaping the attitudes and viewpoints of surrealist-orientated figures like Tanning. Their coexistence is remarkable. Moreover, Patricia Allmer has recently critiqued 'the persistence of androcentric narratives' in surrealist scholarship, as well as the 'critical erasure' and supposed 'rediscovery' of surrealist works by women.[15] The discourse of 'rediscovery' is particularly problematic for Allmer, because it suggests that such figures do not have a critical lineage and are thus little-known or devoid of intellectual appeal, both of which are, of course, now wholly untrue – Allmer goes on to note Peggy Guggenheim's exhibition *31 Women* (1943) as a primary example which contradicts the rediscovery narrative. (Work by Tanning was included in this show.) Allmer also demonstrates how waves of revisionary criticism continued to raise these profiles. Indeed, it must be noted that Tanning et al. are now considered iconic for a younger generation of creative practice, which suggests that revisionary histories have an intergenerational dimension and relevance.[16] The recent death of the feminist art historian Linda Nochlin (1931–2017) makes this discussion all the more topical and timely – in the wake of such revisions and the mass diversification of art education, her famous essay 'Why Have There Been No Great Women Artists?' (1971) is now receiving some equally 'great' responses.[17]

Tanning had her own views on her scholarly 'revival'. In an essay collection, *Surrealism and Women*, co-edited by Mary Ann Caws, Rudolf Kuenzli, and Gwen Raaberg (1991), a short one-page statement by Tanning appears (dated 3 December 1989) – a response, or, more precisely, a retort, to being invited to contribute to an academic compilation on a topic which, for her, was profoundly controversial. Given the lyricism of her other writings and the characteristic poetics of her titles, 'Statement' is surprisingly succinct yet fits with this small but potent, nonconformist contribution.[18] (The short-lived imprint Standard Editions was similarly pragmatic in its titling, a conceptual move, DeJong tells us, to avoid 'fancy baroque names'.[19] This was an interesting redirection for Tanning, whose writing up to this point tended towards the baroque and feminine gothic).[20] As noted earlier, Tanning did not appreciate being referred to as a feminist and certainly did not consider herself a 'woman artist' (nor, one imagines, a 'woman writer'), and she makes her objection to this category clear in this particular statement, arguing succinctly: 'If you lose a loved one does it matter if it is a brother or a sister? If you become a parent does it matter if it is to a boy or girl? If you fall in love does it matter (to that love) if it is for a man or a woman? And if you pray does it matter, God or Goddess?'[21] As Tanning had already argued elsewhere, the seldom challenged category of the 'woman surrealist' had unnecessarily perpetuated the separateness from her male peers, and I am inclined to agree with her that, whilst offering a necessary context for their articulation, such canonical divorcings of female surrealists from their male counterparts 'unnecessarily isolate and perpetuate their "exile"'.[22] This is true too, I would suggest, of the perpetual 'overshadowing' narrative and 'significant other' model – repeated so often in scholarly debate since the 1990s that they have become the accepted truth. Unfortunately, the unrelenting emphasis on Tanning's marginalisation left her unsympathetic to the true aims and values of the feminist project, for it seems she did in fact strongly believe in equality and liberation, and actively sought recognition for her labour.

Further down in her 'Statement', Tanning confronts her general critics, drawing an analogy between their practice and acts of villainy: 'Like the phalanxes of an enemy, myriad assailants converge to bedevil your purpose and bewilder your vision.'[23] The deliberate melodrama of this comment mimics another complaint from her autobiography relating what she perceived as the prevailing lack of understanding surrounding her work: 'Oddest of all, the sad little procession of analyzers, trudging toward the altar of libido ... For example, some paintings of mine that I had believed to be a testimony to the premise that we are waging a desperate battle with unknown forces are in reality dainty feminine fantasies bristling with sex symbols.'[24] For Tanning, reviewers and, more broadly, the historiography of surrealism, seem to have been suspect in their theoretical approach, taxonomical imperative, and heavy reliance on Freudian analytical techniques. In her view, the majority of critical engagements with her work were myopic and did not pay due diligence to her larger themes. She concludes her 'Statement' by shoring up the point that she has 'utterly failed to understand the pigeonholing (or dove-coterie) of gender, convinced that it has nothing to do with qualifications or goals', again suggesting more universalising hopes for humanity. Her discourse on love and loss and gender categories presented here are weighty themes for a relatively short position piece. As with her visual narratives, we find a multifaceted array of themes and the writing is always highly visual; a gender politics located at the intersection of text and image. For instance, her poignant yet comical figurative painting *Woman Artist, Nude, Standing* (1985–87) was painted just prior to 'Statement', offering an eloquent visual commentary on this debate by way of irony and a subversion of the art-historical tradition of the nude genre. Here, a fleshy body, undeniably 'female', attempts to disguise herself, though somewhat conspicuously, with a hat pulled down over her eyes. Her portrayal pokes fun at the predicament of women in the arts and literary scenes in the mid- to late 1980s. Thus, for 'Statement', drafted in 1989, it is interesting to note how Tanning's writings already appear to merge with her concurrent visual

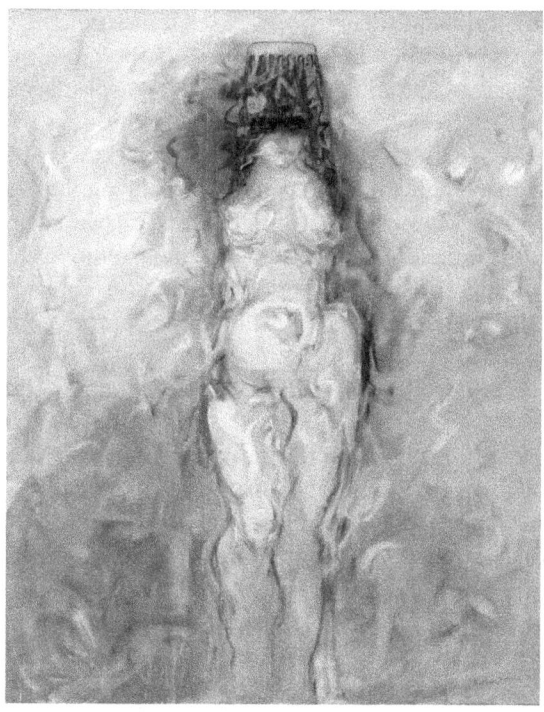

10.1 Dorothea Tanning, *Woman Artist, Nude, Standing*, 1985–87. Oil on canvas.

statements. Such parallels between media become even more apparent in an essay published the same year.

Some parallels

> I ran into Jorge Luis Borges and asked him if it was Ok to quote him in my book.[25]
>
> Constance DeJong

Another piece of non-fiction writing which Tanning prepared around this time was the longer and more self-evaluative seven-page essay on the word/image relationship through the lens of her own artistic experience, again modestly titled 'Some Parallels in Words and Pictures' (1989), for a special issue of *Pequod: A Journal of Contemporary Literature and Literary Criticism*, edited by Mark Rudman. She uses the space of her essay to defend the literary underpinning of art-making. Tanning's writing appears alongside contributions by John Berger and J.D. McClatchy, and edited translations of Boris Pasternak among others, thus placing Tanning directly at the heart of the American literary avant-garde scene to which she was now aspiring. 'Some Parallels' can be read as a retrospective artist's statement outlining her dual artistic and literary practice, while articulating the importance of surrealism for her creative development. Tanning begins by explaining that she is a collector of quotations, and we later learn that these are gleaned from numerous sources. As with much of the subsequent scholarly literature on Tanning, her essay is at first organised biographically and chronologically, with particular focus on her early art and literary education in the Galesburg Public Library in 1927, where she made 'extravagant' discoveries, followed by a stint at Knox College in 1930 where she tells us literature was a 'COURSE' and 'art was the *history* of Art' notably Gainsborough and Reynolds.[26] She writes openly about how her attraction to fantasy images and literature meant that her early works and emergence as an artist were 'a very private matter', with gothic literature being temporarily shelved due to the modernist tastes of the 1930s and 1940s. She expresses a kind of embarrassment around fantasy literature – noting the secretive activity of reading, the shelving of guilty pleasures, and questioning what it might mean for interpretations of her work to confess that aged sixteen she read the horror fiction and ghost stories of the Welsh writer Arthur Machen. In doing so, she owns up to a preference for a counter- or anti-modernism. She goes on to stress how she found a more conducive environment and like-minded crowd in the surrealist movement:

> How can I convey the sense of recognition I felt in seeing a new kind of visual art – pictures, objects, even sculptures – all sparkling with reference to their textual counterparts, all talking with new words. For the first time it was borne upon me that art and literature were inextricably fused. Since forever. Poet and artist bursting the seams of their categories. Art as a metaphor for language.[27]

Such were Tanning's thoughts concerning her initial encounter with surrealism at the Museum of Modern Art's *Fantastic Art, Dada, and Surrealism* exhibition in 1936–37. Ubiquitous surrealist artworks such as Meret Oppenheim's assisted readymade *Object (Breakfast in Fur)* (1936) and Max Ernst's narrative box assemblage *Two Children Are Threatened by a Nightingale* (1924) demonstrated to Tanning the potential 'fusion' which could be achieved between art and literature. For example, we know that Ernst used Freudian literature and that Oppenheim's gesture might be read as the physical manifestation of literary imagery, as, for example, in Leopold von Sacher-Masoch's *Venus in Furs* (1870). Tanning continues her essay with reflection on her francophile imagination and by confirming some of the key sources

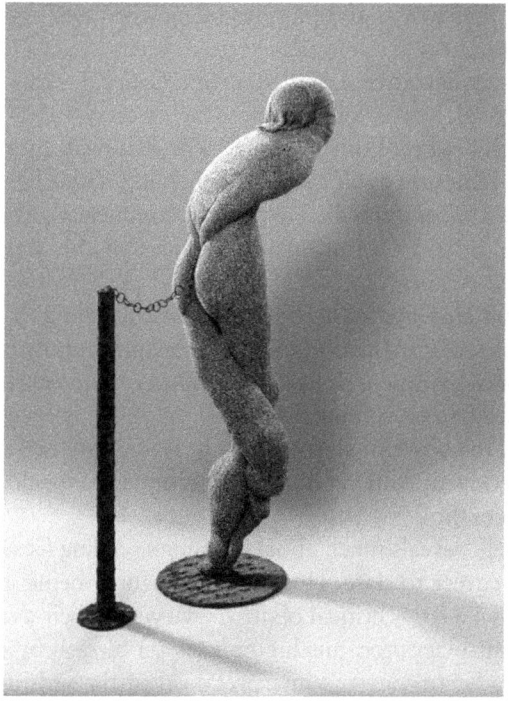

10.2 Dorothea Tanning, *De quel amour (By What Love)*, 1969. Tweed, metal, wool, chain, and plush.

for her artworks – such as the modernist novels of James Joyce and realism of Gustave Flaubert: 'What would Molly Bloom think of Emma Bovary? (My cloth sculpture of 1970, "Emma"?).'[28] Indeed, Tanning's soft sculpture *Emma* is the only illustration reproduced to accompany her writing in this instance. However, towards the end of her essay she also mentions a second example from this soft sculptural output: 'Racine's Ariane turned into a cloth sculpture *de quel amour*', meaning that the absent classical figure from Jean-Baptiste Racine's seventeenth-century French play *Phèdre* (1677) had, for Tanning, become manifest as a soft sculpture with tweedy buttocks chained to a post, *By What Love?* (1969) (Figure 10.2). Her source text becomes an active participant when translated into a literary sculpture. One might note that her soft sculptural output is roughly equivalent in terms of their limited 'edition' to her non-fiction writing – the point being that Tanning was willing to experiment with both soft sculpture and non-fiction writing beyond her better-known practices in painting and poetry. For Tanning, 'Some Parallels' is indicative of the fact that she was fluent in both text and image, her words and pictures being expressed through a range of medial branches.

Tanning's visual narrative *A Mrs. Radcliffe Called Today* (1944) is another artwork highlighted, by way of conclusion to her essay, for its literary referent, namely the gothic writer Ann Radcliffe whose novels enraptured Tanning (save for some temporary self-confessed shelving) from her childhood well into the 1980s. Almost immediately prior to commencing the essay, Tanning had made two collages featuring photocopies of the artist's hands: *Mrs Radcliffe Called Again, Left No Message* and perhaps the most poignant, *Still Calling, Still Hoping* (both 1988). The word 'calling' is significant here, suggesting a séance or evocation of literary inspiration through the lighter-hearted and/or experimental use of 1980s communicative technologies (photocopiers and answerphone machines). 'Hoping' is even more poignant, suggesting that the wisdom she seeks from Radcliffe's literary example has not yet been received. And yet Tanning attempts to 'speak' to Radcliffe by way of intertextuality.

'Some Parallels' reveals much about Tanning's reading lists and perspectives on her artistic career to date. However, it is worth being cautious of such self-analysis. Mieke Bal is critical of artists' views on their own intentionality, concerned that it places too much emphasis on biography and not enough onus on the reader or viewer's interpretation of the writing or artwork in the present tense.[29] As in 'Statement', Tanning may query the labels that critics admonish on her – feminist-surrealist – but, as Bal points out, artists are not the masters of their own legacies. Tanning herself was suspicious of literary theory, although she was certainly an avid reader of cultural news and art criticism. For example, in a letter to the editor of *The New York Review of Books* (1980), Tanning praised Denis Donoghue for his criticism of deconstruction but chastised him simultaneously for his misguided view of surrealism:

> Denis Donoghue's patient explanation of the deconstruction fever [*NYR*, June 12] so rife not only in universities but also in Soho lofts and midtown cocktail parties, really makes it easier for us all, at least for me, to close the dossier and file it away among earlier forgettable fads. I would not, however, be inclined to include the surrealism of the Thirties in this list. In fact I find it grievous that Mr. Donoghue is so reminded.[30]

For Tanning, surrealism was not to be confused with theoretical currencies of the postmodern era. Such delineation is interesting because again it suggests her awareness of the movement's historicisation during the latter part of her career, and again her self-acknowledgement as an eye-witness and, therefore, a primary authority on such matters.

In an earlier 'Letter to the Editor' of *The New York Review of Books* (1967), Tanning defended one of her literary icons, Vladimir Nabokov, claiming a penchant for his 'far-fetched language' in controversial novels such as *Lolita* (1955) and *Pale Fire* (1962).[31] Again, this brief public defence demonstrates not only Tanning's reading of English-language literary reviews during her time in France but her shrewd understanding of the critical reception of avant-garde texts and the power of writing as an expressive vehicle, which she would increasingly tap into.

Purple prose

If Tanning's literary pursuits are historically rooted and highly visual in their content, then it would be true reciprocally to claim that her visual works are very literary, certainly in ekphrastic terms. Her artist's book, *Ouvre-Toi*, could be said to offer an intriguing hinge point in her oeuvre. Prepared as a companion to her soft sculpture show at the Alexandre Iolas Gallery (23 February–18 March 1971), *Ouvre-Toi* comprises a series of aquarelles (originally ink and colour wash drawings). The elongated, frieze format includes several folded pull-out pages that invite the reader to play with her non-linear narratives, flipping between images, many of them abstracted reclining nudes and convulsive, concentric figures (mostly dated between 1965 and 1970). The combination of text and image in *Ouvre-Toi* is noteworthy. Firstly, the handwritten French text has the effect of annotated narrativisation (or comic thought bubbles) for her soft sculptures which appear in sketch form. Here, the artist's book conflates the medium of soft sculpture with a literary outburst – providing narrative readings for her sculptural environments, such as *Hôtel du Pavot, Chambre 202* (1970–73). For example, the words 'Les portes de l'enfer viennent de fermer' ('the gates of hell have just closed') offer an interpretative subtitle to the titular sculpture, *Ouvre-Toi* (1969, now destroyed). Elsewhere, her concentric figures are labelled 'Maternités', confirming readings of these bodies as feminine, and suggesting something voyeuristic about the reader's encounter with these conceptual orgies. These schematic bodies even operate as a form of writing, as a visual language of corporeal motifs. Secondly, anticipating her essay 'Some Parallels', Tanning lists favourite authors by their first names, such as Anatole (France) and Emile (Zola), drawing dotted-line connections between them. These are interspersed with the names of select literary figures, such as 'Irma' and 'Zoë', possibly the heroines of Sigmund Freud's *The Interpretation of Dreams* (1901) and *Delusion and Dream in Jensen's Gradiva* (1907). Tanning makes further dotted links between seemingly

10.3 Dorothea Tanning, page 4 for the exhibition catalogue *Ouvre-Toi*, 1971. Ink, coloured ink, and wash on paper.

disparate examples of ideas for her artworks' titles. For example, 'Dionysos S.O.S.' (which would not be realised as a painting for another sixteen years until 1987), Dante, and *Don Juan's Breakfast* (1972) offer an unusual trio of masculine author and legendary figures associated with excesses of the flesh. The overall effect is an intertextual network or genealogy of literary co-ordinates, markers to those who shaped her thinking, and, in turn, a mind map of future creative directions. As Tanning writes in *Between Lives*: 'I have loved and venerated my references or influences. But to name them would take another book – not just an art book but a book as packed with images as the human brain.'[32]

Not only does this artist's book offer a curatorial rethink of the very notion of the catalogue in terms of exhibition interpretation, it also provides insight into Tanning's experimentation into relationships between her visual artworks and their accompanying literary precursors. The title of the project is significant as well – *Ouvre-Toi* (*Open Sesame*) offers a way in, marking a medial moment where a visual domain yields to a linguistic one. In the fairy tale 'Ali Baba and the Forty Thieves', part of *The Arabian Nights* cycle of storytelling, the term 'open sesame' is famously used as a command or password to unlock the door to a cave.[33] Here the magical words suggest that Tanning reveals the secrets of her practice: the interjection of text into her sumptuous palimpsest of visual languages. Writing on Angela Carter's novels, Anna Kérchy terms this tendency 'grotesque over-writing', an excessive and ecstatic prose that seeks to embed the flesh and 'somaticisation of text'.[34] Carter herself was indignant about the perceived kitsch of her narrative-saturated writing, claiming 'I write overblown, purple, self-indulgent prose. So fucking what?'[35] Tanning's own self-confessed 'purple prose'[36] would, meanwhile, find its fullest realisation in the fictional domain of

Chasm, and within paintings such as *Stanza* (1978) with its abstracted typewriter, but I would suggest that *Ouvre-Toi* provides a self-critical, experimental ground that enabled her promiscuous medial parallels to comingle. The reader opens on to a paradoxical encounter between conceptualism and narrative excess; the mind/body duality is squandered. Whilst Tanning had published her first collaborative suite of prints accompanied by writing, *Les 7 périls spectraux* (*The Seven Spectral Perils*) (1950) with the poet André Pieyre de Mandiargues, at an earlier stage of her career, by 1971 *Ouvre-Toi* is possibly the first time that her own texts and images are so intrinsically enmeshed within her thinking.[37] Printmaking is key to this endeavour but so are writing and its sculptural correspondents. She would go on to make another suite of prints in 1973 entitled somewhat ecclesiastically *En chair et en or* (*In Flesh and Gold*) accompanied by ten of her own French poems. *Ouvre-Toi* serves as a useful tool for unpicking her self-criticism, exploring her text/image intersections, and revealing the mechanics of her writing style which, whether fiction or non-fiction or even in the overlap between the two, is always deeply cerebral and unapologetically 'purple'.

Conclusion: open sesame

All my life I've been on the fence about whether to be an artist or writer ... I've just found that I ultimately had more to say on canvas than on paper.[38]
Dorothea Tanning

The emergence of Tanning's writing practice as a sustained venture coincided with a growing scholarly interest in the work of women associated with the surrealist movement. It is useful to mediate such viewpoints and clashes from a generational angle. What we certainly learn from the study of her critical writings is that she wrote (and rewrote) almost consistently throughout her professional life alongside her better-known visual corpus. There is extensive evidence that one medium informed another and that she was proficient in thinking experimentally late into her career across a range of media. Such intermedial investigations coupled with processes of self-quotation make it difficult to isolate her non-fiction writing from her creative writing, painting, sculpting, and print-making. Tanning once spoke of using art to make 'a little order out of the chaos',[39] and writing seems to have performed a similar function, a method of managing the clutter of dreams, friendships, and the imagination. As such, it is no surprise that Tanning experienced discomfort at being historicised and labelled, despite the fact that the ongoing critical classification of 'woman surrealist' has arguably enabled a solid context for her promotion. Her writing offers an 'open sesame' to fuller understandings of her own position within and beyond the late twentieth-century critical context she was working alongside and through. Texts like those analysed above demonstrate not only an independent mode of thinking but an assertive and self-assured commentary on cultural history. She was nothing if not an important witness to the historical surrealist milieu. Yet she was also in a position to step outside of the movement. As I hope this chapter has made clear, she needs to be better recognised and acknowledged independently as a contemporary writer of experimental insight and literary merit. Focus on her critical writing alongside her multifaceted creative practice presents a case for Dorothea Tanning as a twentieth-century intellectual who has much to offer twenty-first-century feminist discourse.

Notes

This chapter was first presented by invitation from editor Anna Watz for her 'Surrealist Women's Writing in the Later 20th Century' panel at the Modernist Studies Association (MSA) conference in Amsterdam (August 2017). The author would like to thank Anna Watz and Pamela S. Johnson for their comments on the manuscript, and Mimi Johnson for her support.

1 Dorothea Tanning, 'Some Parallels in Words and Pictures', *Pequod: A Journal of Contemporary Literature and Literary Criticism* 28–30 (1989), p. 168.
2 Dorothea Tanning's manuscript for *Chasm* started life as a short story, 'Abyss', first published in *Zero* magazine in 1949, then privately published in 1977 by Standard Editions in New York, before being published by the Overlook Press and Virago in 2004 as *Chasm: A Weekend*. It was subsequently translated into Swedish by Kristoffer Noheden in 2009 for Sphinx Bokförlag as *Avgrund*, and more recently translated into Dutch as *De kloof – een weekend* for Uitgeverij Orlando in 2019. For an extended reading, see my study *A Surrealist Stratigraphy of Dorothea Tanning's* Chasm (New York: Routledge, 2017).
3 See select texts and notebooks in *A Public Space* 24 (2016), ed. Tess Scriptunas and Pamela S. Johnson, p. 37, p. 52.
4 Mieke Bal, 'Autotopography: Louise Bourgeois as Builder', *Biography* 25:1 (Winter 2002), p. 181; Dorothea Tanning in Peter Schamoni, *Dorothea Tanning: Insomnia* (1978), VHS transferred to MP4.
5 Constance DeJong describes her own self-identity of 'writer-artist-performer' as 'hybrid' and the scene as 'porous'. Interview with Jennifer Krasinski, *BOMB Magazine* (3 April 2017), https://bombmagazine.org/articles/constance-dejong/, accessed 24 November 2019. For more on DeJong, see Karen di Franco, 'How Does a Work End?', *So Anyway Magazine* (2019), www.soanywaymagazine.org/spoleto-special, accessed 20 November 2019.
6 Jane Kramer, 'Self Inventions: Dorothea Tanning, Painter Turned Poet', *The New Yorker* (3 May 2004), p. 42; Gaby Wood, 'I've Always Been Perverse',

The Observer (15 August 2004), p. 7. Louise Bourgeois is similarly described as 'the oldest of young artists' by Frances Morris in *Louise Bourgeois: Stitches in Time*, ex. cat. (London: August Projects and IIMA, 2003), p. 10.
7 'Dorothea Tanning Obituary', *The Telegraph* (3 February 2012).
8 Tanning's poem 'No Palms' appeared in *The Yale Review* (1999) followed by further poems published in *Parnassus*, *The Paris Review*, *The Gettysburg Review*, and *The Boston Review*, among others.
9 Dorothea Tanning, *Between Lives: An Artist and Her World* (London and New York: W.W. Norton and Co., 2001), p. 356.
10 Kramer quotes Tanning's thoughts on feminism: 'disgusting'. Kramer, 'Self Inventions', p. 42.
11 This is an example of what Susan Rubin Suleiman terms 'a double allegiance'. Susan Rubin Suleiman, *Subversive Intent: Gender, Politics, and the Avant-Garde* (Cambridge, MA: Harvard University Press, 1990), p. xvii.
12 Whitney Chadwick, *Women Artists and the Surrealist Movement* (London: Thames and Hudson, 1985), p. 12.
13 Griselda Pollock (ed.), *Generations and Geographies in the Visual Arts: Feminist Readings* (London and New York: Routledge, 1996), p. xix.
14 Anna Watz, *Angela Carter and Surrealism: 'A Feminist Libertarian Aesthetic'* (New York: Routledge, 2017), p. 4.
15 Patricia Allmer, 'Feminist Interventions: Revising the Canon', in David Hopkins (ed.), *A Companion to Dada and Surrealism* (Chichester: Wiley Blackwell, 2016), p. 375, p. 373.
16 The writer Kate Bernheimer (2001) and photographer Anna Gaskell (1998) both make reference to Tanning's visual artwork. The exhibition *Three Streets Away* (2019), curated by Alannah Currie, similarly explored Tanning's effect on contemporary art. See also Ann Coxon, 'Another Dimension: Dorothea Tanning, Contemporary Practice and the Legacies of Surrealism', *Dorothea Tanning: Behind the Door, Another Invisible Door* (Madrid: Museo Nacional Centro de Arte Reina Sofia, 2018), pp. 69–81.
17 Linda Nochlin, 'Why Have There Been No Great Women Artists?' (1971), in *Women, Art, and Power and Other Essays* (London: Thames and Hudson, 1991), pp. 145–78. The fact that Nochlin wrote about Tanning makes such connections even more pertinent. See Linda Nochlin, 'Introduction: The Darwin Effect', *Nineteenth-Century Art Worldwide: A Journal of Nineteenth-Century Visual Culture*, 2:2 (Spring 2003).
18 Dorothea Tanning, Cover letter to Mary Ann Caws (3 December 1989). Dorothea Tanning, 'Statement', in Mary Ann Caws, Rudolf Kuenzli and Gwen Raaberg (eds), *Surrealism and Women* (Cambridge: MIT Press, 1991), p. 228.
19 Constance DeJong, 'A History of Modern Love', *Ugly Duckling Presse* (2017), https://uglyducklingpresse.tumblr.com/post/158941870944/a-history-of-modern-love-as-told-by-constance, accessed 24 November 2019.
20 Mary Ann Caws, 'Person: Tanning's Self-Portraiture', in *The Surrealist Look: An Erotics of Encounter* (Cambridge, MA: The MIT Press, 1999), p. 61.
21 Dorothea Tanning, 'Statement', p. 228.

22 Dorothea Tanning cited in Chadwick, *Women Artists*, p. 12, pp. 14–16. See also Dorothea Tanning interviewed by Carlo McCormick where she famously claims: 'Women artists. There is no such thing – or person. It's just as much a contradiction in terms as "man artist" or "elephant artist". You may be a woman and you may be an artist; but the one is a given and the other is you.' *BOMB Magazine* 33 (Autumn 1990), pp. 38–40.
23 Tanning, 'Statement', p. 228.
24 Tanning, *Between Lives*, p. 336.
25 Constance DeJong, *Modern Love* (New York: Standard Editions, 1977), p. 19.
26 Tanning, 'Some Parallels', p. 168.
27 *Ibid.*, p. 169.
28 *Ibid.*, p. 169.
29 Mieke Bal, *Louise Bourgeois' Spider: The Architecture of Art Writing* (Chicago: University of Chicago Press, 2001), p. 36.
30 Dorothea Tanning, 'Letter to the Editor', *The New York Review of Books* (4 December 1980), www.nybooks.com/articles/1980/12/04/deconstruction-an-exchange/, accessed 10 December 2018.
31 Dorothea Tanning, 'Letter to the Editor', *The New York Review of Books* (9 February 1967), www.nybooks.com/articles/1967/02/09/nabokov-2/, accessed 31 December 2018.
32 Tanning, *Between Lives*, p. 328.
33 Marina Warner, *Stranger Magic: Charmed States and the Arabian Nights* (Cambridge, MA: Harvard University Press, 2012), p. 156.
34 Anna Kérchy, *Body Texts in the Novels of Angela Carter: Writing from a Corporeagraphic Point of View* (Lewiston: The Edwin Mellen Press, 2008), p, 12, p. 295; Peter Brooks, *Body Work: Objects of Desire in Modern Narrative* (Cambridge, MA: Harvard University Press, 1993), p. xii.
35 Angela Carter quoted in *Angela Carter: Of Wolves and Women*, BBC Two, 4 August 2018.
36 Grateful thanks to Brenda Shaughnessy for this insight. Tanning frequently used mauve in her sketchbooks (c. 1969). See Caws, 'Person', p. 83.
37 Tanning collaborated subsequently on several artist's books with poets which married text and image: *Accueil* (*The Welcome*) by René Crevel in 1958; *Personne* with Lena LeClerq in 1962; *La Marée* by André Pieyre de Mandiargues in 1970, not to mention single prints for group projects and *Demain* in 1964 with her own poetry.
38 Dorothea Tanning quoted in Michael Kimmelman, 'Interwoven Destinies as Artist and Wife', *New York Times* (24 August 1995), p. 2.
39 Tanning, *Between Lives*, p. 326.

11

Magic language, esoteric nature: Rikki Ducornet's surrealist ecology

Kristoffer Noheden

In her essay 'A Memoir in the Form of a Manifesto', the American writer and artist Rikki Ducornet calls on the necessity for embracing 'the risks of wildness' and the urgent need for forms of storytelling 'in which the world is reinvented, reinvigorated, and restored to us in all its sprawling splendor, over and over again'.[1] This manifesto of poetics evokes the way in which Ducornet, through nine novels, three collections of short stories, numerous volumes of poetry, and many essays, has dreamed worlds into shape that are ripe with the at once subversive and healing qualities of dreams and imagination. Attentive to the mysteries and poetry of nature, Ducornet's writings insert precise descriptions of the mineral, vegetable, and animal kingdoms in narratives bursting with heterodox knowledge. Writing in the tradition of such inventive authors as Jorge Luis Borges and Italo Calvino, Ducornet spins her novels as vast intertextual webs. Threading references to arcane teachings, such as alchemy, gnosticism, and myths, together with literary allusions, encompassing Jonathan Swift, François Rabelais, Raymond Roussel, and many more, she creates literary worlds resplendent with the wild joys of storytelling and animated by forms of knowledge frequently rejected by modern western culture.[2] But above all, her writings evince a surrealist penchant for locating the repressed and the rejected in the material and mental worlds alike; here, esotericism and the secrets of the natural world commingle. Ducornet frequently opposes the magic she locates in nature, language, and imagination to colonialism, industrialism, and Christianity, whose repression of dream and desire is often found to be conjoined with an exploitation of human and non-human animals, as well as the natural world in all its diversity. Here emerges an ecological vision of an enchanted non-human world in peril.

While these tendencies permeate many of her writings, they are particularly prominent in Ducornet's tetralogy of novels based on the ancient notion of the four elements – earth in *The Stain* (1984), fire in *Entering Fire* (1986), water in *The Fountains of Neptune* (1989), and air in *The Jade Cabinet* (1993) – as well as in *Phosphor in Dreamland* (1995), sometimes considered to add a fifth element, variously described as the alchemical quintessence, light, or dream, to the preceding four.[3] Her poetry, in collections such as *The Cult of Seizure* (1989), and in particular her essays, many of which can be found in *The Monstrous and the Marvelous* (1999) and *The Deep Zoo* (2015), bring further perspectives to these topics. Whether plunging into the worlds of Renaissance *Wunderkammern*, the writings of Gaston Bachelard, David Lynch's films, or war atrocities, Ducornet's essays animate many similar themes as her fiction. Reading her novels and essays in tandem as I will do here is not so much to fall prey to intentional fallacy, as though the latter would simply explain the former, but more a way of tracing cross-pollinations that germinate a work in which marvels illumine the throbbing flesh of the Philosopher's Stone.

In this chapter, I argue that Ducornet's writings conjure up possibilities of an imaginative ecology through aligning references to rejected currents of knowledge and criticism of human exploitation, with vibrant descriptions of nature. With an emphasis on the novels *The Stain*, *Entering Fire*, *The Jade Cabinet*, and *Phosphor in Dreamland*, I will show how occult notions of correspondences and ecological insights into the interrelatedness of lifeforms and environments commingle and conjure up a deeply interconnected world. Locating an ecological potential in these pursuits, I look to some of the more speculative tendencies in literary ecocriticism. Introducing a volume dedicated to ecological perspectives on the elements, Jeffrey Jerome Cohen and Lowell Duckert contend that 'with subatomic and cosmic scales have arrived an estrangement from materiality, the reduction into mere utility known as resourcism, and an intensifying ecological crisis rather than greater worldly intimacy, an ethic of nonhuman care, or the ability to acknowledge that the cataclysms that assail us are largely of our own making'.[4] Ducornet's writings confront very similar problems. Here, surrealism's romantic imperative to counter disenchantment and the mechanistic worldview assumes the outline of an ecological strategy.[5] But if Ducornet's writings revive knowledge lost, forgotten, and repressed, they do not merely seek to restore older forms of knowing and being. Acutely aware of the impossibility of simply returning to lost Arcadias, Ducornet rather takes what Michael Löwy and Robert Sayre describe as the radical romantic route of taking a detour to the past on the way to locating a utopian future.[6]

Ducornet's novels are richer than most, relatives of magic realism, Lewis Carroll, and self-reflexive literature from Calvino and Vladimir Nabokov to the author's close friends Angela Carter and Robert Coover. Whilst acknowledging the many directions in which her writings push and pull, I will mainly discuss them in relation to surrealism, a movement in which she has participated from the 1960s and up to the present. In particular, I will place her writings in the context of a little-recognised, albeit fundamental, ecological tendency in surrealism. This surrealist ecological sensibility can be traced through Ducornet's critical treatment of collecting and naming, her interrogation of language's capacity to both dominate and liberate, and the ways in which her intermingling of near-naturalistic observation and esoteric lore brings forth a view of nature as animated by its own forms of creativity, beyond what modern western science and philosophy have been willing to recognise.[7] Before proceeding to develop these thoughts, I will sketch out Ducornet's relation to surrealism.

Rikki Ducornet and surrealism

Born Erica DeGré in 1943, Rikki Ducornet discovered surrealism as an eight-year-old through, as she puts it, 'the back door' of Salvador Dalí's paintings and Jean Cocteau's film *The Blood of a Poet* (1932), whose 'convulsive beauty ... seized [her] imagination'.[8] Chance encounters fortified her attraction to the movement. Growing up on the campus of Bard College, where her father was a sociology professor, she came upon such formative discoveries as rows of bottled animals in formaldehyde, including a human foetus and a two-headed cat, surely priming her interest in the astounding richness of the natural world, and sadness over its being stilled in human collections.[9] One day, as she crossed the green glass bridge leading to the second-storey stacks in the college library, she chanced upon a blue-spined book on the other side. The volume turned out to be Paul Éluard and Max Ernst's early collaboration *Les Malheurs des immortels* (1922).[10] Ducornet notes how Éluard's poems and Ernst's collages are replete with sacred butterflies, totemic snakes, and talismanic birds, thus evoking a world in which there are no clear lines between humans and other animals, while also issuing a frightening portent: 'There are no real birds anymore.'[11] The young girl's mind may have been seeded by Éluard and Ernst's book, as interplays between words and images, imaginative inter-species relations, and intimations of ecological catastrophe recur in her oeuvre as an artist and writer.

Ducornet's initial encounter with organised surrealism occurred in the company of her first husband Guy Ducornet, also an artist and writer, whom she married in 1964. In 1967, the two met several members of the Chicago Surrealist Group at an anti-Vietnam war rally.[12] Ever since, she has participated intermittently in the group's frenzied activities, including contributions to the journal *Arsenal: Surrealist Subversion*, the huge 1976 world surrealist exhibition *Marvelous Freedom, Vigilance of Desire* in Chicago, and Ron Sakolsky's voluminous 2002 anthology *Surrealist Subversions*. Ducornet never settled in Chicago, living among other places in the Loire valley in France from 1972 to 1988, and thus had to contribute to the group's activities from a distance. However, the first exhibition she contributed to was a surrealist collage show in Brno in 1966, and she went on to exhibit with para-surrealist artist groups Fantasmagie, Ellebore, and Phases. In recent years, she has contributed to such exhibitions as *El umbral secreto* in 2009 in Santiago, Chile, *Surrealism in 2012* in Reading, Pennsylvania, *The Chase for the Object of Desire* in 2014 in Quebec, and the retrospective *Revolutionary Imagination* in 2018 in Chicago. All this is to say that her early encounters with surrealist art, poetry, and film have been augmented and nourished by a longstanding participation in the activities of the international surrealist movement.

Having started out drawing, painting, and making collages, much to her own surprise Ducornet turned to writing in the early 1970s, composing the prose poems and poems that would be published in her first volume *From the Star Chamber* (1974). She followed that slim book with a number of poetry collections vibrant with the mysteries of nature and eroticism, short stories marked by black humour redolent of the surrealist cartoonist Roland Topor, and eventually a string of phantasmagoric, iridescently black novels. She describes her writing methods as rigorous, yet resolutely guided by discoveries prompted by dreams and intuition. So strong is her reliance on dreams that she had never even thought of writing a novel before a dream about a girl being born with a hare-shaped birthmark on her face launched her into imagining the fate of Charlotte, the protagonist of *The Stain*.[13] Alchemy is another central source of inspiration for Ducornet. The twentieth-century French alchemist Eugène Canseliet and philosopher of science and imagination Gaston Bachelard inform her view of writing as something akin to organic growth nourished by dreams and refined in the fiery furnace of the imagination, a commingling of mind and matter, human and nature. Many of the resulting writings, as well as her drawings and paintings of flowers, roots, and seeds metamorphosing and breaking out of botanical categorisation, call up a surrealist ecology, equally attentive to the material world and to the ways in which dream and imagination may uncover new dimensions of the mineral, vegetable, and animal kingdoms.

Such ecological pursuits have a long history in surrealism.

Surrealism and ecology

Surrealism is often thought of as an urban movement with decidedly urban interests: arcades, the detritus of modernity, flea markets, odd commodities. But whilst such works as Louis Aragon's *Paris Peasant* (1926) and André Breton's *Nadja* (1928) demonstrate the ways in which Paris and its labyrinthine geography shaped early surrealist experiences, already Aragon's book also dreams of more pastoral vistas. And, as Paul Hammond comments, from the mid-1930s and onwards, many surrealists looked increasingly to nature for answers to political riddles as well as poetic needs.[14] From the outset, surrealism has displayed a remarkable interest in non-human animals, plants, minerals, and their surroundings.[15] Max Ernst's collages and paintings, Luis Buñuel's films, Leonora Carrington's paintings and writings, Toyen's paintings, and Jan Švankmajer's films and collages are but some examples of surrealist works that people the world with new species, display inventive relations between organisms and their environment, or explode naturalistic views with ripples of desire and imagination that incite marvellous transformations. Taken together, this imagery conveys a world in which humans are entangled with their fellow beings and surroundings, and in which other organisms and even presumably inert matter are shown to possess imagination and creativity. The art historian Donna Roberts argues that surrealism has an innate ecological disposition, which can be traced to the movement's opposition to the blind cult of industrial progress, and modernity's eradication of an analogical view of natural interrelations in favour of scientific detachment.[16] Such a take on ecology is more broadly encompassing than the scientific study of environments or environmental activism with which the term is commonly associated, but it recognises their basic premise that humans are part of, rather than separate from, nature. Surrealism has indeed been receptive to both biological and activist forms of ecology.

If surrealist imagery and narratives evince a fascination for nature from the movement's very beginning, surrealism's theoretical articulations of ecological stances have become more elaborate and explicit throughout its long history. It was largely implicit during its first fifteen years or so, took a more pronounced shape during the Second World War, and was explicitly articulated in a variety of ways in the decades following the war. From the beginning, the movement's belief in the egalitarian qualities of the unconscious destabilised humanist and Cartesian views of the coherent self and its mastery of both the subject and its surroundings.[17] When surrealism's opposition to the modern West's worship of the trinity 'family, country, religion' made it look to ethnographic research into indigenous societies, the findings not only enabled the movement to question the presumed supremacy of western civilisation but also undermined the very idea of human exceptionalism.[18] Effie Rentzou describes how, in the 1930s, the surrealist journal *Minotaure* employed an anthropological perspective not only to relativise western culture but also to blur the presumed boundaries between humans and animals, culture and nature.[19] Later surrealist texts explicitly point to anthropocentrism as one of the central problems afflicting this civilisation. In his 1942 'Prolegomena to a third surrealist manifesto or not', published in the wartime journal *VVV*, Breton exclaims that '[m]an is perhaps not the centre, the cynosure of the universe', and suggests that we need new myths of the world to displace humanity from its self-imposed position as the crown of creation.[20] In exile during the Second World War, Breton's interest in nature also intensified. In *Martinique: Snake Charmer* (1948), he lauds the vegetation on the Caribbean island Martinique, exclaiming that its lianas are 'ladders for dreams'.[21] And in his 1945 essay *Arcanum 17*, written during a trip to the Gaspé peninsula, Canada, he lauds the poetry of birds and stones, signalling a new attentiveness to the marvellous intricacies of nature closely observed.[22]

Following the war, Breton came to diagnose the dire political situation and its threat of destroying the world as a consequence of a fractured human relation with nature. In an interview he states that '[Surrealists] in no way accept that nature is hostile to man, but suppose that man, who originally possessed certain keys that kept him in strict communion with nature, has lost these keys, and that since then he persists more and more feverishly in trying out others *that don't fit*'.[23] For Breton, scientific knowledge of nature was not sufficient to re-establish these severed connections. Instead, he turned to alchemy and occultism for new ways of imagining the interrelation of nature and humanity. Occultism's doctrine of correspondences, and the reconciliation of internal desire and external world effected by the surrealist marvellous, henceforth became associated with a proto-ecological potential to conjure up the interconnectedness of human and world.[24] But for surrealism, such creative and reenchanting apprehensions of nature are far from exclusively human abilities. In *Arcanum 17*, Breton writes: 'At the top of the list of initial errors that remain the most detrimental stands the idea that the universe only has intelligible meaning for mankind, and that it has none, for instance, for animals.'[25] If animals, and even other beings and things, are ascribed a capacity to detect a deeper meaning in the universe, then the esoteric Book of Nature is written in a universal language that is constantly read by bacteria, agate stones, and ibises, as well as by humans attuned to surrealism's eco-occultist hermeneutics.

In the decades to follow, other surrealists made more explicit and direct connections between surrealism's revolutionary subversion of the edifices of western civilisation and a liberation of animals and nature from the stranglehold of human exploitation. In the anarchist magazine *Le Libertaire*, Jacqueline Sénard probed the ecological relations between different species, and extended ecological concerns to humans and the mind.[26] Carrington lashed out against the human mistreatment of other animals and the environment in works such as her eco-utopia novel *The Hearing Trumpet* (1974); she also expressed support for the radical environmental movement and its agenda to take back wilderness from the malls and highways that had eradicated it.[27] The Chicago Surrealist Group have likely made the most consistent attempts to bring surrealism's ecological tendencies to bear on environmental activism, in their elaboration of what they called 'a specifically surrealist ecology', or an 'Ecology of the Marvelous'.[28] The co-founder of the group Penelope Rosemont describes how, when making collages, 'my ornithological, entomological and zoological preoccupations have remained in the forefront, immeasurably enhanced by my deepening awareness of ecology'.[29] Naturalistic observation and fascination, then, inform collage methods that reassemble the world in ways that draw out new connections, so illustrating 'a surrealist axiom that the emancipation of humankind and the emancipation of Nature are one and indivisible'.[30]

Throughout these works, surrealists elaborate an ecological approach that rests on the subversion of anthropocentrism, recognition of the intrinsic value of other lifeforms, speculation about non-human minds, and the construction of new models for conceiving of the world's interrelatedness, often through a dialectical relationship between occultism's worldview of correspondences and ecological science's study of the interconnectedness across beings and their environments. Such is the broad scope of surrealism's ecological developments. I am not suggesting that Ducornet has been explicitly influenced by, or even aware of, all these examples. But surrealism's overarching approach to nature forms a significant part of the climate, or ecology if you will, that enables her own writings to shoot out their probing tendrils.

Interrogating domination

Ducornet's debut novel *The Stain* is the story of Charlotte, who is born with a birthmark on her cheek in the shape of a fuzzy, leaping hare. In the small, superstitious village in which she grows up, such marks are considered portents of evil, and Charlotte is doomed to be an outcast. Her mother having died in childbirth and her father being a violent drunkard, Charlotte is left in the care of her fervently religious aunt Edma, who scolds and torments her, and her husband Emile, who is kind and spends most of his time tending to the cabbages in the garden. Taken in by Edma's religious obsessions, Charlotte aspires to become a saint. Meanwhile, the village Exorcist, a man seeking to penetrate the secrets of nature and serving dark lords, takes an interest in her. Assailed by Edma, the Exorcist, and eventually a convent full of oppressive nuns, Charlotte breaks loose of their spell when she sees a huge hare glowing in the sun. Electrified by a sight that indicates an alchemical transformation of her own harelike inscription to luminous gold, she runs away and starts a new life in the forest, where she cultivates a closeness to nature that absolves her of the need for transcendent divinity.

When she began writing her second novel, *Entering Fire*, Ducornet realised that her stories centred on the ancient elements, and she sought inspiration in Gaston Bachelard's rich excavation of what he calls the material imagination. To be sure, Bachelard's intimate readings of the associations conjured by the elements across writings by poets, philosophers, and alchemists suggest possibilities for loving, oneiric experiences of the material world, which resonate with Ducornet's evolving ethics of embracing matter and the body.[31]

Accordingly, *The Stain* is packed full of earth, while *Entering Fire* rages with fire as, through letters, it narrates the rivalry between a womanising, botanist father and his abandoned son turned raging anti-Semite and fascist. Its successor *The Fountains of Neptune* is soaked in water, as it details the fate of a young man awakening from a decades-long coma trying to confront traumatic incidents in his long-gone past. The fourth novel in the tetralogy, *The Jade Cabinet*, is animated by air, Bachelard's element of movement. In it, the two sisters Memory and Etheria grow up with an absent-minded naturalist father intent on unlocking the secrets of language, a mother reduced by crippling illness to a withdrawn existence, and their good friend Charles Dodgson, better known under his *nom de plume* Lewis Carroll. Looming large over the family is the wealthy industrialist Radulph Tubbs, a man who scorns nature and dreams of replacing it with factories. Buying off the father with precious jade figurines, Tubbs spirits Etheria away and marries her. When, eventually, she escapes her abusive husband, Etheria sets a series of events in motion that leads Tubbs to Egypt, where his investments include purchasing a million ibis mummies to be crushed by a machine and sold as fertiliser – a potent image of industrial profanation of the sacred, if there ever was one. Tubbs continues his conquests but is ultimately humbled by his inability to relocate his estranged wife. The wind-torn narrative breathes hope of a world free from industrialists and their conquests, but ends on an ambivalent note as the narrator Memory ends up marrying her sister's former husband Tubbs. Following upon the elemental tetralogy, in *Phosphor in Dreamland* the narrator pieces together elements in the history of the Caribbean island Birdland during the seventeenth centrury. Victims of colonisation, the island's indigenous inhabitants have all but died out, together with an endemic animal called the lôplôp, with an allusion to Max Ernst's famous totem bird, a giant birdlike creature prone to burst into enchanting song. The narrator explores the island's history through recreating the fate of the inventor and poet Phosphor, an orphan raised by Fogginius, a raving madman fuelled by an unholy blend of Christian doctrine, empirical observations of nature, and folk knowledge. Inventing first a primitive camera, then an ocularscope capable of capturing reality in three dimensions on photographic plates, Phosphor is hired by the nobleman Fantasma Fango to join him on an expedition during which they will document island life and nature. Following Phosphor's development through his devotion to science and discovery of poetry, his serving Fantasma's mission to catalogue and capitalise on both humans and nature, and his subsequent discovery of love, *Phosphor in Dreamland* subtly investigates the conditions and constraints of liberty and the human tendency to exploit and dominate other beings. Whilst all of these novels are in conversation with each other, there is also a dialectical relation between Ducornet's fiction and her essays. If her essays sometimes zone in on and diagnose the maladies of this civilisation, her fiction narrates their inherent tensions and shows, if often obliquely, that there are alternatives to them.

Ducornet's writings, then, gravitate around ethical questions about the ill deeds humans commit on each other as well as to other species and the environment. She explains that she considers humanity to fail in being 'unable to sustain a healthy relationship with one another and with the planet. And that failure takes on all kinds of forms, in infinite ways, but primarily in the abuse of authority.'[32] Her narratives and essays probe such infected areas in western civilisation as the mistreatment of children and attendant repression of childhood, the ugly legacy of colonialism, the eros-stifling agendas of puritans of all stripes, the cult of instrumental reason, the hostility to dream and imagination, and the detrimental effects of what has become known as the Anthropocene.[33] While she has described *The Stain* as Manichean in its stark contrasts between religion and freethinking, puritanism and the body, the following novels treat these problems as complex, contradictory, and entangled, refusing easy solutions as much as they refuse to give up hope.[34] All this means that Ducornet's writings can be understood to interrogate the manifold mechanisms of what anarchist theory describes as domination, which the philosopher John P. Clark divides into three overarching elements: 'the systematic use of coercion', 'the systematic denial to persons and communities of real agency in the shaping of their destinies', and 'the systematic imposition of constraints on the self-realization and flourishing of persons, communities, and the natural world'.[35] Such domination forms a system with several distinct forms, including capitalism, the state, patriarchy, and, I would add, speciesism, which interact and exert their influence through institutions, ideology, and the social imaginary.[36] In the following, I will focus in the main on how Ducornet depicts the workings of the human domination of nature through practices of collecting and naming, and how she indicates counter-measures against it through liberatory uses of language and a reshaping of the imaginary through invocations of heterodox forms of knowledge. But much as Clark describes, and as the Chicago surrealists Gina Litherland and Hal Rammel assert in their anti-speciesist tract 'An unjust dominion', such practices are inevitably intertwined with others, including sexism, racism, and capitalism, from which they cannot be extricated.[37] In an interview, Ducornet herself talks about 'the ecological and social ravages so evident since the Industrial Revolution', and proceeds to note that 'the Market exploits the profound connection between nature and autonomy', pointing to patterns in the history of colonialism.[38] Similarly, in Ducornet's fiction, some characters' wrongful acts against other humans mirror the overall human domination and exploitation of nature, and the dismantling of oppression and repression is also a pursuit of a surrealist ecology.

The ambivalence of collections

In her afterword to *The Jade Cabinet*, Ducornet writes, 'I long for my own poetic territory which would include a keeping garden for insects, an extensive zoological library (color plates intact!), a wonder room and a jade cabinet which would, ideally, contain a chimera of mutton-fat jade'.[39] Her novels and essays create precisely such poetic territories. They reanimate extinct species, show possibilities of non-coercive relations with nature, and let loose flashes of repressed gnosis. They also evince an acute awareness of the way in which scientific discoveries both struck blows to bloated human self-confidence and enabled an ever more efficient exploitation and domination of nature. In the essay 'Optical terror', Ducornet describes how '[t]he Enlightenment was preceded by the great voyages of discovery, which revealed a sprawling world, infinitely stranger than previously imagined. Those Nest-building men of the woods … must have badly cracked the egos of those who flattered themselves made in God's image.'[40] In *Phosphor in Dreamland*, she extends this argument, as the narrator waxes about the consequences of similar findings: 'If men and women looked like God and *Semnopithecus nasica* like clownish man, then God had a little of the monkey, too, and the universe illuminated more brightly by monkeyshine, perhaps, than by the flames of votive candles. Darwin, dear Ved, is just a sneeze away!'[41] Here, observations of the antics of monkeys destabilise the Christian worldview, suggesting that play, rather than piousness, may be what makes the world go round. In her fiction, Ducornet relishes in cracking civilised human egos in a similar way, and she frequently amasses the heterogeneous wonders of the natural world against the strictures of Christian, capitalist, and scientific dogma alike.

Ducornet's mention of the wonder room indicates an attraction to Renaissance *Wunderkammern* which she shares with other surrealists. For Breton, such collections embody an analogical principle of arrangement, promising to be a 'key to this mental prison' of alienated modernity with its promise of 'free and limitless play'.[42] Ducornet's writings suggest that ecological interrelations may emerge from playful, analogical associations that reveal the interrelatedness of things kept apart by the logic of identity.[43] Yet, for all the fascination her novels evince with the *Wunderkammer*, replete with premodern analogical arrangements of wondrous animals, stones, plants, and artefacts, they are also attentive to the violence and exploitation inherent in establishing such collections. In *Phosphor in Dreamland*, Ducornet asserts that 'the cabinets reveal an existential stance', which, she has the fictive scholar Alicia Ombos argue, is 'an attempt to seize and fix a universe in constant flux'.[44] The cabinets are symptomatic of an ontological crisis, and reveal 'an incapacity to read – not only the world's body but its metaphysical books of days and dreams and prophesies'.[45] Analogical arrangements, then, if they are ever to be capable of breaking us out of the prison house of identity, need to be paired with an ethical imperative to assert, and embrace, the world's incessant change.

Many of Ducornet's narratives pivot on the characters' approach to nature. An interest in examining and documenting animals and plants is sometimes bound up with a recognition of the myriad other lifeforms surrounding humanity which destabilises anthropocentrism, but in other instances it forms part of a will to power and domination. In *The Stain*, the humble Emile tends to his garden and, gaze low, admits that he is more fond of his cabbages than of humans. The ambitious Exorcist, on the other hand, obsessively documents the world, lest it fall apart. '*Everything* must be on record', he states, counting the mould stains on the wall and the dog hairs on his shoes, pointing his camera towards his own faeces.[46] In many ways the Exorcist, revelling in accursed knowledge, self-proclaimed servant of Satan, and unduly fixated on base matter, is the inversion of the pious Christian outlook represented by Edma. Yet they come together in their strivings to dominate other humans as well as a nature they consider unclean and debased. Fogginius in *Phosphor in Dreamland*, former priest and errant naturalist, furthers this tendency. Obsessively cataloguing the wildlife surrounding his abode, he kills off all the animals as, in his desire to fixate unwieldy life, he transforms them into a mass of poorly executed taxidermy specimens. As it turns out, when not grounded in an ethics of egalitarianism, the mania for documenting the world is eerily similar to the strictures of Christianity, empirical obsession merely the flip side of closed-off hostility to the sensuous world. Both attitudes are complicit in ecological disaster.

Much as Ducornet avoids placing undivided faith in premodern views of nature, her novels take a dialectical approach to modern science. Surrealism has always combined its disdain for positivism and logic with an unabashed fascination with scientific discoveries, from advances in physics to evolutionary biology. As Penelope Rosemont puts it, surrealists 'delight in the discoveries of science – from the deep-sea vents and their life-forms to listening to gravity-waves from the collisions of distant stars'.[47] *Phosphor in Dreamland* abounds with minute attention to zoological, botanical, and mineralogical detail. The narrator gushes forth about a new room in the local museum, stating that he 'cannot express how delightful it is within the oval room to contemplate the bodies of the astraeans, the millepora, the corallines, madrepores, and meandrina that have, over millennia, caused the island to be, and simultaneously contemplate the island itself, as if *magicked* into miniature and pulsing with life'.[48] In this instance, Ducornet shows that the wonder of collecting and naming can be placed in the service of a more ecological vision of the world, attentive to its detail and the intricate inter-relation between life forms and geography, rather than keyed to domination. Scientific inquisitiveness and poetic wonder thus come together through a dialectics in which eros-driven participation in nature combines with dogma-defying search for knowledge.

Charles Darwin, the figurehead of evolutionary biology, shows up in different places across Ducornet's writings. Surrealists have lauded Darwin's discoveries for their dismantling of the myth of human exceptionalism, but also problematised Darwinism for its goal-oriented view of evolution.[49] In Ducornet's writings, Darwin is sometimes lightly mocked. In *The Fountains of Neptune*, a monkey is called Charlie Dee in mock reference to Darwin, but perhaps more as an affront to human conceptions of superiority; it is surely no accident that Charlie irks the novel's charismatic but danger-ous character Tojours-Là so much that he beats the monkey to death. In *Phosphor in Dreamland*, the narrator laments the fact that, whilst evolution proposes kinship across species, humanity hears a more grandiose tune and distorts Darwin in order to perceive itself to be 'Nature's Crowning Glory'.[50] Rather than critiquing evolutionary biology in itself, such instances lampoon those who draw on its discoveries to conceive of humanity as the crown of evolution, a conception of human exceptionalism that ultimately only replicates the Christian image of human superiority over nature. In contrast to such Darwinisms, Ducornet's writings seem to be more attuned to Darwin's own minute attention to the environment and the interactions of different organisms, including their inner lives, and his contention that the difference between humans and other animals is one of degree, not kind. Here, then, emerges an ecological vision of the world, which simultaneously embraces the lessons of evolution, ethological speculation, and the free play of analogical association.

Biology can also counter domination. In *Entering Fire* Lamprias's first visit as a child to the palaeontology museum in Paris makes him realise 'that the species to which I belong is damned'.[51] But he finds an antidote in botany to humanity's domination and exploitation of other species. Refining his skills with methods that are equally scientific and esoteric, he becomes so successful at growing orchids that *Time* magazine dubs him 'the Einstein of biology'.[52] He is seduced by the poetry of the vegetable world in a way that recalls Breton's earlier-mentioned discovery of the oneiric richness of the Martinican vegetation. Lamprias's raging-fascist son Septimus cannot abide his father's interest in messy nature, and destroys many of his biology books: 'my Darwin, Martius and Spix, my Humboldt and Auguste de Saint-Hilaire, my Cuvier, Lamarck and my Lund', a veritable canon of pioneering, empirical investigations into nature, which are here made into strong counterforces against a totalitarian fear of the unpredictable, organic world.[53] Whilst Septimus abhors decadent nature, he directs his own classificatory mania towards humans, as indicated by his bilious injunction to '[d]istrust men with skulls which defy classification'.[54] Fogginius, too, emphasises the close proximity between classifying nature in a spirit of domination and classifying humans in a spirit of racism. As he explains Yahweh's reasons for creating humans differently in different locations, he proclaims: 'The races were meant to be fixed, once and for all, like nails in a door.'[55] The conflict between Lamprias and Septimus plays out the conflicting employments of scientific inquiry, as Lamprias joins botany with alchemy, and Septimus perverts evolutionary biology with fascist ideas.

Non-coercive approaches to knowledge of plants and animals are evinced in *The Stain*. Archange Poupine, an aloof man living by himself in the forest, knows all the names of wild flowers, and their potential uses. His is a knowledge that comes from being with the natural world and being attuned to it, not merely gazing at it as from an outside position. Poupine's is also the knowledge of folk magic and poetry, as is clear from the wild stories he proceeds to tell Charlotte, of jealous crows, angry toads, and the fact that the stone called the Devil's Finger, just outside the village, is 'in truth a pebble that Gargantua the giant had found once, long ago, in his shoe'.[56] Poupine's belief in liberty is also clear when he says: 'Some people are monkeys ... And monkeys, Charlotte, being people, should not be kept in cages.'[57] Poupine's intuition of something similar to Darwin's scandalous discovery of the close kinship of monkeys and humans echoes when Lamprias's Amazonian partner Cûcla in *Entering Fire* says, 'I was brought up to refer to the apes as "Uncle" and "Aunt"'.[58] Poupine and Cûcla appear to suggest that a viable alternative to a culture of collecting and naming in the spirit of domination is an eco-egalitarian immersion in the sensuous world that is predicated on an initiatory transformation of the self, the outcome of which is an enchanted and magical coexistence. The imaginary underlying such coexistence is further explored through magic uses of language that explode utilitarianism.

The eco-magic of language

Rikki Ducornet describes how, at an early age, she was 'infected with the venom of language', when she opened an alphabet book in which 'B was a Brobdingnagian tiger-striped bumblebee, hovering over a crimson blossom, its stinger intact'. This meeting of image and word had such an effect on her that she found herself 'initiated into the alphabet', and its Edenic capacity to both engender and transform reality.[59] As the naturalist and linguistic obsessive Angus Sphery in *The Jade Cabinet* has it, this was a language 'so powerful as to *conjure the world of things*. All of Adam and Eve's needs were seen to by this language of languages which was also a species of magic.'[60] Indeed, Ducornet's novels evince an intimate connection between magic, alchemy, and the secrets of language similar to that proposed by such luminaries as the mysterious alchemist Fulcanelli, and picked up on by Breton in his search for an employment of words that can break the spell of alienation.[61] Ducornet's writings frequently infuse descriptions of nature with the lure of esoteric secrets, relations that are obscured to positivist logic but ripe for discovery by poetically and magically attuned minds. In this, her writing is kin to alchemy's language of birds, built on a bawdy argot that short-circuits the distinction between high and low through a playful dialectics of concealing and revealing.[62] While Ducornet's novels are filled with eggs representing the Philosopher's Stone, animals that can be seen as images of different stages of alchemy's Great Work, and frequent allusions to the processes of dissolution and transmutation that characterise it, her proximity to the language of birds can also be seen in the delight in which she partakes of the kinds of riddles, allegorical expressions, and descriptions of wild associations that Fulcanelli relates back to the Renaissance folk mentality.[63] This magic language relishes in a creative reconstitution of the world, ripe with promises of a reconciliation of human and nature with strong ecological implications.

Ducornet returns time and again to the enchanting prospect of an Edenic language, but some of her characters appear drawn to the powers of language for reasons founded in a will to dominate. Ducornet's most oppressive characters are often capable of concocting tales and spinning words into deceptive nuggets. There is the verbose Exorcist in *The Stain*, the fiery fascist Septimus de Bergerac in *Entering Fire*, the seductive storyteller Tojours-Là in *Fountains of Neptune*, the surprisingly eloquent industrialist Tubbs in *The Jade Cabinet*, and, to crown this troop, Fogginius in *Phosphor in Dreamland*, a man who talks so incessantly that he drives Fantasma's strong man Yahoo Clay out of his mind, makes others stuff their ears to drown out his stream of grotesque wisdom, and, in one of the book's most memorable passages, stops talking only as advanced age finally catches up with him and he disintegrates, 'collapsed with a sigh into a heap of knucklebones and pale ashes'.[64] All these men wield language as an instrument of domination: social, religious, speciesist. Ducornet locates a similar problem in Adam himself, who, she writes in an essay, 'is the son of Yahweh after all, and domination is to his taste. Like a grocer, he parcels out the animals: those that creep upon their bellies and thrive in confusion – the venomous scorpion, the snake – these he despises. The docile cattle he enthralls, and in envy, fear, and ignorance, demonizes the wild beast.'[65] The impulse to catalogue and name rears its ugly head in the myth of the origin of human language, and points to the ecological necessity of recalibrating this linguistic myth.

Phosphor in Dreamland may point to some ways of effecting such a change. The novel is not only permeated with minute attention to the natural world; it also throbs with the magic of language. But Ducornet couples these impulses with the euphoria of play and alchemical transformations rather than with domination. In a letter to his friend V.S. Krishnamurti, the narrator writes, '[I] recall your conceit that all living things carry fables – the fabulous histories of their being within their cells: each creature an encyclopedia written in code. You likened the chromosomes to the Minotaur's maze, the face of the Medusa, a map of Milano, Mars seen from space.'[66] Here is the great play of analogy in action, as cells mirror the mythological maze, cartography, and celestial bodies, in a breathless zoom in and out; the interconnectedness of a world structured by correspondences merges with the interconnections of ecology, as the imagination traverses domains humans are taught to regard as separate. The effect is one of linking up the smallest life forms with the grandest cosmic phenomena, and of associating the richness of the material world with the expanses of the mind. Much as Breton looked to occultism for keys to unlock new human relations with nature, so Ducornet draws on alchemy's notion of a living nature replete with correspondences between the great and the small in order to envision new ecological relations.[67]

In *Entering Fire*, Ducornet has Lamprias read an old manuscript by his ancestor Cyrano de Bergerac. To Lamprias's astonishment, the purported alchemist describes the Philosopher's Stone as vegetal. Lamprias expands on his ravenous, erotic appetite for the minute details of the natural world: 'I am not a botanist by profession, but an enamoured amateur ... I see the future in flowers, which like angels or astronauts spend their entire existence in the sky ... The primary elements – heavy and simple – have been transformed into the airy, the complex. Here I understand the true intent of Eden.'[68] Projecting philosophy and alchemy upon nature investigated in detail and with sympathy, the novel seems to suggest, is preferable to straightforward cataloguing. In that way, Ducornet asserts the continuity between the alchemical and biological investigations of nature; she evokes the necessity of an imaginative participation in the mysteries of the natural world, intertwined with, rather than separate from, the mind.

When the narrator in *Phosphor in Dreamland* proceeds to compare the way in which his friend engaged him with his knowledge, with the way in which he engaged a dolphin by throwing fish to it, he also asserts the connection of language and nature, communication occurring through the transmission of arcane lore as well through tossing fish to a cetacean. If such couplings destabilise anthropocentrism and its attendant notion that, as Breton puts it, the universe only holds intelligible meaning for humans and not for animals and other beings, there are further intimations that the Edenic language of which Ducornet dreams may break the anthropocentric mould.

In the essay 'On Language as Such and the Language of Man', Walter Benjamin evinces his own fascination with conceptions of an Edenic language, as he argues that language occurs everywhere in the world, and that human languages are merely one particular example.[69] Benjamin puts forth a very different linguistic theory from that which has dominated the humanities since the second half of the twentieth century or so, but in recent years his linguistics has gained new relevance for scholars examining the languages of animals and plants. Monica Gagliano points out that the presumed arbitrary relation between signifier and signified in human language (as propagated most famously by Ferdinand de Saussure), which has been put forward as proof of humanity's superior capacity for abstraction, may in fact be exaggerated.[70] Plants communicate, with each other as well as with other species, through colours and patterns, smells and sounds. Non-verbal language – gestures, grunts, laughter, sighs – in both human and non-human animals is embodied. There are, then, indications that there may be a closer material relation between the environs and language than dominant strands of twentieth-century linguistics have acknowledged.[71] Similar perspectives occur in Ducornet's essay 'Natural and Unnatural Books of Nature', in which she describes the intricate patterns of communication that occur between butterflies and birds, and how these resound with the human creation of signs.[72]

A shrinking of the distance between signifier and signified would render human language closer in nature to non-human languages, or what Walter Benjamin called 'language as such'. As Gagliano puts it, 'human language is not more exceptional than the very evolutionary process that shapes it – a natural dance by which the symbolic, yet material, gestures of all living species are perpetually moved unto new and evolving habits of rendering meaning in the world'.[73] Other scholars have looked to esotericism's notion of the Book of Nature for its conviction, so frequently recalled in Ducornet's narratives, that all things are inscribed with a universal language. Kate

Rigby points to how the German mystic Jacob Böhme 'proposed that all creatures disclose themselves, not only to humans but also to one another, through the distinctive resonance or "voice" (*Hall*) that emanates from their corporeal form, drives and appetites'.[74] In a similar vein, Patricia Vieira refers to Böhme's theory of the signature of all things as a prescient intimation of what science has only recently identified as plant language.[75] In extension, these advances in thinking about non-human language give a renewed urgency to surrealism's magic linguistics.

One way in which human language may be bridged with that of other species, plants, and proctists may be precisely through poetic uses. For Böhme, 'human verbal language retains traces of a putative pre-lapsarian mode of speaking, which participated in the primal "sensual language" still "spoken" by other creatures'.[76] Benjamin considered it the task of art and poetry to activate these Edenic remnants, since 'they do not aim to translate the language of things into that of humans, but, rather, to stage an encounter between the two'.[77] Art and poetry, then, 'point in the direction of a non-hierarchical world, where all languages are equally valid and translation moves horizontally, rendering the language of one nonhuman or human being into that of another'.[78] Ducornet frequently imagines such possibilities. In her fictional universe, eroticism is the strongest force able to conjure such enchanted forms of inter-species communication. In *Entering Fire*, Lamprias describes 'an orchid that imitates a spider with such sorcery, the male, seduced by the painted eyes of a lady who is not there ... scurries mad with desire upon the flower ... I see the spider copulate and come, see sperm glisten on her rigid tongue'.[79] A species-crossing eros is also on display in *Phosphor in Dreamland*, where a ritualistic interaction between scallop and starfish parallels the first erotic encounter between the narrator and his lover: 'And when the starfish coaxed the scallop's valves apart, we exhaled simultaneously and turned to one another. I felt my byssal anchors snap as for the first time those salmon-colored lips parted.'[80] This is much more than a metaphorical euology to carnal love. It is a mutual mapping of mollusc and human fate, a tracing of the passions along species-crossing lines that suggest possibilities of new ecologies.

Surrealism's, and Ducornet's, attentiveness to the interplay of beings and things, their willingness to listen to what they communicate, may make their art and writings conducive to such an egalitarian language. In particular, post-Second World War surrealism's desperate insight in the need to mend the world through creating new philosophies and poetics of nature resonates with Vieira's hopeful view that '[a]rt partakes of the things' communitarian nature in its endeavor to bring together nonhumans and humans and make the broken, post-Edenic world whole again'.[81] This is another take on the strategy of going on a detour to the past in search of new, utopian futures so forcefully described by Löwy and Sayre. In this case, doing so requires taking a plunge into nature approached through the dialectics of close observation and esoteric speculation.

A decisive part of surrealist ecology is its refusal to separate mind and matter, waking and dream. As Ducornet expresses it: 'Perhaps this is the Real's greatest paradox: it must be dreamed in order to be lived. After all, to dream the Other is to dispel the shadows of distrust and prepare for the initial encounter.'[82] Surrealism's ecological potential resides in its insistence on merging reality and imagination, which forges a path to increased intimacy with reality, including all those beings we do not yet know, those plants and minerals that would otherwise remain opaque.

Notes

Research for this chapter has been funded by the Swedish Research Council, 2016-01196.

1. Rikki Ducornet, *The Deep Zoo: Essays* (Minneapolis: Coffee House Press, 2015), p. 85. The present chapter is informed by conversations with Rikki Ducornet in Port Townsend, 16–18 February 2018, and in Prague, 22–4 May 2018. I want to thank Rikki for her hospitality, warmth, and generosity.
2. See Wouter Hanegraaff, *Esotericism and the Academy: Rejected Knowledge in Western Culture* (Cambridge: Cambridge University Press, 2012).
3. See M.E. Warlick, 'Rikki Ducornet: An Alchemy of Dreams and Desire', *Cauda Pavonis* 20:2 (2001), p. 25; G.N. Forester and M.J. Nichols, 'Postscript: An Email Interview with Rikki', in G.N. Forester and M.J. Nichols (eds), *Festschrift Volume Four: Rikki Ducornet* (Singapore: Verbivoracious Press, 2015), p. 209.
4. Jeffrey Jerome Cohen and Lowell Duckert, 'Introduction: Eleven Principles of the Elements', in Jeffrey Jerome Cohen and Lowell Duckert (eds), *Elemental Ecocriticism: Thinking with Earth, Air, Water, and Fire* (Minneapolis: University of Minnesota Press, 2015), p. 4.
5. See Michael Löwy, *Morning Star: Surrealism, Marxism, Anarchism, Situationism, Utopia* (Austin: University of Texas Press, 2009), p. 9.
6. Michael Löwy and Robert Sayre, *Romanticism Against the Tide of Modernity*, trans. Catherine Porter (Durham, NC: Duke University Press, 2001).
7. See David Skrbina, *Panpsychism in the West* (Cambridge, MA: MIT Press, 2005).
8. Sinda Gregory and Larry McCaffery, 'At the Heart of Things Darkness and Wild Beauty: An Interview with Rikki Ducornet', *Review of Contemporary Fiction* XVIII:3 (1998), 126–7; italics removed.
9. Carolyn Kuebler and Randall Heath, 'Ducornet in Dreamland: An Interview', in G.N. Forester and M.J. Nichols (eds), *Festschrift Volume Four: Rikki Ducornet* (Singapore: Verbivoracious Press, 2015), pp. 106–7.
10. Rikki Ducornet, 'Brightfellow', *Powell's* (5 July 2016), www.powells.com/post/original-essays/brightfellow, accessed 27 June 2018.

11 Ducornet, 'Brightfellow'.
12 Penelope Rosemont (ed.), *Surrealist Women: An International Anthology* (Austin: University of Texas Press, 1998), p. 346.
13 Gregory and McCaffery, 'At the Heart of Things', p. 131.
14 Paul Hammond, 'Available Light', in Paul Hammond (ed.), *The Shadow and Its Shadow: Surrealist Writings on the Cinema* (San Francisco: City Lights, 2000), p. 2.
15 See Gavin Parkinson, 'Emotional Fusion with the Animal Kingdom: Notes toward a Natural History of Surrealism', in B. Larson and F. Brauer (eds), *The Art of Evolution: Darwin, Darwinisms, and Visual Culture* (Hanover: Dartmouth College Press, 2009), pp. 262–87.
16 Donna Roberts, 'The Ecological Imperative', in Krzysztof Fijalkowski and Michael Richardson (eds), *Surrealism: Key Concepts* (London: Routledge, 2016), p. 217.
17 Katharine Conley, 'Sleeping Gods in Surrealist Collections', *Symposium* 67:1 (2013), p. 8.
18 André Breton, 'Second Manifesto of Surrealism', in *Manifestoes of Surrealism*, trans. Richard Seaver and Helen R. Lane (Ann Arbor: University of Michigan Press, 1972), p. 128; italics removed.
19 Effie Rentzou, '*Minotaure*: On Ethnography and Animals', *Symposium* 67:1 (2013), pp. 30–4.
20 André Breton, 'Prolegomena to a Third Surrealist Manifesto or Not', in *Manifestoes of Surrealism*, trans. Richard Seaver and Helen R. Lane (Ann Arbor: University of Michigan Press, 1972), p. 293.
21 André Breton with André Masson, *Martinique: Snake Charmer*, trans. David W. Seaman (Austin: University of Texas Press, 2008), p. 50.
22 André Breton, *Arcanum 17: With Apertures Grafted to the End*, trans. Zack Rogow (Los Angeles: Green Integer, 2004), pp. 31–8.
23 André Breton, *Conversations: The Autobiography of Surrealism*, trans. Mark Polizzotti (New York: Paragon House, 1993), p. 206.
24 André Breton, 'Ascendant Sign', in *Free Rein*, trans. Michel Parmentier and Jacqueline d'Amboise (Lincoln: University of Nebraska Press, 1995), pp. 104–7. See also Charles Fourier, *The Theory of the Four Movements*, trans. Ian Patterson (Cambridge: Cambridge University Press, 1996); Antoine Faivre, *Access to Western Esotericism* (Albany: SUNY Press, 1994), pp. 10–11.
25 Breton, *Arcanum 17*, p. 58.
26 Jacqueline Sénard, 'Cat = clover', trans. M.B. Rochester, in Rosemont, *Surrealist Women*, pp. 246–7.
27 Penelope Rosemont, 'A Revolution in the Way We Think and Feel: Conversations with Leonora Carrington', in Ron Sakolsky (ed.), *Surrealist Subversions: Rants, Writings & Images by the Surrealist Movement in the United States* (New York: Autonomedia, 2002), p. 186.
28 Franklin Rosemont, Penelope Rosemont, and Paul Garon, 'Surrealism: The Chicago idea', in Franklin Rosemont, Penelope Rosemont, and Paul Garon (eds), *The Forecast Is Hot!: Tracts & Other Collective Declarations of the Surrealist Movement in the United States 1966–1976* (Chicago: Black Swan Press, 1997), p. xxx; italics removed; Franklin Rosemont, *Revolution in the Service of the*

Marvelous: Surrealist Contributions to the Critique of Miserabilism (Chicago: Charles H. Kerr, 2004), p. 6; Ron Sakolsky, 'The Surrealist Adventure and the Poetry of Direct Action: Passionate Encounters between the Chicago Surrealist Group, the Wobblies and Earth First!', *The Journal of Aesthetics and Protest* 8 (2011), www.joaap.org/issue8/Sakolsky_surrealists.htm, accessed 28 June 2018.

29 Penelope Rosemont, *Surrealist Experiences: 1001 Dawns, 221 Midnights* (Chicago: Black Swan Press, 2000), p. 18.
30 Rosemont, *Surrealist Experiences*, p. 18.
31 See e.g. Gaston Bachelard, *Earth and Reveries of Will: An Essay on the Imagination of Matter*, trans. Kenneth Haltman (Dallas: Dallas Institute, 2002), p. 201.
32 J.W. McCormack, 'The Burden of Strangeness: Rikki Ducornet', *Publishers Weekly* (20 May 2016), www.publishersweekly.com/pw/by-topic/authors/profiles/article/70442-the-burden-of-strangeness-rikki-ducornet.html, accessed 28 June 2018.
33 See Christophe Bonneuil and Jean-Baptiste Fressoz, *The Shock of the Anthropocene: The Earth, History and Us*, trans. David Fernbach (London: Verso, 2017).
34 See Gregory and McCaffery, 'At the Heart of Things', p. 132.
35 John P. Clark, *The Impossible Community: Realizing Communitarian Anarchism* (New York: Bloomsbury, 2013), p. 94.
36 Clark, *Impossible Community*, p. 104.
37 Gina Litherland and Hal Rammel, 'An Unjust Dominion', in Sakolsky, *Surrealist Subversions*, p. 376.
38 Gregory and McCaffery, 'At the Heart of Things', p. 129.
39 Rikki Ducornet, *The Jade Cabinet* (Normal: Dalkey Archive Press, 1994), p. 158.
40 Rikki Ducornet, *The Monstrous and the Marvelous* (San Francisco: City Lights, 1999), p. 7.
41 Rikki Ducornet, *Phosphor in Dreamland* (Normal: Dalkey Archive Press, 1995), p. 43.
42 André Breton, *Surrealism and Painting*, trans. Simon Watson Taylor (Boston: MFA Publications, 2002), p. 200. See also Marion Endt-Jones, 'Between *Wunderkammer* and Shop Window: Surrealist *Naturalia* Cabinets', in John C. Welchman (ed.), *Sculpture and the Vitrine* (Farnham: Ashgate, 2013), pp. 99–100.
43 See Jan Švankmajer, 'Cabinets of Wonders: On Creating and Collecting', trans. Gabriel M. Paletz and Ondrej Kálal, *The Moving Image* 11:2 (2011), p. 103.
44 Ducornet, *Phosphor in Dreamland*, p. 43.
45 *Ibid.*, p. 44.
46 Rikki Ducornet, *The Stain* (Normal: Dalkey Archive Press, 1995), p. 71.
47 Penelope Rosemont, 'Thinking like an Octopus: The Surrealist Paranoid Critical Method Applied to the Brain of a Cephalopod', unpublished response to an enquiry on surrealism, nature, and ecology circulated by the author, July 2018.
48 Ducornet, *Phosphor in Dreamland*, p. 35.
49 See Parkinson, 'Emotional Fusion'; Roberts, 'The Ecological Imperative', p. 224.
50 Ducornet, *Phosphor in Dreamland*, p. 13.

51 Rikki Ducornet, *Entering Fire* (San Francisco: City Lights, 1987), p. 46.
52 Ibid., p. 82.
53 Ibid., p. 75.
54 Ibid., p. 77.
55 Ducornet, *Phosphor in Dreamland*, p. 22.
56 Ducornet, *The Stain*, p. 114.
57 Ibid., p. 114.
58 Ducornet, *Entering Fire*, p. 111.
59 Ducornet, *Monstrous and the Marvelous*, p. 1.
60 Ducornet, *Jade Cabinet*, p. 10.
61 Fulcanelli, *Dwellings of the Philosophers*, trans. Brigitte Donvez and Lionel Perrin, www.cista.net/Houses/main.htm, accessed 28 June 2018; Breton, 'Fronton-Virage', in *Free Rein*, trans. Michel Parmentier and Jacqueline d'Amboise (Lincoln: University of Nebraska Press, 1995), pp. 188–9.
62 See Fulcanelli, *The Dwelling of the Philosophers*.
63 Warlick, 'Rikki Ducornet'; Fulcanelli, *The Dwellings of the Philosophers*.
64 Ducornet, *Phosphor in Dreamland*, p. 107.
65 Ducornet, *Deep Zoo*, p. 97.
66 Ducornet, *Phosphor in Dreamland*, p. 3.
67 See Faivre, *Access to Western Esotericism*, pp. 14–15; Warlick, 'Rikki Ducornet', p. 32.
68 Ducornet, *Entering Fire*, p. 31.
69 Walter Benjamin, 'On Language as Such and on the Language of Man', in *Selected Writings Volume 1: 1913–1926* (Cambridge, MA: The Belknap Press, 1996), pp. 62–74.
70 Monica Gagliano, 'Breaking the Silence: Green Mudras and the Faculty of Language in Plants', in Monica Gagliano, John C. Ryan, and Patricia Vieira (eds), *The Language of Plants: Science, Philosophy, Literature* (Minneapolis: University of Minnesota Press, 2017), p. 91.
71 Gagliano, 'Breaking the silence', pp. 86–91.
72 Ducornet, *Deep Zoo*, pp. 16–18.
73 Gagliano, 'Breaking the Silence', p. 92.
74 Kate Rigby, 'Earth's Poesy: Romantic Poetics, Natural Philosophy, and Biosemiotics', in Hubert Zapf (ed.), *Handbook of Ecocriticism and Cultural Ecology* (Berlin: De Gruyter, 2016), p. 50.
75 Patricia Vieira, '*Phytographia*: Literature as Plant Writing', in Gagliano, Ryan, and Vieira, *Language of Plants*, p. 219.
76 Rigby, 'Earth's Poesy', p. 50.
77 Vieira, '*Phytographia*', p. 222.
78 Ibid., p., 222.
79 Ducornet, *Entering Fire*, p. 32.
80 Ducornet, *Phosphor in Dreamland*, p. 134.
81 Vieira, '*Phytographia*', p. 222.
82 Ducornet, *Deep Zoo*, p. 100.

Index

abhumanism 12, 182–4, 185, 189, 194, 196–8, 201, 202, 204–6
Acéphale 94–5, 96, 97
Adamowicz, Elza 20, 45, 63n21
Adorno, Theodor W. 11, 70, 78, 79, 82, 84
Agar, Eileen 1, 171
Alain (Émile-Auguste Chartier) 110–11
alchemy 66n84, 76, 90, 94, 163, 164, 171, 172–3, 225, 226, 228, 230, 231, 232, 237, 238, 239
anagram 9, 144, 146, 149, 153
Andersen, Hans Christian 150
animal 12, 13, 31, 53, 59, 60, 67n95, 73, 123, 124, 125–33, 181, 182, 185, 191, 194, 195, 196, 197, 198–9, 202, 204, 205, 208n43, 225, 227, 228, 229, 230, 235, 236, 237, 238, 239, 240
anthropocentrism 1, 2, 13, 205, 229, 231, 235, 240
anthropology 90, 93, 112, 229
Apter, Emily 144, 145, 151
Aragon, Louis 30, 31, 40n29, 180, 228–9
Arendt, Hannah 11, 70, 71, 74, 75, 80–1
Artaud, Antonin 100, 143, 144, 180
autobiography 6, 8, 9, 12, 13, 17, 37, 93, 99, 100, 123, 143–4, 145, 150, 153, 187, 189, 190, 210, 214
automatism 12, 44, 46, 125, 127, 158, 160–1, 166–7, 170, 171, 173, 174, 177n55

Bachelard, Gaston 226, 228, 232
Bal, Mieke 210, 218
Barnes, Djuna 27
Bataille, Georges 9, 30, 40n29, 83, 88, 89–92, 94–7, 98, 99, 100
Beauvoir, Simone de 27, 46, 47, 185, 197
Bellmer, Hans 9, 143, 180, 191
Benjamin, Walter 20–1, 33, 240, 241
Bernier, Jean 87, 88, 98, 99
bilingual 124, 129, 130, 144
biology 5, 182, 185, 195, 205, 229, 235, 236–7, 239
Böhme, Jacob 141
Borrow, Antony 162, 164, 165
Brauner, Victor 195, 196, 208n48
Breton, André 11, 30–1, 40n29, 42, 43, 44, 45, 46, 47, 48, 50, 52, 54, 56, 61, 62, 62n6, 65n54, 66n73, 75–6, 83, 87–8, 97, 98, 99, 100, 103, 104, 109, 110, 111, 112, 113, 115–16, 120n33, 120n39, 123, 125, 126, 127, 162, 166, 180, 181, 183, 228, 229–30, 234, 237, 238, 239, 240
Bridgwater, Emmy 9, 157, 171
British Poetry Revival 12, 156, 157, 158–9, 160, 163, 165, 166, 170
Buñuel, Luis 229
Butler, Judith 5–6

Cahun, Claude (Lucy Schwob) 6–7, 7–8, 10, 17–41, 125
  photographs
   Je tends les bras 35
   Self Portrait (Crouched Naked in a Rock Pool) 35

Self Portrait (Lower Body, Seaweed, and Le Pere) 26
Self Portrait (Near a Granite Wall) 18
writings
'Amor amicitiae' ('Jeux uraniens') 29–30
'Beware of Domestic Objects' ('Prenez garde aux objets domestiques') 21, 31
'Chanson sauvage' 32
'Confidences au miroir' 30, 36
Disavowals, or Cancelled Confessions (*Aveux non avenus*) 7, 8, 10, 17–25, 27, 30, 32–4, 36–7
'Place Your Bets' ('Les Paris sont ouverts') 30, 31, 32, 33
Vues et visions 28, 30
Caillois, Roger 94, 95, 96
Calvino, Italo 9, 225, 226
capitalism 20, 21, 31, 32, 46, 82, 91, 205, 233, 234
Carrington, Leonora 1, 7, 8–9, 10, 11, 42–67, 68–86, 125, 126, 162, 202, 229, 230
paintings
Femme et oiseau 55–6, 57
Green Tea (*The Oval Lady*) 56, 66n72
writings
'The Debutante' 8, 43, 48, 59–60, 67n89, 67n95, 71
Down Below (*En bas*) 8, 53, 73, 83
'The Happy Corpse Story' 11, 70, 81–3, 84
Hearing Trumpet, The 8, 62n4, 230
House of Fear, The (*La Maison de la Peur*) 11, 42–3, 47, 48, 50, 51, 61–2, 64n39
'The House of Fear' 48–51, 52, 54, 56, 62, 64n39, 64n48, 71
Little Francis 42, 64n48, 66n55
'A Man in Love' 60–1
Oval Lady, The (*La Dame ovale*) 11, 51–62, 64n39
'The Oval Lady' 52–4, 55, 71

'The Royal Summons' 54–5
Stone Door, The 11, 69, 75–81, 82, 83, 84
'Uncle Sam Carrington' 48, 57–9
'White Rabbits' 11, 69, 71–5, 80, 82, 83, 84
Carroll, Lewis 48, 54, 55, 65n68, 67n95, 226, 232
Carter, Angela 9, 212, 220, 226
censorship 107–8, 115, 118n16
Césaire, Aimé 9, 103, 105, 106, 108, 109, 115, 116, 118n23
Césaire, Suzanne 7, 9, 11, 103–21
writings
'Alain et l'esthétique' 110–11
'André Breton, poète' 112, 116
'1943: Le Surréalisme et nous' 112, 116
'Le Grand Camouflage' 111, 112, 113–16, 117n12
'Léo Frobenius et le problème des civilisations' 111, 112
'Malaise d'une civilisation' 113
'Misère d'une poésie' 111
Chadwick, Whitney 1, 43, 66n78, 69, 126, 212
chess 55–6, 65n68
Chicago Surrealist Group 227, 230, 233
childhood 56, 123, 125, 133, 186, 187, 233
Chirico, Giorgio de 28
Christianity 162, 225, 232, 234, 235, 236
Cixous, Hélène 27–8, 179, 180
Clark, John P. 233
Cocteau, Jean 28, 185, 227
collage 2, 6, 7, 11, 20, 28, 33, 42, 44–7, 48–50, 51, 54, 55, 63n12, 137, 159, 171, 172, 173, 177n55, 218, 227, 228, 229, 131
College of Sociology 93, 94–5, 97
colonialism 103–4, 111, 112, 116, 158, 225, 233, 234
Colquhoun, Ithell 1, 7, 12, 156–78
paintings
Linked Islands I 163
Linked Islands II 163
Santa Warna's Wishing Well 163

Colquhoun, Ithell (*cont.*)
  writings
    'Confidential Service' 171
    Goose of Hermogenes 156
    Grimoire of the Entangled Thicket 167, 168, 169
    'Hypnagogic Interior' 171, 173–4
    'Little Poems on the Theme of the Way' 163
    'The Myth of Santa Warna' 162–3
    'Ode to the Philosophical Mercury' 171–3
    Osmazone 171–4
    Sword of Wisdom, The 156
    'Uath' 167–9
communism 21, 30–1, 88–9, 91–2, 108
confession 87, 99–100
convulsive beauty 45, 48, 52, 61, 65n54, 120n34, 222
convulsive identity 11, 45, 47, 50, 52, 54, 56, 61

Dalí, Salvador 142, 146, 227
Darwin, Charles 236, 237
death 11, 76, 87–8, 90, 93, 97, 98–9, 128, 132, 136–7, 140n57, 153, 182, 195, 196, 202, 204
DeJong, Constance 211, 213, 215, 222n5
Derrida, Jacques 33, 149
Desnos, Robert 30
double meaning 12, 54, 124, 129, 130, 131
Dubuffet, Jean 122, 124, 128–9, 130, 140n46
Ducornet, Rikki 7, 9, 13, 225–45
  writings
    Cult of Seizure, The 226
    Deep Zoo, The 226
    Entering Fire 225, 226, 232, 236–7, 238, 239–40, 241
    Fountains of Neptune, The 225, 232, 236, 238
    From the Star Chamber 228
    Jade Cabinet, The 225, 226, 232, 234, 238
    'A Memoir in the Form of a Manifesto' 225
    Monstrous and the Marvelous, The 226
    Phosphor in Dreamland 225, 226, 232–3, 234–6, 238–9, 240, 241
    Stain, The 225, 226, 228, 131–2, 233, 235, 237, 238
Duchamp, Marcel 42, 56, 159
Durkheim, Émile 93

ecocriticism 1, 13, 157, 170, 226
ecofeminism 157, 169
ecology 13, 14n4, 204, 226–7, 228–31, 234–5, 236, 238, 239, 241, 242
Eliot, T.S. 158, 165
Éluard, Nusch 1
Éluard, Paul 27, 88, 180, 227
Ernst, Max 11, 18, 20, 28, 44–6, 47–51, 52, 53, 54, 55, 56, 61, 62, 63n12, 63n21, 64n39, 64n46, 64n48, 65n58, 68, 83, 84n1, 125, 126, 139n27, 140n50, 162, 210, 216, 227, 229, 232
eroticism 28, 111, 144, 187, 192, 228, 241
esotericism 156, 164, 167, 168, 170, 172, 173, 225, 227, 230, 237, 238, 240–1, 242
ethics 70, 75, 79, 116, 152, 197, 204, 226, 232, 233, 235
exile 11, 68–86, 230

fairy tale 58, 66n82, 132, 143, 153, 211, 220
fascism 53, 68, 70, 78, 80, 83, 92, 210, 232, 237, 238
femininity 20, 28, 37n2, 43, 46–7, 55, 56, 58, 60, 61
feminism 1, 2, 3–5, 7, 8, 9, 10, 11, 13, 38n7, 43, 46–7, 59, 60, 61, 62, 67n89, 69, 76, 143, 169, 180–1, 185, 205, 206n6, 208n43, 211, 212–14, 218, 222, 223n10
femme-enfant 46, 50, 62, 64n48, 180
Fini, Leonor 1, 3, 4, 7, 12, 179–209
  paintings
    Angel of Anatomy, The 202, 203, 204

Étude pour Mourmour 188
Les Stryges Amaouri 192, 193, 194
Rogomelec 202, 203
Sphinx Amalbourga 192, 193, 194
Sphinx Philagria 182, 183, 196
Vespertilia 195, 208n48
writings
    Le Livre de Leonor Fini 184, 186, 190, 200, 208n44
    L'Oneiropompe 12, 184, 187, 195–200
    Miroir des chats 184, 186, 190, 191, 207n20
    Mourmour 12, 184, 186–95, 198, 207n19, 207n20
    Rogomelec 7, 12, 184, 187, 200–4
Ford, Charles Henri 69, 162
Foucault, Michel 68, 144
Freud, Sigmund 36, 42, 43–4, 92, 93, 164, 187, 214, 216, 219

Gascoyne, David 156–7, 158, 159
Gauthier, Xavière 179–86, 197, 205, 206n6
Genet, Jean 185, 195–9
gothic 70–1, 72, 73–4, 76–7, 80, 84, 212, 213, 216, 218
Graves, Robert 167
Guggenheim, Peggy 213

Hammer, Barbara 36
H.D. 27
Hirtum, Marianne van 9
historiography 1, 12, 157, 211, 212, 214
Hitchcock, Alfred 146
Holocaust 77, 79–80, 81, 83
Horkheimer, Max 82
Horna, Kati 68, 69
Howgate, Sarah 37
Hubert, Renée Riese 9, 143
Hugo, Valentine 1, 125
humanism 45, 185, 200, 205, 206
humour 45, 60, 67n95, 123, 126, 128, 130–1, 134, 164, 200, 228
hybridity 205, 208n43
hysteria 45–6, 47

intertextuality 12, 26, 48, 54, 145–6, 149, 150, 152, 153, 154, 212, 218, 220, 225
Irigaray, Luce 143, 206n6

Jung, Carl Gustav 164

Kabbala 167, 173
Kaplan, Nelly 9, 10
Keats, John 150
Kermode, Frank 166

Lamba, Jacqueline 30
Larkin, Philip 165, 166
Lautréamont, Comte de 44, 108, 109, 111
Le Brun, Annie 9, 206n6
Legge, Sheila 157
Leiris, Michel 9, 11, 88, 89, 90, 91, 93, 94, 97, 98, 99, 108, 118n19, 120n33
Lepri, Stanislao 185, 187, 190, 191, 201
little magazines 158–9, 160, 163, 165, 166, 168–9
Lomas, David 43–4, 45–6, 49
London Surrealist Group 156, 157–8, 160, 161
Lorde, Audre 27
Löwy, Michael 30, 226, 242
Loy, Mina 28
Lusty, Natalya 10, 50, 51, 64n46, 67n89

Maar, Dora 1
Mabille, Pierre 97, 115
Mac Orlan, Pierre 10, 23–4, 25–6, 27, 33
magic 76, 90, 143, 149, 156, 173, 181, 220, 225, 236, 237, 238–9, 241
magic realism 9, 226
Man Ray 56
Mansour, Joyce 9, 10, 180
marvellous 11, 93, 97, 162, 229, 230
Marxism 30, 180, 205
masculinity 6, 18, 28, 46
masochism 151, 204
Masson, André 83, 162
Mauss, Marcel 93

Maximin, Daniel 105, 106, 115, 117n11, 117n12
mental illness 142, 143, 145
Merleau-Ponty, Maurice 27
Mesens, E.L.T. 157, 160, 168, 170
Michaux, Henri 30, 143
Miller, Lee 1
Mitrani, Nora 9
Molinier, Pierre 180
Monnerot, Jules 94
Montaigne, Michel de 26
Moore, Marcel (Suzanne Malherbe) 7, 8, 18, 28, 36, 37, 38n4
Moorhead, Joanna 8, 47, 57, 59, 60, 69, 78
Moro, César 68
Mouvement de libération des femmes (MLF) 180
myth 11, 12, 20, 23, 28, 29, 34, 76, 97, 150, 152, 162–6, 168, 174, 180, 181, 184, 187, 190, 192, 194, 198, 201, 202, 225, 230, 236, 239

nature 13, 30, 31, 35, 36, 55, 98, 126, 163, 204, 225–45
Nazism 68–9, 70, 71, 73, 77, 78, 79, 80, 152
Negritude movement 105, 111, 115
neo-paganism 156, 157, 162, 168, 169–70
New Age 165, 169, 170
Nietzsche, Friedrich 97, 151
Nochlin, Linda 213, 223n17
non-human 189, 204, 225, 229, 231, 240–1

occult 7, 13, 76, 156, 160, 161–2, 164, 165, 169, 173, 226, 230, 231, 239
Oppenheim, Meret 1, 4, 216
Orenstein, Gloria Feman 1, 126
other 21, 34, 45, 90, 96, 98, 99, 100, 161
outsider art 124, 143, 152

Paalen, Wolfgang 68
Pailthorpe, Grace 157
passivity 11, 42, 44, 46–7, 50, 53, 54, 56, 61, 62, 64n48

patriarchy 179, 233
Peignot, Colette (Laure) 7, 9, 11, 87–102
  writings
    Sacred, The 89, 98, 99
    Story of a Little Girl, The 89, 97, 98
Penrose, Roland 160
Penrose, Valentine 1, 9, 28
Péret, Benjamin 68, 162
perversion 179–81, 185, 187, 191, 199, 205
Pilnyak, Boris 88
Plath, Sylvia 156
Plato 29, 40n48
Platonic love 29, 30, 33
Poe, Edgar Allan 73
politics 2, 5, 6, 8, 10, 11, 13, 17, 19, 21, 24, 28, 31, 36, 43, 53, 69, 70, 71, 74, 75, 76, 78, 79, 80–1, 84, 88, 104, 105, 106, 107, 108, 109, 114, 115, 116, 120n33, 123, 126, 152, 164, 169, 180–1, 182–3, 185, 195–8, 200, 204, 205–6, 212, 229, 230
posthumanism 204
poststructuralism 32, 33
Pound, Ezra 158, 165, 172–3, 177n53
Prassinos, Gisèle 9, 10
psychoanalysis 45, 180
Pucill, Sarah 36–7
puns 149, 151

racism 6, 107–8, 119n23, 233, 237
Rahon, Alice 9, 28
Réage, Pauline (Anne Desclos) 185, 191
refugee 69, 74, 75, 78, 81, 84
religion 19, 43, 165, 169–70, 229, 233
Renzio, Toni del 160, 162
Rimbaud, Arthur 62n6, 97, 108, 109, 111
Rimmington, Edith 156, 157, 171
Rosemont, Penelope 1–2, 8, 9, 13, 14n14, 231, 235

sacred 11, 89, 92, 93–9
sacrifice 201–2, 204

Sade, Marquis de 80, 91, 185, 191
sadism 180, 204
Sage, Kay 1, 7, 12, 56, 122–41
  writings
    'Amorce' 130–1
    China Eggs 133
    'Corbeaux' 133
    Demain, Monsieur Silber 122, 123, 127, 130, 131
    'Demain, Monsieur Silber' 122, 132–3
    'Deux canards et moi' 134–5
    Faut dire c'qui est 122, 129, 130, 133, 134
    'Finis Coronat Opus' 132
    'Funeral in Milan' 128
    'L'Autre côté' 127
    'L'Insomnie' 127
    'Menu' 130
    'Mon ami' 129
    'Mon oiseau et moi' 135–7
    Mordicus 122, 124, 126, 128, 130, 135, 137
    'Répétition' 133, 135
    'Souvenirs d'enfance' 133
    The More I Wonder 122, 123, 128
    'Vive la vache' 128–9, 131
Said, Edward 11, 68, 70, 72, 73, 74, 75, 77, 81
Saussure, Ferdinand de 90, 240
schizophrenia 144
Schneemann, Carolee 199, 209n60
Schwob, Marcel 17, 23, 186
science 227, 228, 229, 230, 231, 233, 234, 235–6, 237, 241
self 10, 17, 19, 20, 21, 22, 23, 24, 27, 29, 31, 32, 33, 36, 43, 46, 47, 48, 50, 53, 54, 61, 62, 96, 98, 100, 119n29, 123, 125, 130, 142, 143, 174, 186, 202, 204, 218, 229, 237
Seligman, Kurt 83
sexuality 2, 5, 8, 21, 50, 99, 133, 151, 180, 182, 185, 189, 205
slang 122, 124, 126, 127, 129, 130, 131, 134, 135–6, 174
Smith, Ali 8
Soupault, Philippe 127
Souvarine, Boris 88–9, 91, 92, 97

Spivak, Gayatri Chakravorty 6, 146, 149
Stein, Gertrude 27
Suleiman, Susan Rubin 10, 223n11
Švankmajerová, Eva 9
Švankmajer, Jan 229

Tanguy, Yves 122–3, 124, 125, 129, 130, 132, 134, 136, 137, 139n27, 140n57, 141n72, 141n77
Tanning, Dorothea 1, 3, 4, 5, 7, 8, 13, 49, 56, 125, 126, 130, 139n27, 140n50, 210–24
  visual works
    A Mrs. Radcliffe Called Today 218
    De quel amour (*By What Love*) 217
    Don Juan's Breakfast 220
    En chair et en or (*In Flesh and Gold*) 221
    Hôtel du Pavot, Chambre 202 219
    Les 7 périls spectraux (*The Seven Spectral Perils*) 221
    Mrs Radcliffe Called Again, Left No Message 218
    Stanza 221
    Still Calling, Still Hoping 218
    Woman Artist, Nude, Standing 214, 215
  writings
    Between Lives: An Artist and Her World 210, 220
    Birthday 210
    'Blind Date' 210
    Chasm: A Weekend (*Abyss*) 210, 211, 212, 221, 222n2
    'Dream It or Leave It' 210
    'Some Parallels in Words and Pictures' 211, 215–19
    'Statement' 211, 212–15, 218
    Ouvre-Toi (*Open Sesame*) 211, 219–21, 220
Thomson, Rupert 37
Topor, Roland 228
Toyen 1, 180, 229
translation 7, 8, 12, 143–55, 241
transmediality 145

Tropiques 9, 11, 103–10, 114–16, 118n23, 119n24, 119n29, 120n37
Trotsky, Leon 30, 31
Tzara, Tristan 30

unconscious 7, 19, 42, 44, 50, 61, 79, 144, 160–1, 164, 165, 229
untranslatability 12, 144, 151

Vaché, Jacques 87
Varo, Remedios 1, 68, 69
Vergine, Lea 3

Wearing, Gillian 37
Webb, Peter 186, 198
Weil, Simone 88, 92
Weisz, Emerico 'Chiki' 68–9, 75, 76, 80

Woolf, Virginia 27, 38n7
wordplay 12, 19, 54, 124, 128, 172

Yoyotte, Simone 9

Zürn, Unica 7, 9, 10, 99, 142–55
   illustrations
      Das Haus der Krankheiten 147
      Plan des Hauses der Krankheiten 148
   writings
      Dunkler Frühling (*Dark Spring*) 142, 151–2
      Das Haus der Krankenheiten (*The House of Illnesses*) 142, 143, 146–51
      Die Trompeten von Jericho (*The Trumpets of Jericho*) 143, 152–3

EU authorised representative for GPSR:
Easy Access System Europe, Mustamäe tee 50,
10621 Tallinn, Estonia
gpsr.requests@easproject.com

www.ingramcontent.com/pod-product-compliance
Lightning Source LLC
Chambersburg PA
CBHW070609170426
43200CB00012B/2636